EMBODYING MEXICO

Currents in Latin American & Iberian Music

WALTER CLARK, SERIES EDITOR

Nor-tec Rifa!
Electronic Dance Music from Tijuana to the World
Alejandro L. Madrid

From Serra to Sancho:
Music and Pageantry in the California Missions
Craig H. Russell

Colonial Counterpoint:
Music in Early Modern Manila
D. R. M. Irving

Embodying Mexico:
Tourism, Nationalism, and Performance
Ruth Hellier-Tinoco

Embodying Mexico

Tourism, Nationalism & Performance

Ruth Hellier-Tinoco

OXFORD
UNIVERSITY PRESS

Oxford University Press, Inc., publishes works that further
Oxford University's objective of excellence
in research, scholarship, and education.

Oxford   New York
Auckland   Cape Town   Dar es Salaam   Hong Kong   Karachi
Kuala Lumpur   Madrid   Melbourne   Mexico City   Nairobi
New Delhi   Shanghai   Taipei   Toronto

With offices in
Argentina   Austria   Brazil   Chile   Czech Republic   France   Greece
Guatemala   Hungary   Italy   Japan   Poland   Portugal   Singapore
South Korea   Switzerland   Thailand   Turkey   Ukraine   Vietnam

Copyright © 2011 by Oxford University Press, Inc.

Published by Oxford University Press, Inc.
198 Madison Avenue, New York, New York 10016

www.oup.com

Oxford is a registered trademark of Oxford University Press.

Library of Congress Cataloging-in-Publication Data

Hellier-Tinoco, Ruth.
Embodying Mexico : tourism, nationalism, and performance/ Ruth Hellier-Tinoco.
    p.   cm.—(Currents in Latin American and Iberian music)
Includes bibliographical references and index.
ISBN 978-0-19-979081-4 (alk. paper)
1. Folklore—Performance—Mexico.   2. Folk dancing, Mexican.   3. Folk music, Mexican.
4. Popular culture—Mexico.   5. Culture and tourism—Mexico.   6. Politics and culture—Mexico.
7. Culture and globalization—Mexico.   8. National characteristics, Mexican.
9. Mexico—Social life and customs.   I. Title.
GR115.H45 2011
972—dc22   2010010477

Cover: Embodying the iconic *Dance of the Old Men*, José Evaristo Gabriel of Urandén Island, Lake Pátzcuaro, and members of his family, Jesús, José Refugio, and Luis Alberto, pose for a photo on the roof of their home in Mexico City in 2010.

Recorded video examples (marked in text with ⬤) are available online at www.oup.com/us/embodyingmexico
Access with username Music3 and password Book3234
For more information on Oxford Web Music, visit www.oxfordwebmusic.com

This book is dedicated to
all the musicians, dancers and their families
of Lake Pátzcuaro, Michoacán, Mexico

and
to my mum, Margaret
who taught me how to love through pain
(Rest in peace—Q.E.P.D.—Que en paz descansa)

Acknowledgments

IN THIS BOOK I narrate stories of individual lives, of journeys and border crossings, of connections through time and space, of capturing memories and re-presenting them, and of shaping identities. Here I acknowledge the hundreds of individuals who have been involved in shaping my own journeys and memories during the last fifteen years, a fragment of which I present here in this book. Myriad people have contributed to this ongoing project and to the multiple areas of my life that are thoroughly enmeshed in it. I began to write this acknowledgment a couple of years ago. At that time I registered those whom I had known, but who, in the course of the passing years, had died, with the usual mark Q.E.P.D.—Que en paz descansa— rest in peace. As I come to amend this page before publication, and as I look through the names, there are so many more who also have passed on. It is with profound sadness that I acknowledge their passing—Q.E.P.D. On this page I have decided not to distinguish these individuals, but instead I simply record each name.

In one overarching gesture, I extend my most profound gratitude to all the many people in Mexico, the UK, the United States, and elsewhere who have supported me, shared their wisdom and time with me, and shown me overwhelming kindness, hospitality, and patience. Here I name many of those who have been most influential, and I also include names and institutional support in two appendices. I offer my heartfelt thanks to:

All the many musicians, dancers, and friends from the Lake Pátzcuaro region and the wider P'urhépecha region: Don Dimas Esteban Mangato, Don Felipe Ramos Santiago, Don Rodríguez Candelario Pantaleón, Juan Francisco Calixto, Juan González Ramos, Oliberto Matías Domínguez, and all their families, especially Nana Ma. Luisa, Tata Felix, Mari, Lucy, Israel and Javier, and all the children * Pablo Alejo Reynoso and his family, Rosa, Zintlali, Yvon and Gris, and Sergio, Vidal and Arsenio and their families on Pacanda * Adela Alejo and Cecilio Gabriel and family of Urandén * Aurelio and Moisés de la Cruz and family of Janitzio * José Dimas, Angela and Guadalupe of Santa Fe de la Laguna * Pedro Dimas and family of Ichupio * the Gabriel and Camilo families of Urandén and Mexico City, and in particular, José Evaristo * Gervasio, Atilano, and Pedro López and family * the family of Nicolás B. Juárez, especially Rafael Juárez, and Adelaida Bartolo, Gilberto Cázares Ponce, and Enedina Ponce * Abel Orozco and family * Raúl and Manuel Candelario * Cruz Guadalupe, Pedro Antonio, Nicolás Constantino, Rosendo Cristóbal, and Isidro Ramírez of Jarácuaro * Gerardo Guzmán and family of Pacanda * the Cortés family and Francisco López of Janitzio * Jesús Morales and family of Tecuena * Antonio Pablo Villegas of Cucuchucho * Ezequiel Diego of Yunuén;

Many individuals in Morelia, Pátzcuaro, Mexico City, and elsewhere including: Leobardo Bartolo Ramos and family for welcoming me to Jarácuaro and for guiding me in Mexico City * the Bautista family of Paracho and Morelia, in particular Javier, Joaquín, Juan, Carlos, Joaquín and Ceci* Ben and Patty Warren for their unbridled care * Ireneo Rojas Hernández and family* Wicho * Fernando Nava * Arturo Chamorro * Mario Kuri-Aldana * Henrietta Yurchenco * Alvaro Ochoa * Clarissa Malheiros and Juliana Faesler (La Maquina de Teatro) * the family Cervantes in Pátzcuaro;

Friends and colleagues in Santa Barbara, including Francisco Espinosa * Madeline and all the Blickleys * Juan and Lola* Carlos and Azalea * Paul * Simon and Euzetta * Ali and John * Dave and Winnie; Sarah; Gabriela and Stefan.

The Ramírez Tinoco family in Toluca and Morelia, who always showed me such love and care (César, Irma, Lalo, Irma, Carlos, Israel, Erick, Liliana, and Christian, spouses, children, aunts and uncles, Sandra, my ahijado Martincito, Ulisses, B.), and César, with, and through whom I learned so much about life and Mexico;

All those in the UK who have influenced my scholarly pursuits and laughed with me through difficult times, including Caroline Bithell, Katherine Brown, Steve Cottrell, Peter Johnson, Mark Lockett, Laudan Nooshin, Tina Ramnarine, Henry Stobart, Jonathan Stock (and so many others in the British Forum for Ethnomusicology); to my colleagues at the University of Winchester; Rosemary Dooley; my friends in "the Spanish group"; Tony, who first journeyed through Mexico with me; all the bikers who shared my thrills in the Alps and Pyrenees; my dear friends Margaret, Doreen and Nick, Ann and Antony;

The whole Cooley clan;

My dad Ken, sister Joy, brother Brian, and families;

and my wonderful husband, Tim.

Contents

About the Companion Website

www.oup.com/us/embodyingmexico

Oxford has created a password-protected companion Web site to accompany *Embodying Mexico*. As dances, visual imagery, and iconography form the core of this study, accessing exemplars in photographic form will enable the reader to engage further with the narratives that are woven through this text. The video material includes ensembles performing the *Dance of the Old Men* both in Mexico and the United States.

Access with username Music3 and password Book3234

PART I

Setting the Scene
Many Mexicos

Introduction

¿Que hay detrás de la máscara, qué es aquello que anima al personaje?
What is behind the mask, what is it that gives life to the character?

La Llama Doble, Octavio Paz

Mexico and Mexicanness are constructs created, shaped, and performed through discourse, photographs, dances, places, peoples, words, bodies, colors, foods, languages, musics, texts, films, journeys, stones, and memories. Mexico and Mexicanness are a sense of national belonging, a notion of authenticity, an expectation of difference, a collective identity, a real soul, a tourist destination, an amalgam of past and present, a crossing of borders, an impression of death, an optimism for the future, an imagined community, a question of hybridity, a folkloric culture, a trace of pre-Conquest civilizations, a confidence in diversity, an idea of otherness, an indigenous presence, a desire for tradition, a history of superimposition....

Two corporeal acts, the *Dance of the Old Men* and *Night of the Dead*, from two tiny islands on Lake Pátzcuaro, Michoacán, have both been deployed as efficacious, iconic embodiments and referents of Mexico and Mexicanness from the postrevolutionary era of the 1920s to the present day, within complex and contradictory performism frameworks and strategies, for interfacing nationalist and touristic agendas. Both were appropriated for, and disseminated within, collections of embodied activities and visual imagery for performing Mexico and Mexicanness.

At the heart of the *Dance of the Old Men* and *Night of the Dead* are two corporeal figures: a dancing old man and a kneeling woman. The face of the old man is a mask—a wooden mask that covers the flesh-and-blood face of a living person, disguising and concealing the individual and transforming him into a collective indigenous and folkloric material icon of the nation of Mexico. The face of the kneeling woman is not a mask—it is the flesh-and-blood visage of a living person, yet the blue shawl that envelopes and frames her face conceals her individuality, transforming her also into an embodiment and representation of Mexico. Both the *Dance of the Old Men* and *Night of the Dead* have profound connections with individual dancers, musicians, and villagers, and with two little island-communities on Lake Pátzcuaro, yet both iconic practices are spectated, witnessed, exhibited, projected, performed, reproduced, remembered, and disseminated in multiple and multifarious contexts inside Mexico's national borders and globally.

In this book I weave together narratives of these dancing men and kneeling women, and their role in the politics and poetics of nationalism and tourism. I trace, analyze, and discuss the processes and actions by which the *Dance of the Old Men* and *Night of the Dead* of Lake Pátzcuaro (home of P'urhépecha peoples) were used to perform, image, construct, and imagine Mexico and Mexicanness, for the multiple objectives of incorporating disparate peoples, enabling economic development, fashioning a future, attracting tourists, and creating collective identities. As the island of Janitzio and the body of water that is Lake Pátzcuaro have also performed a major role as sights and sites in the network of signification surrounding the *Dance of the Old Men* and *Night of the Dead* since the 1920s, I encompass these locations within my study. Throughout this book I focus on mapping a ninety-year trajectory and tracing the development of the frameworks surrounding these practices, sights, and sites as they were promoted as nationalistic and touristic iconic referents, icons, performances, and attractions.

The five words of the title form a structuring and theoretical through-line. Each term is conceptual, indexing a network of ideas that is political, pragmatic, and processual, and that both stands alone and operates fundamentally through interrelations with the others. Tourism and nationalism are all-encompassing terms that reflect multiple and multifarious notions, yet it is significant that they are both –isms, for they convey the idea of both doctrine and process, engaging with an ideological and philosophical perspective, and also with ongoing strategies and activities that move an idea into practice. Attaching the suffix *-ism* focuses the attention on the ideology or philosophy surrounding the element to which it is joined. I therefore coin the term performism to frame discussion in this study, engaging with the broadest conceptual understandings of performance, performing, and performativity. My aim is to draw attention to the multiple cohering and cumulative political, ideological, epistemological, ontological, and aesthetic ideas, processes, actions, and strategies that created the performance of Mexico and Mexicanness, as evidenced in the uses of the *Dance of the Old Men* and *Night of the Dead* through the last ninety years.

My analysis is rooted in the specifics of Mexican political and ideological contexts of the twentieth and early twenty-first centuries, and is inherently concerned with tracing and analyzing designations of indigenous and indigenousness, and constructions of folklore and *folklórico*. A thread that runs through this study documents how the *Dance of the Old Men*, *Night of the Dead*, and the people of Lake Pátzcuaro came to be labeled as folkloric, and with what consequences. I merge a synchronic and diachronic approach by mapping a ninety-year period of decision-making processes, even as I focus on detailed embodied, dramaturgical, and textual analyses. The trajectory begins in the aftermath of the revolutionary wars, fought between 1910 and 1920. In the early 1920s, both the *Dance of the Old Men* and *Night of the Dead* of Lake Pátzcuaro were appropriated, theatricalized, photographed, and disseminated through official state channels within postrevolutionary political and ideological frameworks of fervent nationalism and burgeoning tourism. In the 1930s both practices were incorporated into wider national structures and staged as scenes of everyday life in Mexico City, even as the island of Janitzio (and the surrounding body of water) was simultaneously developed as a tourist destination. By the Golden Age of the 1940s and 1950s, the role of the *Dance of the Old Men* and *Night of the Dead* as constructs of authentic Mexicanness had been firmly established. After the 1968 massacre and staging of the Olympic Games in Mexico City, both were deployed with vigor within the populist agenda. Through the subsequent four decades of mass migration, economic instability, neoliberalism, global tourism, and community fragmentation, the *Dance of the Old Men* and *Night of the Dead* have been performed and exhibited in a plethora of contexts in Mexico, across the border in the United States, and in multifarious European and international contexts.

I am particularly interested in the value of connections, lattices, networks, and fragmented narratives and scenarios; of the relationship between the micro and the macro; and of the constitution of centers and peripheries. Throughout this study I therefore move between the micro and the macro, between the grand narratives and individual lives, and the associated ramifications and consequences in local, regional, national, and transnational contexts. I encompass the lives of individual villagers, teachers, dancers, presidents, folklorists, politicians, musicians, journalists, photographers, musicologists, fishermen, mask-makers, writers, and anthropologists. Some names will be familiar to those cognizant of Mexican contexts (President Lázaro Cárdenas, Francisco Domínguez, Rubén M. Campos), whereas many others will be unfamiliar, obscured by the anonymity of folkloric contexts (Gervasio López, Juan Francisco, Juan González, Evaristo Gabriel).

Although two embodied activities are at the heart of this study, I analyze multifarious modes of representation, actualization, and transmission, encompassing live events, printed texts, films, photographs, objects, and experiences. In more specific terms this includes: theater performances, a Disney film, *Mexican Folkways* magazine, National Geographic guides, Ballet Folklórico companies in Mexico and the United States, printed theater programs, postcards, press releases, didactic dance books, populist magazines, academic journals, tourist guidebooks and pamphlets, newspaper reports, Web sites, a Mexican Tourist Board marketing poster in Europe, and an interactive exhibition in the Mexican Pavilion at the World's Fair.

As this is fundamentally an interdisciplinary study, I engage with a range of discursive communities using theorizations drawn principally from performance studies, ethnomusicology, dance studies, theater studies, anthropology, and tourism studies. I particularly explore notions of folkloricization, ideological refunctionalization, embodiment, essentialization, gaze, authentication, commodification, commoditization, and traditionalization. As an integral element of performism surrounding the *Dance of the Old Men* and *Night of the Dead*, processes for creating and sustaining an officially sanctioned lattice of discourse and imagery formed an essential strand of activities in the postrevolutionary era, and has continued ever since. In shaping the *Dance of the Old Men* and *Night of the Dead* as national icons and cultural practices, a particular set of meanings was molded, circulated, and reproduced. At the heart of the success of the iconicity of the two practices lies this web of communicative significances, relying on associations, both implicit and explicit, with locations, landscapes, histories, corporeal activities, and somatic types, predominantly concerned with perceptions of indigenous, authentic, and different people and practices. It is therefore pertinent to engage the notion of embodiment as a central theorization in order to discuss and interpret these processes that relate to the signifying power of human bodies in representational acts, and the incorporation of disparate people into a unified national body. Through appraisal of these profound contexts I examine epistemological issues, concerning knowledge bases, subjectivities, and processual modes of knowledge, closely connecting personal, political, and representational processes. In these processes the viewer, spectator, or reader performs an active role—an embodied role—a performing role.

The scene opens in a village—on an island—in Mexico.

CHAPTER 1

Beyond Your Expectations

Twenty-First-Century Mexico

There was another dance of old men, which they danced hunched over, with masks of old men, which is more than a little funny and amusing and makes one laugh because of its manner.

—Father Diego Durán, sixteenth-century Spanish priest in Mexico

As the silvery moon rises high over the glistening waters of Lake Pátzcuaro, I catch on the wind the echoes of music: vigorous strumming on a *vihuela* (small round-back guitar), melodic strains of a violin, a pulsating line on plucked *tololoche* (double bass), and the rhythmic tapping of dancing feet. Reflected in the lake's glassy surface I see the undulating hills embracing the body of water and the six little stepping-stones of land, all shapes and sizes, which are the islands of this lake region and home for centuries to P'urhépecha peoples.[1] Far in the distance I glimpse long motor launches chugging across the waters between the island of Janitzio and the dock in the town of Pátzcuaro, piloted by one-time fishermen, whose coarse brown hands tell of harsh hours heaving strong nets.

In the village of Jarácuaro, outside the church and village office a rough wooden stage has been erected in the atrium, and lights have been strung from tree to tree.[2] Out of the shadow emerges a straggly line of four old men, their backs curved with the weight of the years, supporting themselves on roughly hewn walking sticks sculpted from upturned roots. Toothy grins light up their rosy faces, which display the crevices of age. Long white hair hangs over their shoulders. A hush of anticipation descends over the expectant crowd. With faltering steps the men stumble and shuffle to the center of the platform, seemingly devoid of energy and strength. Clothed in white shirts and baggy trousers (neatly embroidered in geometric cross-stitch around wrists and ankles), and covered by a warm and bright woolen *gabán* (poncho), the old men seem comfortable in these everyday garments. On their heads are large straw hats, with ribbons tumbling over their faces, adding a splash of color and fun to the occasion. Finally they take their places center stage, facing an audience of some two thousand people, huddled in the darkness of the night, wrapped in shawls and ponchos. Abruptly a strident chord on violin, vihuela, and tololoche shatters the muted silence and the old men begin to dance, the vigorous rhythm of their footwork equal to that of the music. Stamping, hopping, and creating complex figures, the dancers display a remarkable degree of energy for such seemingly ageing humans.

These are the *Viejitos*[3] (Old Men) and this is *La Danza de los Viejitos* (The Dance of the Old Men), "the most representative demonstration of the folklore of Michoacán" (García Contreras 1986:25).[4] With light on the faces of the dancers one can see that their wide toothy grins are permanently this way. These visages are not frail, human flesh, but masks expertly carved from wood, their rosy-pink complexion contrasting with the brown hands that grasp the walking sticks. These are not the elders of the community, but men and boys with agile bodies; villagers who dance expertly to entertain the crowd that has gathered for the Festival of Music and Dance on the island of Jarácuaro to celebrate *Night of the Dead*.

"Have You Seen the *Dance of the Old Men* Yet?"

As a foreigner living in the city of Morelia in the mid-1990s, I was asked the same question by numerous people: "Have you seen the *Dance of the Old Men* yet?" The question was always posed with the same sort-of earnest concern, the implication being that if I hadn't seen it, then I had really missed out on something most important. I had indeed seen the *Dance of the Old Men*, the intentionally humorous dance, in which masked old men figures hobble into the spectated area and then proceed to execute precise and rapid rhythmic footwork usually to the accompaniment of one or two violins, double bass, and vihuela. Not only had I seen *The Old Men*,[5] but I had also found it hard to miss the images of the masked wizened guise of the Old Man dancer, with beribboned straw hat and multicolored poncho. This image was utilized frequently, emblazoned on tourist literature and souvenirs, advertising this event or that product. A stroll through *El Mercado de Dulces* (The Candy Market) revealed T-shirts, key-rings, mugs, pens, postcards, embroidered wall-hangings, and numerous other knickknacks and artifacts displaying the Old Men figures. The *Dance of the Old Men* was depicted in various configurations: with a group or line of dancers; with just one dancer or a musician; and in some cases with only the masked face and hat. These visual representations were unmistakably *The Old Men* from Lake Pátzcuaro, Michoacán. In case any doubt was possible, the phrase "*Los Viejitos*" or "*La Danza de los Viejitos*" accompanied the visual depiction, sometimes with the addition of a locational term, usually "Morelia," "Pátzcuaro" or "Michoacán" (figures 1.1, 1.2, 1.3).

In the city of Morelia, *The Old Men* had a presence in many contexts—danced live in five-star hotels, at folklore festivals, and for political events; captured in photographs on postcards and tourist brochures; disembodied in Old Man masks on sale in craft markets. Everyone I came into contact with knew about this dance; nearly all had seen it, and some had danced it at primary school, most often for

Figure 1.1 An array of souvenir objects displaying the *Dance of the Old Men* (*La Danza de los Viejitos*) of Lake Pátzcuaro. Objects include: T-shirt, mug, pen, embroidered hanging, miniature wooden figure, mask, and hat, bookmark, postcards, and bottle case. One postcard incorporates both *The Old Men* and *Night of the Dead* within the frame, and one T-shirt depicts the two Old Men figures as skeletons. Locational markers indicate Pátzcuaro, Michoacán, and Mexico. The central wooden figure has the word "Mexico" embroidered on the poncho.
Photo by Timothy J. Cooley, 2010.

a Mother's Day concert. This dance seemed to have a presence and an accepted ubiquity that made it special and significant, yet also quite simply part of the fabric of life.

Locationally, *The Old Men* is associated with a state—Michoacán; a city— Morelia; a town—Pátzcuaro; a lake—Lake Pátzcuaro; and two islands—Jarácuaro and Janitzio (figures 1.4, 1.5, 1.6). The state of Michoacán, which forms part of the western central area of Mexico, is a large and diverse region, steeped in preincursion, colonial, and postcolonial history. Prior to the arrival of Spaniards, the invincible P'urhépecha Empire dominated present-day Michoacán and the surrounding states. During the fourteenth and fifteenth centuries this empire had as its capital the city of Tzintzuntzan, located on the shores of Lake Pátzcuaro. Remains of pyramids still mark the presence of this remarkable civilization. Although decimated

Figure 1.2 A composite postcard from Lake Pátzcuaro, with the slogan "Saludos desde Janitzio" (Greetings from Janitzio). Images depict: the *Dance of the Old Men* performed by Gervasio López and his ensemble posing outside the Hotel La Posada de Don Vasco, Pátzcuaro, where they initiated hotel performances in the 1960s (top right); women on Janitzio posing as they undertake the work activity of weaving *fajas* (belts) (top left); an aerial view of Janitzio, Lake Pátzcuaro, clearly showing the island surrounded by water, and the statue of Morelos standing on top (bottom).

by the Spanish incursion, the P'urhépecha peoples survived and today form an important element of contemporary Michoacán and Mexico. The home of many dancers and musicians of *The Old Men* is the small village of Jarácuaro, in Lake Pátzcuaro, which lies some thirty-five miles to the west of Morelia. The Lake Pátzcuaro region has its own distinctive characteristics, not least because of the lake environment, with its inhabited islands and gently rolling hills. Numerous villages are dotted around the edge of the waters of Lake Pátzcuaro, many of which date back to preincursion eras. The colonial town of Pátzcuaro is located near the shores of Lake Pátzcuaro, where low-level colonial buildings line the narrow cobbled streets and elegant colonnaded arches surround the two plazas (14 🔊). Within the waters of Lake Pátzcuaro lie six islands of varying shapes, sizes, and populations (23 🔊). Each island also has its own distinctive elements: Jarácuaro is flat and expansive and connected to the mainland by a causeway; Pacanda is farthest from Pátzcuaro, and is large and verdant; Yunuén has steep sides, leaving little room for cultivation; Tecuena is the tiniest of the islands; Los Urandenes are small and separated from the shore by just a thin strip of water; and finally Janitzio has a distinctive, conical

Figure 1.3 A four-image composite postcard depicts aspects of the town of Pátzcuaro and the lake region, displaying human bodies in each: the performers of the *Dance of the Old Men*, with Gervasio López's ensemble (top left); a stone statue of sixteenth-century Spanish priest Vasco de Quiroga (center); the stone statue of independence leader Morelos, in the center of the island of Janitzio (top right); a grand interior of a local church with a saint's icon inside a glass case (bottom). The live bodies of the dancers and musicians of the *Dance of the Old Men* cohere with the monumentalized iconic bodies.

shape that makes it highly visible as it rises up out of the water.[6] Although Lake Pátzcuaro itself has iconic status, it is Janitzio that is a major tourist attraction and destination, captured and reproduced endlessly in nationalistic and tourist paraphernalia, and in the twenty-first century, visited by over one hundred thousand tourists for the once yearly event of *Night of the Dead*. Throughout this region, the many villages have a great richness and diversity of dances, music, and celebratory socioreligious practices and activities. Fiestas and festivities take place throughout the year, marking notable dates in the Catholic and civil calendar. Music and dance are an essential element of each fiesta, and music ensembles and dancers proliferate in this area. Yet despite the multiplicity of practices, only one dance is associated with this region and promoted as the most representative dance of Lake Pátzcuaro—the *Dance of the Old Men*.

In contrast to the Lake Pátzcuaro region, Morelia is a large bustling city, 195 miles from Mexico City, whose center is designated a UNESCO world heritage site due to the remarkable presence of two hundred historic buildings, all of which were constructed in the region's characteristic pink stone. Built between the sixteenth and early eighteenth centuries, the plazas, arcades, impressive houses, dazzling cathedral, and more than a dozen churches form this site of colonial construction. It is impossible to ignore

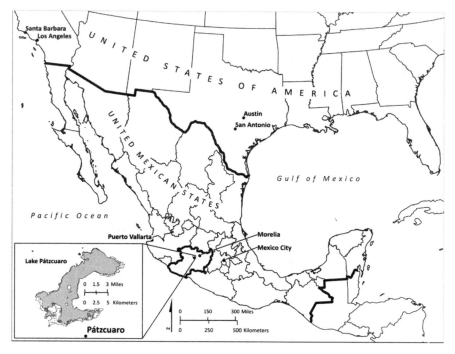

Figure 1.4 Map of Mexico and southern United States, with inset of Lake Pátzcuaro.

Map by Indy Hurt, Department of Geography, University of California, Santa Barbara.

the histories of this location in which Spanish colonization, independence, and revolution are woven into the very fabric of the place. Heroic men provide the source of names for streets, buildings, and even the city itself.[7] It was in Morelia that my involvement with *The Old Men* began in the mid-1990s, when I met one ensemble of the dance from Jarácuaro, directed by Juan Francisco Calixto (music director and violinist) and Juan González Ramos (dance director and dancer). Forming the music ensemble, three other musicians played under Francisco's direction: Oliberto Matías Domínguez (violin); Dimas Esteban Mangato (tololoche), and Felipe Ramos Santiago (vihuela). Under González's direction, the other dancers were Rodríguez Candelario Pantaleón, Israel Francisco (son of Juan), and Miguel González (son of Juan). Each weekend these Jarácuaro residents performed in the center of Morelia, in the Peña Colibrí, a venue for live music, good food and drink located in a large colonial house one block away from the central plazas. As an informal setting a *peña* offers a range of regional and international musics in a casual atmosphere. The Peña Colibrí opens its doors to local, national, and international clients, who are attracted by the daily performances of small music ensembles whose repertoire consists mainly of Latin American and Caribbean popular musics. As a regular part of the program *The Old Men* provides a draw to visitors. Late Friday and Saturday night, the ensemble from the village of

Figure 1.5 Map of the State of Michoacán, Mexico, marking the capital, Morelia, Lake Pátzcuaro, and communities referred to in this study.
Map by Indy Hurt, Department of Geography, University of California, Santa Barbara.

Jarácuaro stages the dance. Tables fill up quickly, with some hopeful clients even being turned away at the door. The master of ceremonies introduces the performance with the words "authentic," "traditional," "indigenous," and "P'urhépecha," guiding the audience in their reception and interpretation of the dance. An air of excitement pervades the room as the musicians take their place on the tiny stage. Below the stage, tables and chairs are pushed back in preparation for the entry of the dancers. Following a few *pirekuas* (songs in the P'urhépecha language) and P'urhépecha *sones* (slow and lyrical instrumental numbers) a side door opens and the Old Men shuffle and shamble into the space.[8] Cheering and clapping greets them, as though welcoming in old friends. The Old Men position themselves carefully before the waiting audience, and proceed to execute precise, rapid, and highly skilled footwork and figures. After a frenetic set piece, involving leaps and jumps, the Old Men almost collapse from apparent exhaustion, providing much hilarity and eliciting great laughter. A few moments later they have composed themselves again and proceed to undertake the next set piece. In their final pièce de résistance, *El Trenecito* (the Little Train), the dancers form a one-behind-the-other line by holding walking sticks, and weave their way around the space (and the guests), gradually increasing their pace from walking, to jogging, to frantic running, frequently leaving the last dancer hanging on for dear life. The

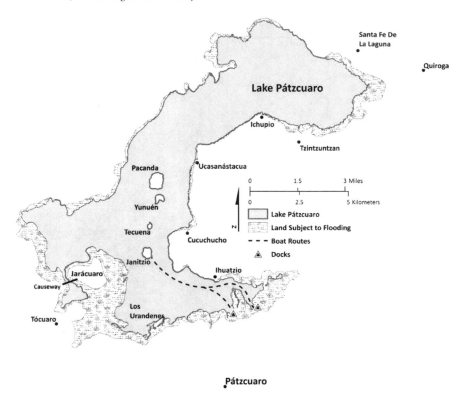

Figure 1.6 Map showing Lake Pátzcuaro, Michoacán, Mexico, with salient communities and features.
Map by Indy Hurt, Department of Geography, University of California, Santa Barbara.

audience whoops and applauds as finally the hunched and worn-out figures hobble back through the side door. As the clients continue to drink and eat, in the side room the dancers remove their masks and costumes, and spread out their ponchos on rough mattresses on the floor in preparation for sleep. Each week, these eight men and boys make the hour-and-a-half long bus journey from their Lake Pátzcuaro village to perform in Morelia (00–07, 15–16 ◓).

In the mid-1990s, in the early hours of the morning each weekend, after the clients had gone home from the Peña Colibrí and before the musicians from Jarácuaro retired to sleep, I joined in some jam sessions with the group and with other musicians who had performed during the evening. Juan Francisco invited me to play violin with their ensemble, and so over a number of years I had the opportunity to share with the lives of these musicians, dancers, and their families, and experience something of their role in performing *The Old Men* in folkloric and touristic contexts (figure 1.7). I was provoked to consider many questions emanating from this milieu, revolving around the hows, whys, and with what consequences did this one dance come to hold the place of the most representative of

Figure 1.7 Cover of CD "Los Viejitos de Jarácuaro. Danza tradicional de Michoacán con el conjunto de cuerdas los Purépechas de Jarácuaro" (the Old Men of Jarácuaro, traditional dance of Michoacán with the string ensemble the Purépechas of Jarácuaro). The CD comprised music for the *Dance of the Old Men* composed by Aurelio Calderón, Gervasio López, and Juan Francisco, and also non-dance compositions by Nicolás Bartolo Juárez. The author played violin with this ensemble for many years and is positioned in the center of the photo. The performers are: l to r, back row: Dimas Esteban Mangato, Felipe Ramos Santiago, author, Juan Francisco Calixto; Oliberto Matías Domínguez; front row: Miguel González, Israel Francisco, Rodríguez Candelario Pantaleón, Juan González Ramos. Original photo taken inside the Hotel Alameda, Morelia, 1998 (César Ramírez Tinoco).
Photo from author's collection.

the state? My interest concerning the aura around *The Old Men* led to searches through archives, documents, and magazines; to spectating and playing for live events; and to multiple conversations with organizers, musicians, dancers, and spectators in Mexico, the United States, and Europe.

Mexico: Beyond Your Expectations

In major cities across Europe in 2006, the wooden toothy-grinned mask of the Old Man, covering the face of a dancer from Jarácuaro,[9] with beribboned hat perched on head, gazed out from the center of huge billboard posters beneath the advertising slogan "Mexico: Beyond Your Expectations," "México: Más de lo que imaginas," or a translation of this sentiment in the relevant language (figure 1.8). Within the frame of the photo, a brown-skinned hand clutching a rustic walking stick contrasted with the pink hue of the carved wooden mask. Although the Old Man dancer was given center stage, the photo was juxtaposed with two other quintessential iconic referents of Mexico: the snowed-covered volcanic mountain of Popocatépetl, with the domed colonial church of Cholula in the foreground; and the stereotypical Mexican landscape of towering cacti and rolling hills, with carefully manicured green fairways of a golf course in the foreground. With these images the Mexican Tourist Board launched their major advertising campaign in Europe, promoting Mexico as an enticing attraction in a global marketplace. With this poster, *The Old Men* performed a potent role as a nationalistic and touristic signifier, embodying Mexico on a global stage. In an equally

Figure 1.8 Huge European advertising campaign poster created by the Mexican Tourist Board, displayed in many cities in 2006. This poster was located in Barcelona, Spain, with a slogan stating "México: Más de lo que imaginas"— Mexico: Beyond Your Expectations.
The Old Man dancer of Jarácuaro is given center position, juxtaposed with the volcano Popocatéptl and the colonial church at Cholula (r.), and rolling mountains, iconic cacti, and golfers (l.). The dancer is Bulmaro Paleo of the island of Jarácuaro, Lake Pátzcuaro. The Old Man photograph was taken by professional photographer Bruce Herman many years prior to the deployment in this advertising campaign.
Photo by Ruth Hellier-Tinoco.

compelling display, in October 2010 an exhibit of the iconic mask and beribboned hat of *The Old Men* was chosen as a quintessential representative essence of Mexico for EXPO 2010, the World's Fair, Shanghai, China.

The *Dance of the Old Men* has never held the status of *the* national dance of Mexico—this position is still reserved for the *jarabe tapatío* (known in English as the Mexican hat dance), much as the rumba in Cuba (Daniel 1991 and 1995) or the tango in Argentina (Savigliano 1995, Taylor 1987). Nevertheless, it is *a* national dance of Mexico, one of a small set of representative dances that is used as an essence and representation of the nation of Mexico in multiple contexts. A brief overview of contemporary venues and documentation demonstrates the role of *The Old Men* in local, regional, national, and international settings. In Pátzcuaro the dance is a tourist attraction: danced on the dockside as visitors wait to be transported to the island of Janitzio, and in hotels, restaurants, and other tourist locations throughout the town (figure 1.9). Paintings of the Old Man mask and dancer adorn the walls of the restaurant in the Best Western hotel La Posada de Don Vasco, where national and international travelers can watch *The Old Men*

Figure 1.9 Abel Orozco and family, of Jarácuaro, perform the *Dance of the Old Men* in La Casa de los Once Patios (House of Eleven Courtyards) in Pátzcuaro, Michoacán. As a location listed as a "must see" in tourist guides it attracts a regular flow of visitors. Tourists capture *The Old Men* with still and video photographic equipment, performing their role in circulating the representational imagery in global arenas.

Photo by Ruth Hellier-Tinoco, 2005.

while eating their meals. Tourist brochures and posters display the dancing figures as an essence of Michoacán, and in the markets souvenir objects and knickknacks are adorned with the unmistakable mask, beribboned hat, and poncho. In Morelia, dancers from Jarácuaro and the lakeside villages of Santa Fe and Ichupio perform in folkloric and tourist events, in restaurants, the convention center, the cultural center, and museums. Here too hotels and restaurants display the image of *The Old Men*, even using it as a familiar sign to indicate the men's bathroom in an expensive hotel.

In Mexico City, the Gabriel family from the island of Urandén (who migrated to the metropolis in the 1960s to play mariachi music) dance *The Old Men* in government-organized folkloric events and in private fiestas for fellow Michoacanos (figure 1.10 and cover image) (31–34 ◐). On the grand stage of the government-run, white marble, Art Nouveau Palacio de Bellas Artes (Palace of Fine Arts), in the heart of the city, the Ballet Folklórico de México (Folkloric Ballet of Mexico), a troupe of highly trained professional dancers and musicians, performs *The Old Men* as an indispensable facet in a repertoire of state-sanctioned dances that purport to capture

Figure 1.10 J. Evaristo Gabriel of the island of Urandén, in his home in Mexico City, wearing the costume for the *Dance of the Old Men*, holding an old clay mask from the village of Santa Fe de la Laguna. A photo of Rufino Gabriel, Evaristo's father who taught him the dance, and a painting of men with butterfly fishing nets on Lake Pátzcuaro can be seen in the background. The Gabriel family make their living in Mexico City with their mariachi ensemble (31–37 ◐).

Photo by Ruth Hellier-Tinoco, 1998.

and represent the essence of Mexico for audiences of national and global visitors. In tourist resorts such as Cancún, Acapulco, and Puerto Vallarta, where the lure of sun, golden beaches, turquoise waters, and a fully-inclusive hotel package draw Mexican and international tourists, as part of an evening of entertainment *The Old Men* appears in staged events by small folkloric dance ensembles hired by hotels and restaurants (00–07 ◐). Descriptive narratives and photographs of *The Old Men* are published in major international tourist guide books: the Lonely Planet guide to Mexico includes a reference to *The Old Men* in a section entitled "Indian Dance" (Noble 1995:51); and a National Geographic guide features two photos of the dance (Onstott 2006), embedding it in the consciousness of travelers as a *must-see* element of the Mexican experience.

Within a national sensibility, *The Old Men* is presented as traditional and indigenous. Nationalist folkloric festivals and official events encompass *The Old Men* within the repertoire, and school children and amateur dancers in Ballet Folklórico groups throughout the country don mask, poncho, and sandals to hobble, shuffle, and stamp their way through the dance, accompanied by live musicians or an audio recording of a music ensemble from the village of Jarácuaro. In a schoolbook entitled *Michoacán*, published by the Department of Public Education, and issued free to all school children, the dance is depicted in text and photos (1992:234, 257). In an elaborate publication entitled *Tradiciones mexicanas* (Mexican Traditions), a description of the dance is accompanied by a full-page glossy photo of the ensemble of musicians and dancers led by Juan Francisco and Juan González from Jarácuaro (Vertí 1991:387, plate between 272 & 273).

In the United States of America, the *Dance of the Old Men* is deployed in many contexts as live event and visual icon. At Mexican, Chicana/o, and pan–Latin American festivals, ballet folklórico ensembles dance *The Old Men*, costumed in carved masks, embroidered trousers and shirts, colorful ponchos, and beribboned hats often imported from the Lake Pátzcuaro region of Michoacán. In Saint Paul, Minnesota, *The Old Men* was performed each December from 2004 to 2007 as part of a folk dance version of *The Nutcracker*, enacting the role of representative of Mexico, produced and danced by the Ethnic Dance Theatre (Andrea Conger: personal communication).[10] In Santa Barbara, California, the Grupo de Danza Folklórica Quetzalcóatl (folkloric dance group) includes *The Old Men* within its repertoire, led by master dancer Francisco Espinosa, who learned *The Old Men* in Mexico City in his youth in the Grupo de Danza Marcelo Torreblanca, before migrating across the border (figure 1.11) (48 ◐). On numerous concert stages, a masked Old Man dancer performs with the most famous mariachi ensemble in the United States—"Nati Cano and Mariachi Los Camperos"—for their Michoacán medley.[11] As a deliberate marketing strategy, the distinctive image of beribboned hat and Old Man mask serves as a memorable logo for the bakery and deli Los Tarascos in Santa Barbara, appearing on both sides of the bilingual business card.

Returning the spotlight to Mexico, in the village of Jarácuaro *The Old Men* is part of the way of life: little boys, with hat on head and stick in hand, rehearse their *zapateado* (rhythmic footwork) in the living room to the accompaniment of their father's vihuela; men and women embroider intricate panels with cross-stitch

Figure 1.11 Taken in 2009 in Santa Barbara, California, United States, director Francisco Espinosa poses with boys of the Grupo de Danza Folklórica Quetzalcóatl after a weekly rehearsal of the *Dance of the Old Men* in the Franklin School. Espinosa learned the dance as a youth in Mexico City, in a direct line of transmission that links with the first theatricalized event in the 1920s, danced by Marcelo Torreblanca as taught by Nicolás Bartolo Juárez of Jarácuaro (48 ◐).
Photo by Timothy J. Cooley.

as decoration for the wrists and ankles of the costume, and iron white shirts and trousers, and tie string onto masks; children and adults weave long lengths of palm into braided strands, then transform them into straw hats, adding rainbow-colored ribbons, ready to be sold as souvenirs or used in live enactments. For these families on Jarácuaro, *The Old Men* is part of a tradition of nationalistic and touristic folklore begun in the 1920s and still in full flow in the twenty-first century.

Soul of Mexico: *Night of the Dead* as Public Show

As night closes in, a mist hangs low over the surface of Lake Pátzcuaro and darkness falls on the diminutive island of Janitzio. Thousands of candles flicker gently in the shadowy night air, lighting up the tiny cemetery that clings to the side of the sharply sloping face of the island. Shrouded figures of women kneel beside graves, their heads bowed in prayer and meditation, each covered with a distinctive blue *rebozo* (shawl) that frames their brown-skinned faces. Bundles of bright orange *cempasuchitl* (marigold) flowers, baskets of bread of the dead, and ornate *ofrendas* (offerings for the dead) adorn the tombs. This is the scene each year during the night of the first of November as the islanders commemorate *Noche de Muertos* (Night of the Dead), a communal event of remembrance.[12]

Yet, as the moonlight reflects off the glassy water, illuminating the little island, one can see that these women are not alone in the cemetery for this one special night of the year. Thousands upon thousands of other bodies join them in this remarkable scene: visitors and sightseers crowd onto this diminutive island, attracted by the expectation of observing and experiencing a unique, indigenous ritual, enacted by authentic P'urhépecha inhabitants. Performing the role of a memento mori, this is the biggest tourist event of the year, drawing over one hundred thousand national and international visitors to the Lake Pátzcuaro region, with the ultimate destination of the island of Janitzio. These crowds of onlookers have come to experience and witness a mystical, corporeal event. While the women and children of Janitzio remain on the island to enact their ritual roles by the gravesides, men of the island sit in their small dug-out canoes decorated with candles, holding *mariposa* or butterfly-shaped fishing nets as a display for the audience, while others ferry the never-ending stream of visitors across the water in large motor launches.

Figure 1.12 A large advertising poster for *Noche de Muertos* (Night of the Dead), created by the Michoacán and Mexican Tourist Boards in 2005, and sponsored by many state and private enterprises. It was situated near the jetty on Lake Pátzcuaro that is used for traveling to the island of Janitzio. A single woman's body, identifiable as simply P'urhépecha indexed through the blue rebozo, creates the central focus, as she is surrounded by candles and the bright orange *cempasuchitl* flowers. The slogan announces "Michoacán. Noche de Muertos…nuestra más viva tradición" (Michoacán, Night of the Dead…our most living tradition) (and also includes the exhortation "be nice to tourists").

Photo by Ruth Hellier-Tinoco.

In the twenty-first century, the romanticized imagery of this once-a-year event appears in tourist brochures, guide books, postcards, and posters. One image holds center stage: a kneeling shawled woman. She is usually depicted with head bowed, beside a grave, surrounded by marigolds and offerings, in the darkness, yet illuminated by the glow of candles. Other representations of Janitzio capture P'urhépecha men in their canoes with butterfly fishing nets, and the island–form itself, with its distinctive conical shape. As a tourist attraction on a year long basis, the island draws visitors to wander the narrow streets, to view the surrounding islands and hills, to sample the freshly-caught fish and hand-made tortillas, and to observe the residents as they go about their everyday lives (figures 1.12, 1.13, 1.14, 1.15).

In 2000, 3D representations of the kneeling women of the island of Janitzio undertaking *Night of the Dead* were exhibited in Hannover, Germany, at *Expo 2000*, the World's Fair, in a filmic display entitled *Soul of Mexico*. In 1999, throughout

Figure 1.13 A delicate line drawing depicting a single woman commemorating *Night of the Dead* on Janitzio, as published in the program for *Hamarándecua*, a theatricalized costumbrista event in Mexico City in 1930, in which *Night of the Dead* on Janitzio was represented on stage. The line drawing, by artist Carlos González, portrays the anonymized woman kneeling, in backview, with candles and flowers. Under the direction of both González and Francisco Domínguez the same corporeal embodiment was reenacted on stage.
Courtesy of COLMICH.

85. The cemetery on the island of Janitzio, Lake Pátzcuaro, Michoacán, after midnight on All Saints' Day.

86. Los viejitos of Michoacán.

Figure 1.14 A single page from the widely disseminated 1947 publication *A Treasury of Mexican Folkways* by Frances Toor. Both the *Dance of the Old Men* of Pátzcuaro and *Night of the Dead* on Janitzio are brought together and framed within a single border, effecting both a designation as *folk* and a pairing that continues to this day. The book circulated widely in Mexico and the United States. (Although the caption states All Saint's Day, All Soul's Day is recognized as the equivalent of Day or Night of the Dead). In the background, Negritos masks are also visible, a dance that continues to be enacted in many P'urhépecha villages.

Courtesy of CENIDIM and Biblioteca de las Artes, Mexico City.

Figure 1.15 A giant advertising poster in the heart of Mexico City deploying a P'urhépecha fisherman with a *mariposa* (butterfly) fishing net on Lake Pátzcuaro to market Mexico's largest cellular phone company. The slogan reads: "Todo México Es Territorio" (All Mexico Is Our Territory—or more colloquially, We Have Mexico Covered). The iconic form of the island of Janitzio is distinctive in the background, firmly signaling the exact location. The image engages notions of backward preindustrial and premodern separation, signified through an embodied indigenous P'urhépecha fisherman cut-off temporally (of the past) and spatially (through a body of water), to sell the latest cutting-edge technology. The campaign ran in print form and on television (43 ❧).

Photo by Ruth Hellier-Tinoco, 1999.

the night of the first of November, the activities of the Janitzio islanders in the cemetery were captured on film over a durational period, using a sophisticated configuration of cameras. These images were displayed in the form of a living diorama to an audience of international visitors at *Expo 2000*. Within the Mexican pavilion, an "immersive gallery" projected 3D real time images of *Night of the Dead* on Janitzio onto screens using technology that was able to "plunge visitors into the heart of this celebration of the dead so that they feel 'as if they were there'" (www. mexico21.org.mx and Hanover 2000: Press Release). Visitors could walk through the tunnel as if walking through the cemetery, observing the P'urhépecha women kneeling and praying, lighting candles, and laying flowers, at the "ancestral celebration" (ibid.) (figure 1.16). In a virtual reality, interactive depiction, women on Janitzio enacting *Night of the Dead* were given the role of embodying Mexico at the World's Fair, performing an essence of Mexico in a global arena.

Figure 1.16 *Soul of Mexico*, the 3D interactive film exhibition of *Night of the Dead* on Janitzio, projected in the Mexican Pavilion at *Expo 2000*, the World's Fair, Hannover, Germany. Relying on the idea of a living diorama and being there, spectators wore glasses to see the 3D effect. Interestingly, without the glasses (and as with this photographic reproduction) the images and bodies appear blurred and ephemeral, cohering with multiple descriptions configuring the women on Janitzio as phantasmagorical figures. Using a complex arrangement of cameras, filming took place in the cemetery on the island of Janitzio, Lake Pátzcuaro for the duration of *Night of the Dead* in 1999.
Photo courtesy of Philippe Chiwy.

After the Revolution: Imaging and Embodying Mexico

In the twenty-first century, the *Dance of the Old Men* and *Night of the Dead* of Lake Pátzcuaro are engaged as iconic embodied referents of Mexicanness and of authentic and indigenous Mexico in multifarious national and global contexts. Yet in 1922 neither activity was a public spectacle for the attention of outsiders. Dances of old men in the Lake Pátzcuaro area took place in an ad hoc way for local villagers during fiestas, being danced in the streets for hours on end in the communities of Jarácuaro, Cucuchucho, and Santa Fe. Night of the Dead on the island of Janitzio was a private celebration, with no onlookers and no outsiders present. Any visitors who did journey to the islands were treated with great suspicion and regarded as "the enemy" (León 1934:162).

Nevertheless, by the 1940s both *The Old Men* and *Night of the Dead* of Lake Pátzcuaro had become prominent public spectacles and well-known icons, with the status of unambiguous representations of indigenous P'urhépecha life. U.S. anthropologist George Foster, who carried out fieldwork in the Lake Pátzcuaro region between 1944 and 1946, described the *Dance of the Old Men* as "really typical and characteristic of the Tarascan [P'urhépecha] region and one of the most entertaining of all Mexico," and also observed that *Night of the Dead* on Janitzio "has become one of the most famous spectacles of Mexican indigenous life.... Great crowds of tourists have come, and the Tarascan women show no hesitancy in talking with them" (1948:208 & 220–21).[13] In 1947, photos of both *The Old Men* and *Night of the Dead* of Lake Pátzcuaro appeared together on a single page of the influential book *A Treasury of Mexican Folkways* by Frances Toor (1947, photos 85 and 86, no page) (figure 1.14).

In the crucial period between 1920 and 1940, the postrevolutionary era of nationalism and burgeoning tourism, events and activities were undertaken that transformed *The Old Men* and *Night of the Dead* of Lake Pátzcuaro from a local dance and a private ritual into public spectated events and iconic embodied referents of Mexico and Mexicanness. To contextualize this, between 1910 and 1920 the Mexican Revolution fractured the country. When the revolutionary civil wars drew to a close, ambitious and far-reaching strategies and programs for nation-building and capitalist modernization were formulated and implemented. The demographic of Mexico included diverse communities of peoples, which necessitated the unification of a wide-ranging populous, many of whom were considered to be in states of "backwardness" and therefore in need of incorporation. At the heart of much policy-making were issues of ethnicity and race, in which the movements of *indigenismo* and *mestizaje* were fundamentally embedded. Whereas indigenismo entailed both valorizing and incorporating indigenous peoples and cultures (past and present) into the newly developing nation state, mestizaje concerned the concept and practice of creating a mixed, authentic Mexican nation.[14]

In documenting and analyzing the postrevolutionary period, many scholars of Mexican history and popular culture have made generalized observations concerning processes and policies in which indigenous practices and peoples were appropriated and nationalized; were performed as staged folkloric representations; and were established as part of national folk culture (García Canclini 1993:43; Rowe and Schelling 1991:5, 64; Knight 1990:82; Dawson 1998:29; Zolov 2001:253). These general ideas are wholly applicable to *The Old Men* and *Night of the Dead* of Lake Pátzcuaro. Within postrevolutionary political and ideological frameworks, both practices were appropriated, commodified, and disseminated through official state channels, and circulated in representational contexts away from the villages in the P'urhépecha region of Michoacán, within a nationalist, modernizing political agenda as embodiments of folkloric nationalism, and simultaneously deployed within tourist contexts. Both were thoroughly bound up with ideologies concerning ethnicity and race, indigenismo and mestizaje.[15]

Initiating the transformation in the early 1920s, state-sponsored intellectuals, artists, and politicians visited the island of Janitzio to observe Night of the Dead, and also witnessed a dance of old men on the island of Jarácuaro. In 1924, as a result of these visits, both the *Dance of the Old Men* and *Night of the Dead* of Lake Pátzcuaro were represented and performed in theatricalized events on a stage in Mexico City organized by government institutions. Simultaneously photographs and articles with an ethnographic focus were published in populist magazines and academic journals. In one decisive action, one man from the island of Jarácuaro, Nicolás Bartolo Juárez, was taken to Mexico City to teach *The Old Men*. In the ensuing months, years, and decades, the *Dance of the Old Men* and *Night of the Dead* were thoroughly incorporated into the national sensibility as essences of authentic Mexico.

Which Mexico? Many Mexicos

It is clear that *The Old Men* and *Night of the Dead* did not spontaneously emerge as public spectacles and icons of Mexicanness. They were shaped, promoted, and manipulated by individuals, groups, organizations, and institutions. Since the initial appropriation in the early 1920s, both practices have been performed, represented, and deployed continually in regional, national, and international events, for national and global tourists, for local residents and foreign dignitaries, and for Mexican presidents and international audiences. They have been taught to schoolchildren, and taken on tour to many countries; and they have been documented and reproduced, inscribed as words, photographs, and drawings, in books, magazines, newspapers, films, publicity material, and souvenirs. In this study my aim is to examine the activities and strategies of nationalist and tourist performism by tracing and analyzing the trajectory of *The Old Men* and *Night of the Dead*, from the immediate postrevolutionary years through to the present day. Engaging with Scott's observation that "any carefully detailed empirical case is always far richer than the generalizations that can be extracted from it" (1994: ix), I maintain a focus on the ninety-year course of the two practices, concentrating on "micro analyses" (Geertz 1988:39) that are in constant dialogue with macro contexts, where the micro informs the macro and vice versa. Examining the course of the two practices therefore involves integrating the micro-workings of these practices into the macro context of Mexican cultures, histories, ideologies, and politics.

In short, I trace the practices of the *Dance of the Old Men* and *Night of the Dead* of Lake Pátzcuaro as they were molded and developed as iconic and emblematic representations of Mexico, discussing their role in constructing and shaping notions of Mexico, in embodying the *Soul of Mexico*, and in promoting "Mexico: Beyond Your Expectations." Significantly, contexts of both nationalism and tourism require the formation of a set of iconic referents and stereotypes, comprising visual images, dances, music, food, sites, clothing, and other cultural practices that become representative and recognizable. Through processes of essentialization significant units of recognition are created and produced, by reducing and neatly classifying images, repertoires, discourses, and peoples into a set of nationally familiar and easily identifiable types. In terms of postrevolutionary Mexican nation-building, these representative types were specifically related to perceptions of *mexicanidad* (Mexicanness) and *lo mexicano* (that which is wholly and authentically Mexican). In a similar vein, attracting international tourists to "destination Mexico" and national tourists to particular areas of Mexico also necessitated a carefully shaped set of emblematic sights and sites. Both *The Old Men* and *Night of the Dead* formed essential elements as representative icons for nationalistic and touristic agendas.

Both practices were promoted as referents of indigenousness, authenticity, pre-Hispanicity, rurality, folklore, tradition, the past, ritual, and pagan beliefs. They functioned as signifiers of places and associated peoples ranging from the local (Lake Pátzcuaro) to the national (Mexico), and reception and interpretation revolved around a network of associations and significations. Of vital importance to this network was the notion of bodies, for at the heart of both iconic practices were bodies with potent symbolic status. These bodies (which indexed people) were framed to be read as authentic indigenous bodies, folkloric bodies, and bodies of the past. Importantly, the lattice of significations and connotations generated in the early 1920s is still in place today.

Examining the hows and whys of the processes and significances of the *Dance of the Old Men* and *Night of the Dead* involves grappling with the multiplicity and complexity that is Mexico. Mexico is a country and peoples of contrasts and contradictions, with a population in 2010 of around one hundred ten million people, encompassing over sixty languages, and diverse lifestyles, where colonial cities rub up against rural communities, and mountain ranges drop down to crystal coastlines. In this nation one quarter of the population lives in the capital, Mexico City, where skyscrapers, modernist blocks, and colonial churches jostle for space within crowded urban neighborhoods, and where stones of ancient pyramids and verdant green parkland stand alongside universities, opera houses, and cantinas. Mexico is a country of movement, migration, and journeys: millions of Mexicans migrate within the territorial limits and millions more live across the border in the United States as both documented and undocumented residents. Mexico is not only a nation within the territorial boundaries, but Mexico as people thrives north of the border in the United States. Perhaps most crucially for this study, Mexico is a nation where concepts, discourses, and representations of ethnicity and race, of past and present, of preinvasion and colonial, of indigenous and mestizo weave in and out of everyday life, and are inescapably and thoroughly embedded in all contexts. Such heterogeneity and multiplicity has therefore necessitated the continuation of essentialist and stereotypical icons and embodiments of a contained and constructed Mexico, for, as Stern has noted, "'Mexico' is a half-fiction, a patchquilt of 'many Mexicos' stitched together as much by political fiat and cultural proclamation as by unity of experience, memory, and identity" (Stern 1995:23–24).[16]

Three-element Approach: Art, Institutions, and People

In order to appraise and consider the complexities of performism encompassing *The Old Men* and *Night of the Dead*, I engage three parameters of study as proposed by Cynthia Novack: "the 'art' (the choreographic structures, movement styles, and techniques of dance), the institutions (local, national, global) in which it is practiced and performed, and the people who participate in it as performers, producers, spectators, and commentators" (Novack 1995:181). This three-element approach appears throughout my study as a framework within which to analyze and understand some of the principal issues—aesthetic, political, personal, ideological, and economic—concerning *The Old Men* and *Night of the Dead* as practices of ideological refunctionalization for folkloric nationalism and touristic exhibition. Such a framework enables me to move from the fine detail of individual lives and specific events, to the cultural, social, political, and aesthetic contexts within which they functioned.

In relation to the idea of art, I extend this to the broader notion of spectated event, undertaking dramaturgical analyses of the two practices in a range of settings and contexts, both live and mediated, from the early twentieth century to the present day. Within this concept I include representations of the practices in writing (program notes, newspaper articles and Website material); as visual photographic images (postcards, magazines, guide books, films); and as objects (tourist souvenirs). For the second element, institutions, I principally focus upon state and governmental institutions and departments, particularly those engaged with education and research—schools, universities and research institutes, predominantly those involved with the disciplines of anthropology, folklore studies, music and dance—and those concerned with tourism. I also include the notion of "place and space," examining the importance of venues and locations in shaping and framing reception and interpretation of performances. For the third element, people, I encompass the lives, publications, and performances of Lake Pátzcuaro residents, politicians, government employees (in particular, anthropologists, folklorists, and artists), pedagogues, and tourist-industry personnel.

Methodologies: Canoes, Archives, and Artifacts

For a study such as this, with a historical span of ninety years and a geographical area covering villages, towns, cities, and a nation within a global context, the sources of data and methods of collection were, by necessity, many and varied, and might be regarded as eclectic and even serendipitous. My research led me from island village to capital city, from sound collections to live event, from home of the former state governor to the General Archive of the Nation. The resulting presentation that is this book provides glimpses of realities of complex historiographies. Moving between the micro-contexts of the lives of Juan Francisco, Juan González, and the many other residents of the Lake Pátzcuaro region and the macro-contexts of national politics and presidents serves to reinforce the personal and individual consequences of seemingly unimportant local activities.[17]

The overall context is an interdisciplinary one, where the boundaries between practices (music, dance, theater) and fields (performance studies, ethnomusicology, dance studies, theater studies, history, anthropology, tourism studies) are blurred. Similarly, this study comprises material from a diverse range of sources that include: literary objects (published books, academic journals, magazines, newspapers, programs, state papers, and tourist brochures); music transcriptions (published and unpublished manuscripts); audio artifacts (musical sound recordings—commercial and private; spoken interviews and radio programs); film artifacts (private and institution-made recordings); photographs (in books, journals, magazines, newspapers, and private collections); and miscellaneous artifacts (tourist souvenirs and paraphernalia). I attended and participated in many live events in a range of venues, and an indispensable element involved playing the violin with various ensembles, particularly that of Juan Francisco and Juan González. As my violin went with me to each place, so I was invited to join in with many different groups of musicians in the Lake Pátzcuaro region. In Mexico City, Morelia, Pátzcuaro, and villages throughout the P'urhépecha region, I carried out interviews with musicians, dancers, state officials, cultural activists, organizers, archivists, and family members. In multiple locations I sorted through state papers, newspaper and sound archives, performance artifacts, and literary documentation.[18] Issues concerning my own narratives and roles in these research and subsequent representational processes are complex, contradictory, and dichotomous. Embedded in these descriptions and accounts are my own interpretations and experiences, even as I draw on the narratives, explanations, and stories of others. In chapter 10 I discuss aspects of these complexities, particularly in terms of reciprocity and consequences.

Trajectory Through This Book

At heart this book combines and interweaves an analysis of twentieth-century cultural histories and politics with dramaturgical analyses. The course of the book is to a large extent chronological, tracing performism processes through a ninety-year period from 1920 to 2010. However, as I move between the micro-analyses of the specific practices and processes encompassing *The Old Men* and *Night of the Dead*, to the macro-context of Mexico and a global marketplace, this chronological approach is interspersed with more detailed explorations of particular moments, practices, events, and lives. My central thesis is that twenty-first century contexts that engage *The Old Men* and *Night of the Dead* as folkloric, indigenous icons are intrinsically and fundamentally connected to the formational period of the 1920s, with profound ramifications in local, national, and international arenas. With an awareness of the recent scholarship that aims to challenge the writing and analysis of Mexican twentieth-century history in terms of continuity and lack of change (see Schmidt 2001:29), the focus of this study concerns the endurance and recycling of images and rhetoric from the early 1920s to the first decade of the twenty-first century. With a historical study spanning a ninety-year period, there is a need for periodization to enable discussion of particular movements and moments; however, having to separate out eras, or demarcate temporal boundaries, inevitably leads to false divides. I argue that the deployment of *The Old Men* and *Night of the Dead* in each period leads to the next, therefore, the policies and strategies of the postrevolutionary years provided the framework around which all latter uses were constructed.[19]

In order to deal with issues chronologically and theoretically, I have divided the book into three parts, covering conceptual and basic historical ideas in part I, a chronological account in part II, and a combination of theoretical, illustrative, and analytical cases in part III. It is therefore possible to engage with part II or part III separately, tracing either the chronological path or delving into particulars of constructing notions of indigenous bodies, illustrative cases, and dramaturgical elements. In many instances in part II, I have included dramaturgical analyses (of films, staged events, and documentation) within the historical discussion, therefore it would be possible to focus upon each element separately, for even as they constitute each other, the two elements can also be examined apart.

Part I comprises two chapters: in this opening chapter I have given an overview of contemporary contexts in which *The Old Men* and *Night of the Dead* as images, ideas, and live events are circulated and performed, and I have described the initial processes of the postrevolutionary era that transformed these practices from local seasonal activities to public, national spectacles. In the following chapter, I outline theorizations of the principal areas of focus as salient and applicable to this study, dealing with nationalism, ethnicity, identity, tourism, performance and performism, and embodiment.

Part II of this book is roughly chronological dealing with the periods of 1920 to 1940 (the postrevolutionary era); 1940 to 1968 (the Golden Age and growing unrest); and 1968 to 2010 (post-massacre and postmodernism).

In chapters 3 to 6, I deal with the period from 1920 to 1940, which were the foundational and constructional years of nation-building and burgeoning tourism. In chapter 3 I contextualize the historical, political, and ideological trajectory through eras of pre-Conquest, colonization, and independence (with burgeoning forms of nationalism and indigenismo), leading to a period of revolution in the early twentieth century. I draw out some of the salient and momentous political, ideological, and cultural issues of the postrevolutionary period with particular reference to issues of ethnicity, race, nationalism, folklore, education, music, theater, and dance. Chapter 4 covers the events and people involved in the initial processes of appropriation, commodification, display, and theatricalization of the two practices in Mexico City as staged folklore within nationalist contexts and for the growing tourist industry. I discuss the visits of state officials to *Night of the Dead* on Janitzio and the subsequent dissemination through photos and written texts in publications such as *Mexican Folkways* and *Ethnos*. I also analyze aspects of a Regional Theater event in the highland town of Paracho, and discuss collecting and representational processes. I single out for special attention the Jarácuaro musician and composer Nicolás Bartolo Juárez and the musicologist Rubén M. Campos. The transformation of *Night of the Dead* and the island of Janitzio into touristic and folkloric attractions is the focus of chapter 5. In chapter 6 firstly I focus upon major theatricalized events in Mexico City in which both practices were staged. Secondly, I discuss events across the border in the United States, analyzing elements of a didactic book for staging the *Dance of the Old Men* and an event in San Antonio, Texas in which performers from Lake Pátzcuaro enacted *The Old Men* for "Mexicans abroad."

Chapter 7 deals with the period known as the Golden Age (1940 to 1968). Firstly I discuss the development of notions of folklore and folklórico and the incorporation of *The Old Men* into the repertoire of regional Mexican dances. Secondly, I analyze elements of national and international dissemination of images of Lake Pátzcuaro, *Night of the Dead*, and *The Old Men* in books and films, and relate this to the flourishing tourist industry in Lake Pátzcuaro encompassing the initiation of hotel performances and the Festival of Music and Dance for *Night of the Dead*. Thirdly, I give an overview of didactic and pedagogical regional dance publications and events, and describe the founding and influence of the professional Ballet Folklórico de México.

Chapters 8 and 9 cover the period from the late 1960s to 2010, dealing with a plethora of representational practices encompassing *The Old Men* and *Night of the Dead* and the consolidation of their roles as embodiments of Mexico. In chapter 8 I turn the spotlight on the Lake Pátzcuaro region again, discussing developments in tourism, *Night of the Dead*, Festivals of Music and Dance, and other staged and spectated contexts. Chapter 9 deals with a discussion of European tours, Mexico City staged events, *The Old Men* in museums, festivals, and international folkloric tours, and publications. I describe media dissemination of *The Old Men* through television, books, recordings and guides, and I conclude with a glance across the border to the United States discussing the proliferation of Mexican Folkloric Dance ensembles.

In chapter 10 I consider the ninety-year trajectory of *The Old Men* in relation to the residents of Lake Pátzcuaro, particularly in terms of migration, transmission, reappropriation, and cultural revitalization. I use the P'urhépecha Artistic Festival of Zacán as a specific focus for discussion, and also reflect upon my own presence and impact as a musician and researcher, particularly related to the making of an audio recording and the consequences of this for one member of the Bartolo Juárez family.

Part III encompasses theoretical discussions and detailed dramaturgical analyses. In chapter 11 I turn my attention to analysis of the reception, interpretation, meanings, and significations of *The Old Men* and *Night of the Dead*, firstly placing emphasis upon the concept of bodies, embodiment, and difference, and the construction of the idea of indigenous bodies; secondly I examine the network of ideas surrounding Lake Pátzcuaro, pre-Conquest ancestry, and the exhibition of work and everyday life; and thirdly I discuss specific elements of both *Night of the Dead* and *The Old Men* as corporeal activities.

I analyze visual images in chapter 12: firstly, postcards circulating in the Lake Pátzcuaro and Morelia area; secondly, Las Tarascas fountain, and advertising using fishermen on Lake Pátzcuaro; thirdly, the marketing poster of the 2006 European campaign of the Mexican Tourist Board; and fourthly, *Soul of Mexico*, the filmic exhibition of *Night of the Dead* on Janitzio at the World's Fair, Germany in 2000.

In chapter 13 I reflect upon the ninety-year trajectory of *The Old Men* and *Night of the Dead* in terms of symbolic and economic production, and relationships of power.

CHAPTER 2

Discursive Communities

Performism, Nationalism, and Tourism

FROM THE 1920S onward, two embodied activities, the *Dance of the Old Men* and *Night of the Dead* of Lake Pátzcuaro, were deployed as public spectated practices and iconic referents within multifarious nationalistic and touristic contexts. Through this study my aim is to document and discuss many of the processes, events, lives, and activities involved in this trajectory. In order to explore the courses of action and their ramifications I engage with a range of discursive communities. As a way of introducing some of the issues under discussion, here I briefly outline theorizations of the principal areas of focus as salient and applicable to this study, namely: nationalism, identity, and ethnicity; tourism; performance and performism; embodiment; and dance and music in nationalistic and touristic contexts. Finally I include a few key elements of other conceptual ideas in relation to the Mexican contexts that form the core of this inquiry, encompassing appropriation, representation, framing, gaze, essentialization, authentication, commodification, commoditization, hegemony, and centers and peripheries.

Nationalism, Identity, and Ethnicity

The interrelated concepts of nationalism, identity, and ethnicity are central to this study; however, one of the problems in discussing the "amorphous concept of nationalism" is the "extensive disagreement over virtually everything in the general literature on nationalism" (Morris 1999:364), with recognition that nationalism is not a coherent ideology, but a broad cultural frame in which a variety of contradictory claims are made. Despite the divergences in thinking over nationalism, one area of concurrence concerns the concept of the socially constructed nature of various types of peoplehood and the tenuous links to historical formations, such that nations and national cultures are "plastic constructs not cultural givens" (Fox 1990:4). Notions of fluidity, invention, and construction are fundamental to an understanding of the processes at work by governments and institutions in nationalization activities, with most courses of action encompassing the authenticating or traditionalizing of products (Hobsbawm and Ranger 1983). Thus, shaping, constructing, building, inventing, and imagining a nation, community, and national identity are all central concepts.[1] Shaping and creating national identity often takes place through the formulation of ethnic identity, so much so that nationalism and ethnicity are seen to be intrinsically related, and regarded as modern phenomena inseparably connected with the activities of a modern centralizing state (Brass 1991:8). Identities may be regarded as social and historical constructions that are therefore layered and multiple, and capable of shifts and transformations. Concepts of the formation, formulation, manipulation, and maintenance of identity through processes that involve "signifying identities" (Cohen 2000) is central.

Ethnicity is seen as "an arguable and murky intellectual term" (Chapman, McDonald, & Tonkin 1989:11) and a "problematic word" (Stokes 1994:6), observations which attest to certain complexities of nation formation invoking this concept. As ethnicity is regarded as arising from the social organization of cultural difference (Barth 1969) so a focus upon issues of constructed identity are paramount, engaging notions of power struggles and hegemonic processes. According to Brass, ethnicities are social and political constructions, and are frequently the creation of elites and those in positions of power, who draw upon, distort, and sometimes fabricate materials from the cultures of the groups they wish to represent in order to protect their own well-being or existence or to gain political and economic advantage for their groups as well as for themselves (Brass 1991). Thus the idea of the tactical management of ethnic identity (Cohen 2000:3) for nation-building relates to hegemonic processes as a means of shaping and controlling notions of nationhood. For nationalist purposes, these processes involve the formation or appropriation of uniting symbols, myths, and figures around which the nation as people can gain a sense of community and belonging.

Tourism

Processes and theories of tourism primarily concern issues of travel and journeys, involving ideological shaping, economic impact, and social consequences. Recognizing the sheer manipulative influence of tourism is essential, for "tourism is not just an aggregate of merely commercial activities; it is also an ideological framing of history, nature, and tradition; a framing that has the power to reshape culture and nature to its own needs" (MacCannell 1992:1). People make journeys and then return home having engaged in an encounter with difference, shaped through notions of home and other. In regional, national, and international environments, tourism therefore "profoundly influences the ways we define place, *foreignness*, and ourselves" (MacCannell 2001:380). Behind the anonymous "it" of tourism are multiple agencies, institutions, and people. Significantly, one principal agency is often a state-controlled government tourist board. Aspects of economics, commercialism, commercialization, and capitalism are central to tourist contexts. Processes and issues of commoditization—of turning practices and peoples into commodities—are fundamental, with sophisticated tourist productions forming a significant element of many tourist sites. As ethnic identity is central to processes of nationalism, so ethnicity and ethnic identity are common elements of tourism. A tourist *attraction* becomes the motivation to leave home, and the attraction for the journeying frequently involves an experience of *otherness* (ibid.). Otherness, exoticism, and foreignness are regarded as a basic commodity and appeal of tourism. In ethnic tourism the marketing of peoples, cultures, and places as indigenous forms a primary element, with products, practices, and bodies/people acquiring a monetary exchange value for consumers. Peoples designated as indigenous are frequently utilized in tourist packages, forming tourist attractions through exotic representations for both foreign and domestic travelers. Exoticism and foreignness tend to rely upon state-constructed notions of ethnicity, for although there are multiple institutions mediating the relationship between tourism and ethnicity, the state is the largest of them (Wood 1997). Such a system also affects the distribution of resources through issues of structures of political access, for if the state is dominant in the political construction of ethnicity by means of official designations, so the state predominates in relation to economic decision-making (Nagel 1994).

Concepts and processes of production, construction, commodification, and commoditization are therefore central to tourism, entailing the generation of images of the Other, the creation of "natives" and "authenticity," and the consumption of images, and myths and fantasies (Crick 1989:330–329). Methods for engendering "ethnicity-for-tourism," and for creating an ethnic attraction and destination, whether as place or peoples, involves transformational processes which MacCannell designates as site sacralization (1999:43–48), involving cultural appropriation, authentication, and the staging of authenticity (MacCannell 1999:91–107). Tourist productions are generated through a network of attractions (Kirshenblatt-Gimblett and Bruner 1992:300), which often relies upon notions of *type*, *stereotypes*, and essentialist expressions, foregrounding symbolic and iconic references. One of the significant elements for ethnic tourism in nations with large indigenous populations is the linkage between past and present (Kemper 2001:250), allowing visitors to experience a sense of difference through preindustrial and premodern notions.

Performism, Performance, and Performativity

Notions of performance are fundamentally important to this study, however, as with nationalism, the concept of performance continues to be permeated with ambiguities despite cogent attempts at definition. "Performance" as a term is used in multiple academic fields and areas of life, from business to sport, from theater to linguistics, from disability to ethnography, from physics to dance, from history to psychology, and from music to communication studies. Cognate terms of "performer," "to perform," "performative," and "performativity" all contribute to the richness and complexity of uses. Trying to tease out and interrogate the multifarious possibilities has been undertaken many times (c.f. Bell 2008, Campbell 1996, Schechner 2002). As performance studies scholar Diana Taylor has observed, "performance" is a polysemic term that has multiple definitions and uses, that encompasses a diverse array of ideas and practices, and that covers an "extraordinarily broad range of behaviors...from the discrete dance to conventional cultural behavior," simultaneously connoting "a process, a praxis, an episteme, a mode of transmission, an accomplishment, and a means of intervening in the world" (Taylor 2003: 6, 15). My own rationale for engaging the term "performance" is precisely due to the multifarious applications, usages, and therefore possibilities that it offers. Drawing on multiple and even divergent uses encompasses and highlights the complexities and contradictions inherent in any context and process. For this study I mainly draw on the broadest theorizations and applications from performance studies, but I also engage with more conventional usages in ethnomusicology, musicology, dance studies, theater and drama studies, and also uses in history, anthropology, cultural studies, film studies, and tourism studies.

In order to provide a broad outline, here I mention a range of salient areas of performance and its cognates as applicable to this study. As a generalization, performance may be regarded as a human activity that works in three principle ways: firstly, as *poiesis*, constructing and making culture (c.f. Butler 1990 and 1993, Derrida 1990, Turner 1982); secondly, as *mimesis,* representing, imitating, or reflecting the world (c.f. Bourdieu 1984, Schechner 1988); and thirdly, as *kinesis,* intervening, and remaking social and political rules (c.f. Conquergood 1995, 2002). Conventionally, in terms of music, dance, and theater, performance is a framed event, an enactment out of tradition, and a discrete object of attention in which the framing is inherently part of the event itself. Temporally, it has a beginning and an end, and spatially it has a marked boundary around it. It may entail practices and events that involve theatrical, rehearsed, or conventional and event-appropriate behaviors, and it is listened to, viewed, and gazed upon for communicatory and affective purposes. Using Richard Schechner's distinction, such events would be designated "is-performance" (2002:38). Performance also refers to the informal scenarios of daily life. All human, everyday practices are *performed*, so that any action at whatever moment or location can be seen as a public presentation of the self. Schechner called this application "as-performance" (ibid.), referring to ways in which behaviors and practices can by analyzed and interrogated as performance, even though conventionally (according to a specific local context) they would not fit a classification of performance. This concept relates to the idea of the performative turn, which concerns an awareness of the relations between everyday life and stage performances.

The notion of the performative and performative utterance, as introduced by Austin, and developed by Derrida, concerns a philosophy of language, conceptualizing how a spoken or written text can bring about human interactions in the very process of speaking or writing/reading. Judith Butler's theory of performativity is particularly useful, because it concerns the constitution of identity, and pays special attention to bodies (1990). Performativity deals with how identity is performed, and how each person performs multiple and shifting identities in history, language, and material embodiments. In the original work, Butler's use of performativity concerned how a *gendered* identity is constituted, observing that performers onstage materialize characters in and through their bodies. Butler therefore used the term "materialization" to refer to the body's appearance, and to acting and doing, rather than deploying the term "construction," with all the implications of social construction of identity. Broadly, performativity is a theory of identity; a strategy of critique; and a political practice, and is valuable for the way in which it embraces and attempts to interrogate and investigate multifarious areas of cultural, social, political, and economic life. According to theories of performativity, ethnicity, race, class, and gender are all constituted in and through performance (everyday practices), through a complex matrix of normative boundaries, boundaries that are created in language, enacted in institutions, and produced by technologies that generate certain relationships. All make explicit claims about what is normal, and also therefore what is other/different. Although performativity may be useful for understanding gender, constructions of race and ethnicity are not so easily understood or explained through performativity, for "race/ethnicity is a different kind of performative enacted *through the visual*" (Bell 2008:198).

According to Alan Hyde, race is "a kind of domination of the body by the eye. Race is thus not a thing or a state but a relationship, and the question is always not just what state has been constructed, but who is doing the construction and for what purpose?" (Hyde 1997:223). Such an observation is central to my study, drawing attention to issues of looking, viewing, spectating, watching, and witnessing. I return to this aspect presently in relation to embodiment.

In this study I am specifically interested in tracing and analyzing contexts, strategies, processes, agents, individuals, and institutions implicated in shaping, disseminating, receiving, and interpreting iconic referents for twentieth and twenty-first century Mexican nationalism and tourism. I therefore find it useful to coin a new term—"performism." Performism encompasses matters of process, practice, doctrine, and theory. As an *–ism* it conveys the idea of both doctrine and process, indexing a network of ideas that is political, pragmatic, and processual. In other words, it engages with an ideological and philosophical perspective, and also with the ongoing strategies, activities, and processes that move an idea into practice. Relating to both nationalism and tourism, the term references a broad complex of notions, yet at the core is a concept of "perform" associated with accomplishment. With the term "performism" I aim to foreground doctrines, policies, programs, and processes of shaping and constructing a multifaceted matrix of performed significations and iconic referents, in a spectrum from micro to macro contexts.

I encompass the previous delineations of performance and performativity, but place the focus on the wide-ranging processes and practices that together cohered, and cohere, to shape and construct gazed upon, listened to, experienced, and viewed iconic referents. The doctrine concerns the production of iconic referents or performances in the broadest sense, taking in the idea of performance as a spectrum rather than distinct categories (encompassing, but not limited to, films, staged events, physical locations, work activities, theater productions, political edicts, tourist guide books, magazines, and souvenir objects). By deploying the word "performism," I seek to draw attention to the fluid and extensive range of meanings and practices, and highlight the ever-present processual aspects of accomplishing a composite of performances, through the shaping, molding, constructing, disseminating, and interpreting of boundaries, frames, and gazes. Although the term "folkloricization" is useful for considering processes of shaping emblematic collections of conventionally conceived performance practices (music and dance) through display and institutional involvement, my intention in coining the term "performism" is to broaden the concept of performance, perform, and performer to include a much wider range of applications. Performism takes in the multiple presentational and representational processes and practices involving signification, meaning, and experience, for political, ideological, economic, social, and experiential functions and objectives. Performism encompasses written and spoken linguistic text, corporeal practices, geographical locations, visual and sonic images, and material acts. Performism enables me to interrogate the complex milieu of activities and events of nationalism and tourism of the twentieth and twenty-first centuries, within which two corporeal activities (the *Dance of the Old Men* and *Night of the Dead*) and a geographical place (Lake Pátzcuaro and the islands) were deployed.

Significantly, the vocabulary of conventional is-performance imbues discourse concerning both nationalism and tourism. Mauricio Tenorio-Trillo has applied this to Mexican nationalism, describing the nation-building process as a performance and a shared and comprehensive drama, in which the essence of the nation was gradually created through the concerted acts of the Mexican population (1996:245). In a similar vein, cultural historian Derek Sayer, in his discussion of Mexican state forms, describes the hegemonic projects as "enactments," asking the question "who is the audience for this performance" (Sayer 1994:369,376). Historian Mary Kay Vaughan, in her compelling final reflections for the seminal volume on the politics of culture in Mexico since the 1940s, refers to the intense, multilevel negotiations that were necessary to consolidate the postrevolutionary state, noting that "notions of *lo mexicano* as nation, region, village, and subject were mutually inscribed in the actors of the time in diverse but meaningful ways…" (2001:473). In tourism studies, Dean MacCannell suggests that tourism is a "spectacle in which we all have bit parts" (2001:380). By engaging these applications, vocabulary and analytical positions, the role of embodied actions, undertaken by individual and multiple performers or actors, becomes a potent and accessible scenario for detailed scrutiny. Performism therefore not only takes in these applications but also makes them inherently part of the same interrogative processes.

Although the term "performism" might have as a cognate "performist," I prefer to redeploy the term "performer" to encompass all those involved as organizers, decision-makers, recipients, readers, viewers, witnesses, producers, directors, and publishers. Cohering with the terms "nationalist," "tourist," and "indigenist" (as applicable to this study), a performist would be a person who actively supports and participates in the project at hand. However, by using the term "performer" I engage with performance in the broadest sense, and therefore relate this to performing a role, in other words, carrying out and accomplishing an activity (however, passive or unconscious). So, for example, each person who captures, publishes, and views a photo is performing a role. As is now commonly recognized in reader, reception, and audience theories, the role of audience member, or viewer, reader, and listener is something performed, consciously or otherwise. A reader, viewer, or listener is actively involved in the signification of the communication, and indeed, creates meaning through their reception and interpretation, as they are engaged with spectating, experiencing, and participating. Here, I seek to explore the dynamic individual and collective actions and interactions performed by a diverse range of performers, including presidents and teachers, fishermen and musicians, students and film-goers, Web site readers and attendees at public events.

Finally, in coining the term "performism" I relate to three other –isms that are central to this study: tourism, nationalism, and indigenism (*indigenismo*). Significantly, all three reference a complexity of ideas and practices that shift and transform in specific contexts. Tourism is a doctrine, concept, set of policies, and activities concerned with traveling for pleasure and providing tours and services for tourists (in this case, a tourist does the tour-ing). Nationalism, as a concept, doctrine, set of policies, and activities is concerned with commitment to the interests or culture of a nation (a nationalist is part of the project as a primary activist). Indigenism pertains to a doctrine, discourse, set of policies, program, and activities concerning indigenous peoples and practices (an indigenist (*indigenista*) supports and shapes the ideological movement).

Embodiment

In conjunction with performism, concepts of embodiment are wholly appropriate for examining and engaging with the nationalistic and touristic uses of *The Old Men* and *Night of the Dead*. Three applications of the notion of embodiment are useful: firstly, to be in the body and take form in human flesh; secondly, to make an idea actual or discernible, and to represent, stand for, symbolize or express something abstract in tangible or material form; and thirdly, to make something part of a system or whole. The first definition of embodiment is particularly relevant for this study due to the centrality of human bodies as primary signifiers. At the heart of my analysis is the presentation, re-presentation, and reactualization of symbolic systems through living bodies. I aim to examine the potency and efficacy of the body in these representational practices, where the bodily practices are used to produce meaning, and where the weight of history is felt in, on, and through the body. In each context of display and representation, live bodies and mediated and inscribed bodies (moving and still bodies in photos, drawings, models and written accounts) were viewed, read, and interpreted. I am therefore using the term "body" in order to examine how a human being becomes classified, and how bodies are read as Mexican, or indigenous, or different. So, bodies/people[2] are designated "indigenous" (through external designation or self-designation), and somatic traits (and therefore human beings) are labeled "indigenous."

Although the notion that the body acts as the central element may appear somewhat obvious, the idea of "naturalness" can lead to overlooking the complexities and constructed nature of the communicating factors and the signifying power of the concrete body (Butler 1993). In many contexts, the body generates a metalanguage for communication, with physical traits and phenotypic characteristics providing signifying elements. Divisions of race, cultural identity, and gender are often founded upon the body as a material sign of social difference, and the body itself, as a physical entity, acts as "the ultimate signifier of identity and the final authenticator" (Desmond 1999: xiv–xv). In processes of nationalism and tourism, people/bodies have been deployed and exhibited through events and activities that, for their efficacity, relied upon notions of bodily difference, exoticization, and othering. Practices of corporeal display have not only involved live presentation but also exhibition through mediated reproduction, mostly in the form of photographs, films, and artwork, all of which has been utilized for molding ideological patterning, and for shaping and creating constructions of identity. In both nationalist and tourist contexts there has been a tendency toward the objectification of peoples designated indigenous as a national symbol and as a tourist attraction. In both contexts, which merge and interface in terms of this study, the bodies/people on display have often been framed as ethnographic objects, yet, as Barbara Kirshenblatt-Gimlett has observed, "ethnographic objects are made, not found, despite claims to the contrary. They did not begin their lives as ethnographic objects. They *became* ethnographic through processes of detachment and contextualization.... Live exhibits as a representational mode make their own kinds of claims. Even when efforts are taken to the contrary, live exhibits tend to make people into artifacts because the ethnographic gaze objectifies" (1998:55). In conjunction with Kirschenblatt-Gimblett's work, I draw on Jane Desmond's studies in relation to tourist industries and tourism contexts, in which she highlights "the centrality of the body in marketing, staging, and audience reception," calling for further research in this area "if we are to better understand the powerful attraction and huge ideological impact that these industries have" (1999:xvi).

The first definition of embodiment (in the body) is absolutely central to the study. However, I am examining this in relation to the second designation, focusing on the use of bodies in dramatizing, reproducing, and representing ideological and political positions (for example, Mexicanness, indigenousness, difference, incorporation). Significantly, one of the ideological positions references definition three—to make something part of a system or whole. Assimilation, integration, and incorporation of bodies designated as indigenous (and therefore problematic), were strategies of nation-building. (Significantly, the very term "incorporate" (*incorporar*) includes the word *corp* (body) within it.) Simultaneously, and dichotomously, those same bodies/people were also exoticized and appropriated as national symbols of authentic Mexicanness.

Dance and Music for Nationalism and Tourism

Although I engage the term "performance" to refer to multifarious activities, rather than a conventional dance, music, theater, and performing arts usage, it is also valuable to connect with studies, primarily in the areas of ethnomusicology, dance ethnography, and dance anthropology, in which discrete practices of dance and music have been analyzed in terms of identity formation, nationalism, and tourism, often also encompassing issues of folklore. While nationalism and tourism are dealt with separately in many of these studies, it is significant that there are many overlaps and interrelationships, particularly when engaging the concept of folklore. In general terms, dance and music are widely accepted as highly efficacious practices for signifying and shaping identities (Buckland 2001, Cowan 1990, Desmond 1993/4 and 1997a, 1997b, Erdman 1996, Hutchinson 2009, Meyer 1995, Ness 1992, Reed 1998, Rodríguez 1996). In contexts of modern nationalism, dance, musical practices, and musical instruments have been deployed as representative and emblematic within strategies for unification. Subsequent to processes of state-sponsored and institutional collection, composite versions of music and dance practices have been created as a demonstration of a unified identity, creating links between a government and the masses (Lau 1996, Manuel 1989, Pegg 1995). Dance and music *revival* is a common aspect within contexts of nationalism, particularly encompassing forms designated as *traditional*. Typical processes for revival involve collecting, archiving, presentation of concerts, publication of literature and recordings, and the formation of educational enterprises (Blaustein 1993:263, Castelo-Branco and Freitas Branco 2003, Dacosta Holten 2005, Goertzen 1997, Nettl 1978, Rosenberg 1993). Of central importance is the recognition that revival "consciously selects and intensifies certain values while casting its present endeavours within the framework of the traditions of the past" (Jabbour 1993: xiii).

The idea of *folklore* as a political tool is particularly common within agendas of nationalization, unification, and identity-construction. I draw on the insights of Steven Feld, who described hegemonic folkloricization as a process in which "dominating outside parties legitimate condensed, simplified, or commodified displays; invoke, promote and cherish them as official and authentic custom, while at the same time misunderstanding, ignoring, or suppressing the real creative forces and expressive meanings that animate them in the community" (1988:96). These outside parties have been widely documented as encompassing state-sponsored officials, scholars, intellectuals, artists, and politicians. The role of folklorists and musicologists in shaping society, alongside and in collaboration with political leaders, is also commonly recognized (Seeger 1994:11; Ramsey 1997). As governments and institutions are necessarily implicated in the promotion and manipulation of folklore (as practice and concept), so processes of folkloricization are intrinsically connected with control and power relations (Harker 1985, Kamenetsky 1972, Poole 1990, García Canclini 1993).

Although folkloricization is a standard trope of nationalism (folkloric nationalism), primarily concerned with incorporating carefully selected dance and music practices, it is also wholly applicable to tourism, and to processes of creating ethnic attractions and destinations. Dance and music often play a significant role in tourist destinations, particularly in defining and constructing concepts of place and otherness. State-run tourist institutions are centrally involved in promoting *folk* culture, particularly through festivals and competitions, and are fundamentally concerned with the shaping and constructing of cultural politics and practices in relation to the tourist industry. Dance and music have a presence in tourist contexts in a variety of ways: as living exhibitions, museums, and as reenactments; as folkloric shows to entertain; as the focus and draw of an event such as a carnival or festival; and as a purportedly *everyday* element of a local situation (Cooley 2005, Davis 1994, Desmond 1999, Duany 1994, Goertzen 1997, Kaeppler 1977, Ramsey 1997, Rosenberg 1993 Saragoza 2001, Zolov 2001). Timothy Cooley's study relating to southern Poland has been particularly influential in my own work, providing many points of reference in terms of tracing the shaping and "brokering" of ethnic identity through music by ethnographers for a tourist market (2005). Similarly important is Jane Desmond's work on Hawaii, in which she analyses "bodies on display" and "the linkage of performance, photography, tourism, and the production of the iconic image" (1999:105). In a slightly different vein, but related to contexts of both nationalism and tourism, I draw on Néstor García Canclini's notion of ideological refunctionalization in order to call attention to economic aspects. Through a range of strategies, a unified system of symbolic production is generated specifically for modernist nationalism and capitalist development (1993:viii).

Strategies, activities, discourses, and programs of nationalism and tourism that I discuss in this study were common to many areas of the world in the twentieth century; however, an awareness of analogous contexts in Latin America and the Caribbean is particularly pertinent. In this vast region there are common threads that connect countries, histories, and situations, particularly in relation to indigenous peoples, invasion, conquest, colonization, and settlement. A generalized model for mestizo Latin America that is applicable to many contexts, including Mexico, is founded on the use of "indigenous communities [as the] prime site from which to obtain the 'raw materials' needed to elaborate a set of national styles" (Scruggs 1999:302). In the Andean region of Peru folkloricization processes were based upon delineation of indigenous and mestizo practices (Mendoza 1998, 2000, 2008, Mendoza-Walker 1994, Turino 1984, 1993). Brazilian contexts in the 1920s and 1930s encompassed state-sponsored "folkloric" music and dance, in processes that were aimed at constructing a national identity (Reily 1994). "Folkmusic" was used in nationalist processes in Nicaragua after 1930, with the dance of the marimba being promoted as Nicaragua's "national dance" (Scruggs 1999). In Haiti, processes of folkloricization, involving the staging of folklore and music, were essential elements in the construction of national identity (Averill 1989, 1991, 1994, Ramsey 1997). The *merengue* was transformed from rural idiom to transnational mass music in the Dominican Republic (Austerlitz 1997, Davis 1994, and Duany 1994). In Cuba, music and dance have been used as prominent national symbols by state institutions, while processes of folkloricization transformed Afro-Cuban *santería* (O. A. Rodríguez 1994, V. E. Rodríguez 1994, Daniel 1991, 1995, 1996, and Hagedorn 2001). *Música tropical* was used in the shaping of notions of nation-hood and race in Colombia, specifically in relation to constructions of blackness in Colombia (Wade 2000).[3]

Pertinent Processes of Performism in Mexican Contexts

Through this study I engage the range of discourses outlined above, considering them valuable for analyzing the specific contexts of the *Dance of the Old Men* and *Night of the Dead* of Lake Pátzcuaro through the twentieth century and up to the present day, however, certain processes were particularly productive throughout the ninety-year period under consideration, and so I turn to this lattice of inter-secting practices as a way of highlighting the most important aspects in terms of Mexican contexts. These include: appropriation, representation, framing, gaze, essentialization, authentication, commodification, and commoditization. In the postrevolutionary era, appropriation generally entailed collecting and then re-presenting practices and peoples designated as indigenous and rural, and was typ-ically undertaken by artists, folklorists, anthropologists, and other intellectuals acting on behalf of the government. While processes of selection sometimes involved highly systematized decision-making efforts, this also happened through fairly haphazard methods, relying on already known places, locations, and people. Following collection, processes of representation involved displaying and exhibit-ing appropriated practices and peoples in a range of contexts, from live events to mediatized documentation. There was a tendency toward anthropological and ethnographic representation, with the link between anthropology and the study of indigenous peoples being particularly notable. Each context of representation formed, and continues to form, part of a complex of processes that frame recep-tion, and that generate a body of activities and images referencing Mexicanidad. Acts of framing guide perception, reception, and communicative processes in each representational context (Goffman 1974), and frames were, and continue to be actively adopted and manufactured, emphasizing a deliberate choice. Thus, "frames are principles of selection, emphasis and presentation composed of little tacit theories about what exists, what happens, and what matters" (Gitlin 1980:6). As the choice of certain aspects over others makes those elements more prominent in a communicating text, therefore selection promotes a particular interpretation (Entman 1993:52).

Engaging the notion of frameworks and structures draws attention to the importance of juxtaposition and the relational presence (and absence) of images and bodies inside frames. Such juxtapositions construct and shape signification through the presentation of ideas and ideological positions in specific contexts. This idea is applicable to numerous framing processes discussed in this study, including theatricalization, publication, event venues, tourist locations, reper-toires of dances, and souvenir contexts. Juxtapositions are inherent in staged folk-loric events (through multiple dances and music on one stage in one temporal and spatial moment); in publications (in ethnographic and tourist guide books and postcards); and in tourist material and contexts (souvenir stands). Live events involve stage-areas that are bounded spatially. Photographs and artwork in magazines, postcards, and tourist brochures rely on iconic juxtaposed images, while literary communication in journals, newspapers, books, and pamphlets utilizes similar processes with written text.

In conjunction with framing, frameworks, and juxtaposition, notions of gaze, drawn from tourism and film studies, are useful for understanding how recurring images and discourse generate ideas of "the most representative." A tourist gaze involves a specific mode and particular way of looking, concerning what is important about a place (Urry 2002:12). Gaze also concerns the directed way in which a camera frames the images presented, directing the eye of the viewer to certain objects, people, or images, rather than to others (Mulvey 1975). Through a collective tourist gaze, tourists are directed to believe, through careful reinforcement of particular images and ideas, that one attraction is the more representative (Urry 2002:45–46). Notions of the tourist gaze are equally applicable to nationalist contexts as to tourist environments. Shaping constructs of official nationalism engaged the same processes, creating a collective nationalistic gaze. In all contexts, the collective gaze is created through processes of reproduction, representation, and signification, using networks of signs, imaged in photographs, films, brochures, souvenirs, and postcards. The gaze can be endlessly reproduced and recaptured, relying on and perpetuating the notion of "the most representative" and "typical." Creating a collective gaze may also be considered in terms of essentialization, involving a reduction of diversity to significant units of recognition and to icons that are shorthand for a set of peoples, for a region, or for a nation. For agendas of Mexican nationalism and tourism, essentialization involved the production of stereotypes, and the reduction and neat classification of the country into regions each with its own typical food, dance, music, clothes, and other cultural practices that were regarded as representative. Local and regional features became part of a set of nationally accepted standards, and specific ethnic cultural expressions were transformed in a larger category of what García Canclini calls "type" (1993:65). In nationalizing processes, states were essentialized in order to create national unity, highlighting the dichotomy of maintaining difference while also incorporating difference into the nation. As García Canclini observes, "The need to homogenize and at the same time preserve the attraction of the exotic dilutes the specificity of each village or town...into the (political) unity of the state—Michoacán, Veracruz—and each state into the political unity of the nation" (ibid.). Such a configuration was, of course, also crucial for the tourist industry and essential for generating tourist attractions. Thus, what was unique and specific to a region or ethnic group became "typically" Mexican, with resultant homogenization, as other forms were ignored, forgotten, and standardized. Even the diversity of Mexican foods was reduced to a few stereotyped dishes, becoming "La comida Mexicana" (Mexican food) through the construction of national cuisine (Pilcher 1998:156). Significantly, regional cuisines were not obliterated, even as they were relegated to an unimportant role in a national scenario, in much the same way that local P'urhépecha dance and music practices remained current, even as *The Old Men* and *Night of the Dead* were reified to the status of national icons.

For essentialized practices to become accepted, they were generally subject to processes of authentication by which they acquired and earned the label "authentic." The designation "most representative" relates to the formulation of, and desire for authenticity, which is present in processes of nationalism and tourism. Authentication involved the framing and promoting of practices, bodies, and locations as authentic, frequently through naming, description, and contextual placing, signaling to the audience and viewer that the practice, body, or location should be read and interpreted as authentic. Once a sight/site (or sound, taste, movement) comes to be regarded in this way, maintaining the framework around it and continuing a trajectory that presents and receives the practice, body, or place as authentic is relatively uncomplicated. Within an agenda of Mexican nationalism, the notion of authentically Mexican was developed in opposition to purportedly inauthentic foreign entities, both internal and external, which were usually perceived as European[4] and from the United States. In a similar vein, the notion of authentically Mexican was crucial in tourist configurations, for an "authentic experience" acts as a driving motivation for many tourists (MacCannell 1999:101). As with nationalist processes, this engaged an opposition to European and United States facets, and also invoked an opposition to ideas of urban and modern, therefore in many Mexican contexts the icons and cultural practices developed as tourist attractions related specifically to peoples, places, and activities designated as pre-Hispanic, indigenous, and rural. Here also the concept of "staged authenticity" is wholly applicable (MacCannell 1973). Now regarded as a ubiquitous element in tourism processes, this notion encompasses the tourist quest for the authentic, as tourists desire to enter into a backstage region of social space. These environments are therefore framed in such a way that results in presenting an aura of authenticity, while at the same time being staged and enacted with a specific gaze in mind.

Processes of commodification, entailing the alteration or modification of a practice to suit a particular agenda and enactment venue, are standard in nationalist and tourist contexts. In displaying and staging appropriated practices in theater spaces, schools, and political and tourist contexts, dramaturgical and scenographic elements of the music, dance, or ritual are altered in some way from other versions that may be considered to be original.[5] John MacAloon suggests that commodified forms tend to be "empty forms" in which the practices are disconnected from the values in their indigenous cultural contexts, turning them into something suited for "travel abroad" or taken "back into their original places to be reappropriated through novel local meanings or traditionalisms created for the task" (1995:35). Although the concept of commodification is applicable to contexts involving *The Old Men* and *Night of the Dead* in the twentieth century, the situation is deeply complex, and the so-called empty forms are often laden with value for those who perform them, both in terms of the cultural affirmation that they afford and certain economic returns that they make possible. Processes of commoditization concern ways in which an area of life not primarily regulated by economic criteria becomes commercialized, drawing the activity in the economic domain (Greenwood 1977:130). This economic domain may be local, national, or indeed international, and it is quite likely that there is a simultaneous tension between providing a service and fulfilling a political and ideological agenda. Issues of exchange and economic value are central in most tourist contexts, and were also inherent in Mexican twentieth-century nationalist processes in which capitalist development was of paramount importance. Symbolic production and economic factors were inextricably linked in virtually all contexts encompassing the *Dance of the Old Men* and *Night of the Dead*, with elements of commoditization and reconstructed ethnicity present. MacCannell's notion of "reconstructed ethnicity" (1984, 1992) is a strategy that aims at maintaining and preserving ethnic forms for the entertainment of tourists within a framework of folkloric nationalism. Reconstructed ethnicity and ethnic identity invariably involve the objectification and reification of ethnic images and are produced particularly through a process that engenders a global network of interaction. As such, ethnic groups begin to utilize their traditions and practices, whether "original," newly created, or lying somewhere between these two poles, becoming commodities to be sold to tourists, and also acting as rhetorical weaponry in internal dealings (MacCannell 1992:168). An engagement with this final concept runs as a thread throughout this study.

What should be apparent from this brief overview of strategies, tactics, methods, and practices is their interrelatedness, such that one process reinforced the potency and efficacy of another. As I discuss below, these were not necessarily planned through wholly coherent strategizing processes, yet they formed part of webs of ideas and discourses of performism that enabled them to be perpetuated.

Projects of Performism: Hegemony, Centers, and Peripheries

In concluding this foundational chapter, I refer to two further networks of concepts that I deal with throughout the study, namely hegemony, and centers and peripheries. In postrevolutionary Mexico, creating Mexicanness and lo mexicano were government-inspired, directed, and implemented processes and projects, valuable for uniting the nation and for tourist enterprises, undertaken and executed through government agents. Strategies and policies were developed and put into action through government departments and institutions, and enacted by state employees, politicians, academics, and artists. Such a conceptualization engages the notion of hegemony and hegemonic projects, both of which have been heavily debated in relation to Mexican politics, history, and culture in the twentieth century. Some scholars are "deeply suspicious of any grand claims to the existence of hegemonic projects" (Sayer 1994:371, see also Scott 1994), while others see the usefulness of this as an analytical approach, noting that "if we conceive a hegemonic process and common discursive framework as...state *projects* rather than state *achievements*,...we can advance our understanding of 'popular culture' and 'state formation' in relation to each other" (Roseberry 1994:365). I apply this notion of government-led processes and projects to highlight issues of power relations, particularly as subordinated peoples were incorporated, appropriated, and represented in processes within which the principal response was a utilitarian one. I engage with the notion that "what hegemony constructs is not a shared ideology but a common material and meaningful framework for living through, talking about, and acting upon social orders characterized by domination" (Roseberry 1994:360–61), for both *The Old Men* and *Night of the Dead* became elements of common material within frameworks of lo mexicano, indigenismo, and ethnic-tourism.

Recognizing and acknowledging that the actions of government officials in performism processes often gets subsumed within the term "the state," I specifically name individuals in relation to activities of appropriation and promotion. When I do refer to "the state," this always indicates the role of particular individuals within organizations and institutions who operated under the auspices of the government, all of which functioned within a network of authority through public activities, therefore performing a form of cultural power, for as Sayer observes, "'the state' does not exist...'the state' *is* an ideological project (rather than an agency that *has* such projects)....The state is not the reality behind the mask of political practice, the state *is* the mask" (1994:371). I emphasize the localized and individual decision-making processes of specific governmental employees, particularly in terms of constructing and shaping notions of indigenousness, ethnicity, and folklore, therefore highlighting their role in creating histories and narratives of the nation. The state endorses "a particular narrative of the nation that moves in tandem with the march of 'civilization.'...As much as these histories affiliate a group of people, they generally order them into hierarchies reflecting differences in class, race, gender, and national space. As they create centers of power, knowledge, culture, progress, and authority, they fashion peripheries of backwardness and subordination. While they 'include,' they simultaneously 'exclude' and 'other' non-members" (Vaughan and Lewis 2006:6). By tracing and examining the narratives and histories generated through the multiple representational practices embodying *Night of the Dead* and the *Dance of the Old Men*, I aim to focus on the agents of the state and explore issues of centers and peripheries, as experienced and lived by villagers of Lake Pátzcuaro, and as played out on local, national, and international stages. Issues concerning who undertakes the shaping of framing are key to understanding hegemonic processes. The dynamics of representation and the power relations inherent in any presentational context are central to understanding how representation forms part of a complex environment, involving who has the power to represent whom (Kirshenblatt-Gimblett and Bruner 1992:303).

Claudio Lomnitz, in his exploration of Mexican nationalism, has noted that "it is now commonplace to recognize that centers and peripheries have historically constituted each other" (2001:165). This assertion is fundamentally important to this study in which two distinct practices from a purportedly peripheral location and peoples, and their interface with, and constitution of a centralized Mexican nation are the focus. Locationally, the nation of Mexico and the capital city of Mexico have acted as the center, while indigenous and rural villages and villagers have acted as the periphery. In relation to the general populus, the elite, and middle classes have taken the role of center, while peoples designated as indigenous perform as periphery (in need of incorporation into the center, and useful for the construction of identity of those in the center). As I make evident throughout this study, the interface of center and periphery as performed through the processes and peoples surrounding the *Dance of the Old Men* and *Night of the Dead* of Lake Pátzcuaro have indeed constituted each other. The ongoing and consequential relations are by no means equitable, however, and so I engage in discussions concerning issues of economic status, power relations, identity and cultural belonging; the tension between utilizing performances, peoples and bodies framed as *of the past* for touristic and nationalistic ends; and the effects and consequences for those implicated in such representation in local, regional, national, and global transactions and relationships.

With these issues and processes of performism opened up, I now turn to discuss the role of the *Dance of the Old Men* and *Night of the Dead* through the twentieth century and into the twenty-first, analyzing how these cultural actions came to be called folklore, and how this designation was perpetuated and propagated through multiple representational practices, with inherent consequences and effects.

PART II

Tracing Ninety Years
of Performism

CHAPTER 3

Forging the Nation

The Postrevolutionary Years

CERTAIN ERAS ARE so momentous that everything that comes afterward cannot be understood or imagined without it. Such is the case with the postrevolutionary period of the 1920s and 1930s, when the *Dance of the Old Men* and *Night of the Dead* were appropriated as nationalist cultural artifacts and transformed into public spectacles within both nationalist and tourist contexts. In order to examine and comprehend these processes and their consequences, I draw out some of the salient political, ideological, and cultural issues of the period as pertinent to this study. It is necessary to dwell upon the postrevolutionary forms because, in the twenty-first century, political and ideological positions concerning ethnicity, race, and indigenousness still relate directly to earlier configurations. It is also important to appreciate that although the postrevolutionary period was a new political phase (and is central to this study as the era in which both the *Dance of the Old Men* and *Night of the Dead* of Lake Pátzcuaro were appropriated for national use), constructions of ethnicity and race, and notions of nationalism and the imaging of the nation in a global arena were drawn directly from previous models. Therefore, although my principal focus in this chapter is on the postrevolutionary decades, I begin with a brief contextualization of the historical, political, and ideological trajectory that led to the period of revolution in the early twentieth century. I then turn specifically to the postrevolutionary period, focusing on issues of ethnicity, race, nationalism, folklore, education, as well as music, theater, and dance.

Incursion, Spanish Rule, Independence, and Revolution

Prior to the arrival and incursion of explorers, *conquistadores*, and missionaries from Europe, the landmass of present-day Mexico, and vast areas of the whole American continent, were home to diverse peoples and civilizations. Hundreds of cultural and ethnic groups and societies inhabited the land, speaking a multiplicity of languages, and manifesting expertise in writing, monumental architecture, mathematics, astronomical studies, and militarization. Of relevance for this study is the preincursion civilization of the P'urhépecha (also known as Tarascan), who inhabited an immense region totaling 27.6 thousand square miles, covering an area west of present day Mexico City, in the states of Michoacán and part of the neighboring states of Guerrero, Guanajuato, and Querétero. Tzintzuntzan, the thriving capital city of the P'urhépecha empire on the edge of Lake Pátzcuaro, had a population of forty thousand, and in the Lake Pátzcuaro region the population was between seventy thousand and ninety thousand prior to the arrival of Spaniards.

The year 1492 marked the arrival of the Italian Cristoforo Columbo (Christopher Columbus) in the Bahamas, followed by numerous other European explorers. In 1519, a Spanish expedition led by Hernando Cortés[1] set down in the landmass that was subsequently designated Mexico. The Spanish overthrow of the Mexica (Aztec) civilization in 1521 marked the beginning of a three-hundred year period of Spanish colonial rule. For the P'urhépecha empire, the devastation began in 1522 with the arrival of Cristobal de Olíd and his regiment of Spanish *conquistadores* in the area. Within a few years, the thriving capital Tzintzuntzan was reduced to a tiny village of a few thousand inhabitants.

In 1535 the viceroyalty of New Spain was established and with this action, a Spanish political entity was superimposed upon preexisting indigenous states and subdued peoples, bringing with it the transformation and destruction of many lifestyles, cultures, practices, and knowledges. A crucial element of the colonial period involved classifying and ordering people according to perceptions of race. Mestizaje (miscegenation) resulted from the perceived racial mixing of peoples, so a set of defined racial categories was imposed, and a complex caste system was brought into operation that sought to categorize all forms of race, through the principal groupings of *indios*, Europeans, Africans (mostly slaves), and Creoles (Spaniards born outside of Europe). Integral to these named categories were indications of defining roots and mixing, related specifically to skin color and somatic types (with terms such as *indomestizo* and *afromestizo*).

By the late colonial period (end of eighteenth and beginning of nineteenth centuries) forms of nationalism and indigenismo were being fashioned and shaped. Criollo nationalism was constructed around the superiority of Creole citizens, and indigenismo celebrated the roots of American civilization, without making connections between living indigenous people and the past (see Brading 1985). These positions left an ideological legacy that persisted through the twentieth century and that continues to impact in the twenty-first century, which directly relates to the central tenet of this study concerning ideas of indigenous peoples and practices, and the narratives and images of the preincursion past as embodied in *The Old Men* and *Night of the Dead*. One specific embodied image that played a central role throughout the period of colonial rule, and which therefore had a bearing on discourse, policy, and ideology concerning ethnicity and race, was that of the Virgin of Guadalupe. Her brown-skinned corporeal figure is believed to have appeared to an indigenous peasant, Juan Diego, in 1531, remaining on his cloak as a permanent visual representation. The physiognomy of the image of the Virgin of Guadalupe encompassed a syncretic form, mixing an embodied representation of indigenousness and Europeanness, creating ideological cohesion for uniting disparate peoples for Catholicism, and acting as the most extraordinarily powerful icon in generating a sense of shared belonging, a role that continues to the present day.[2]

In 1821 formal independence from Spain was recognized, following the establishment of a republic between 1810 and 1821 under the leadership of Miguel Hidalgo and José María Morelos y Pavón. At this point Mexican territories still extended much farther south and north than present borders demarcate. A nationalist ideology prevailed and the symbol of the Virgin of Guadalupe continued to serve as a corporeal embodiment for uniting the country. Between 1846 and 1848, a war between Mexico and the United States followed an invasion by the U.S. Army. In 1848 Mexico lost almost half of its territory to the United States, creating tensions that are still being played out in the twenty-first century and that impact deeply upon Mexicans and Mexican-Americans living in the United States, particularly in the southwestern states. France invaded Mexico in 1864 and occupied the country until 1867 (under the rule of French-supported Emperor Maximilian I of Austria, in collusion with Mexican monarchists). The year 1868 marked the beginning of an era of great significance for indigenous representation in national politics when Benito Juárez, a man of Zapotec ethnicity, became president. He was the first indigenous person to lead a country in the Americas in three hundred years, paving the way for future presidents in other Latin American nations; however, none has yet followed him in Mexico.

Between 1877 and 1910, under the presidency of dictator and elitist Porfirio Díaz, the emerging concept of an ideal modern Mexican nation was developed, encompassing progress, science, and industry. At this time Mexican nationalism included strategies for cultural patrimony and a national culture, however, the foremost cultural and intellectual model for the elite was France. Race, ethnicity, and skin color were of fundamental importance in shaping the perception of Mexico on a world stage, and in an era of Darwinism and evolutionary processes, the Mexican elite followed the lead taken by European figures. The superiority of the white European race was forcefully promoted and if Mexico was to take its place among major nations, it needed to represent itself as "white," for if a nation was to be considered modern and cosmopolitan, "whiteness" was important. During this era, Mexican exhibits at the world's fairs demonstrated the role and position of peoples classified as indigenous as a component of Mexican nationhood. Indigenous images, artifacts and peoples were put on display for international perusal and consumption, but only as exhibits of a glorified ancient *past*, demonstrating indigenismo as the reification of images of the past. The "scientific" inferiority of contemporary indigenous peoples (and mixed-blood peoples, who together made up the majority of the population) was regarded as an advantage for the development of a modern nation (Tenorio-Trillo 1996:88).[3] As this was also an era of an incipient trend of travel and tourism, with European and U.S. travelers exploring Mexico on a quest for the exotic and the ancient, displays of

Mexican Otherness acted as forms of promotion for the nation.[4] The interface between European ideas and Mexican notions of race and ethnicity were particularly
apparent in the worlds of art, theater, and dance. European influences were upper-
most in Mexico, yet the styles and genres of spectated events were constructed
around notions of nationality and ethnicity, which presented a dichotomy between nationalism and cosmopolitanism, despite the prevailing culture being profoundly Europeanized (Lavalle 1988:70). In Mexico City, opera and ballet were
prominent, drawing on European, and in particular French models, with a desire
on the part of the Mexican elite to become part of European movements, yet
simultaneously drawing upon vernacular Mexican styles (such as the *jarabes*). As
I discuss presently, transformation of rural, social, and ritual dance forms into theatricalized shows generated an especially dichotomous arena for the display of
ethnicities, races and also classes.

After the Revolution: Forging a Nation

In 1910, President Porfirio Díaz's power was challenged, and the Mexican revolution (also known as the Revolutionary Civil Wars) was initiated as a rebellion
against Díaz. A rapid process of foreign-led modernization and the perceived
discrimination by foreign-managers led workers in industries of textiles, railroads,
and mining to rise up, along with significant portions of the dislocated and dis-
possessed peasantry. During a decade of civil wars and revolution, factions and
revolutionary forces fought battles for control of territory and people. Although
fighting continued until 1920, the Constitution of 1917 was put in place (under the
leadership of President Venustiano Carranza [1917–1920]) and remains to this day.
From the chaos of the revolution, a new nationalistic and idealistic era emerged, in
which the great diversity and multiplicity of peoples in Mexico was to be unified
and guided into a modern age of economic development and political stability.
The Constitutionalists believed in a unity of new principles capable of producing
a real nation, which would see the inclusion of social rights, and economic and
social equality, engaging the state in the role of chief promoter of the improvement of the public process.

   During this complex and tangled period of crisis and corruption, movements,
ideologies, and policies were varied, ambivalent, and contradictory as Mexico
struggled to define itself.[5] Above all, the need for unification remained central to
the revolutionary institutions. Between 1920 and 1940 diverse and radical governmental programs were put in place in an attempt to create a united and enlight-
ened Mexico, and to shape a Mexican identity by *forjando patria*, "forging a nation,"
an objective propounded by Manuel Gamio, one of Mexico's most highly influential contemporary politicians and anthropologists (1960 [1916]). Significantly for
this study, Gamio's role in shaping strategies for forging the nation of Mexico was
fundamentally important in relation to the processes surrounding *The Old Men*
and *Night of the Dead*, encompassing educational and anthropological issues, and
involving pronouncements on folklore and indigenismo, as I discuss presently.

Forging the Mexican nation and creating a national identity, understood as *lo mexicano* (distinctively Mexican) and *mexicanidad* (Mexicanness), involved generating a series of roughly shared assumptions and a set of symbols, icons, discourses, and places through processes of appropriation, dissemination, and celebration (Vaughan 1997 and Vaughan and Lewis 2006:2). Paramount within these symbolic practices and discourses were notions of a relationship with the past to generate a sense of belonging in the present in order to build a prosperous future. Primary processes therefore entailed reorganizing and reinventing the past, including incorporating continuities from the prerevolutionary era. Politically, economically, and culturally those charged with Mexican state formation reacted to and with global trends, and utilized a network of media and strategies familiar in many world contexts, encompassing education, art, radio, rhetoric, the press, mass mobilization, sport, social reform, and party organization. In this aspect, Mexico was comparable to any other developing nation and there are many similarities and parallels with processes that took place in diverse areas of the world in the twentieth century as nations endeavored and strove to articulate and define themselves. In Mexico as the dominant classes attempted to mold the entire culture of the society and provide cultural, moral, and ideological leadership, so the role of the state was simultaneously interventionist, paternalist, and instrumentalist. Through hegemonic processes the government endeavored to create a national identity through the management of symbolic practices that were wholly sanctioned by the state for the development of the whole society; a situation that eminent Mexican writer Carlos Monsiváis referred to as "state control of the significance of being Mexican" (1987:13; see also Bartra 1989).

Indigenismo and Incorporation

Crucial to creating notions of Mexicanness and central to processes of modernizing development were issues concerning the perceived ethnicity of peoples, their practices, and their contribution to the nation. The movements and ideologies of indigenismo and mestizaje were again reformulated within the postrevolutionary framework. As concepts of race, class, and ethnicity were at the very heart of many ideologies and policies, it is significant that a major problem in discussing these issues is that not only were the ideologies paradoxical in their temporal setting, but that their subsequent treatment by scholars has perpetuated the dichotomies involved. In this study I therefore particularly focus upon the specific constructions of ethnicity and indigenousness that encompass *The Old Men* and *Night of the Dead* and the peoples of Lake Pátzcuaro. These formulations were shaped and reinforced specifically through multiple processes of embodied display, and photographic and literary textual dissemination. Since the Spanish incursion in the sixteenth century, issues of the *place* of indigenous peoples in Mexico has been deeply embedded in the Mexican psyche and politics. Transformational processes were essential to postrevolutionary ideology and policies, and key concepts included fusion, integration, incorporation, and emancipation. People classified as indigenous were required to integrate because the sheer diversity and "back-wardness" were regarded as problems if Mexico was to transform itself into a modern, capitalist nation. Simultaneously (and paradoxically), indigenous peoples were seen as a "factor for progress" and therefore were to be incorporated into the nation.[6]

Indigenismo formed a central ideological movement, and although it was not a new movement, its use in the postrevolutionary era signified that a fundamental basis of the movement had radically shifted, for whereas previous indigenists made no correlation between living indigenous peoples and the past that they celebrated as their own, postrevolutionary indigenismo valued the cultures of living indigenous peoples. Herein lies the basic paradox of indigenismo: the incorporation of the indigenous population into society coupled with the preservation of assets of traditional culture that were deemed positive (Mörner 1970:226). However, in the postrevolutionary era, classifications and interpretations of race, ethnicity, and class were undertaken with widely differing criteria, with a "slip" between terms such that racial characteristics were generally social rather than biological (Knight 1990:73).[7] The nature of indigenous/mestizo status was subjective and therefore the ethnic status of both individuals and communities was not immutable (ibid.). Thus, the term indigenous was sometimes used to refer to one race, whilst at other times differentiation was made according to location. Mestizaje referred to biological fusion, and also cultural and social fusion, therefore a person designated as indigenous could become or achieve a mestizo status through a process of mestizaje. One aim was therefore to incorporate, integrate, and transform the indigenous populations and to "mestizo-ize" them (Knight 1990:87). The mestizo was to provide the key to the future development of Mexico, being neither indigenous nor European, but quintessentially Mexican. In 1925, prominent intellectual and former secretary of education José Vasconcelos published *La raza cósmica* (the cosmic race) in which he presented his concept of forming a new mestizo race as the ideal racial type (1948 [1925]).[8] President Plutarco Elías Calles (1924–1928),[9] in his inauguration promise, expressed his aim "to incorporate the Indian into modern civilization" (Sáenz 1928:75), and Lázaro Cárdenas, as governor of Michoacán (1928–1932), stated that schools on the shores of Lake Pátzcuaro were involved in "the incorporation of the *indio* to civilization" (*Informe* 16.9.1931:12). This objective, to "Mexicanize the Indian, not indigenze Mexico," was later underlined by Lázaro Cárdenas in his inaugural speech for the Department of Indigenous Affairs and the National Indigenist Institute (Barre 1983:93).

As the boundaries between racial and ethnic definitions were constantly blurred, so too class-based distinctions were often merged with ethnic and racial definitions and used in their place. Indigenous peoples, who for the most part lived in rural areas, were therefore frequently classified as *campesinos* (rural peasants), a term that included all rural dwellers, disregarding any ethnic or racial distinctions. This classification was utilized to draw attention to the poor economic status and preindustrial methods of production of such people, who were therefore regarded as in need of integration into national society through transformation from passive subjects to active citizens (González 1981:117–128,

Knight 1990:106). It is therefore significant that the region and communities at the heart of this study, namely Lake Pátzcuaro and the islands and P'urhépecha lakeside communities, were categorically and overtly rural.

Although policies regarding race and ethnicity are the most significant for this study, two other ideological positions are also noteworthy in relation to the post-revolutionary era, namely anticlericalism and the anti-outsider policy. Within the doctrine of anticlericalism, the Catholic Church was regarded as an antinational force and problematic for a developing national context (Knight 1994a:396). The emphasis was therefore upon secularization, and syncretic and pre-Hispanic religious and spiritual practices, all of which were important to the presentation and reception of *The Old Men* and *Night of the Dead* as purportedly pre-Catholic and pagan rituals. Regarding the anti-outsider policy, the general focus was to display distrust toward foreign interests and external domination, in particular Europe and the United States. This enabled formulations of an "authentic" Mexican identity based around indigenous peoples, in the belief that by eradicating the imitation of foreign ideas a genuine national culture would emerge (Rowe and Schelling 1991:165).

Institutions, Intellectuals, and Artists

Governmental institutions, and artists, intellectuals, and politicians working in an official capacity through state organizations performed central roles in implementing strategies for shaping indigenismo and mestizaje. In discussing the activities of key figures and organizations involving education, popular culture, and specific academic disciplines, it is striking to note the overlapping, interweaving, and interfacing relationships and functions, highlighting the ways in which a core of individuals and departments were able to formulate and disseminate highly influential practices and doctrines. Artists and intellectuals adopted interventionist positions and used their artistic and scholarly practices for overtly ideological and political agendas, and there was an acceptance of the notion of polymaths and intellectuals, as boundaries between professional roles were frequently blurred. For example, Manuel Gamio and Moisés Sáenz both held the post of undersecretary of education and also held scholarly positions as university academics, while muralists, such as Diego Rivera and David Siqueiros, and composers, such as Silvestre Revueltas, promoted explicitly political and ideological positions in their artistic work.[10]

The academic disciplines of anthropology, ethnology, folklore, history, and archeology had a particularly high profile, and research-based studies in these areas were profoundly influential, drawing on a pattern going back to the 1860s. Applied anthropology in particular was given precedence, with the setting up of a new government-backed school that focused on the study of contemporary indigenous communities and their ancient predecessors. The dominant paradigm for both theoretical and applied anthropological work involved taking an interventionist role, particularly in terms of molding perceptions of ethnicity. Most anthropologists and archeologists believed in the need to incorporate indigenous peoples into modern national development (Tenorio-Triollo 1996:236). Crucially, many middle-class artists, academics, and politicians adopted a position of power, speaking with social scientific authority, and presenting themselves as experts.

Both Gamio and Sáenz were central to the advancement of anthropology and archeology, which then fed both artistic and populist indigenismo.[11] Gamio, known as the "father of anthropology," was a great champion of indigenismo and as early as 1916 had pronounced on what he called "The Indian Problem" (Gamio 1960 [1916]).[12] The declared objective of indigenismo, as defined by Gamio, was the incorporation of the indigenous people into Mexican nationalism (Stavenhagen 1979:45).[13] As I noted above, Gamio's discourse is of particular importance for this study because of his role in formulating and disseminating notions of folklore, specifically invoking the peoples and practices of Lake Pátzcuaro. His 1925 article "The Utilitarian Aspect of Folklore," published in the populist, bilingual magazine *Mexican Folkways*, illustrated the interventionist and instrumentalist role of intellectuals and the place of folklore in nationalizing processes. A brief example captures the core of Gamio's ideas:

> A magazine like this one, devoted to make known the thousand mysterious and fantastic paths through which flow the ideas of those Mexicans who for various reasons still remain in backwards cultural stages, deserves all our appreciation and enthusiastic praise. All that may appear on its pages should be carefully consulted by anthropologist, sociologist and the statesman if they sincerely wish to know the true aspects of the soul of the people. (1925:6–7)

In order to draw people out of the "backwards cultural stages" Gamio suggested a solution to the problem that involved forging an Indian soul (1960 [1916]:93), through a program of behavioral modernization and extensive investigation of indigenous peoples by ethnographers, anthropologists, demographers, teachers, and artists. Part of the "forging" process was undertaken by folklorists, musicologists, and artists such as Francisco Domínguez, Rubén M. Campos, Carlos González, and Frances Toor whose work in the Lake Pátzcuaro region was pivotal in shaping perceptions of Lake Pátzcuaro music and dance practices, and in placing *The Old Men* and *Night of the Dead* in a public arena.

The Secretariat of Education, Collecting, and Disseminating

The creation of the Secretaría de Educación Pública (SEP), the Secretariat of Public Education, in 1921 was of profound significance and played an absolutely central role in processes of performism (encompassing folkloricization and ideological refunctionalization), enabling intellectuals, artists, pedagogues, and politicians to wholly commit to didactic and interventionist actions. As the department responsible for education and culture, many of the activities discussed in this study involving the *Dance of the Old Men* and *Night of the Dead* of Lake Pátzcuaro were organized, enacted, and promoted under the auspices of SEP. Significantly, SEP was formed under the leadership of Vasconcelos, who is recognized as the founder of modern education in Mexico (Paz 1972:152), and whose central pedagogical principle "to educate is to redeem" (Keen 1996:284) underpinned the many fervent and mission-like strategies of this ministry. SEP embraced a wide range of activities and departments, all of which were engaged with ideological and political activism.

Schools and pedagogical institutions were seen as efficacious settings for fostering nationalism, effected by shaping ideological positions and molding model citizens through behavioral modification. Revolutionary educational policy sought to inculcate literacy, nationalism, notions of citizenship, sobriety, hygiene, and hard work, and was specifically related to the policy of indigenous incorporation (de la Torre Otero 1933, Guzmán Gómez 1991, Knight 1990:81, Lewis 2006:191, Vaughan 1982 and 1997, Educational Work of the National League of Peasants 1928). Under the auspices of SEP, Vasconcelos initiated the *Misiones Culturales* (Cultural Missions) in 1923, consisting of teams of teachers who lived and worked in rural, and often remote, communities.

Many forms of media and presentation were used to disseminate and inculcate officially sanctioned ideas, including populist and scholarly publications, staged festivals, radio programs,[14] regional dance and music competitions, regional theater, films, and sport.[15] Dance and music were taught in all schools as an integral element of the nationalization processes (Lavalle 1988:97).[16] Under the auspices of SEP, processes for collecting, studying, centralizing, and disseminating music and dance practices and other material concerning indigenous peoples and practices were undertaken by teachers, folklorists, anthropologists, artists, and scholars. Accounts by three contemporaneous individuals all attest to SEP's activities in this area: musicologist Rubén M. Campos indicated that the Department of Fine Arts (a SEP institution) many times sent young musicians to collect songs and *sones* from Michoacán (Campos 1928:85); musicologists Gabriel Saldívar and Elisa Osorio Bolio also noted that collecting of dance was done by SEP (Saldívar and Osorio Bolio 1934:156);[17] and Marcelo Torreblanca, a trainee-teacher and later one of Mexico's leading dance researchers, observed that "the teachers of the *Misiones Culturales* taught the teachers of physical education the dances that they had learned in their work, and for many years they were disseminated in the schools of Mexico City" (Torreblanca 1980).[18]

As material was appropriated, assembled, and disseminated, so collections of officially sanctioned practices and images were molded as national repertoires and as representations of lo mexicano. Central to these nationalising processes was the idea of patrimony of the nation, in which both cultural practices and living indigenous peoples were regarded as the heritage of the whole nation.[19] In part, these were seen as integrationary tactics, aimed at incorporating indigenous peoples into the nation, encompassing both a benevolent notion of "care" and also an inherent concept of control. Two pronouncements by leading politicians illustrate the point: Vasconcelos (secretary of education) referred to indigenous peoples as "our Indians" (1926:77–79), and Lázaro Cárdenas (governor of Michoacán) described P'urhépecha peoples as "our tarascan race" (Informe 16.9.1931:20).

In the early 1920s, Vasconcelos worked with a team of intellectuals, artists, and musicians who particularly engaged strategies of folkloricization as part of the educational and cultural project. Recognizing the importance of theater as a didactic tool in national life, Vasconcelos supported and financed the movements of the *Teatro Regional* (regional theater), *Teatro Folklórico Mexicano* (folkloric theater), *Teatro Sintético Mexicano* (synthetic theater) and *Teatro al Aire Libre* (open-air theater) (Bullé Goyri 2003, Londré and Watermeier 1998). Of great importance for this study are two central figures in these theatrical movements: Francisco Domínguez and Carlos González. Both men worked for SEP and regarded their artistic tasks as inherently political, and both were instrumental in organizing the initial theatricalized staging of the *Dance of the Old Men* and *Night of the Dead* in Mexico City.[20]

Mexican Folkways: Reaching a Bilingual Readership

Printed matter played a particularly significant role in constructions of indigenousness and folkloric nationalism, with publications aimed at many strands of society reaching a diverse readership, all dedicated to the dissemination of anthropological, indigenous, and rural themes. The wide array ranged from academic and scholarly ethnographic books and articles to more populist magazines and newspapers. The magazine *Mexican Folkways* was particularly influential in shaping the concept of Mexican folklore, and in establishing an inherent association between notions of folklore and indigenousness. *Mexican Folkways* was promoted as a "bi-monthly magazine, in English and Spanish, dedicated to indigenous traditions and customs" (all editions). Writing in 1939, U.S. folklorist Ralph Boggs observed that "nearly all phases of Mexican folklore are described and discussed in the files of this periodical, vividly illustrated with pictures and reproductions of texts" (Boggs 1939:159). Produced between 1925 and 1937, this magazine included articles, photos, artwork, and musical transcriptions, all of which evoked romantic idealistic images of a rural, indigenous population, and also encompassed an ideological position that regarded the backwardness of certain indigenous peoples to be in need of development. *Mexican Folkways* specifically engaged and blurred an ethnographic and artistic frame to present indigenous and rural practices and peoples, imaging notions of lo mexicano and folkloric Mexico. Of fundamental importance to the central tenet of this study is the inclusion of articles and photos in *Mexican Folkways* that represented activities and peoples of Lake Pátzcuaro, including *Night of the Dead* on Janitzio.

Frances Toor, a U.S. expatriate folklorist and anthropologist, was the founding editor,[21] and significantly, the production of the magazine was partly subsidized by the Mexican government, indicating the relationship between the content of publication and state-sanctioned notions of ethnic and racial ideologies and folklorism. *Mexican Folkways* provided a forum for many indigenist intellectuals, with contributors forming an eclectic roll call of polymaths, who successfully blurred distinctions between roles as artist, intellectual, and politician. As I noted previously in this chapter, Manuel Gamio, undersecretary of education, disseminated his views on the utilitarian aspects of folklore in the very first edition of *Mexican Folkways* (1925:6–7). In 1926, the muralist and political activist Diego Rivera became the magazine's art editor (Mendoza 1956:49), demonstrating the notion of national art and ethnographic subjects. Under Rivera, coverage of the arts expanded to include the work of contemporary artists working in Mexico, such as José Clemente Orozco, Edward Weston, and Tina Modotti. Other contributors included Sáenz (previously mentioned as undersecretary of education), SEP-employed artist Carlos González, U.S. anthropologists Robert Redfield and Ralph Beals, Mexican anthropologists Carlos Basauri and Dr. Atl (Gerardo Murillo), and SEP-employed composer and folklorist, Francisco Domínguez.

As *Mexican Folkways* was published in both Spanish and English, the magazine was significant in influencing a Mexican and U.S. readership. Evidence that *Mexican Folkways* was appreciated in the United States in this period is provided by a note made by U.S. poet Carl Sandburg in his seminal 1927 publication *American Songbag*, who referred to *Mexican Folkways* as "the magazine so ably and humanly edited by Frances Toor in Mexico City" (Sandburg 1927:294). The impact in the United States encompassed the shaping of a potential tourist audience and enhancement of the developing artistic rapprochement with U.S. patrons, artists, and intellectuals concerning the investigation, preservation, and revitalization of folkloric culture and arts in Mexico (Vaughan and Lewis 2006:14, Sandoval 1998:33).

Performism for a Burgeoning Tourist Market

As exemplified by *Mexican Folkways*, shaping a notion of authentic Mexicanness through representations of indigenous and rural life served a developing tourist agenda both nationally and internationally. Imaging the nation for tourism took place through a range of processes that interfaced and merged with those of nationalism, continuing a trajectory begun several decades earlier. World's fairs were intrinsically important in this area, developing a propaganda network in order to build up transnational relations. Even in 1900, a publication entitled *To Mexico: Studies, Notes, and Useful Advice for Capitalists, the Immigrant and the Tourist*, produced for the Paris World's Fair, was targeted directly at potential tourists (Gostkowski 1900).[22] By the postrevolutionary era, tourism formed a central element of governmental development strategy, with activities promoting tourism and developing tourist attractions being the business of many governmental institutions, not only those specifically charged with tourist matters. Governmental initiatives included the creation of the National Committee for Tourism in 1928 followed by an expansion of the state's role in tourism in 1934 when Lázaro Cárdenas assumed the presidency, and the setting up of the Department of Tourism in 1936, with the regulation and licensing of hotels, travel agents, tourist guides, and restaurants (Saragoza 2001:101). In the 1920s, specific regions were selected by governmental bodies as being particularly suitable for touristic development, and were consequently subject to programs and policies for development. SEP urged teachers to engage their communities in developing tourist facilities and in promoting their region as a tourist destination, thereby inculcating pride in their region (Waters 2006:229). Drawing on a long trajectory of imaging Mexico developed since the mid-1800s by ethnographers, explorers, lithographers, painters, scientists, and travelers, the principal iconography of the postrevolutionary era incorporated Mexico's green valleys, snowcapped volcanoes, cactus plants, colorful market vendors, and the romantic, exotic Other (Vaughan and Lewis 2006:5).[23]

Artistic, Musical, and Theatrical Nationalism

Shaping nationalistic artistic and aesthetic sensibilities and constructing notions of what constituted indigenous and folkloric practices was central to many artistic, sculptural, and architectural endeavors. In the field of art, mural painting engaged indigenous themes, with artists using the walls of public buildings to glorify indigenous peoples, past and present. Diego Rivera, David Siqueiros, and Juan O'Gorman all practiced their art form with overtly ideological inspiration (Eggener 2000:33).[24] Architecture and architectural styles similarly employed notions of an indigenous past and present (Vasconcelos 1963:9, Olsen 1997). In discussing "el nacionalismo musical mexicano" (Mexican musical nationalism) in his *Panorama de la música mexicana* (Panorama of Mexican music), the Spanish musicologist Otto Mayer-Serra observed that the " 'folklorista' current in many countries had led to the formation of national schools and that composers in Mexico also took this on board" (1941a:96). Nationalist composers, most notably Carlos Chávez, Silvestre Revueltas, Miguel Bernal Jiménez, José Pablo Moncayo, Manuel M. Ponce, and Blas Galindo, incorporated "folk" elements in their compositions (Garland 1991:51), which drew on indigenous musical practices.[25]

Staged and theatricalized productions also engaged with nationalistic themes and representations, and state artists used the material of customs, legends, indigenous topics, and popular ideology to create their works. Even by the end of the nineteenth century and into the early years of the twentieth century, images of a rural and purportedly exotic Mexico were utilized in theatricalized performances. In the centennial independence celebrations of 1910, a set of popular dances, costumes and types were performed and exhibited as representations of regional identities (Vaughan and Lewis 2006:5). In Mexico City and other urban centers large-scale events, ballets, operas, and pantomimes presented treatments or representations of pre-Hispanic Mexico (Campos 1930:200).[26] A large-scale staged event representing aspects of preinvasion Aztec culture took place in 1925 in the open-air Theater of the Pyramids of Teotihuacán, close to Mexico City, and a presentation of Maya culture was staged in 1929 in Oaxaca (Campos 1930:201). Other major themes included the armed revolution and social transformation (Audiffred 2000, Tortajada Quiroz 1995, 2000).

SEP-sponsored theater movements previously mentioned (*Teatro Regional, Teatro Folklórico Mexicano, Teatro Sintético Mexicano* and *Teatro al Aire Libre*), all embraced themes of rural and indigenous life. Significantly for the trajectory of the *Dance of the Old Men* and *Night of the Dead*, a genre of literature emerged that also impacted upon the course of staged, folkloric performances—the *costumbrista* genre, which focused upon "capturing the environment and characters of the pure popular type" and "nuestra gente campesina" (our peasant people) (Sol 1938a). Drawing on the notion of local *costumbres* (customs), and using rural life and people as its resource, the national literary genre was transferred to the stage. *Cuadros costumbristas* (scenes of customs) or "scenes of everyday life" with no central musical or dance elements were dramatized and represented. Both the *Dance of the Old Men* and *Night of the Dead* were presented as public practices through theatricalized costumbrista performances in 1924, as I discuss in the following chapter.

Prior to this, in 1921, two major exhibitionary events were staged in Mexico City as part of the huge state-sponsored centennial festivities celebrating independence: *Noche Mexicana* (Mexican Night) and the *Exhibición de Artes Populares* (Exhibition of Popular Arts). They are important in the context of this study because they provided models for subsequent exhibitions and staged occasions involving *The Old Men* and *Night of the Dead*, and for their overt display of P'urhépecha objects within a nationalist setting. Although centennial celebrations were held in 1910, further events were staged after the revolutionary wars had come to an end, all of which were rooted in rural popular culture, with the terms "folk culture" and "indigenous culture" frequently being invoked in connection with this context (López 2006:24). *Noche Mexicana* took place in Chapultepec Park and was modeled on regional *ferias* (fairs) that involved stalls selling food and performances of dance and music. Small stages were set up around the park, and a large stage was constructed within the lake, which formed the centerpiece of the park.[27] The *Orquesta Típica del Centenario* of Miguel Lerdo de Tejada, with 350 musicians, was engaged to accompany regional dancers (ibid.:26). One hundred performers danced the *jarabe tapatío* (a dance from Jalisco) as part of a choreographic section entitled "Fantasía Mexicana," drawn directly from a theater event of the same name staged in 1919 in Mexico and the United States, in which the renowned ballerina, Anna Pavlova, had danced the jarabe tapatío en pointe.[28] Importantly, for the 1919 performances of *Fantasia Mexicana*, a representation of a utilitarian object from the P'urhépecha region was utilized as a central scenographic element in scenery designed by Adolfo Best Maugard. The object, a *jícara* (a brightly painted gourd or flat wooden dish from Uruapan, a town in the P'urhépecha upland area), was painted as a hugely enlarged form on the stage curtain. Representations of P'urhépecha jícaras were subsequently deployed as iconic referents of indigeneity in folkloric performances, particularly as a prop held by female dancers in Ballet Folklórico ensembles in Mexico and the United States performing P'urhépecha dances, including the *Dance of the Old Men* (see 174) (42 ◗).

In *Noche Mexicana*, placing the jarabe tapatío dance on stage within a state-organized, overtly nationalistic event authenticated the position of this dance as quintessentially national, simultaneously consolidating it as a dance to be performed by multiple dancers in a staged setting. As part of this event, P'urhépecha jícaras were also on display, identical to those imaged on the painted curtain in *Fantasía Mexicana*; however, this time they were used for serving refreshments, rather than as a solely scenographic element. As reported in the newspaper *El Universal*, lower-class refreshments were served "'in gourds beautifully decorated by the Indians of Pátzcuaro' by elite white women" (López 2006:25). Curiously, the objects were erroneously associated with the Lake Pátzcuaro region (rather than the P'urhépecha uplands region), creating a network of associations that linked indigenous peoples of Lake Pátzcuaro and the jícara. In this context overtly indigenous images from Lake Pátzcuaro were placed within and juxtaposed with a centralized, modern, and folkloric sensibility.

The other large-scale event, the *Exhibición de Artes Populares*, involved a series of musical performances and dioramas, regional singers, Yucatecan dancers, Lerdo de Tejada's Orquesta Típica del Centenario again, and galleries full of objects (ibid.:32). The aim of the exhibition was to create an aesthetic encyclopedia of Mexico, teaching visitors to recognize authentic popular arts and to identify them as indigenous and "muy nuestro" (uniquely ours), all of which engaged a knowledge-based discourse (ibid.:31–33). In order to generate material, organizers undertook collecting expeditions to areas that they knew, which included the Lake Pátzcuaro region. Therefore, as with *Noche Mexicana*, objectified representations of the peoples of Lake Pátzcuaro were exhibited as cultural heritage, establishing and promoting the place and peoples as authentically Mexican and indigenous within a national framework. A central element of the exhibition involved conveying the idea that not just the objects but also the entire way of life they represented was on display. By framing the objects as representations of the lives of indigenous peoples, the whole event enacted a containment activity. High-level politicians (including the president), foreign envoys, elite and middle-class public, and the press attended, emphasizing the political and ideological role of the event and the processes of dissemination to both national and international audiences.

Both events reveal strategies in which indigenous and rural practices were incorporated into a national sensibility, and in which distinctively P'urhépecha artifacts were deployed in a nationalist context as displays of indigenous life. Unmistakable are processes of collecting, appropriation, authentication, commodification, exhibition, and nationalization of objects and peoples of Lake Pátzcuaro within a Mexican paradigm. However, even within this setting many complexities surrounded the ideological and pragmatic aspects of indigenous representation, for the organizers and critics held "contrasting visions of the role that indigenous cultures should play in the formation of the national self. They clashed in their assumptions about the relationship between Indianness and Mexicanness" (ibid.:23–24). Two positions were evident: firstly, the use of popular and rural aesthetics as a base or germ for the creation of Mexicanness; and secondly, popular arts as the embodiment of the ultimate expression of primordial Mexicanness (ibid.:30). As I discuss through this study, it was the latter position that was taken up in the ensuing processes of performism encompassing the *Dance of the Old Men* and *Night of the Dead* as embodied representations of indigenousness, Mexicanness, and Mexico, even as the two events of 1921 laid the foundations and set the course for the public spectacles of *The Old Men* and *Night of the Dead* as displays of P'urhépecha life.

CHAPTER 4

Appropriation
and Incorporation

From Island Village to Capital City

IN THE FIRST years of the 1920s, a small group of state representatives visited the
Lake Pátzcuaro region, witnessing both Night of the Dead on the island of Janitzio
and a dance of old men on the island of Jarácuaro. So began the transformation of
these two activities into iconic referents of Mexico, changing from private events
into publicly spectated performances. Embedded within the complex cultural,
political, and ideological contexts of nation-formation, a few individuals played
an influential and significant role in constructing and shaping notions of folklore,
indigenousness, and Mexicanness by engaging these practices. In this chapter my
main focus is upon considering the events and people involved in the initial
processes of appropriation, commodification, display, and dissemination.
Following a brief overview of the P'urhépecha region, I discuss the practices of
Day/Night of the Dead, and dances of old men prior to nationalist appropriation.
I then trace the paradigmatic moment of the shift from local to national in the
1920s, comprising: the visit of state officials to witness Night of the Dead on
Janitzio and the subsequent publication of photos and texts; the first theatrical
events in which the *Dance of the Old Men* and *Night of the Dead* were staged in
Mexico City; and the Teatro Regional event of the *Fiesta of Song and Dance* in the
P'urhépecha town of Paracho. Finally, I discuss two influential figures, musicolo-
gist Rubén M. Campos and Jarácuaro teacher, musician, and composer, Nicolás
Bartolo Juárez.

P'urhépecha Peoples: Decimation and Survival

At the start of the sixteenth century, the city of Tzintzuntzan, on the edge of Lake
Pátzcuaro, was the thriving capital of the powerful P'urhépecha empire. This was
reduced to a tiny village of a few thousand within a few years of the arrival of

Cristobal de Olíd and his regiment of Spanish conquistadors in the area in 1522. The ruins of *yácatas*, (round preincursion ceremonial constructions) in Tzintzuntzan became an important element in configuring the location as a pre-Hispanic site of interest in the twentieth century. Similarly, the remains of a preinvasion site at nearby Ihuatzio, on the edge of the lake, situate the region as inherently pre-Hispanic. In the sixteenth century, Pátzcuaro was established as the new capital of the region, and became a place first for religious orders, and then for the criollo elite. Despite the decimation of the P'urhépecha population, a sense of stubborn resistance and the influence of the sixteenth- century priest Vasco de Quiroga enabled the P'urhépecha heritage to survive better than many indigenous cultures and peoples in other areas of Mexico (Zárate Hernández 1993:209–210). Vasco de Quiroga's influence led to the shaping of craft and cultural practices in the area, particularly in the Lake Pátzcuaro region.

Culturally and topographically there are many variations in the P'urhépecha region, differences that are reflected in the division of the territory into four areas: the Sierra or Meseta (the uplands); La Cañada de los Once Pueblos (the valley of eleven villages); la Ciénega de Zacapu (the marsh of Zacapu); and el lago de Pátzcuaro (Lake Pátzcuaro). The Lake Pátzcuaro region is distinctive and demarcated through the presence of the lake, the island villages within the waters, and many little communities around the lake edge. Throughout the region the P'urhépecha language acts as a unifying feature, and is also a tangible piece of audible evidence for the notion of continuity with the past, even though the language spoken today is very different to that in the sixteenth century (Márquez Joaquín 1997:219).[1] In the twentieth century there was a reduction in numbers of people speaking P'urhépecha, although in the last two decades various initiatives have promoted the teaching and use of the P'urhépecha language in schools in the area. In the Lake Pátzcuaro region, the older generations are bilingual, speaking both P'urhépecha and Spanish, while the younger generations tend to speak mainly Spanish. Additionally, through extensive and nonpermanent migration to the United States, many people in the area also speak English. Economically the region is sustained through craft production (for example, hat-making and pottery), agriculture and fishing (although this has declined considerably), the service sector (small shops and businesses), and the tourist industry. Migration had a major impact throughout the region during the twentieth century, with a notable increase in the 1940s as the braceros program enabled and encouraged organized migration to the United States.[2] Encompassing transitory, seasonal, or permanent migration patterns, popular destinations have been urban centers, such as Mexico City, Guadalajara, and Morelia; agricultural regions such as the northern state of Sonora; and the United States, particularly the southwestern and bordering states.

Dances of Old Men and Days of the Dead

Local celebrations of fiestas and national days are an important feature of life, with celebratory events marking the major feast days of the Roman Catholic calendar.

Roman Catholicism forms the basis for religious beliefs and practices, although these often take on a syncretic form. The season of Christmas, New Year, and Three Kings (6 January) is a prime time for continuous celebrations, along with Corpus Christi and the Patron Saint day of the village. Music and dance form an integral part of these fiestas, which often encompass a Mass, feasting, and fireworks, and go on for three days. Both unmasked and masked dances are a regular feature of many celebrations. A great variety of masks exists throughout the region, with certain archetypes being used more than others, particularly el diablo (the devil), la maringuía (the virgin Mary, costumed as a young P'urhépecha woman but danced by a man), and viejos (old men). As an archetypal genre, masked dances of old men were danced in the region informally as part of religious celebrations and weddings, with lines of dancers performing in the streets, moving from house to house, and dancing inside and in front of the church[3] (26–27 ◐). Old men characters appeared (and continue to be used) in pastorelas, dance-drama pieces performed during the Christmas season. Set pieces of dialogue were interspersed with dancing, often without fixed choreography or with minimal choreography. These were considered to be religious-educational pieces, encompassing issues of Christian doctrine, but always with a humorous element. Dialogue for various versions from the nineteenth and early twentieth centuries exists in print.[4] At the beginning of the twentieth century, forms of old men dances in the Lake Pátzcuaro region existed mostly in two lakeside villages: Santa Fe de la Laguna and Cucuchucho. In Cucuchucho a group of roughly twenty villagers performed as old men, dancing for the fiestas of Christmas, New Year, and Three Kings. The director of the group accompanied on the guitar-like jaranita or jarana and also danced.[5] In Santa Fe de la Laguna, dances of old men took the same format with groups of young men dancing in the streets. Masks were crafted from clay, as pottery work was the principal source of income for Santa Fe villagers. Although masks were always used in the dance they were not always placed over the face, but were sometimes worn hanging over the chest (as still happens in various dances in Santa Fe and the island of Janitzio).

In the late nineteenth and early twentieth century, Felipe Dimas, organist and choir director of Santa Fe, directed a dance of old men and accompanied by playing a chordal pattern on a ten-string jarana. For a few years this dance ceased to be presented in Santa Fe, but in about 1920 it was revived for the wedding of Dimas's first son, Lucas, as a form of humorous entertainment for the assembled guests. Subsequently, the dance continued to be enacted for local fiestas. Other dances also became part of these seasonal events, with many groups of dancers creating their own choreography and musical accompaniment.[6]

Events that led to the initial process of appropriation of a dance of old men into the national arena took place on the island of Jarácuaro, a village on the opposite side of the lake to both Cucuchucho and Santa Fe. Concurring accounts by villagers from Jarácuaro suggest that the transmission process from Santa Fe to Jarácuaro happened through the temporary migration of two young brothers from Jarácuaro, Andrés and Simón Orozco, in about 1920. Both were choristers who sang for mass in the church of Jarácuaro. As part of their training they spent time in Santa Fe undertaking choral and singing classes and while there they saw a dance of old men being enacted, accompanied by a ten-string jarana. The Orozco brothers observed the villagers dancing from house to house, where they were given gifts of fruit. On their return to Jarácuaro, Andrés and Simón decided to organize a similar dance for the Christmas season, using clay masks that they had taken with them from Santa Fe. During this season other dances were also presented on the streets, such as the Dance of the Apaches using black painted clay masks also from Santa Fe.[7] Soon after this initial presentation of a dance of old men by the Orozco brothers on the island of Jarácuaro, another family also formed a group to enact a dance of old men. This was the Bartolo Juárez family, and in particular Nicolás. Under the direction of their father, the Bartolo Juárez family had already formed a music ensemble, performing on the island and for nearby villages, gaining a reputation for their expertise both as musicians and composers. It was this reputation that was the grounds for the visit of Mexico City–based folklorists, musicians, and artists to the island of Jarácuaro in the early 1920s, which led to their witnessing a dance of old men.

In the same way that dances of old men took place informally in villages all over the P'urhépecha region, on 1 and 2 November the yearly celebration of Day/Night of the Dead was commemorated not only in communities in the P'urhépecha region but also in cities, towns, and villages throughout Mexico. As part of the Roman Catholic calendar, All Souls Day and Day/Night of the Dead were marked as national feast days of memorial celebration, with the enacting of a ritual of collective mourning for the remembrance of all deceased adult family members and friends. *Los Angelitos* (the little angels), a ceremony held on 31 October, marked the remembrance of children who had died. Despite the secularization of the postrevolutionary era, All Souls Day, Day/Night of the Dead, and other traditional religious fiestas were incorporated into the radical calendar. Day/Night of the Dead was celebrated throughout Mexico in a multiplicity of manners, and in many places was linked with preincursion practices that manifested a variety of syncretic forms.[8] For most Mexicans the occasion encompassed two locations: the home and the cemetery. In the home the family created a small shrine or altar on which were placed photographs, votive candles, food, flowers, and any other offerings to recollect and recall specific likes associated with the deceased individual. Correspondingly, family members took food, drink, candles, and offerings to the cemetery where the commemoration either lasted for many hours (during the night or day) or simply entailed a short visit (see figures 1.12 to 1.14). Other public activities also took place involving displays, altars, streets events, and a Mass. In the P'urhépecha region the observance varied from community to community, but still encompassed similar focal elements: the presence of an altar in the home, and passing the day or night in the cemetery, often with the attendance of a priest who officiated for prayers and for Mass. Prior to the early 1920s the occasion of Night of the Dead on the island of Janitzio was marked in just this way—as a night of offerings, bread, food for the dead, candles, prayers, mass, and hymn-singing. The only non-islander present was a priest who solemnized the occasion.

Appropriation, Publication, and Theatricalization:
Visits and Dissemination

By the early 1920s, the Lake Pátzcuaro region had already been brought to the attention of Mexico City–based government intellectuals, folklorists, ethnographers, anthropologists, artists, and politicians, through dissemination in publications and staged events, as exemplified in the use of P'urhépecha artifacts in both *Noche Mexicana* and the *Exhibición de Artes Populares* in Mexico City in 1921. In terms of postrevolutionary ideology, the P'urhépecha peoples served as an ideal model of indigenousness, whose practices were regarded as authentic but who were also in need of incorporation, assimilation, and modernization. The region was sufficiently accessible to allow urban intellectuals to visit from the state capital of Morelia and from Mexico City, and yet also evoked an impression of remoteness suitable for embracing ideas of authenticity.

In relation to this study, four people in particular who visited the islands of Janitzio and Jarácuaro on collecting visits were thoroughly involved with shaping processes of performism through staged events and publications. They were Rubén M. Campos (musicologist), Carlos González (artist and producer), Francisco Domínguez (folklorist and composer), and Frances Toor (anthropologist and folklorist). Their visits to the island of Janitzio for Night of the Dead initiated the "in situ" spectacle for visitors, and resulted in appropriation for theatricalized performance and dissemination through publication. In parallel processes, as a consequence of their visits to the island of Jarácuaro, a dance of old men was appropriated for theatricalized performance in Mexico City. I discuss the influence of these four individuals in this and subsequent chapters.

The visit to the island of Janitzio for Night of the Dead by the group of state officials in the early 1920s was profoundly significant. Toor, González, and other visitors all presented their experiences in nationalistic and touristic dissemination processes. Descriptions and photographs of the tour were published by two members of the party (González 1925, 1928a; Toor 1925a, 1928). The act of visiting the island and subsequent representation in literary and photographic form marked the beginning of the process of transformation of the ceremony on the island of Janitzio from intimate, private ritual (Night of the Dead) into a public spectacle, national and touristic icon, and patrimony of the nation (*Night of the Dead*). A description of several elements of the visit to Janitzio serves to exemplify major aspects, encompassing journeys, witness, and observation. In order to make their way to the island, the small group of visitors from Mexico City and the United States crossed the lake by large wooden canoe and disembarked on the island. Once on the island, the group wandered through the narrow streets, looking inside the church, peering into houses where P'urhépecha families were sleeping or preparing for their night-time celebration, and finally making their way to the cemetery (Toor 1928). In the cemetery the visitors observed the Janitzio inhabitants sitting and kneeling around the gravesides, placing their offerings, talking, singing hymns, and praying. One member of the group took photographs of the event. After passing a few hours on the island, the visitors boarded the canoe and journeyed back across the lake to the shore of Lake Pátzcuaro. The presence of the visitors on the island was not pre-arranged by the Janitzio inhabitants, and interaction between hosts and guests was minimal. As one of the visitors noted: "at no time do these fisherfolk welcome visitors, and less for this intimate occasion" (Toor 1928:68). The group that journeyed to Janitzio was made up of official representatives of the state, including Carlos González, Moisés Sáenz (undersecretary of education), and Dr I. L. Kandel, a scholar of comparative education from Columbia University (New York), as guest of honor (ibid.). The composition of this party demonstrates a model for the workings of the performism processes encompassing political, artistic, educational, and academic elements. The presence of both Sáenz and González, as SEP representatives, illustrates the interfacing and overlapping roles of government, pedagogy, scholarship, and cultural matters. Sáenz was inherently involved in shaping governmental policy on indigenous peoples, and was also a contributor to *Mexican Folkways* magazine (Sáenz 1928). González collected material for ethnographic and popular representation in photographic, artistic, and theatrical forms. The presence of Dr I. L. Kandel, a high-level pedagogue and scholar from the United States, exemplifies the importance of cross-border, international, collaborative initiatives.

As the prototype for all future tourist excursions to Janitzio for *Night of the Dead* (leading directly to the presence of over one hundred thousand visitors in the twenty-first century), the visit in the early 1920s encapsulates all the principal features of the journey to the island and the presence of non-P'urhépecha spectators of the ritual. There was no expectation that the visitors would participate in the rituals, but rather that they would remain on the outside, performing a role as voyeurs, onlookers, and witnesses. In the very act of visiting the ceremony and observing the ritual commemoration, two groups of people were present—actors and viewers—transforming the event into an activity for exhibition, display, and observation. In this scenario, people living in the present moment were framed and read as from the past, with an unequivocal presentation of the inhabitants of Janitzio as an idyllic and romantic Other, an idea that was subsequently disseminated widely through ethnographic, popular, and tourist publications.

As the act of the visit to the island created a pattern for all future journeys, so too the published visual and literary accounts demonstrated a linguistic and photographic style and tone of representation which created a paradigmatic model for all future events and reports, leading directly to the utilization and framing of this occasion in the twenty-first century. Two published articles were particularly important for the network of ideas and significations that they depicted. One account, by González (1925), appeared in the Mexican scholarly journal *Ethnos*, whose founder and director was Manuel Gamio (anthropologist and undersecretary of education). As a journal "dedicated to the study and improvement of the indigenous population of Mexico," the political and ideological framing of the peoples and practices was overt. The second account was published in *Mexican Folkways*, in a section entitled "The day of the dead in Janitzio" (Toor 1928). Although the two publications had distinct readerships, both articles engaged a descriptive and objectifying ethnographic approach, also employing elements of romantic idealization and a clear ideological stance. Notions of *otherness* imbued the writing and photos, and both the ritual and peoples were characterized as authentic, mystical, and pre-Hispanic.

A few examples from the *Mexican Folkways* article serve to illustrate the style and ideological positioning presented. Toor began her article by describing the journey to Janitzio "in a huge fishing canoe," remarking that "no signs of life were visible as we approached," and then playing with linguistic signifiers of distance and travel to another time and place, characterizing the island as an "unreal world" and "a distant world of fantasy," where the events "made the scene weird and fantastically beautiful" (Toor 1928:68–9). Toor engaged the phrase "the Tarascan fisher folk" to describe the inhabitants of Janitzio, placing them in a rural, working environment and specifically labeling them with the term "folk." In these few sentences the people of Janitzio and the event of *Night of the Dead* were decisively positioned outside of contemporary and modern Mexico, existing in the same temporal space, yet confined to a state of a dream, and therefore not real. The event was described as "*un cuadro*" and "a scene" (both the Spanish and English terms appear in the original text), indicating a framed experience, ripe for spectating and viewing from the outside: "The scene of the night was like a strangely beautiful dream in an unreal world" (ibid.). The P'urhépecha ritual was also specifically presented as "pagan" and as a non- and pre-Catholic religious practice, a depiction that ensured that both the peoples and practices could be usefully deployed within a framework of indigenismo.

Of great significance for the future trajectory of the reproduced imagery of *Night of the Dead* on Janitzio were the photos taken by González (1925, 1928a). These black and white framed illustrations depict small groups of women in the cemetery, enfolded in their *rebozos* sitting by the gravesides with their offerings of flowers and candles. One photograph is a close-up taken from behind a group of kneeling women in which the backs of their heads, wrapped in rebozos, form a clear embodied outline. The iconography of this image was subsequently deployed countless times in tourist and folkloric literature, and continues to be reproduced to this day. Another photograph, taken at a greater distance, encompasses not only small clusters of women huddled around gravesides, kneeling and sitting on the ground with candles and flowers, but also the wall of the cemetery, a few tiled roofs of houses, and most significantly, part of the lake. The inclusion of water within the frame serves to establish and reinforce these shawled and kneeling P'urhépecha women as ethnically and authentically *other* through the notion of separation, boundaries, and isolation.

The *Mexican Folkways* article was not only significant on its own terms for the literary and visual iconography that it presented, but also for the juxtaposition of three other photographic images and printed text that were not wholly part of the article, but which acted as intertextual signifiers influencing reception and interpretation. The first of these is a photograph, taken by art photographer Tina Modotti, which directly precedes the account of *Night of the Dead* in the magazine. The photograph depicts three pieces of "Bread of the Dead," with the caption "Every family on the island of Janitchio [sic.] bake and form [sic.] their own bread.

They make mostly animals with great skill" (Modotti 1928:64). Although special bread is a common feature of celebrations for Day and Night of the Dead in many parts of Mexico, the Modotti photograph created associations specifically with the island of Janitzio. Closely connected with art photographer Edward Weston (whose photographs of the island of Janitzio taken in the mid-1920s still circulate in international art exhibitions[9]), Modotti's work exemplifies the process of a middle-class artist taking the everyday and ritual objects of indigenous peoples and displaying them in a transformed art frame, much as the painted jícaras for *Fantasía Mexicana*.[10]

In the second example of juxtaposition, two ethnographic and "specimen" photos of women from Janitzio are embedded in the article on *Night of the Dead*, even though they are not directly related to the content (Toor 1928:68, 69). In one photo, an unnamed woman stands in profile to the camera, and the caption describes the clothes that she is wearing. In the other photo, two sisters (as stated in the caption) stand side by side, one with her head turned to the ground (appearing to be shy of the camera). As photographic studies of physiognomy and clothing, they present the women as ethnological objects and curiosities for display in the public arena of the magazine.

The third example is an article by Moisés Sáenz, entitled "Rural Schools and the Progress of the *Indio*," which directly follows the Toor article on *Night of the Dead* (1928). Sáenz's article presents a deeply ideological view of indigenous peoples, implicating the P'urhépecha peoples of Lake Pátzcuaro within the rhetoric. As undersecretary of education, Saenz's own ideological positioning was highly influential, so the dissemination of his policy of integration and transformation, openly set out in *Mexican Folkways* just a few pages after the account of *Night of the Dead*, was of great import. Saenz was known as one of the "social surgeons" who believed that by eliminating elements of indigenous peoples that were supposedly obstacles to modernity, and by stimulating those that were positive, the Mexican nation could modernize itself (del Val 1995:52).[11] In his article in *Mexican Folkways*, Sáenz comments on the results of experiments relating to indigenous and mestizo schools, and refers to "the inhabitants of the regions of superior indigenous culture—Jalisco, Michoacán, Oaxaca, Yucatán" (1928:75), even as the very title indicates the need for progress through transformation. As *Night of the Dead* and the peoples of Lake Pátzcuaro became part of these transformational processes, so the dissemination of images and representations such as those published in *Mexican Folkways* performed processes of shaping perception and reception. In a dichotomous context, the islanders of Janitzio were valued for their other-worldliness even as they were considered to be in need of incorporation. From the outset, concepts of ethnicity and racial formation and the complexities and polarities that drove policy-making were inherently part of the political and ideological framework encompassing the appropriation and dissemination of *Night of the Dead* on Janitzio.

With high-ranking government officials, artists, and academics acting as key players in processes of folkloricization and ideological refunctionalization, the official visits to the island for *Night of the Dead* and the dissemination of details of the event in literary and photographic form instigated both the ceremony of *Night of the Dead* on Janitzio and the inhabitants of Lake Pátzcuaro as artifacts of cultural heritage and authentic visitor attractions, available and accessible to all for the good of the nation. Significantly for the future role of the island and event as a tourist destination and attraction, the published descriptions of the initial visit to the ritual celebration contain the very core of the tourist experience—a journey from one place to another and back again. Not only did the journey to the island of Janitzio encompass travel across water in a canoe, from one shore to another, but the conceptualization of the living islanders and their ritual of *Night of the Dead* as other worldly, magical, mystical, and phantasmagorical also allowed for an experience of traveling to another world. These remained essential elements of the tourist experience and the marketing imagery since that time.

Putting It on Stage: Island Village to National Capital

The group of government officials that visited Janitzio in the early 1920s for *Night of the Dead* also journeyed to the island of Jarácuaro, drawn by the reputation of the Bartolo Juárez family (and in particular Nicolás) as great musicians and composers. These visits to Jarácuaro were undertaken for the purpose of collecting material for publication and dissemination through SEP for nationalist agendas. As with the trips to Janitzio, the group crossed the lake by canoe, an experience depicted by eminent musicologist Rubén M. Campos, who documented these events and his esteem for Nicolás Bartolo Juárez writing, " 'This is the child Mozart' I said to the painter Carlos González one day when we were crossing from Erongarícuaro to Jarácuaro by canoe to hear the Juárez Quartet" (1928:86). Campos was intensely interested in the Bartolo Juárez family ensemble, writing about the family and their music in his seminal 1928 publication *El folklore y la música mexicana* (Folkore and Mexican Music) (ibid.). While on the island, however, the visitors were witness to a dance of old men, which they consequently decided to collect for re-presentation in a staged public performance in Mexico City. Two men in particular were pivotal: Carlos González and Francisco Domínguez. Both González and Domínguez were heavily involved with the Teatro Regional and Teatro Sintético movements, and were seeking suitable material for their theatricalized events. Frances Toor later commented on the role of these two men in *Mexican Folkways*, noting that "Francisco Domínguez and Carlos González were both sent by the Ministry of Public Instruction in 1923 to study folklore in the State of Michoacán" (1930:108). As a result of their excursions to Michoacán, in 1924 they staged two events in Mexico City that were profoundly significant as the first instances of theatricalized performances of the *Dance of Old Men* from Jarácuaro and *Night of the Dead* from Janitzio.

Following the visits to Jarácuaro the process for staging these theatricalized performances, (an overt process of nationalist folkloricization) involved taking the young musician and dancer, Nicolás Bartolo Juárez, to Mexico City in 1924, to teach his version of the *Dance of Old Men* to a small group of trainee-teachers at a government-run institution. After training and rehearsing, the students performed the *Dance of the Old Men*, as taught to them by Bartolo Juárez of Jarácuaro, on stage in the building of the Cine Olímpia in Mexico City, for an audience of foreign officials from Chile, in a state-sponsored event organized by SEP. Vasconcelos, in his role as secretary of education, sponsored and funded the event. The student-dancers wore costumes and masks from Jarácuaro, and one of the students, Marcelo Torreblanca, replicated Bartolo Juárez's role by acting as lead dancer and musician, accompanying the dance on the jaranita. An account written by Torreblanca himself serves as a valuable description of the most important aspects:

> A little history—in the 1920s the Secretary of Education had an engage-
> ment to present a ceremony for a contingent of Chilean delegates who
> were visiting Mexico and the old *Cine Olímpia* was offered [as a venue].
> From Jarácuaro, the authorities brought the best musician and dancer of
> this dance [The Old Men], who was the great Nicolás Juárez.
> ...they chose various [students] from the National Preparatory School
> who at the same time were studying in the Elementary School of Physical
> Education.... Nicolás Juárez directed the students and left the rehearsals to
> one of them, the one who had demonstrated most interest and discipline.
> As well as teaching him to play the *jaranita*, he was put in charge of direct-
> ing the dance. The clothes were made in Jarácuaro and were, of course,
> original and authentic.
> I believe that this was the first time in Mexico that a group of
> watered-down performers [*aguados*] danced this dance in the Federal
> District, Mexico City and it was initiated in a great way, because they
> learned directly from the authentic dancer who did not allow his dance to
> be distorted, and who also taught how to respect the dance and perform it
> with indigenous feeling and thought. (Torreblanca 1980)

As I discuss below, this experience in 1924 had a profound impact on the young Torreblanca, who went on to become one of Mexico's most respected and influential researchers and teachers of dance. Torreblanca's work continues to have an impact on folkloric ensembles in Mexico and the United States as they perform *The Old Men* in the twenty-first century.

Encompassed in the Cine Olímpia event of 1924 were features of performism processes that provided models for ideological and aesthetic parameters that have been present in contexts using *The Old Men* ever since. Here I outline the principal features. Appropriation procedures involved the collection, transfer, and recontextualization of a dance and music practice, and objects (clothes and a mask) presented as indigenous. A P'urhépecha villager was engaged to undertake the transmission process of teaching the dance and music, which was then commodified by middle-class artists for use on a stage with nonlocal dancers and musicians. Trainee-teachers took the role of actors for the live spectated event, and subsequently as teachers and transmitters of the dance in multiple school environments, establishing the diffusion of a repertoire of regional and national dance and music through school contexts. Processes of appropriation and re-presentation formed part of centralization and incorporation strategies, with government officials working for SEP as the instigators and organizers. Their role was to take this artifact of music and dance to the national capital for display purposes within a state-organized, officially sanctioned context of communicating, imaging, and embodying ideas of Mexicanness. At its core the Cine Olímpia spectacle entailed enacting a dance and music practice framed as indigenous on a stage as a representation of authentic Mexicanness for a foreign audience. Through this event, a form of dance of old men became "fixed," and a specific choreography was created which transformed a free-form durational and processional dance into a temporally and spatially limited set of short pieces, each with its own defined patterns. It was this form that became the model for future performances of the *Dance of the Old Men* danced both by folkloric ensembles in Mexico City and by local groups in the Lake Pátzcuaro region.

The staged spectacle at the Cine Olímpia encompassed a commodifying and interventionist position, engaging a discourse concerning indigenous practices and transformational processes. Traditional practices and peoples were seen to be in need of transformation by middle-class educators and artists, and the dance was treated as a practice that could be molded and shaped to suit the nationalist agenda. However, issues of aesthetic boundaries, ideological referencing, and the function of dance, music, and craft practices in nationalizing processes were highly debated. Taking Bartolo Juárez to Mexico City enacted a form of intervention, in which cultured artists were regarded as necessary to transform indigenous practices into art. As López has noted, Vasconcelos "did not consider the vernacular industries to be 'art'.... True art could not 'arise spontaneously from the people.' It had to be nurtured and required 'intervention by cultured artists.' It also demanded state patronage, 'since artists cannot produce anything when abandoned to their own resources, and only the government' was able to direct and systematize artistic production" (López 2006:29).

Yet within a commodifying agenda, a concept of authenticity also figured as a central element, and was preeminent in the discourse and reception of *The Old Men*. Authentication processes ensured that the practice and costume were framed as authentically indigenous, validated through transmission by a genuine indigenous person. It is useful to draw upon Torreblanca's own delineations of his contemporaneous understanding of the teaching process and staged event, as captured in written documents and radio programs. Torreblanca indicated that instead of using authentic people (los verdaderos)—in other words, dancers from the villages of Lake Pátzcuaro—SEP committed a crime by using trainee-teachers as performers (Radio Educación C665). These dancers were "watered-down" or inauthentic, in contrast to Bartolo Juárez who was an "authentic dancer" (Torreblanca 1980). However, the practice *was* perceived to be authentic on account of the authenticity of the person who taught it and the process of teaching, thus the student teachers were taught by an "authentic dancer" who did "not allow his dance to be distorted" and taught "how to respect the dance and perform it with

indigenous feeling and thought" (ibid.). So the practice of Bartolo Juárez was perceived to be the original and authentic form, and his way of feeling and thinking
could be taught in the same way that the movements and music of the dance could
be taught. Less controversially, the costumes and masks were regarded as authentic
because of their origin and production in the Lake Pátzcuaro region.

A Synthetic Theater: Everyday Life on Stage

With the theatricalized performance of the Cine Olímpia spectacle *a* dance of old
men of Jarácuaro was transformed into *The Dance of the Old Men*. Using a fixed
choreography, and displayed for a seated audience, the framed and contained set
of movements and music were initiated into their role as an embodied icon of
indigenousness and Mexicanness. Following on from the success of the Cine
Olímpia occasion, another performance event was organized that incorporated
not only the *Dance of the Old Men* but also *Night of the Dead* of Janitzio. I draw on
the words of Torreblanca again to provide an outline:

> From this [the Cine Olímpia event] was born what was called *el Teatro
> Sintético del Murciélago* [the Synthetic Theater of the Bat], in which sum-
> marized costumbrista scenes were presented, including Night of the Dead
> from Janitzio, the Dance of the Old Men and Dance of the Moors. The stu-
> dents performed The Old Men again accompanied by a *jaranita* with four
> strings. (Torreblanca 1980)

As for the Cine Olímpia occasion, *The Old Men* was danced on stage in a commodified form by nonlocal performers. As before, Bartolo Juárez was invited and taken to
Mexico City, where he taught *The Old Men* and also the *Dance of the Moors*, a dance
enacted for the celebratory fiesta for the Patron Saint of Jarácuaro. As I discuss presently, although the *Dance of the Moors* was performed and promoted in the 1920s and
1930s as a nationalist dance alongside the *Dance of the Old Men*, after the 1940s it was
only infrequently incorporated into national dance repertoires (44–45 ⬤).

The principles and practices of the Teatro Sintético event provided a model for
formulating future folkloric occasions, and actually drew on a form of dioramic
exhibition and dance display that had already been utilized in performances in
Mexico City and at world's fairs. The Teatro Sintético or Folklórico movement was
founded for the purpose of synthesizing a variety of popular performance styles
and so-called *folk customs*.[12] As a government-sponsored theatrical form that operated within ideological and political frameworks, aesthetic principles and discourse
encompassed overt notions of authentic indigenousness. Carlos González and
Francisco Domínguez were two of the principal organizers. Aesthetic ideas of a
synthetic theater were drawn from the Futurist Theater of Italy, involving very
brief ideas compressed into a few minutes (Marinetti et al. 1995 [1915]).[13] Of
particular significance was the way in which the theater event included not only
overt dance and music practices, but also costumbrista scenes, or "scenes of

everyday life" and "local customs" with no central musical or dance elements. These scenes entailed the representation of a ritual celebration, a custom, or an element of everyday life within the bounded frame of a stage.

The "scene" of *Night of the Dead* on Janitzio had no conventional dance or music elements, yet it was re-presented and re-created on stage and framed as a spectacle and display. The activities of this nonobserved ritual were theatricalized and acted out on stage for an audience. As the visit of the governmental officials to Janitzio for *Night of the Dead* transformed the occasion into a public spectacle *in situ*, the Teatro Sintético event changed it into a theatricalized spectacle and staged exhibit. Through processes of commodification, a private, durational, collective ritual of remembrance held within a walled cemetery was converted into a brief theatricalized show on a stage for public viewing, transforming indigenous P'urhépecha life into an ethnographic exhibit, showcase, and living diorama. Displaying scenes of P'urhépecha life in this way encouraged reception and interpretation involving ethnological curiosity, by providing a window onto the lives of indigenous others. Despite the student-actors standing in for the *real* bodies of Janitzio residents, a process of indexation referenced an original context elsewhere, emphasizing issues of authenticity. Significantly, Nicolás Bartolo Juárez did sing in the Teatro Sintético event, also permitting a concept of authentic indigenousness (and a development that pointed toward the growing importance of incorporation of authentic performers in events designated as folkloric). With the anthropological frame taking the representation out of the realm of entertainment, the dioramic display of *Night of the Dead* facilitated an interpretation of the activities as a reenactment of something that took place in a different place, prompting audience members to seek out possible meanings and symbolic actions and properties. As with the dissemination of *Night of the Dead* on Janitzio in the photographic and literary accounts of González and Toor, for the theatricalized performance those aspects of the ritual that were most useful for contexts of indigenismo, folkloric nationalism, and authentic Mexicanness were highlighted for the audience-gaze: women swathed in rebozos kneeling by gravesides, surrounded by flowers and candles in a dimly lit atmosphere became the prime dramaturgical and scenographic elements.

The import and consequences of the display of the *Dance of the Old Men* and *Night of the Dead* in the Teatro Sintético event are profound. Crucially, *Night of the Dead* on Janitzio was enacted within the same frame as *The Old Men*, setting up the pairing that has remained in place ever since. Correspondingly, this event promoted both activities as practices of authentic Mexicanness, initiating a trajectory of utilization in multifarious twentieth- and twenty-first- century nationalist and tourist contexts.

Mexican Life: Regional Theater and the Fiesta of Song and Dance

In 1924[14] another government-sponsored, staged event incorporating P'urhépecha dance, music, and ritual took place: *La Fiesta de la Canción y de la Danza*, the *Fiesta of Song and Dance*. However, unlike the Cine Olímpia and Teatro Sintético performances, this event was staged far from Mexico City, over two hundred miles away in the P'urhépecha highland town of Paracho. As part of the Teatro Regional movement the *Fiesta of Song and Dance*, as described by Rubén M. Campos, was "the first tentative representation of Mexican life" (1930:200). Although it did not include a staging of *The Old Men* or *Night of the Dead*, it is important to include a brief summary in this study because of the multiple connections with processes of performism surrounding these two practices. The *Fiesta of Song and Dance* was part of the Teatro Regional de Paracho (Regional Theater of Paracho), directed and organized by Francisco Domínguez and Carlos González, both of whom were working in an official capacity for SEP. As part of the Regional Theater movement, the Paracho theater was sponsored and funded by SEP, under the leadership of Vasconcelos in his capacity as secretary of education.

All the principal elements of staged folklore were present including the theatricalization of local customs; the use and idealization of indigenous peoples as a national symbol; the role of urban leaders as main organizers; and politicization and ideological framing. The event was significant for shaping and disseminating postrevolutionary ideas concerning indigenismo, folkloricization, and the performance of Mexicanness, which included formulating an official notion of "P'urhépecha." Musicologist Rubén M. Campos attended the Fiesta in his capacity as a representative of the Department of Fine Arts (part of SEP), and delivered a "Eulogy to Song and Dance" in which he presented an ideologically informed discourse on the theme of ethnicity and folklore. Details of Campos's speech, and descriptions and photographs of the theater event, were subsequently disseminated to a wide intellectual readership (Campos 1928, 1930). Significantly, the format of the Fiesta provided a model that was engaged from the 1960s onward for the Festival of Music and Dance on Janitzio as staged entertainment for visitors at *Night of the Dead*.

The *Fiesta of Song and Dance* was principally a presentation of cultural practices of designated indigenous peoples in an open-air theatrical setting. A stage was constructed in the atrium of the ruined church in Paracho, using a proscenium arch design, decorative panels to frame the spectated area, and an operational curtain and a painted backdrop. Audience members were accommodated in temporary seating in front of the stage area constructed specifically for the event. Local villagers made up a small element of the audience; however, the majority were intellectuals and government officials from Morelia and Mexico City who had made the arduous journey for the event. The program comprised music and dance "re-constructions" (Campos 1930:200), with the inclusion of music from areas of Mexico other than the P'urhépecha region.[15] Most of the participants, however, were young P'urhépecha women from the town of Paracho.

An overt element of ethnographic showcasing permeated the staged event as boundaries between enacting and real life were blurred. Such a context is exemplified through a brief discussion of the costumes and actors. Although the costumes had purportedly been *designed* by the artist Carlos González (ibid.:201), the clothes were those worn by P'urhépecha women as part of everyday life.[16] By regarding these clothes as a theatrical costume and by framing them within a staged representation, their significance was therefore transformed, clouding a distinction between everyday life and theatrical re-presentation. Such obfuscation was even more problematic with regards to the women dancers and musicians. Framed onstage for the gaze of the audience, the women were on display as essentialized indigenous and authentic specimens, utilized for constructions of Mexicanness by middle-class audience members who had journeyed great distances to see and hear them.

Significantly, the issue of authentication and blurring of boundaries was emphasized in subsequent photographic documentation of the event (Campos 1928 and 1930). A set of photos encapsulated and classified three specific sets of clothes: firstly, on stage, young women from Paracho wore the clothes of P'urhépecha women; secondly, off-stage, a young P'urhépecha woman was depicted wearing a long skirt, embroidered waist-band and blouse, and labeled with the title *india michoacana* (indigenous Michoacán woman), a generic essentialist description; and thirdly, a group of young non-P'urhépecha women off-stage were depicted wearing urban-style 1920s dresses (1928:85, 93, 97–99).

Heightening the political framing of the Fiesta, Campos's "Eulogy to Song and Dance" served as an overt form of ideological and cultural doctrine for the live event. Subsequently publishing the full transcript in his influential 1928 book *El folklore y la música mexicana* enabled a much wider dissemination process (94–100). Campos's eulogy encompassed an unmistakable sense of idealistic, ideological, and political positioning, and the overall style of the speech was both poetic and rhetorical, with a distinctive impression of a rallying call. Significantly, Campos set out the formula and framework for many future uses of indigenous practices and peoples in nationalistic and touristic contexts, and provided a succinct résumé of the principal constructions around which the success of the utilization of such activities relied. What is striking is the way in which these associations and perceived characteristics became attached to, and remained central to interpretations of *The Old Men, Night of the Dead,* and the lives of the P'urhépecha villagers of the Lake Pátzcuaro region as they continued to be framed in relation to nationalistic and touristic contexts, through guide books, magazines, political rhetoric, and staged representations.[17] Here I simply highlight a few specific concepts that are useful as indicative of aspects of indigenismo and notable for the formulaic and formational elements connected to folklore movements in many countries.

Campos emphasized the origins of the P'urhépecha race, noting a continuous link between preincursion and contemporary times.[18] He regarded the strengths of a country to be "tradition" and "all that is its own." Campos described postconquest Mexican history as "three centuries of barbaric domination and one century of disorder," observing that the indigenous people have continued to suffer from being in a position of inequality. He characterized the P'urhépecha people as a "strong, beautiful, artistic race," in whose music and dance "purity and sincerity" are displayed, qualities which he then contrasted with the "high art music of the city" and the "maelstrom of the city" with its "deafening noise of the modern life."[19] Campos placed the trained musicians and scholars of the cities in opposition to rural dwellers, portraying the latter as having innate musical and dance abilities, and "magic fingers." According to Campos, the rural dwellers were "artists by a gift of God," however, this was not the Christian God, but Dionysus. Finally, he observed that the songs and dances of the rural and rural-indigenous peoples had healing properties for curing the ills of the modern city. Relating these concepts to the individuals and practices in this study, in the following section I return to these ideas, discussing how Campos applied them specifically to Nicolás Bartolo Juárez of Jarácuaro and his family.

Nicolás Bartolo Juárez and Rubén M. Campos: Influential Individuals

As the theatricalized events in Mexico City and Paracho were crucial for creating models and patterns for future uses of *The Old Men* and *Night of the Dead*, so Nicolás Bartolo Juárez and Rubén M. Campos were profoundly important in the ideological refunctionalization processes of the 1920s and 1930s in their own ways. In the final section of this chapter, I focus on both individuals, particularly in terms of the connections between them. As the Teatro Regional event of the *Fiesta of Song and Dance* in the upland P'urhépecha town of Paracho and the Teatro Sintético in Mexico City represented a geopolitical periphery and center, so Bartolo Juárez and Campos embodied similar notions: one was a Lake Pátzcuaro island-dweller and the other a Mexico City urbanite. Bartolo Juárez came to the attention of Campos through his family's musical reputation, which led to Campos visiting the island of Jarácuaro, writing about Bartolo Juárez, and transcribing some of his compositions. These visits also led to Bartolo Juárez teaching *The Old Men* to students in Mexico City. Although Campos was not directly involved with appropriating and promoting *The Old Men*, he was highly influential in the postrevolutionary era in shaping aesthetic and ideological notions of folkore and in drawing attention to certain musics as indigenous (including those of the Bartolo Juárez family).

Campos was a musician, composer, musicologist, and folklorist who worked for the government as part of SEP. He was an extremely prolific, persuasive, and skilled writer, and his definition of folklore was seminal in setting boundaries in Mexico (Stevenson 1999:701). *El folklore y la música mexicana*, published in 1928 through SEP, was a major work that had a wide readership amongst the Mexican middle class (Boggs 1938:177), with endorsement and acknowledgement for his work from both the president of Mexico and the minister for education (Puig Casauranc 1928: no page). Of great significance for this study is the fact that Campos's book included a section recording details of the Bartolo Juárez family. In this and other publications Campos delineated aesthetic and ideological aspects of music and dance that were taken up in many subsequent contexts. He described the popular music of Michoacán as "folkloric production," indicating attributes and qualities that he connected with such music—thus, Mexican songs "should be simple and sincere," in contrast to what he called "artistic artifice," the lack of which was compensated for "by inspiration" (1928:80). Such concepts of inspiration emphasized the spontaneity and naturalness of "folkloric" musicians, who were perceived to be untrained, in direct opposition to the urban, middle-class musicians. He also indicated that "the lack of contrapuntal, polyphonic knowledge is compensated for with sentimentality" (ibid.). In an article entitled "Las Danzas Mexicanas" (Mexican Dances), Campos made an overt link between indigenous dance and folklore, stating that "as the foundation of our folklore, as progression from other eras, alive, beating, the joy of children and the elderly, of the cultured and the simple folk, indigenous dance is the only surviving element of the Aztec soul" (1932:25). Significantly, this article was published in a magazine entitled *Nuestro México* (Our Mexico)—"A monthly magazine exclusively Mexican"— within a section on the theme of "Mexicanization," emphasizing the role of indigenous dance within a nationalizing ideology. Campos applied his general ideas concerning indigenous music and dance to Nicolás Bartolo Juárez in particular, so here it is appropriate to discuss representations of Bartolo Juárez in Campos's publications in terms of dissemination of ideas. Before turning to Campos's words, however, I commence with an overview of salient aspects of Nicolás Bartolo Juárez's life.

Nicolás Bartolo Juárez was born in about 1895 on the island of Jarácuaro. As with all inhabitants of the Lake Pátzcuaro islands, he grew up fishing on the lake and cultivating a small plot of land.[20] He made straw hats, and performed and composed music. He later worked as a music teacher in Jarácuaro (at the Escuela Rural Clase C [Correspondence: 28 Nov. 1939]), Paracho, and Tarétin. In common with many families in the region, the Bartolo Juárez family were competent musicians and played for local fiestas in P'urhépecha communities. Nicolás' father, Hipólito Bartolo, formed a quartet with his three sons, Alejandro, Esteban, and Nicolás. With other family and village members they also had an *orquesta de cámara* (chamber orchestra), which had its roots in the musical groups that proliferated in towns and villages throughout Mexico from the time of the rule of Emperor Maximilian of Austria (1864–1867) and then through the Porfiriato (with its distinctive European influence). These orquestas comprised violin, viola, cello, double bass, flute, clarinet, trumpet, and trombone (figure 4.1). Most villages included someone who could play the violin, making this a ubiquitous rather than an elitist instrument. Given the reputation of the Bartolo Juárez family, their skills and techniques were clearly superior to others in the region, and their playing and composing abilities were specifically judged against others in the region through contracted, competitive village fiesta events known as *serenatas* or *concursos*.

The Juárez Quartet comprised father Hipólito on double bass, and sons Alejandro on violin, Esteban on clarinet, and Nicolás on cello. Nicolás was also a competent musician on other instruments including double bass, violin, and clarinet. They were all skilled readers of musical notation and capable of playing a range of styles of music, including European classical music (for example, Beethoven, Mozart, Haydn) and popular European dance music—the standard repertoire of quartets and orquestas in Mexico at the time. Alejandro and Nicolás also composed original pieces, notating them themselves. These compositions included P'urhépecha *sones* (in 3/8 time) and *abajeños* (in 6/8 time), *paso dobles*, and marches. Many compositions by Nicolás were published both by Domínguez

Figure 4.1 The Juárez Orquesta on the island of Jarácuaro, c. 1930. L. to r. the musicians are: Alejandro Bartolo Juárez (violin); Aurelio Calderón (viola); Cesario Bartolo (cello); Nicolás Bartolo Juárez (double bass); Bonfilio Bartolo (trombone); Enrique Bartolo (clarinet); Rafael Juárez (flute).

Photographer: unknown. Courtesy of Adelaida Bartolo.

(1925 and 1941) and Campos (1928 and 1939). In 1937 Nicolás also arranged for the publishing of two books of his own compositions: *sones isleños del Lago Pátzcuaro* (island *sones* of Lake Pátzcuaro), and *canciones isleños del Lago Pátzcuaro* (Island Songs of Lake Pátzcuaro). Notably, they were published by el Departamento Autónomo de Prensa y Publicidad, DAPP (the Independent Department of Press and Publicity), which was created by President Lázaro Cárdenas to coordinate government broadcasting, to regulate media content, and to organize government information activities. From 1937 to 1939, the DAPP produced thousands of posters, pamphlets, leaflets, advertisements, and musical shows, and was involved in the series of staged events entitled *Danzas Auténticas Mexicanas* (Authentic Mexican Dances) at the Palace of Fine Arts in 1937 and 1939 in which *The Old Men* was performed (see chapter 6.) Both of Bartolo Juárez's publications of 1937 made overt and inextricable links with the Lake Pátzcuaro region, utilizing references to the lake in the title of both books, and using the words "Isla de Jarácuaro" (Island of Jarácuaro) on the front cover. The cover artwork depicts Lake Pátzcuaro, distinctive through the towering statue of Morelos atop the conical island of Janitzio, with the costumed dancers of the Old Man and a Moor (figure 4.2).

One striking aspect of Nicolás Bartolo Juárez's life concerns the connections that he had with high-ranking politicians, most significantly two Michoacán state governors, General Francisco Múgica (governor 1920–1924)[21] and Lázaro Cárdenas.

Figure 4.2 Front cover of *Sones isleños del Lago Pátzcuaro* (Island *Sones* of Lake Pátzcuaro), a book of musical compositions by Nicolás Bartolo Juárez of Jarácuaro, published in 1937 by the DAPP (Independent Department of Press and Publicity). The colored front-cover painting depicts a *Dance of the Old Men* masked dancer (with *jaranita*, as Bartolo Juárez himself danced this in the 1920s); a *Dance of the Moors* dancer; and the island of Janitzio in the background.

Courtesy of INI, Pátzcuaro.

Both lived on the shores of Lake Pátzcuaro, close to Jarácuaro, and not only visited the various communities of the Lake Pátzcuaro region frequently but also invited the Juárez Quartet to play for fiestas in their homes. A relationship between the Múgica household and the Juárez family is borne out in the dedication of compositions by brothers Nicolás and Alejandro to Múgica and his wife, Carolina[22] (47 ◐). When visiting Mexico City, Nicolás stayed at the home of Múgica's sister-in-law, Margarita, and in his capacity as governor of Michoacán, General Múgica promised to ensure that his family would want for nothing while he was away. Connections between Bartolo Juárez and Cárdenas were particularly strong in the 1930s, as I discuss presently.

Campos on Bartolo Juárez: Indigenous, Intuitive, and Spontaneous

After the three state officials (Campos, Domínguez, and González) had visited Jarácuaro in the early 1920s, discovering it to be a valuable location on their collecting itinerary, various activities followed that involved the documentation of Bartolo Juárez's life and music, and his invitation to go to Mexico City "to be known and valued" (Campos 1928:88). Yet what Bartolo Juárez became known and valued for had to fit the political agenda of the state. In tracing trajectories of representation, mapping the selections that were made for ideological and political purposes are possible when alternatives are also clear. In the case of Nicolás Bartolo Juárez, observing the choices reveals elements of the ideological shaping processes. In Jarácuaro, Bartolo Juárez performed most frequently on the cello with the quartet, playing a wide range of musical styles with a high level of skill, and also composing his own music. In Mexico City this versatile, competent, and skilled musician and composer was mostly limited to teaching *The Old Men*. Although Bartolo Juárez sang his own compositions for the Teatro Sintético spectacles, Campos represented him as a man who belonged in his rural idyll, emphasizing the return to his native Jarácuaro home, and also remarking on his authenticity as an indigenous island dweller (1928:88). Alongside this literary text, Campos included a photo of the island of Jarácuaro, with the waters of Lake Pátzcuaro clearly visible, indicating notions of separation, authenticity, and even utopia.

Campos was evidently taken with the musical skills of Nicolás and the Bartolo Juárez family, dedicating a whole section to them in his 1928 book, and including a photo of Nicolás Bartolo Juárez, as well as several compositions in transcription. Yet it is striking how Campos represented and characterized the music and musicians, creating a construct of *folklore* that fitted entirely with European nationalist formulations, and portraying Bartolo Juárez as having certain natural skills, which were the consequence of his location and position. He expounded the concept of nontraining and folkloric musicians, and made the point strongly in relation to Bartolo Juárez, specifying that his music "is composed by a musician who has not studied harmony or counterpoint, who does not know the rules of musical composition, who has never heard a musical chamber group and has no knowledge of the high musical forms, one of which is the quartet" (1928:87). Although many of

Bartolo Juárez's musical skills were similar to those of Campos and Domínguez with regards to playing, composing, arranging, and transcribing competence, nevertheless, his social and ethnic position, as rural and indigenous, was used to emphasize certain perceived attributes or qualities—and lacks. Thus, Campos paints the Bartolo Juárez family as natural or spontaneous musicians who "are contrapuntalists by nature, by marvelous intuition...each one divining his role.... The musicians of Jarácuaro do not know why they are poets" (1928:86–87). Campos attributed Bartolo Juárez's compositional stimulation to inspiration from the rural and natural location, noting that "inspiration is what suggests themes like 'El Lago'[The Lake], 'La Canoa Más Ligera'[The Lightest Canoe], 'La Golondrina'[The Swallow]—in his little poet world he was lucky; for Lake Pátzcuaro is one of the most beautiful landscapes that the author of these lines has been able to compare with the alpine lakes of Italy....The rusticity of Lake Pátzcuaro is the most appealing of features...one feels the charm of the sonorous waters where poetry is bathed without being overwhelming" (Campos 1928:87).[23] Such a romanticized and ideologically descriptive narrative created a fixed, tangible, and influential representation not only Bartolo Juárez, but also of all the peoples of Lake Pátzcuaro, and by extension, all indigenous peoples.

Even as Campos shaped and disseminated constructs of folklore within a nationalist context through his writing and photographic images, so he also, inadvertently perhaps, promoted the Lake Pátzcuaro region as ripe for development as a tourist destination, and fostered the idea of the peoples of Lake Pátzcuaro as perfect embodiments of authentic Mexicanness. In brief, the 1920s was the decade in which *The Old Men* and *Night of the Dead* were transformed into public spectated practices, and into referents of indigenousness, tradition, and authenticity. In the following chapter, I turn to examine the processes through which the Lake Pátzcuaro region and inhabitants were shaped for nationalist and tourist utilization, with profound ideological and political objectives, incorporating *The Old Men* and *Night of the Dead* as icons of and for the Mexican nation.

CHAPTER 5

Destination Lake Pátzcuaro

Creating a Tourist Attraction with an Island and Night of the Dead

SIGHTS AND SITES are of major importance in tourist contexts. Since the first dissemination of official state visits to the island of Janitzio for *Night of the Dead* in magazines, books, and journals in Mexico and the United States, and the theatricalized staging of *The Old Men* and *Night of the Dead* in Mexico City in the early 1920s, Lake Pátzcuaro has been an ever-present element. With its island communities and shoreline villages of P'urhépecha inhabitants, Lake Pátzcuaro has formed a central sight and site in the network of signification surrounding *The Old Men* and *Night of the Dead* from the inception of their roles as public icons of Mexicanness. During the 1920s and 1930s, through multiple channels of diffusion, all the requisite foundational stones were put in place and frames of reference established that promoted the place, peoples, and their practices as indigenous, P'urhépecha, and traditional. The lake region was represented as an authentic space and place, where tradition, ritual, and everyday life merged into one. Such authenticated sites/sights were efficacious for nationalistic and touristic agendas, with authentication processes relying on ethnic and racial constructions and embodied classifications. Crucially, the formulation of indigenousness as it related to the people of Lake Pátzcuaro was of central importance. Significantly, during the decade of the 1930s, the ceremony of *Night of the Dead* on Janitzio became an increasing attraction for visitors, drawing tourists, scholars, politicians, and artists to Lake Pátzcuaro and to the island of Janitzio.

Tracing the shaping of this location as an iconic referent of authentic indigenousness is important to developing an understanding of processes of performism surrounding *The Old Men* and *Night of the Dead*. In the previous chapter I focused on appropriational and representational activities in the 1920s involving *The Old Men* and *Night of the Dead*, and in this chapter I turn to the development of the Lake Pátzcuaro region in the 1930s both as a tourist destination and a location for the study and incorporation of indigenous peoples. Firstly, I briefly delineate the policies of integration, assimilation, and indigenismo, as well as certain strategies used to achieve them. Secondly, I consider the ethnic and racial delineation of P'urhépecha characteristics. Thirdly, I discuss the role of Lázaro Cárdenas and the building of a statue on Janitzio. Fourthly, I give an overview of dissemination through still photography, films, and other textual material. And finally I return to *The Old Men*, noting local initiatives for performances by Lake Pátzcuaro residents.

Measuring Heads and Admiration for the Exotic

By the late nineteenth century, the Lake Pátzcuaro region was already identified as a destination and location of special interest. Foreign travelers and intellectuals who visited the area documented their experiences of the place and the peoples. Frederick Starr, a U.S. anthropologist, visited Lake Pátzcuaro and Janitzio in 1897 and included a description of the island in his English-language publication of 1908 entitled *In Indian Mexico* (published in Spanish in 1995, see 1995:89–95). Like other anthropologists of his time, Starr was drawn to undertake investigations in Mexico through "a certain curiosity, folkloric 'ánimo' or 'soul' and energy, romanticism and admiration for the exotic" (Scharrer Tomm 1995:13). Coming from a physical anthropological position, Starr's research included a focus upon somatic types, and his methodologies included measuring P'urhépecha people (mostly men) to establish links between linguistic families and distinct racial types (ibid.:15). Throughout his fieldwork Starr was accompanied by a photographer who captured images of people "as specimens," demonstrating use of photographic mediation and documentation as an essential aspect of the processes of representation of Mexican indigenous peoples and practices for imaging Mexico.[1]

Building on previous repute, in the postrevolutionary era the Lake Pátzcuaro region became a focus of attention for two distinct yet interrelated nationalist policies: firstly, an indigenista policy, which encompassed the utilization of appropriate indigenous peoples, practices, and artifacts as models of authenticity for constructing the Mexican nation; and secondly, an integrationist policy that required local indigenous and rural populations to move from their "backwardness" to be integrated into the national arena in order to facilitate capitalist development. In the Lake Pátzcuaro region, this involved a double-action of firstly, visits of outsiders (tourists, intellectuals, artists) to the area, and in particular to Janitzio; and secondly, dissemination of the region as cultural capital to outsiders through multifarious means, effectively drawing the location into a national capitalist market and encouraging economic development. As I described in the previous chapter, visits to the island of Janitzio for *Night of the Dead* and to the island of Jarácuaro to hear the Bartolo Juárez ensemble by an official group of state representatives in the early 1920s (including González, Domínguez, and Campos), led directly to the appropriation of *Night of the Dead* and the *Dance of the Old Men* for imaging Mexico.

The Lake Pátzcuaro region became a privileged space for the experimentation and implementation of official development programs (Zárate Hernández 1993:215), and with the heavy intervention of the state, the expectation was that the area would change both economically and culturally. One objective of these programs was capitalist development, to be accomplished partly through the breaking of traditional practices and ties that were considered impediments to this development. The strategy of intervention of state institutions had a clear ideological function of both legitimating the patrimonial state and presenting it as a benefactor state. To this end, a series of national institutions was established, including the Cultural Missions, "whose central objective [in the Pátzcuaro region] was to 'bring out of their backwardness' the inhabitants of the lake region" (ibid.:216). Another significant initiative involved the setting up of the research program *El Proyecto Tarasco* (The Tarascan Project) in the mid-1930s, through the collaboration of representatives from the University of California, the National Polytechnic Institute of Mexico, and the Bureau of Indian Affairs of Mexico, all of whom agreed to undertake a "cooperative program in anthropology in the area inhabited by Tarascan speaking Indians" (Beals, de La Borbolla and Rubin 1940:708; see also Pérez-González 1997). Nationwide, archeological projects were a central element of the state's indigenista vision, and although this mostly concentrated on the "great" civilizations (Aztec, Maya, Zapotec), other indigenous groups were also embraced, including the P'urhépecha of Michoacán (Saragoza 2001:96). From the 1930s onward in the Lake Pátzcuaro region, archeological explorations were initiated in Tzintzuntzan and were later undertaken in Ihuatzio (another lakeside community), with the express objectives of excavation, rescue, and restoration (Cortés Zavala 1995:54).

All these initiatives and strategies involving assimilation, intervention, and development relied upon the delineation of racial and ethnic distinctions and characterizations in relation to the P'urhépecha inhabitants of the Lake Pátzcuaro communities. In these characterizations, racial and ethnic formations and constructions from the prerevolution era were prevalent. Documents published in the postrevolutionary era delineated the principal ideological and strategic issues, which generally comprised the two-stranded and somewhat contradictory elements of the need for P'urhépecha assimilation and change due to backwardness, coupled with a sense of suitability and adaptability for the newly evolving nation. Two such accounts, authored by renowned intellectuals Nicolás León and Lucio Mendieta y Núñez, published in 1934 and 1940 respectively, provide useful illustrations. Although Mendieta y Núñez's work came at the end of the period under consideration, not only were the ideas thoroughly embedded in postrevolutionary ideology and therefore pertinent to this discussion, but also Mendieta y Núñez was an important figure for the role he played as an indigenista: from 1925 and as indigenista; from 1925 as editor of the previously cited academic journal *Ethnos* (established by Gamio) in which González published the first article documenting *Night of the Dead* on Janitzio; and as director of sociology at the National University (UNAM) from 1939. As I noted in the previous chapter, *Ethnos* was "dedicated to the study and improvement of the indigenous population of Mexico," encapsulating the objectifying, interventionist, and developmental objectives of state-controlled intellectuals, particularly anthropologists, ethnographers, folklorists, linguists, and pedagogues.

León, a physician and anthropologist from the Porfirian era and "a veteran measurer of Indian heads" (Tenorio-Trillo 1996:215), published an account entitled *Los Tarascos* (The Tarascans) in 1904, through the National Museum of Mexico (in his capacity as Professor of Ethnology at the museum).[2] In this volume he documented historical, ethnic, and anthropological facets, encompassing "primitive history, discovery and Conquest" (1904:1). In 1934 León published an ethnographic volume entitled *Los indios Tarascos del Lago de Pátzcuaro* (The Indigenous Tarascans of Lake Pátzcuaro). In this publication León described how the P'urhépecha inhabitants of Lake Pátzcuaro "have been assimilated a great deal into the modern civilization" but also "hold onto the customs and practices of their people" (132). He highlighted the suitability of the P'urhépecha for integration, for example, noting that "these indigenous people have...accepted many of the modern advances...and they have a good idea of their political rights and duties, and are always abreast of the march of national government" (164). However, he also framed their practices as part of a premodern complex, explaining how the people of Jarácuaro occupy their time with fishing and agriculture (162). León delineated his understanding of the P'urhépecha people in racial terms, describing them as being "mixed with the *criollo* race" (163), noting that "their [the P'urhépecha race's] mixture with the whites has greatly improved their descendants" (157).

Turning to the publication *Los Tarascos: monografía, história, etnográfica y económica* (The Tarascans; Monograph, History, Ethnography and Economics) by Mendieta y Núñez (1940), clear assimilationist ideas linked to notions of race and ethnicity were again prevalent. Mendieta y Núñez's book, described as a Mexican authority (Mörner 1970:226), was influential in terms of shaping perceptions regarding P'urhépecha peoples. Mendieta y Núñez made particular ideological positions clear in his text, asserting that transformation of an indigenous person into a citizen is more necessary from the view of national society than from the view of the indigenous person (157). He stated that indigenous people were not on the same "level" as the rest of the population, and therefore they had to be brought "up" to the standards of other Mexicans (158). The strategy for transformational processes becomes clear in his "Final Observation":

> The Tarascans are an indigenous group that is easily adaptable to a superior life. They don't offer great resistance to innovation. We have seen how pure race tarascos have raised themselves above the level of their brothers, and have set up workshops, have gone to the cities and have partly changed their customs. Others, in the countryside, demonstrate anxiety at betterment. The problem of their incorporation into the national life fundamentally consists in modernizing their customs and their ideas, in taking them from the Colonial times to the Mexico of today. The job is not easy. However, with determined educational work, it could produce, perhaps, great results. (264 & 282) [3]

Not only is Mendieta y Núñez's work significant for the general formulation and dissemination of ideas concerning P'urhépecha peoples, but crucially for this study, Mendieta y Núñez includes photos of dances of Old Men (ibid.:173–74) and a short description of *Night of the Dead* (ibid.:83) within his account of the peoples of Lake Pátzcuaro. These specific activities and practices were therefore represented in photographic form within a published document that boldly declared an assimilationist strategy for nation-building objectives.

Tata Lázaro: State Governor and President of the Nation

Whereas both León and Mendieta y Núñez's accounts demonstrate a generalized need for state intervention, the most highly influential intervener in the Lake Pátzcuaro region was Michoacán state governor and later president of the republic, Lázaro Cárdenas.[4] Having mentioned him in the previous chapter in relation to the Bartolo Juárez family, I now consider some of the broader implications of his involvement in performism processes. Cárdenas is important in relation to this study for four principal reasons: firstly, his policies as state governor and then president of the republic played a fundamental role in shaping forms of nationalism and tourism in which *The Old Men* and *Night of the Dead* were disseminated as emblematic icons; secondly, he took a specific interest in the Lake Pátzcuaro region, and in particular focused his energies upon the islands of Janitzio and Jarácuaro, attempting to implement strategies for development (with varying success); thirdly, he knew the Bartolo Juárez family; and fourthly, his son and grandson continued the Cárdenas legacy as governors of the state of Michoacán, promoting *The Old Men* through governmental channels into the twenty-first century.

Cárdenas's home, "Eréndira," was on the edge of Lake Pátzcuaro, and it was there that he preferred to live while acting as governor and president. At a later period, in 1951, he donated the building and grounds to the continent-wide pedagogical institution CREFAL (which I discuss in chapter 7 for the impact both in hosting events involving *The Old Men* and in acting as an international center for academic study of the Lake Pátzcuaro region). As governor of Michoacán, Cárdenas established "an enviable record for honesty, compassion, and concern for commoners" (Keen 1996:287), and he is particularly remembered for his role in promoting the rights of the indigenous and rural populations of Mexico, and for attempting to put in place policies that would improve their economic situation. He favored policies of creating self-sufficient rural populations who could participate in the national economy while still conserving their "indigenous way of life" (Mosk 1950:54). Part of this self-sufficiency plan involved the creation of small industries in rural areas, and the island of Jarácuaro was one of the communities chosen by Cárdenas for industrialization. He gave thirty-five pedal sewing machines and two large presses to the community for their hat-making production, and he aspired to build a bridge to the island to facilitate easier transportation for trade. He financed the construction of the school (Dinerman 1974:129) and gave many musical instruments to the community. Cárdenas visited Jarácuaro from time to time, and Braulio González and other villagers living in the 1990s recalled dancing *The Old Men* in the late 1920s for such visits, with the Orozco brothers, Simón and Andrés, accompanying on the sexta and the jarana. Jarácuaro villagers who met and knew of Cárdenas referred to him with the term of endearment and respect "Tata" (Tata Lázaro), indicating his benefactor and paternalist role. This role was particularly significant given his endorsement of staged events in Mexico City in the 1930s at which *The Old Men* of Jarácuaro was danced, indicating his personal involvement in officially sanctioning this practice and people within a nationalist environment. As I noted previously, it was during this period that Cárdenas came to know the Bartolo Juárez family, including Nicolás. Poignantly, Nicolás Bartolo Juárez and President Cárdenas exchanged letters and communication in 1939, revealing an important element of the relationship between the micro and the macro, between a Lake Pátzcuaro villager and the most powerful man in Mexican politics.[5]

Building a Gigantic Body on an Island

Although Cárdenas's attempts to intervene in production processes on Jarácuaro only resulted in partial success, his interventions involving the island of Janitzio had a far greater impact. Janitzio was singled out for tourist development and promoted as a tourist attraction, fitting the description of tourist locations "whose initial growth [was] induced from the outside" (Cohen 1988:383). Through the intervention of state governors, presidents, state-employed intellectuals and artists, and local business leaders, this island was transformed from a quiet fishing village into an oft-visited and frequently imaged tourist destination. The rationale for the suitability of this location resided primarily in its preinvasion indigenous history, the sense of continuity embodied in the P'urhépecha population, and the notion of remoteness and mysticism of the place perceived through its location in the lake.

By the end of the 1920s Janitzio was visited by a growing number of tourists, artists, and scholars (ethnographers, folklorists, and anthropologists), none of whom was received well by the local inhabitants. As mentioned previously, when recalling her visit for *Night of the Dead* in 1923, Toor observed that "at no time do these fishermen welcome visitors, and less for this special occasion" (1928:68). Although the Janitzio residents regarded tourists as a problem in the 1920s, the state implemented policies and strategies to develop tourism in the area and to create a tourist attraction. For Cárdenas the aim was to promote tourism and "so support and help the population to better their level of life" (Zizumbo 1986:163). In the annual State Report of 1931 the governor of Michoacán called for more work to be done "to attract a more intense flow of tourists each day," and noted that improvements had been made to the spa of Chupícuaro on the shores of Lake Pátzcuaro, even mentioning that the president of the republic had used it on his tour of the State of Michoacán (*Informe* 16.9.1931:21–22). In creating an attraction for tourists, emphasis was placed upon the concept of an indigenous presence. In a newspaper article entitled "En Pro del Turismo en lugares indígenas" (In favor of tourism in indigenous places) one contemporaneous journalist noted that tourists who visited Lake Pátzcuaro were "eager to know the habits, customs and folklore" of the indigenous peoples (1938). Although the Lake Pátzcuaro region encompassed many features that were efficacious for the burgeoning tourist market, one strategy undertaken by Cárdenas in 1930, involving a giant stone body, changed the face of Janitzio forever, and created a long-term impact with consequences that were influential in many future representations invoking *Night of the Dead* and *The Old Men*.

In an act of overt and tangible ideological proclamation, Cárdenas ordered the construction of a gigantic statue in the center of the tiny island. The 132-feet-high effigy embodied the Independence hero, José María Morelos y Pavón (1765–1815). Morelos, Michoacán's most famous "son" and hero, was born in the state's capital city Valladolid, renamed Morelia in 1828 in his honor. Morelos embodied all that was noble and national, performing the role of hero of the Mexican nation and of the liberal state, and specifically symbolizing independence from Spain. By erecting the statue of Morelos in the center of the P'urhépecha island, with the waters of Lake Pátzcuaro encircling the tiny land mass, Cárdenas utilized this human body, sculpted and monumentalized in stone, to perform a role in shaping both nationalism and tourism. The process of monumentalization and the creation of heroes was a fundamental element of nationalizing strategies (Knight 1994b:407), with statues of heroes being located throughout Mexico in public places, in an effort to generate a sense of popular identification, and to create icons for a unified Mexican nation. The statue of Morelos in the center of Janitzio is one of the most remarkable examples of the audacity and potency of the postrevolutionary monumentalization strategy, fulfilling the original objectives of generating both symbolic significance and economic development for the area.

From the moment of construction, the statue became an instantly recognizable iconic body, disseminated through photographs and films both nationally and internationally. An interpretation of the signification of the statue would propose that the ultimate embodiment of Mexican independence and authenticity, materialized in the stone body of Morelos, merges into the island itself. The great patriarchal figure of "Mexico," personified in Morelos, symbolically stands guard over the indigenous P'urhépecha islanders, protecting and watching over them. Associations between the Independence hero and anonymous indigenous peasants—shielded from the damaging effects of colonization on their island home, surviving against all odds, and relying on their own resources, specifically fishing, to ensure their continuation—provided a powerful signifier. Even the corporeal position of Morelos's stone body invited readings of accomplishment, power, and victory as he stood upright, his right arm raised high and his fist clenched. With a hollow body, visitors could climb the stairs inside "him" and emerge at his wrist, to look down up the island of Janitzio, with a bird's eye view of the surrounding lake and peoples below.

The very action of constructing the statue performed a mode of integration of the P'urhépecha peoples of Lake Pátzcuaro into the national body, with the center of power leaving its mark on the periphery, incorporating the islanders of Janitzio into a state-sanctioned role forever. As the embodied practices of *The Old Men* and

Night of the Dead were taken to Mexico City for incorporation into the nation by encapsulating them inside the frame of a governmental theater, so the island of Janitzio was assimilated into the nation through the placing of a corporeal representation of a national heroic icon on the territory. Through the body/monument of Morelos, the island of Janitzio and the P'urhépecha inhabitants of Lake Pátzcuaro became part of "Mexico," putting Janitzio "on the map" for tourists.

In examining the processes by which Janitzio, Lake Pátzcuaro, and the inhabitants were transformed into tourist attractions during the postrevolutionary period, the concept of site sacralization as delineated by Dean MacCannell is valuable (1999). In this pertinent theory, MacCannell outlines five stages by which a tourist attraction and destination is created, involving naming, framing and elevation, enshrinement, mechanical reproduction, and social reproduction. Processes of naming, involving authenticating and marking off the attraction as worthy of special attention by signage or decree, took place through state visits of official representatives, who deemed the place to be of value. Framing, elevation, and enshrinement related to the building of the statue of Morelos, which acted as a form of demarcation. Mechanical reproduction was undertaken through dissemination in journals, magazines, and guide books (as literary and photographic text) and through films and musical compositions. Finally, processes of social reproduction involved the naming of groups of people after the island and lake. MacCannell's concept also encompasses a process in which the attraction is placed inside a tangible structure or given special security measures. Although no new tangible structures or security measure were put in place (to enclose the island of Janitzio, the practice of *Night of the Dead,* or the inhabitants), through processes of demarcation as a site/sight of special interest, the existing waters of the lake, the edge of the island, and the walls of the cemetery were transformed into material boundaries and borders that validated and substantiated the sacralization processes, marking off the experience for visitors.

Films, Photographs, and Music

With rapidly increasing photographic technology, many visitors (both tourists and state officials) transported their equipment across the lake and captured images of the peoples of Janitzio, thereby creating reproducible copies and representations that acted as souvenirs, marketing material, and ethnographic evidence. Yet it is clear that the Janitzio islanders were opposed to the photographic processes, and to the visits of outsiders. When anthropologist and physician León visited in the 1920s to undertake research for his publication on the indigenous Tarascans of Lake Pátzcuaro (1934), he utilized photography as a central element of his investigative processes, and, not wishing to be sullied by the reputation of tourists, he attempted to make distinctions between his own role as a scholar, and that of the tourists. He described how he presented himself to inhabitants of Janitzio as their brother by speaking a few words of the P'urhépecha language. In this way the islanders did not confuse him with tourists, "their enemy," and he saved himself and his camera from being thrown into the lake (León 1934:162). Significantly he noted that "in each tourist they see an agent of their ruin and believe that photographic apparatuses are a cause of this" (ibid.). Such a sentiment is highly compelling when considered in the context of twenty-first century tourist practices in Janitzio.

During the 1920s, and increasingly in the 1930s, illustrations of, and references to Janitzio and Lake Pátzcuaro appeared in numerous published outputs, generated by artists, anthropologists, journalists, politicians, and tourist-industry personnel. Developing the imaging of Janitzio through a network of literary and visual depictions was vital to promotional processes, with the network of artistic and ethnographic images generating and circulating a construction and essentializing of place and peoples useful in both nationalistic and touristic contexts. These depictions particularly captured four aspects: the island of Janitzio in profile; P'urhépecha fishermen using *mariposa* (butterfly-shaped) fishing nets; P'urhépecha women wrapped in rebozos; and the red-tiled, adobe houses. U.S. modernist art photographer Edward Weston captured *art* images of Janitzio in 1926, which were exhibited in Mexico, the United States, and Europe (Arts Council Collection 1999:8). Ethnographic articles and photographs of Janitzio and Lake Pátzcuaro were published in populist magazines, such as *Mexican Folkways*, and academic journals, such as *Ethnos*. In his monograph on the indigenous Tarascans of Lake Pátzcuaro, León painted a romantic picture of Janitzio, describing it as the "pearl of this beautiful lake" (1934:162). Silvestre Revueltas, preeminent nationalist composer of the postrevolutionary era, entitled one of his short orchestral pieces *Janitzio* (1933) after spending time in the Lake Pátzcuaro region, and making connections with villagers, particularly through his interest in the violin (and undoubtedly visiting the Bartolo Juárez family).[6] Revueltas was not only inspired by the region but was also struck by the burgeoning tourist industry, revealing his skepticism through a comment that accompanied the composition: "Janitzio is a fishermen's island in Lake Pátzcuaro. Lake Pátzcuaro is filthy. The romantic travellers have embellished it with verses and music of the picture postcard type. Not to be outdone, I too add my grain to the sandpile. Posterity will undoubtedly reward my contribution to national tourism" (quoted in Slonimsky 1946:250). Agustin Lara composed a song entitled "Janitzio," with deeply poetic imagery of fishing and love.

Film played a significant role in cultivating and circulating a national and international awareness of Janitzio and Lake Pátzcuaro. Cárdenas's government saw the potential of film as a means of social and political influence, so in this period state-funded films were used to promote a particular version of indigenismo. Joanne Hershfield has described these works as "pseudoethnographic films....that reinforced stereotypical representations of racial and ethnic divisions that defined Mexico's social strata....The indigenista films portrayed Mexico's indigenous peoples as pure and simple, like children who had to be led to social (and revolutionary) consciousness by the intellectual elite" (2006:266–269). One such film, entitled simply *Janitzio* (1935), specifically referenced and promoted the Lake Pátzcuaro region and inhabitants, focusing distinctively on Janitzio and

Night of the Dead. Directed by Carlos Navarro, *Janitzio* involved the retelling of the La Malinche/Malinalli story, which explicitly concerned issues of race, ethnicity, conquest, and indigenous peoples (Standish and Bell 2004:127).[7]

Cultural Missions and Dance Contests

As the island of Janitzio and *Night of the Dead* were shaped for public viewing through the decade of the 1930s, simultaneously there was an increase in dissemination of the *Dance of the Old Men* of Jarácuaro as a folkloric and nationalistic dance form through governmental channels. In the following chapter I return to focus on *The Old Men*; however, in concluding this chapter on the Lake Pátzcuaro region, it is appropriate to briefly mention a few activities that took place in the region, and also more widely in Michoacán, involving villagers from Jarácuaro and other Lake Pátzcuaro villages. *The Old Men* was increasingly performed at overtly political events in Michoacán, and was simultaneously publicized through reporting of such occasions in local and regional newspapers. In 1938, for example, *The Old Men* was danced at a fiesta to honor two state officials, General Gildardo Magaña, Michoacán state governor, and General Félix Iréta, chief of military operations. Although the event took place in the town of Ario de Rosales in the *tierra caliente*, outside of the P'urhépecha region, it was reported throughout Michoacán in a statewide newspaper, effectively performing a role in promoting and advancing the authenticity of *The Old Men* as a representative dance (Front page photo: *Heraldo Michoacano*, 29 Oct.1938).

Villagers from Lake Pátzcuaro, including Nicolás Bartolo Juárez of Jarácuaro, also performed *The Old Men* in their local region in the context of events organized by the Cultural Missions. From the mid-1920s onward, the Cultural Missions formed an important strategic element of the nationalizing government under the auspices of the Secretariat of Education (SEP). With a fervent, almost religious nature, the primary task of the missionary-teachers was to reach every small community in Mexico, with the objective of bringing about social change through pedagogical practice. During the 1920s and 1930s, the Cultural Missions played a role in transmitting *The Old Men*, and had a presence in the Lake Pátzcuaro region, organizing activities that incorporated *The Old Men*. Interestingly, Néstor García Canclini has suggested that it was the action of the Cultural Missions that "gave this dance a clearly defined choreography for exhibiting it as a spectacle" (1985:39). However, although the choreography did become fixed through activities instigated by SEP, it was not under the auspices of the Cultural Missions, but rather the theatricalized events in Mexico City. Significantly, Nicolás Bartolo Juárez was influenced by the staged events in the Cine Olímpia and Teatro Sintético, which led to adjustments to his own performances in the Lake Pátzcuaro region when danced within the context of contests organized by the Cultural Missions.

At one such event, Nicolás Bartolo Juárez's version of *The Old Men* was notated, further fixing the choreography. For this occasion in October 1931 a dance contest was managed by the Cultural Mission based in Tzintzuntzan. Bartolo Juárez's ensemble from Jarácuaro, dancing *The Old Men*, won first place, and an ensemble of dancers from the nearby village of Cucuchucho won second place. Three teachers of the Cultural Missions, Fernando Gamboa, Luis Felipe Obregón, and Santiago Arias Navarro, made a detailed record of *The Old Men* as performed by Bartolo Juárez and his ensemble, documenting the choreography (floor patterns, steps and figures), costume, and brief history of *The Old Men* (Gamboa et al. n.d.). This archival record was subsequently used as a pedagogical resource by other teachers of SEP, particularly through the General Direction of Indigenous Affairs. The events in Tzintzuntzan were part of civil and state celebrations marking the first anniversary of the granting of the status of municipality to the town by the governor of Michoacán, Lázaro Cárdenas. This dance contest established the use of *The Old Men* in connection with this state holiday, and, according to U.S. anthropologist George Foster, the participation of dancers from the nearby village of Cucuchucho became a regular feature of this occasion (1948:188). Locating these dance contests in Tzintzuntzan, the former capital of the P'urhépecha empire, was a deeply symbolic act. As staged, competitive, and exhibitionary performance events for local dancers and musicians, these occasions provided a model for future music and dance festivals which became a central feature of the *Night of the Dead* festivities in the region from the 1960s onward, organized by the tourist board and local government. This trajectory leads to twenty-first century contexts, in which villagers from Jarácuaro perform *The Old Men* in Tzintzuntzan on specially erected wooden stages for festivities of *Night of the Dead*, attracting crowds of hundreds of thousands of spectators.

By the end of the 1930s, Lake Pátzcuaro, and particularly the island of Janitzio, with the gigantic stone body of Morelos atop, was recognized as an authenticated site and sight for nationalistic and touristic agendas, and was disseminated through reinforcing visual images and references in films, magazines, music compositions, and journals. The ceremony of *Night of the Dead* on Janitzio had became a major attraction for visitors, and the lake region was regarded as an indigenous place, where tradition, ritual, and everyday life merged into one; and where *Night of the Dead* and the *Dance of the Old Men* were integral elements of an ancient and pristine lifestyle.

CHAPTER 6

Authentic Mexican Dances

In the Palace of Fine Arts and Across the National Border

AS THE 1920S was the decade of initial appropriation of the *Dance of the Old Men* of Jarácuaro, so the period between 1930 and 1940 was one of burgeoning uses, both in Mexico and across the border in the United States. In this chapter I turn to significant activities that were undertaken to continue to mold and publicize both *The Old Men* and *Night of the Dead* as icons of Mexicanness throughout the 1930s. Firstly, I move the spotlight back to Mexico City, where the model that had begun with theatricalized costumbrista events in the 1920s was continued and developed through the 1930s. I focus on two staged performances as exemplars of the state-sponsored, theatricalized, and folkloric framework that incorporated both Lake Pátzcuaro and Mexico City–based performers: *Hamarándecua* (1930) and *Danzas Auténticas Mexicanas* (staged in 1937 and 1939). Secondly, I discuss performism processes concerning the circulation of images, dancers, practices, and discourse across the border in the United States, emphasizing the notion of multiple crossings and journeys, and outlining political, pedagogical, and ideological dissemination of *The Old Men* through educational and tourist publications. I focus particularly on one didactic book, and one government-sponsored event in Tuscon for which an ensemble from Jarácuaro crossed the border to perform *The Old Men*. Finally, I contrast the *Dance of the Old Men* with the *Dance of the Moors*, a dance form that was ultimately not apposite for iconic uses.

Theatricalizing P'urhépecha "Customs" in Mexico City

In April 1930 a performance entitled *Hamarándecua* ("customs" in P'urhépecha), was staged in the Open Air Theater of the Social and Sports Center Venustiano Carranza in Mexico City. Along with the Sintético, Regional, and Indigenista theater movements, Teatro al Aire Libre (Open Air Theater) was another educational, theatrical form that was developed in the early 1920s under the auspices of SEP.

Just as they had for the *Fiesta of Song and Dance* in Paracho in 1924, Carlos González and Francisco Domínguez jointly directed the event, with González taking the role of artistic director and scenographer, and Domínguez acting as composer and musical director. Significantly, the venue for this event was named after the first postrevolutionary president, Venustiano Carranza, providing an overt political and ideological framing. Continuing a practice of the Teatro Sintético, the staged event comprised a series of brief scenes from P'urhépecha life and from Michoacán mestizo life, which included *The Old Men* and *Night of the Dead* from Lake Pátzcuaro. This was a state-organized and state-endorsed occasion, with high-level governmental involvement that included the governor of Michoacán, Lázaro Cárdenas, the undersecretary of agriculture (indicating the importance of agrarian matters), the municipal president of Pátzcuaro, and Jesús Romero Flores, a folklorist working for the Department of Fine Arts.[1] Other governmental organizations included the Governing Body of Mexico City and the General Office of Educational Action.

To generate material for the theatricalization, González and Domínguez drew on their collecting experiences in Michoacán, and in particular the Lake Pátzcuaro region, selecting what were purportedly scenes of everyday P'urhépecha life, including dances and music. In the first section of the performance, entitled "Pátzcuaro," the setting was a village plaza, conveying the notion that the actions taking place were everyday activities. A local market and a wedding celebration were both re-created on stage, with the *Dance of the Old Men* as part of this scenario. As a way of highlighting an indigenous presence alongside a mestizo presence, after *The Old Men*, the bride and groom danced a *jarabe* accompanied by the musical grouping of the *Arpa Grande* (harp, violin, guitar, and bass). A printed program complemented the event, enabling Domínguez and González to guide audience members in their reception and interpretation. By stating that "the '*jarabe*' is performed in the whole of Michoacán" (1930), the directors were able to establish a contrast between this dance and *The Old Men*, which was therefore depicted as being a specifically P'urhépecha tradition. In the second half of the event, the ceremony of *Night of the Dead* on Janitzio was staged. This involved recreating the scene in the cemetery compressed into a short time period, portraying women kneeling by gravesides, wrapped in rebozos, lit by candles, and holding bunches of flowers. The only musical element was the soft singing of prayers and hymns that accompanied the gentle movement of the women in the space. In terms of theatricalizing practices from the P'urhépecha region, two other noteworthy inclusions were the *Dance of the Moors*, and the P'urhépecha practice of *Las Canácuas*, or Fiesta of the Crowns (rites of hospitality). Domínguez and González had included Las Canácuas in their *Fiesta of Song and Dance* in the Regional Theater in Paracho in 1924, and Campos (1928), Domínguez (1930a/b), and Toor (1930) all wrote ethnographic accounts of this ritual.[2] I return to a brief discussion of the *Dance of the Moors* at the end of this chapter.

Two other important aspects of *Hamarándecua* concerned the status of the dancers, musicians, and actors, and the institutional involvement. Musicians and dancers who participated were drawn from a broad spectrum of society and comprised professional musicians, students from Mexico City, and, most importantly, performers from Michoacán, including dancers from the island of Jarácuaro, led by Nicolás Bartolo Juárez. Three groups of students were from a Reform School (young women), an Industrial School (young men), and the School of Popular Music, all state-run establishments dependent upon the government of the federal district of Mexico City, again evidencing the role of pedagogical institutions and individuals in folkloricization and theatricalization processes. Music was provided by a Police Band and the Orquesta Típica of Miguel Lerdo de Tejada, the same ensemble that was engaged to perform in 1921 for *Noche Mexicana* and the *Exhibición de Artes Populares*. As an official state-sponsored ensemble of Mexico City, this orchestra was very popular in the 1920s traveling to "all the cities of the United States" (Campos 1930:184) and using instruments that Campos described as "typically Mexican" (ibid.).

As the Orquesta Típica of Lerdo de Tejada represented a centralized, Mexico City–based, and typically Mexican ensemble, so the involvement of dancers from the villages of Jarácuaro and Pichátaro (a settlement close to Jarácuaro, located midway between Lake Pátzcuaro and the uplands), represented an authentic indigenous, rural, and peripheral element. Bartolo Juárez led the group of Old Men dancers, acting as musician and director, while performers from Pichátaro danced the *Dance of the Moors*. In a contemporaneous edition of *Mexican Folkways* the process of authentication, incorporation, and participation was clearly delineated in an article by Frances Toor. Describing aspects of *Hamarándecua*, she noted that "recently the Canacuas have formed part of a complete program of Michoacán folk customs, dances and music given by the Central Department of the Federal District in the open air theater of the new Workers' Park Venustiano Carranza....Mrs Angela Alcaraza taught the dance [the Canácuas]. Mrs Alcaraza is from Michoacán where she has often seen the Canacuas, but in order that it might be reproduced as authentically as possible, Indian girls were brought from Michoacán to Mexico City to help in the teaching" (1930:108).[3] Engaging villagers from the P'urhépecha region enabled a demonstration of the literal, embodied inclusion and incorporation of indigenous people as active participants in a state-sponsored performance in Mexico City, placing them in the heart of the nation. The framing of these participants and the practices was carefully shaped to guide audience members toward a reading of authenticity, clearly explained in the printed program. For example, Bartolo Juárez was credited as the musical director, rather than choreographer or composer for *The Old Men*, indicating that neither the music nor the choreography were created by him, but were collectively and traditionally passed on, validating *The Old Men* as authentically anonymous (Domínguez and González 1930).

In the printed program, an elaborate nineteen-page booklet, Domínguez and González deployed a deeply poetic literary style and included delicate line drawings throughout that idealized and romanticized P'urhépecha people and their practices.[4] Through literary text and images Domínguez and González expressed their ideological and political positioning. Clear explanations of authenticity, ethnicity, and historical perspectives on racial issues were evident, which stressed the importance of the Lake Pátzcuaro region, and referred explicitly to processes of appropriation, commodification, and adaptation for staged and theatricalized enactment. In commodifying the *Night of the Dead, The Old Men*, and other practices for the stage, González and Domínguez were open about their processes of adaptation and stereotypification. Their aim was "to reproduce the most typical of the customs of the indigenous people of the tarascan region, not from past...but simply to present scenes of nowadays, adapted to the demands of theatrical technique, with all the implication of hybridity and of superimposition" (1930). This focus upon contemporary practices contrasted with many of the descriptions of the rituals, music, and dance, which deliberately and overtly highlighted the inherent presence of the past. Thus, Domínguez and González depicted current P'urhépecha cultural practices as hybrids, formed as a result of the intervention of the "upstart" Spaniards, yet recognizing links back to the pre-Hispanic past and "the unmistakable mark of an aboriginal civilization." The Spaniards were portrayed as "the dominators," while the P'urhépecha people were characterized both as "the popular soul of Mexico" and also oppressed peoples, who had suffered four hundred years of servitude under the *conquistador* then under the landowners, surviving a double oppression that was economic and religious. The values of the contemporary P'urhépecha peoples were unambiguously presented: their survival; their resistance to oppression; their ability to maintain and perpetuate their own pre Hispanic characteristics and practices; and the "spirit of the race."

Aspects of authenticity were recurrently accentuated and, somewhat contradicting their notion of hybridity, Domínguez and González draw a direct line from the "first tarascan epochs" to the present-day customs, which they regarded as "untainted" and "the richest and least adulterated folk-lore." They emphasized the survival of authentic artistic expression that had been more successful in the Lake Pátzcuaro region than in the upland region. Domínguez and González also highlighted the "survival" and "noble" aspects of the P'urhépecha peoples, portraying them as being "awake to all the interests of a Mexico wracked with the eagerness of renewal," thereby affirming them as useful to the progress of the nation.

By describing and explaining various scenes from *Hamarándecua* in the printed program, Domínguez and González indicated frameworks and significations for interpreting and reading the performance. Thus, *The Old Men* was a "rare demonstration of the tarascan sense of humor" and conveyed "the naïve comic sense of the tarascan race." The inhabitants of Lake Pátzcuaro were portrayed as distinctly non-Catholic, even pagan, and the account of *Night of the Dead* was, in many ways, the most overtly essentialist, with the ceremony described as a non-Christian, mystic event. According to Domínguez and González, the Catholic priest was not present for the ceremony, having "escaped before sunset." A short example of the text exemplifies and demonstrates the poetic style and ideological framing:

In the funerary offering [Night of the Dead] of the islanders of Janitzio, the pagan attitude towards death re-emerges, an attitude of friendship, or respectful and trusting communion with the dead: the indigenous person [*indio*] only uses the Christian weeping of the candles that drip in the middle of the night on the graves, as a new element of beauty to exalt still more the serene alliance of life with death. (1930)

This narrative and others added weight to the idea that the practice of *Night of the Dead* and the P'urhépecha peoples of Lake Pátzcuaro connected directly to preinvasion times, through the notion of death and ancestors, and through the contemporary practice of a ceremony purportedly undertaken unchanged for centuries or even millennia. Thus, it is not the people who weep in a Christian way, but the candles. In a similar vein, Domínguez and González described the ceremony of Canácuas as "a shoot of the past that is not extinct," emphasizing its connection back to a preconquest era. In conjunction with the textual descriptions of *Night of the Dead* on Janitzio, a simple line-drawing by González encapsulated an embodied image of a single P'urhépecha woman participating in the ritual (figure 1.13). Captured in back view, the woman is depicted in a kneeling position, her head covered with a rebozo, and accompanied by candles and flowers. The drawing replicated the key elements of González's photographs, circulating this very particular corporeal image, and further establishing the embodied representation of *Night of the Dead* on Janitzio as iconic. Significantly, the practice of fishing was also given prominence in the published program, furthering its importance as one of the key images, activities, and concepts for the network of associations surrounding *The Old Men, Night of the Dead*, and Lake Pátzcuaro. In the form of a visual image, the front cover of the program illustrated three P'urhépecha women, heads draped in blue rebozos, selling fish. In literary form, Domínguez and González characterized the P'urhépecha peoples as "a race of fishermen and highlanders, craftsmen and musicians."

Through the live event and the literary and visual texts in the program the notion of "exhibiting P'urhépecha life" was predominant. Although the directors of *Hamarándecua* set out to present *contemporary* P'urhépecha life, the spectacle and program obfuscated the boundaries between contemporary and prencursion indigenous peoples, intermingling present and past. In this context the presence of purportedly authentic indigenous bodies/people performing rituals and practices that were said to be *of* and *in* the past effected a blurring of interpretation that led to reading the people/bodies as also *in* and *of* the past. This interface of presenting past and present indigenous life in performance is particularly potent given the material that formed the basis of other contemporary theater events organized by artists such as González and Campos that explicitly dealt with scenes of pre-Hispanic Mexico. Those performances, often pantomimes and ballets, drew directly upon preincursion imagery, recreating and imagining notions of a preconquest past. In the same year that *Hamarándecua* was produced, Campos and González worked together to present a ballet (with choirs) entitled *Quetzalcóatl* in which pre-Hispanic Atzec dances were represented (Bruno Ruíz no date: 73 & Campos 1930:201).

Both González and Domínguez had influential roles in shaping aspects of indigenousness and folkloricization in Mexico, making their political and ideological objectives, as well as their artistic and aesthetic objectives, central to their endeavors. Both were directly concerned with the promotion of *The Old Men* and *Night of the Dead* through staged events and publications, and both were major figures in the four SEP-supported, didactic theater movements (Regional, Indigenista, Sintético and Aire Libre). Domínguez also promoted P'urhépecha music through publication and performance. As a musician and folklorist who worked for the Musical Archives of the National Institute of Fine Arts (part of SEP), one aspect of his position involved collecting musical material. In 1921 and 1923, he travelled to the state of Michoacán to study and undertake research (Campos 1928:85, 99, Domínguez 1941:n.p, Mendoza 1956:49, and Toor 1930:108). Rafael Juárez, Nicolás Bartolo Juárez's nephew, who was a teenage musician at the time, recalled the collecting visits of Domínguez to Jarácuaro, pointing out that Domínguez had asked him many questions but had only given him a tip for the information he gave (Personal communication: 1996). As a result of these and other field trips, Domínguez published three albums of transcribed music through SEP, comprising music collected in Michoacán (1925), including two compositions by Nicolás Bartolo Juárez. In another publication that circulated at a slightly later period, Domínguez's ideological framework was evident. *El álbum musical de Michoacán* (A Michoacán musical album), published by SEP in 1941 to mark four hundred years "from the Spanish incursion," incorporated transcriptions of pieces by various composers of the Lake Pátzcuaro region, including a selection by Nicolás Bartolo Juárez.[5] Domínguez also included a short biography of the Bartolo Juárez family, with a particular focus on Nicolás. He engaged a distinctive ideological and aesthetic stance, associating the music of the Bartolo Juárez family with that of P'urhépecha feeling and sensitivity, noting a specific link to nature, and articulating the notions of "traditional destiny" and "natural inspiration" which reflected the beauty and serenity of Lake Pátzcuaro and the Lake atmosphere (Domínguez 1941). In a noteworthy moment of unequivocal positioning, a dedication at the opening of the publication, written by an unspecified representative of SEP, placed an emphasis on "the exceptional aesthetic qualities that are an authentic message of the Indigenous Tarascan Race" (1941: n.p.).

"Indigenous Dancers in the Palace of Fine Arts" (Mendoza 1939)

As *Hamarándecua* presented *The Old Men* and *Night of the Dead* as theatricalized customs within the context of P'urhépecha and Michoacán life, in the second half of 1930s staged events were organized that placed *The Old Men* into the wider context of Mexico, establishing it as authentically Mexican within an all-encompassing frame of *nation*. Unlike previous costumbrista events such as *Hamarándecua*, these occasions consisted of a series of unconnected dances, enacted one after the other, much in the form of a festival presentation. They incorporated customs and practices not only from Lake Pátzcuaro and Michoacán, but from diverse regions and states of Mexico, thereby performing, embodying, and representing, in temporal and spatial form, a Mexico that was united and held together within the frame of one single occasion. In a similar vein to the 1921 centenary event of *Noche Mexicana* in Chapultepec Park, a performance-event with the same title was presented on a stage in the waters of Lake Chapultepec in 1935. Using floating scenes, the event was, in essence, a celebration of Mexicanness, utilizing practices from various regions of Mexico. *The Old Men* and the *Dance of the Moors* were staged under the direction of Bartolo Juárez. As for the theater event *Hamarándecua*, the musicians accompanying the *Dance of the Moors* were from Mexico City. In order to aid them in their playing, Bartolo Juárez transcribed the music for the musicians, demonstrating his own musical proficiency. However, as Rafael Juárez recollected in the 1990s, the written transmission process was not publicized because it did not fit with the folkloric image of oral transmission (personal communication).

Two years after *Noche Mexicana*, an event entitled *Danzas Auténticas Mexicanas* (Authentic Mexican Dances) was staged in the Palacio de Bellas Artes (Palace of Fine Arts), Mexico City, under the auspices of SEP. It comprised a series of performances in which fourteen groups of dancers and musicians from various regions of the country each presented a dance. *The Old Men* from *"Pátzcuaro"* was included (Los Viejitos, Pátzcuaro Mich.), establishing its place within a limited selection of representative Mexican regional dances. Of greatest significance was the influence of these performances on the formation of the repertoire of Mexican folkloric dance ensembles, including the Ballet Folklórico de México, a professional company founded in the late 1950s and based in the same theater.[6] The printed program for *Danzas Auténticas Mexicanas* sets out many of the major elements of the occasion:

> For the first time in the history of art in Mexico, the Department of Public Education...brings together in this city groups of dancers from diverse regions of the country. Authentic dance, the genuine demonstration of the popular soul, today finds shelter in the Palace of Fine Arts, where a select public will appreciate the vigor and the strength of a people who, in spite of many years of outside domination, knew how to conserve through time the magic thread of their tradition, bringing to our lifetime the sad, melancholic or wild *sones* of the indigenous people (*los indígenas*), who also transformed the cadences and rhythms imposed by the conquistador, in a faithful demonstration of the mestizo and young soul, as a wonderful expression of the artistic and emotional resources of our race.
>
> It is not a review that is being presented, in which the dances are more or less stylized and modified, no. Rather, the dance of the village plaza, a great attraction of simple peasants in popular fairs and fiestas; picturesque and colorful dances which, in little plazas full of sun in villages, satisfy the soul of the people—this is what has been brought here...
>
> [these dances] allow us to feel, experience, and know our people (*nuestro pueblo*), diverse, always young, enthusiastic, and so beautiful, which have awoken enormous and justified interest beyond our borders (*nuestras fronteras*).
>
> (1937)

Authenticity was obviously an essential constituent. Naming the event Authentic Mexican Dances unambiguously indicated the central issue, shaping and affirming notions of authenticity in terms of ethnicity, indigenousness, performance practices, and nationalism. All the performers were drawn from villages and towns in diverse parts of Mexico, enabling the dance practices, the artifacts, and the bodies of the dancers to be formulated as authentic. A later publication documenting fifty years of performances in the Palace of Fine Arts succinctly recorded that the musicians, music, and costumes for the event were "*autóctonas*" (autochthonous, native or indigenous) (*Cincuenta años de danza* 1984:3).[7]

Returning to the printed program, scattered throughout the text were numerous phrases and concepts formulating and shaping the meaning of authenticity in terms of ethnic, social, and racial identity. Thus, the dances were associated with "the magic thread of tradition" maintained by the "indigenous people," who were portrayed as the great preservers, having managed to perpetuate their practices in spite of the Spanish invasion, or who had transformed the imposed practices of the Spaniards to suit their own ends. Authenticity was also expressed in terms of unadulterated practices. Original and authentic dances existed in village plazas—sites and locations of a primary socioreligious function—and it was those dances that were simply being enacted in a different context. An emphasis was placed upon the idea that the dances were not "stylized and modified" and were therefore "authentic." Quite unlike the recognition of Domínguez and González, the directors of *Hamarándecua*, that the theatricalization of scenes involved adaptation to the technical demands of the theater, the directors of *Danzas Auténticas Mexicanas* chose to make a claim that no such process took place with the event in the Palace of Fine Arts. Yet despite such assertions, the dances were fundamentally subject to processes of commodification, having being appropriated and brought together by the state, and then altered spatially and durationally to suit a theater audience and gaze. Throughout the program text, locations and peoples were characterized in specifically romanticized and essentialized ways. Significantly, the words and phrases connected with the purported original enactment contexts were those that have been most associated with folkloric practice in Mexico: "picturesque," "colorful," "soul of the people," "full of sun," "simple," and "popular."

Of central importance was the literal demonstration and embodiment of the state policies of centralization, integration, assimilation, and incorporation. By bringing together villagers from diverse regions of the country, the bodies of disparate peoples from throughout Mexico were spatially and temporally incorporated into the Mexican nation and corporeally framed together on the stage and within the walls of the theater of the state-controlled Palace of Fine Arts in the center of the capital of the nation. People that had been hidden away in villages throughout Mexico were present, in flesh and blood, in Mexico City, the heart of the nation. Given that *The Old Men* and P'urhépecha villagers from Lake Pátzcuaro were an essential element of this context, this further established and disseminated the role of this dance and these people as representative of Michoacán and Mexico. The contextualization of *Danzas Auténticas Mexicanas* was particularly noteworthy in terms of conceptualizing difference through notions of genre, performance, and "art," by placing it within a context of "high" and "modern" artistic practice. In the year in which *Danzas Auténticas Mexicanas* was presented, other events in the same theater included ballet, opera, modern dance, and contemporary dance (*Cincuenta años de danza* 1984:3). Not only did the National Institute of Fine Arts have its own modern dance company which performed in the theater, but another event involved ballerina Eva Beltri dancing the *jarabe tapatío* (the "popular" dance) in ballet form en pointe, following the model established by Anna Pavlova in *Fantasía Mexicana* in 1919 (ibid.).

Even the building itself contributed to interpretations of the events staged within it. Performing in the Palace of Fine Arts placed the focus upon resignifying indigenous practices as "art." The architecture of the Palace formed another performative role, for as an extravagant cathedral-like white marble edifice, with a huge stage and sumptuous surroundings, complete with grand murals by renowned postrevolutionary artists, the very fabric of the place encompassed representations of the state. The Palace had been commissioned by Porfirio Díaz (the dictator ousted during the revolution), and was planned as a European-style national theater, which was due to be completed for the grandiose centennial celebration of Mexican independence in 1910; however, it was not completed until 1934.[8] The very building was given the role of "protector," projecting the state as a benevolent guardian of indigenous cultural heritage, a point that was specifically referenced in the program through the expression that "authentic dance...finds shelter in the Palace of Fine Arts." As a state-owned and state-run venue, both the dancers and the dance practices were managed by the government. High-level political organization was also evident through the involvement of the governmental Department of Press and Publicity (DAPP) which promoted the event (and which in the same year published two books of compositions by Nicolás Bartolo Juárez), and through endorsement by Amalia Solórzano de Cárdenas, the wife of Lázaro Cárdenas, president of the Republic of Mexico.

Media reporting and representation in the popular press was also influential in shaping perceptions and interpretations, with articles and advertisements appearing in newspapers. A series of advertisements in *El Nacional*, a major newspaper in Mexico City, placed the event alongside motorcycle races, cinema listings, radio programs, and concerts by the Sinfónica de México (the Symphony Orchestra of Mexico) conducted by renowned musician and composer Carlos Chávez (figure 6.1). Advertisements and articles, many written by Mexico City–based intellectual Moisés Mendoza, engaged romanticized and essentialist ideas concerning notions of authenticity. Thus, for example, in one article Mendoza reported that "today...the nation of Mexico [*el pueblo*][9] has entered the theater of the Palace of Fine Arts, through dancers of popular dancers with their authenticity intact, and without modification [*mixtificaciones*], professional choreographers or theatrical tricks....From remote places in the country...in an exhibition of absolute purity, with simple music and colorful costumes this is a beautiful national tradition" (Mendoza 1937). Advertisements engaged similar ideas: "Today, at 5:30 and 8:30, in the Palace of Fine Arts, sees the departure of the extraordinary and

Figure 6.1 Advertisement for *Danzas Auténticas Mexicanas* (Authentic Mexican Dances), a series of theatricalized events staged in the Palacio de Bellas Artes (Palace of Fine Arts) in Mexico City in 1937 and 1939. The *Dance of the Old Men* of Lake Pátzcuaro was performed for both these events, within a repertoire of national dances. Promoted in the newspaper section "Espectáculos para Hoy" (Shows for Today), the advert for this staged, theater event ran alongside promotions for car and motorcycle racing, film programs in modern movie theaters, and a concert by the Symphony Orchestra directed by Carlos Chávez. Note: The correct title for the event was *Danzas Auténtics Mexicanas*, although in this advert the words were inadvertently transposed (*El Nacional*, 22 July 1939).

unique Authentic Mexican Dances, with their authenticity intact, without modification, and with all the joy of the village fiestas. All the time and money in the world are not sufficient to see this spectacle that will not return."

The "spectacle" did return, however, just two years later, in an almost identical format to the 1937 series. Advertisements were again printed in *El Nacional* encompassing the same ideas: "Authentic Mexican Dances, with dancers brought from their far off places of origin, with authentic costumes, instruments and music ... [will] perform in the Palace of Fine Arts]." As before, Mendoza published a long article in *El Nacional* under the title "Danzantes Indígenas en Bellas Artes" (Indigenous Dancers in the Palace of Fine Arts) (1939). Mendoza specifically referred to *The Old Men*, observing that it had been disseminated in the whole country as a visual symbol of the state of Michoacán and noting that it originated in Cucuchucho,

Jarácuaro, and Santa Fe as a fluid form of ritual and celebratory dance. Interestingly, Mendoza did acknowledge that it was created in the twentieth century rather than presenting it as a pre-Hispanic dance; however, he continued to perpetuate the concept of indigenous authenticity and tradition as thoroughly associated with the dance.

Through these live events and printed materials in Mexico City *The Old Men* was thoroughly incorporated into a controlled and limited repertoire of regional Mexican dances, establishing indigenous dancers as an authentic element of real Mexico. The legacy of these activities was the dissemination of *The Old Men* through pedagogical and folkloric organizations, leading to its inclusion in the repertoire of the Ballet Folklórico de México, and the folkloric uses of *The Old Men* by hundreds of dance ensembles in Mexico and the United States.[10]

Across the Border in *El Norte*

Processes of performism, which encompassed imaging the nation through corporeal acts and creating a repertoire of representative authentic dances, were not only vital within Mexico, but also across the national border in Mexico's neighboring territory to the north. Four elements are of particular relevance to discussions of the postrevolutionary era: firstly, the inculcation of a continued sense of Mexicanness in both Mexican migrants and Mexican descendents in the United States by the Mexican government; secondly, the development of folkloric performances of dance and music in the United States by non-Mexican inhabitants; thirdly, the promotion of Mexico as a tourist destination for U.S. travelers; and fourthly, Mexican-U.S. political, intellectual, cultural, and economic relationships. In this section I particularly focus on elements one and two, even as three and four are encompassed within the activities under discussion. In previous chapters I have already noted aspects of political and intellectual relationships, as exemplified in the visit of Professor Kandel to Janitzio for *Night of the Dead*; the collaborative research venture of the Tarascan Project; and literary and photographic representations of Mexico for a U.S. readership in the magazine *Mexican Folkways*, with a U.S. editor working in Mexico City. This third example encapsulated not only a political, intellectual, and cultural relationship but also a touristic and economic one, performing a role in presenting images of Mexico that would entice travelers south across the border.

While the process of constructing and disseminating a repertoire of representative regional dances was underway in Mexico, accomplished through the work of SEP, by the 1930s this collection of dances was also circulating north of the border in the United States. In Mexico, the strategy centered on ideas of unifying a disparate population and generating a sense of Mexicanness through the corporeal act of dancing the same steps, accompanied by the same music. In the United States there were two sets of objectives, one which led to Mexican folklórico ensembles that burgeoned in the 1960s (and to which I return to in later chapters), and the other being concerned with developing a relationship with Mexico by understanding the customs of the "neighbors" across the border (and also, for many citizens, understanding their neighbors in the same city). It is this second context that I deal with here. For many people in the southwestern states their experience of Mexico included face-to-face dealings with Spanish-speaking Mexicans and Mexican descendants living in the United States (those whose families had occupied the land prior to the shift in political control and also more recent migrants to the area).

Pedagogical institutions and cultural organizations developed events and programs for disseminating understandings of Mexico, Mexicans, and Mexican ways of life, and also taught the Spanish language. These programs often involved enactments of music, dance, and the equivalent of cuadros costumbristas or scenes of everyday life. Such performances were incorporated into special events that were organized to celebrate Pan American Day, a multination occasion to acknowledge and mark a sense of solidarity throughout the nations of the American continent (north and south). Such events tended to encompass a recognition of *difference* and heritage, particularly in terms of race and ethnicity. In order to illustrate the developing content of such events and performances in the United States, I discuss a publication of 1935 entitled *Regional Dances of Mexico*, which included detailed instructions for staging *The Old Men* and P'urhépecha customs. The author, Edith Johnston, was a teacher of Spanish language at Austin High School, Texas, and published the book as a pedagogical tool both for Spanish-language teachers and for directors and teachers of cultural groups and clubs.

Essentially the book provided detailed information for creating staged enactments of Mexican music, dances, and scenes of everyday life (including dialogue) that could be "program numbers for club work, public performances, assemblies, and luncheons" (1935:i) The whole project was framed by the notion of "Our Neighbor Mexico" and Johnston's approach was romantic and benevolent (ibid.). Accounts and notation were given for the dances and music, with full descriptions and line drawings to enable the construction and re-creation of costumes and staging. Rationalizing her project, Johnston noted that "the need for varied and authentic numbers, specific instructions for copying costumes, music for accompaniments, and clear, simple instructions for dance formations has occasioned the work and study in this collection. Every number included in this book has been tested by many performances and worked out in detail to make its presentation a success" (1935:iii). As with the staged performances in Mexico City, a concept of authenticity was central to the premise of the book. Johnston made a point of emphasizing the authenticity of transmission processes, noting that the music, dance, and scenes were "obtained first-hand during travels in Mexico...[and] the melodies which constitute the basis for the accompaniments were taken down as heard: they have been arranged in a simple form and the songs transposed to a suitable key" (ibid.). Particularly noteworthy for this study is the focus on P'urhépecha peoples and practices—including *The Old Men*—as material for representation. The publication itself and the events re-created through it were instrumental in the construction and representation of Mexico in the United States, contributing to establishing *The Old Men* as a Mexican regional dance, and linking it specifically with indigenous Mexico.

Both Johnston's book and the events and activities that it generated were influential in both cross-border and local perceptions of, and relationships with Mexicans and Mexico. Johnston's location in the state of Texas, and in Austin in particular, is significant in terms of the concept of Mexican nationalism in the area, linked specifically to the complex history of changing allegiances and governance. From the early sixteenth century the land passed from indigenous territory to Spanish and then Mexican rule. It formed part of Mexican territory until 1836, subsequently becoming independent, and eventually taking membership of the United States of America. The populace of Austin therefore included both English and Spanish speakers, many of whom had recent and ongoing relationships with Mexico. In conjunction with this agenda, as there was an increasing interest in, and cultivation of Mexico as a tourist destination for U.S. citizens, strategies for generating images of a folkloric and indigenous Mexico were also important. Indeed, during the 1930s, in order to market Mexico as a viable and attractive destination for U.S. tourists, and to assist and service the growing flow of tourists journeying to Mexico, various publications and guide books were produced, such as *National Geographic Magazine, Your Mexican Holiday*, (Brenner 1932), *Motorists' Guide to Mexico* (Scully 1933), and *Terry's Guide to Mexico* (Terry 1935).

In a very specific tourist-oriented section of Johnston's book, one "program number" specifically depicts a tourist setting (although the tourist is not from the United States, but from England). In a scene entitled "Lo que es regatear (How to barter)," involving the English tourist and an "Indian" *sarape* (poncho)-vendor from the city of Oaxaca, the poncho is configured as a tourist souvenir. In her staging notes, Johnston gives the instruction that "the Englishman should carry a guidebook, dictionary, umbrella and should use a monocle. The Indian should wear a suit of unbleached muslin and carry a load of sarapes on his shoulder. The Englishman is passing and is attracted by the bright colors" (59).[11] Four elements are particularly noteworthy in this example: firstly, the representation of the "suit of unbleached muslin" as the everyday clothes of an indigenous person, which was also the costume for *The Old Men*; secondly, the configuration of the poncho as a souvenir article and representation of "Mexico," transforming an item of utilitarian clothing (an essential warmth-giving garment of everyday use for many rural Mexicans), and also a component of costume for *The Old Men*, into an object of exchange value for display by foreign travelers; thirdly, the explicit association between an indigenous object (the poncho) and colorfulness; and fourthly, the tourist-host relationship of economic transaction between a foreign traveler and an indigenous Mexican.

Throughout the publication there is an emphasis upon, and association between Mexico and indigenousness. In one section entitled "Supplement for club use. A program on Indian Mexico," Johnston recommends that "an interesting club program may be built on the topic of 'Indian Life in Mexico' using the following numbers: 1. 'Los Viejitos', dance of the Indians of Michoacán [The Old Men]... 2. 'Lo que es regatear'" (60). Linking these two "numbers" together created a framing of *The Old Men* as an authentic indigenous practice and a tourist commodity. Within this section Johnston also suggests including telling the story of Benito

Juárez, "the Zapotec man who became President of Mexico in 1858." In one overt form of essentialist representation, Johnston states that "the Indians of Mexico are masters of beautiful handcraft.... The words most frequently heard in Mexico are *¡Que bonito!* (How pretty!)" (67). There are many references to Michoacán and to the "Tarascans," with the inclusion of various sections labeled as a "Cuadro Regional" (Regional Scene) which purport to encapsulate a scene of everyday life in a P'urhépecha village. As scenarios of *otherness* and *difference* they convey the idea of ethnographic display and a living diorama, re-created and reenacted by students in the United States. Music notation and lyrics for P'urhépecha and other Michoacán songs were provided, including "Flor de Canela" (which developed into the most representative P'urhépecha *pirekua* (song)), "San Miguel Tzitziki," "Jícaras de Michoacán,"and "El Jarabe Michoacano." Musical references were also depicted in the line drawings, with one illustration portraying a musical ensemble consisting of double bass player and two violinists standing outside the cantina Flor de Mayo "Playing 'Adelita,'" one of the most famous *corridos* (narrative ballads) from the revolutionary era (opp.3).

Constructions of P'urhépecha culture appeared in both literary and visual depictions. As an example, Johnston describes "Tarascan Indians dress" as being of "handwoven muslin" with a "woolen gabán" [poncho] (73). Deploying images and music from previous nationalistic performances of *Noche Mexicana* in 1921 and the *Fiesta of Song and Dance* of the Regional Theater in Paracho in 1924, Johnston referenced the *jícaras* (painted gourds) from Uruápan, and Las Canácuas (the P'urhépecha ritual of hospitality). In one scene to be enacted with dialogue, a P'urhépecha family is portrayed going to the market in the city of Morelia to sell their wares. This section includes *The Old Men*, and gives full details for representing and performing the dance, including choreographic and musical notation (37–44). In the musical notation (written for piano), the sectionalization of *The Old Men* is given as five sixteen-bar sections, and the rhythmic accompaniment, without a melodic line, is strikingly different to the later developments of *The Old Men* when the violin was incorporated into the accompanying ensemble. *The Old Men* is characterized as "a very funny dance from the shores of Lake Pátzcuaro" and a ritual dance that is part of every day life. It is particularly noteworthy that the "shirt and trousers of unbleached muslin" are described as both the costume for *The Old Men* of Lake Pátzcuaro, and the daily wear of the "Indian" in Oaxaca, thereby portraying the costume for *The Old Men* as a pan-indigenous set of everyday clothes.

Crossing the Dividing Line: Mexicans Abroad

As staged enactments of *The Old Men* performed a role in the shaping of the perception of Mexico and Mexicanness for non-Mexicans in the United States, the same dance was deployed for the development and inculcation of Mexicanness in "Mexicans abroad" who were living in the United States. On 12 October 1938, an ensemble of villagers from Lake Pátzcuaro performed *The Old Men* in San Antonio,

Texas, for activities marking *Día de la Raza* (literally "Day of the Race")[12] for an audience consisting of Mexicans and Mexican-Americans. As part of the com-memoration, an evening of entertainment was presented in the Auditorium of San Antonio, which included a performance by the Mexican Choir of San Antonio; an official speech by the director of the National Library of Mexico; and a reading of a political message from the governor of Michoacán, General Gildardo Magaña. The event was organized by the owners of a Mexican media company, La Prensa, based in San Antonio, United States. The journey and enactment of *The Old Men* was given an official Mexican state seal in the form of a "scroll" containing the message from General Gildardo Magaña. The events north of the Mexican border were reported in Mexico through an article in the Michoacán newspaper *Heraldo Michoacano*. With this case in point, multiple performism processes were present, through many forms of representational practices, journeys, and border crossings, drawing attention to the circulation and dissemination of ideas, images, peoples, and practices, and the generation a particular course and movement from Michoacán, Mexico, to Texas, United States, and back again. Significantly, at the heart of these journeys and representations were live dancers and musicians from Lake Pátzcuaro and the practice of *The Old Men*. The role of the performers in embodying and shaping notions of Mexicanness through live display in the United States, and through textual and photographic imaging in a newspaper in Michoacán, exemplifies performism processes through dissemination of networks of signifying ideas and images.

In the previous section, I briefly noted the significant history of the state of Texas. Here again the focus is on Texas, with events taking place in the city of San Antonio. Like Austin, San Antonio underwent the transformation from Mexican territory to U.S. territory. In the early twentieth century, the population of San Antonio included significant numbers of inhabitants who were directly associated with Mexico. Some were of Mexican ancestry through predecessors who had occu-pied the land as Mexican territory and who saw the border or "dividing line" move as political control shifted. Others had migrated from Mexico to the United States and settled in San Antonio. In 1920, San Antonio contained the largest number of Mexican residents in the Southwest (nearly 41,500) (Sánchez 1993:65), many of whom had migrated after the Mexican Revolution.[13] From a Mexican govern-mental perspective and a migrant position, there was a need to shape and develop both a Mexican national identity and an identification with the government and people of Mexico. Writing of the U.S. context in the 1920s and 1930s George Sánchez observed that "Mexican government representatives along with members of the expatriate community, anxious to promote nationalist sentiment engaged in a ... campaign to keep emigrants loyalties linked to an emerging Mexican nation" (1993:11). One strategy for enabling this was through the cultivation of cultural practices, including music and dance. Developing an imagined community through the idea of nation-as-people enabled the inculcation of unity by bringing together Mexicans on both sides of the border through symbolic acts. *The Old Men* was therefore selected as an essential and efficacious component of Mexican national identity that all Mexicans should know about, in an effort to shape and promote Mexicanness and a sense of belonging. Through the enactment of *The Old Men* in San Antonio, the authentic national body of Mexico went to the United States in the bodies of the P'urhépecha villagers of Lake Pátzcuaro. The event was framed as a true representation of the nation, with indigenismo embodied in the authentic bodies of live, indigenous people and their practice, engaging the discourses of folklórico and lo mexicano. Generating connections between those designated as Mexican both within and beyond the geopolitical border was central to creating lo mexicano and a shared sense of belonging. Engaging the Lake Pátzcuaro villagers as embodiments of the journey between Mexico and the United States provided a poignant symbolic act, referencing the formation of identity through a sense of territory, place, space, and location.

The paternalist and interventionist role of the state was evident through endorsement by the Michoacán state governor. The ideological position of cultural patrimony was performed through the action of "sending" indigenous musicians and dancers as a representation of the state to the United States, demonstrating control, ownership, and integration. In conjunction with the display of *The Old Men*, the reading of the scroll containing the message of the state governor performed an essential role, framing and shaping the event and emphasizing cross-border relations, nationalism, and Mexican identity. Integral to the speech and to the presence of the P'urhépecha villagers was the categorization and incorporation of the audience members as Mexicans, even though the event took place in the United States. A section of the speech exemplifies principal elements of approach and ideology:

> In recognition of the anniversary of the date on which the Caravels of the bold admiral, symbolic messenger of another civilization, arrived on our shores; in the name of the people and Government of Michoacán, who feel the most profound and sincere warmth for the Mexicans resident in the Great Republic of the American Union, we send a warm greeting…with wishes for the prosperity and well-being of 'Mexico Abroad', and hopes for the development of continental solidarity, towards which Michoacán wishes to actively contribute, we invite you to know Michoacán and offer you the most open and loyal hospitality.
>
> Morelia, 10 October 1938. General Gildardo Magaña.
> (*Será Ejecutada la Danza de 'Los Viejitos'* 1938)

Reporting for Mexicans at Home

Even as the gathering of Mexicans abroad for the concert of *The Old Men* was taking place in the United States, representations of the occasion were circulating back across the border in print form to Mexicans at home, performing yet another vital role. The event was reported in an article in *Heraldo Michoacano*, a statewide daily paper with a readership of mostly middle-class citizens, influential in the inculcation and construction of a sense of Michoacán and Mexican regional and national identity. Through the article, the iconic importance of *The Old Men* as a symbol of Michoacánness and Mexicanness was reinforced, presenting an overtly ideological message. Significantly, the newspaper article included the full text of the scroll of the governor of Michoacán that accompanied the P'urhépecha performers to San Antonio, thereby uniting locationally disparate Mexicans on both sides of the border through a material connection and a shared message, accessible to Mexicans abroad and at home. A short example from the newspaper report gives an idea of the stylistic tone and ideological framing:

> The presence of the unique dancers in the Texas city was greeted with great enthusiasm, because this is the first time that a group of indigenous artists from the P'urhépecha region has crossed the dividing line (*la línea divisoria*) to perform in their special costumes. (Ibid.)

By describing the crossing of the dividing line by the P'urhépecha artists, an explicit notion of nation-as-people (as opposed to territory) was expounded, with the bodies of the musicians and dancers and the practice of *The Old Men* forming tangible elements in nation formation. In both the text of the article and the scroll of the governor, the identity of those living in San Antonio as Mexican was emphasized through references to "Mexicans resident in the Great Republic of the American Union" and "Mexicans abroad," thus extending Mexican identity and nationality outside the territorial boundaries. Perhaps of greatest significance is the explicit presentation of the concept of a dance practice as a fundamental element in the construction of national identity, framing *The Old Men* as an important and well-known element of Michoacán and Mexican life that those Mexicans living in the United States should experience and know in order to be truly Mexican and to maintain their Mexicanness.

> According to the news that has been received, there is great enthusiasm in San Antonio in admiring our dancers, because most of "Mexico abroad" does not know "The Old Men." (Ibid.)

The *Dance of the Old Men* was given the manifest symbolic role of national unifier, particularly emphasized through the suggestion that those Mexicans who did not know it were missing out on something of great significance for their Mexican identity. Strategies of cultural patrimony and state organization were evident in reference to the P'urhépecha villagers, who were described as "our dancers," demonstrating a dual role of control and pride associated with both state ownership and paternalism. As with *Danzas Auténticas Mexicanas* in Mexico City, however, presenting the P'urhépecha performers as "indigenous artists from the P'urhépecha region" also highlighted the repositioning of folklore, traditional, and indigenous practices as *art*, and the performers of such practices as *artists*. Nevertheless, this repositioning of musicians and dancers and *The Old Men* of Lake Pátzcuaro in terms other than folkloric was not perpetuated in ensuing decades.

In an interesting correlative article published in the same newspaper just two weeks prior to the piece covering the San Antonio event, a similar ideological position was expounded concerning the place and signification of P'urhépecha people and their music and dance practices. The article, entitled *"Las 'Canacuas'"* described the way in which songs and dances of the P'urhépecha people were representative of "the tarascan race...because in these one can perceive the sentiments and joy of that race, which was for many years the dominator of this region of Mexico and of which, in spite of the fact that the civilization has lost what is typical and autochthonous, some customs still remain" (*Las 'Canacuas'* 1938). As a demonstration of ownership and cultural patrimony, the P'urhépecha peoples were referred to as *nuestros indios* (our indigenous people) and in another telling phrase, the formulation of *us and them* was delineated with the statement that "this group of artists...allows us to remember past times." Thus, P'urhépecha peoples were explicitly framed and promoted for their usefulness in enabling the construction and shaping of Mexican identity and lo mexicano through memory of the past as embodied in living people, a formulation that continued through the remainder of the twentieth century and into the twenty-first.

Not An Iconic Dance: The Dance of the Moors

Even as I trace the iconicity of the *Dance of the Old Men*, noting the non-iconicity of another dance enables some understanding of why one form rather than another is established in a place of prominence. In the burgeoning folkloric nationalist events of the 1920s and 1930s, *The Old Men* was invariably performed in conjunction with another dance, *La Danza de los Moros*, the *Dance of the Moors*. In 1924, the *Dance of the Moors* was danced in the Teatro Sintético together with *The Old Men*, with both forms being taught by Bartolo Juárez. Through live events and publications, the *Dance of the Moors* became associated with the Lake Pátzcuaro region of Michoacán, and was promoted even more than *The Old Men* in the 1920s. Yet by the end of the 1930s, it had returned to an almost exclusively local village use. Many forms of a *Dance of the Moors* (often as *Moros y Cristianos*— Moors and Christians) existed throughout Mexico, enacted as part of local village and town celebrations for the Patron Saint of the community, with dancers being drawn from the neighborhood who generally danced to fulfill a *manda* (promise) to a saint (Harris 2000, Núñez y Domínguez 1927, and Warman 1972). González, Domínguez, and others witnessed a *Moors Dance* on Jarácuaro, leading to Bartolo Juárez being invited to teach this alongside *The Old Men* in Mexico City (Radio Educación A354/535 and Campos 1928:88). Both dances were performed in the Mexico City staged events of *Hamarándecua* (1930) and *Noche Mexicana* on Lake Chapultepec (1935).

Two overtly ethnographic accounts of the peoples of Lake Pátzcuaro included references to and descriptions of the *Moors Dance* (León 1934:157, and Mendieta y Núñez 1940:173) and Campos also included brief details in his book on folklore and Mexican music, giving a description of the Moors dance and costume in

Michoacán, and also reproducing an illustration of a mural painting by Carlos González entitled "Danza de los Moros en el lago de Pátzcuaro" (Dance of the Moors in Lake Pátzcuaro) (1928:31, 35, 39). In one edition of *Mexican Folkways* González dedicated a whole article to the *Moors Dance*, focusing almost entirely on the version performed on the island of Janitzio (1928b). González described the costume of the dancers in detail (which comprised a suit of silks and velvets, beads, veils, and fringes) and also gave an account of the context and practice. Although the *Moors Dance* was always part of a Catholic celebration, specifically honouring the patron saint of the community and often danced inside the church during Mass and certainly in the atrium after Mass, González stated that the dance was not religious in character, but profane, being danced around the village in the patios of houses (1928b:32). This representation is in keeping with the policy of secularization and the need to characterize indigenous peoples—particularly those so tangibly separate from urban influence as were the islanders of Lake Pátzcuaro—as continuing to carry out pre-Catholic religious practices. Although the dance was performed throughout Mexico in village celebrations, González's article located it firmly in the Lake Pátzcuaro region. González's own photographic images that formed part of the article served to construct the essential folkloric notions of the event, showing P'urhépecha men in costume standing (not dancing) in front of an abode-walled house. It was a depiction of a romanticized setting of the island location, encapsulating the rusticity of the houses, the basic equipment of the fishermen, and the exotic costumes. The juxtaposition of the elaborate costumes contrasted with the abode walls and the dirt floor. Including the images of the preindustrial fishing methods and equipment also shaped the context as authentic and indigenous, and located the dance within a setting of working lives. A photo with the caption "A View of the Island of Janitchio" framed the dance within the specific locale of Janitzio (1928b:36).

In her highly influential book *A Treasury of Mexican Folkways*, Frances Toor published a description of the *Moors Dance* of Lake Pátzcuaro, drawing on the articles in *Mexican Folkways* (Toor 1947:349). Representations and images of the *Dance of the Moors* and the *Dance of the Old Men* appeared together not only in staged settings but were also circulated by other means, such as a front page photograph in a newspaper article depicting an event in Michoacán in 1938 (La Conmemoración 1938) and the painted image on the front cover of one of the books of compositions by Bartolo Juárez (1937b) (figure 4.2). In these documents and depictions the *Dance of the Moors* was always presented as a local, ritual dance, used as part of specific village celebrations. As *The Old Men* was also promoted as being part of the same local, P'urhépecha village context so it too was received and interpreted as an authentically traditional P'urhépecha ritual dance.

Despite all the dissemination in the 1920s and 1930s, the *Dance of the Moors* did *not* continue to be an integral part of the folkloric repertoire, nor was it utilized in connection with the tourist industry. It does not appear on postcards or in guide books, and is not used to market Mexico or to generate notions of Mexicanness.[14] However, it does continue to be danced as an integral element of Patron Saint fiestas in the Lake Pátzcuaro region, mostly unseen by tourists and visitors. While it is unclear how consciously it was deselected, two obvious elements of the *Dance of the Moors* demonstrate its non-suitability and lack of efficacy as a representation of an authentic and indigenous Mexico. Firstly, unlike *The Old Men*, it referenced an overtly Spanish origin, as opposed to an indigenous one, and secondly, the *Moors Dance* utilized exotic and fantastical costumes, rather than pan-indigenous and overtly everyday clothes. This comparison and juxtaposition with *The Old Men* enables a clearer idea concerning the elements of *The Old Men* that were valuable as ideals of the political and ideological framework (44–45 🌑).

Toward the Golden Age

The 1920s and 1930s were foundational years in which multiple representational practices generated a network of signification encompassing *The Old Men* and *Night of the Dead*, presenting them as national icons and as symbolic production useful for indigenismo, nationalism, and tourism. In the 1930s with the major staged events of *The Old Men* in Mexico City and in the United States, P'urhépecha villagers from Lake Pátzcuaro were placed center stage in nation-building processes. Simultaneously, tourists were enticed and encouraged to visit the island of Janitzio to view *Night of the Dead* as the authentic event in situ, causing a shift in the attitude of the islanders toward the tourists. Dissemination in journals, newspapers, magazines, and books in Mexico and in the United States performed multiple roles in advancing the iconicity of *The Old Men* and *Night of the Dead* of Lake Pátzcuaro as essential elements of "Mexico." All of these processes and practices created an efficacious framework that fed directly into the ideological and political necessities of the Golden Age of the 1940s and 1950s.

CHAPTER 7

Films, Visual Images, and Folklórico

Belonging, Difference, and Bodies

OUT OF THE chaos and struggle of the revolution, through the immediate postrevolutionary decades, a newly formulated nationalism and a burgeoning tourist industry provided a shape and framework for a developing nation. From the incipient uses of *The Old Men* and *Night of the Dead* as public spectacles—efficacious for generating notions of a shared community through remembering a pre-Conquest past and for incorporating so-called backward indigenous peoples into a capitalist modernizing environment—multiple representational contexts were developed. Both *The Old Men* and *Night of the Dead* continued to be woven into the multifaceted tapestry of the Mexican nation through complex performism processes, and the peoples of Lake Pátzcuaro remained the focus of attention for government policy, research projects, films, and photographs. On a national scale, *The Old Men* continued on its path of ever-widening national and international usage, through publication and through enactment in educational and folkloric contexts. Disseminated and taught in schools as an essential element in the repertoire of regional dances, it became an indispensable component in the repertoire of the Ballet Folklórico company in Mexico City.

In this chapter I discuss a selection of salient peoples, events, and practices of the period from 1940 to 1968, beginning with an overview of state policies regarding indigenismo, indigenous peoples, and assimilation; the role of government institutions; and the development of notions of folklore. Secondly, I turn to national and international dissemination of images of Lake Pátzcuaro, *Night of the Dead*, and *The Old Men* in books and films. Thirdly, I focus on the transmission of *The Old Men* in the Lake Pátzcuaro region, notably: the burgeoning array of performances for local, private, and political occasions; the initiation of hotel performances; and the Festival of Music and Dance for *Night of the Dead*. Fourthly, I give an overview of didactic and pedagogical regional dance publications and events, and finally, rounding off the chapter, I describe the founding and influence of the Ballet Folklórico de México.

Being Mexican, "Our Mexico," and "Our Indigenous"

The 1940s and 1950s are considered to be a Golden Age, characterized by a sense of development, modernization, urbanization, and industrialization, as well as by the dual movements of mass migration north of the border to the United States, and the influx of U.S. tourists south of the border (Joseph et al. 2001). This period led to unrest in the 1960s and ended with the massacre of students and workers in Tlatelolco, Mexico City, in 1968, just prior to the staging of the Olympic Games in Mexico. Throughout this time Mexico continued as a one-party state under the Institutional Revolutionary Party (PRI).[1] In general political terms there was a shift from radical redistribution of wealth to a policy of capital accumulation, which required a heightened sense of patriotism in order to enable political stability. Therefore, maintaining a sense of a shared community, national identity, and nationalistic sensibilities continued with vigor into the 1940s and 1950s. Imaging and imagining lo mexicano was of primary importance for evoking cultural belonging through a sense of shared assumptions, and by the 1950s there was a generalized sense of pride in the historical act of being Mexican.[2] Cultural production, reception, and consumption were inculcated and disseminated through a range of media and institutions, notably public education and schooling, new governmental institutions, patriotic celebrations, monuments, print journalism and television, consumer culture, and tourism. Of particular importance was the promotion of nationally validated regional tourist sites and folkloric displays. In creating a shared community, issues of national integration and assimilation, cultural patrimony, and the role and place of indigenous peoples were central, and indigenismo remained an important element of national ideology. As before, this was a highly complex and contradictory milieu, embracing a continuing tension between the poles of integration, assimilation, and modernization at one end, and exoticism and indigenismo at the other. The lives of peoples of Lake Pátzcuaro and the activities of *The Old Men* and *Night of the Dead* were therefore enmeshed in this ongoing situation, with these practices being regarded as cultural patrimony, useful for both for national politics and touristic ends.

Significantly, the First Inter-American Indigenist Congress was held in Pátzcuaro in April 1940, with the inaugural speech given by former President Cárdenas, who declared that the indigenous population was a factor for progress and should therefore be incorporated into the nation, effectively Mexicanizing them to create national citizens.[3] In general, the overall goal of assimilation of indigenous peoples was not questioned, rather the strategies required to undertake such aspirations were under discussion. Organizations were set up with the aim of enabling cultural change of indigenous peoples by way of integral action in areas of education, economics, infrastructure, social and political organization, ways of life, and consumption patterns. In a continuation from the postrevolutionary period, pedagogues, artists, linguists, anthropologists, and other social science specialists working in governmental institutions were the chief performers and activists in shaping and disseminating representational and interventionist practices concerning indigenous peoples. As before, the anthropological and social scientific focus gave a theoretical foundation to the politics of indigenous assimilation into the dominant mould of the nation.[4]

Universities, research institutions, and museums were also engaged with processes of study and display, and audio recordings, photographic images, musical transcriptions, and ethnographic writing were all inherently part of the ongoing processes. Publications about music and dance played vital roles in constructing and framing notions of indigenous practices and peoples. Even as peoples and practices designated as indigenous were validated through acknowledgement of their significance, they were also exhibited and analyzed. Concepts of folklore and lo folklórico were fleshed out as part of the same framework for developing a coherent form of nationalism, with folklorists, anthropologists, and other governmental researchers perpetuating a scientific and developmental approach that promoted notions of fixed and essentialized sets of practices and peoples that continued to be shaped and constructed in line with European and U.S. formulations. Two U.S. scholars were highly prominent in this area: Ralph Boggs, who founded the Folkloric Society of Mexico and whose articles on folklore were profoundly influential (1939); and Robert Redfield, whose essay entitled "La Sociedad Folk" (The Folk Society) was published in the *Mexican Journal of Sociology* in 1942 (see also 1947).[5]

As educational activities continued to be instrumental in molding a Mexican sense of belonging, so SEP was influential in providing venues for regional dance and music events, and in publishing information about these practices (Slonimsky 1946:224). SEP continued with radio broadcasts in the form of instructional and cultural programs, aiming to construct a national sensibility through a "panorama" of musical traditions and regional songs, thereby authenticating SEP's official version of national culture (Hayes 2006:250, Schmidt 2001). Similarly, films and vinyl records circulated throughout the country, promoting auditory and visual representations of rurality and nostalgia while simultaneously engaging with modernity and capitalism. In terms of musical genres, even though certain styles such as tango, swing, and mambo were being heard in urban areas, particularly Mexico City, endorsement of *la cultura nacional* (national culture) focused upon other forms that could be regarded as authentically Mexican, including mariachi and romantic ballads, circulated through balladeers such as Pedro Infante and Augstín Lara (Martínez 2001:379). Under the auspices of el Instituto Nacional de Bellas Artes (INBA)—the National Institute of Fine Arts—*labor folklórico-musical mexicana* (Mexican folkloric-musical work) (Solórzano and Guerrero 1941 and Mendoza 1941) was carried out through the Section for Music Research, whose mission was to promote national artistic expression.[6] In 1947 the Academy of Mexican Dance was also founded as a component of INBA. The company included two dancers who were subsequently highly influential in the course of the dissemination of *The Old Men*: Josefina Lavalle, who became director of the National Foundation for Dance Research (FONADAN); and Amalia Hernández, founder of the professional Ballet Folklórico de México.[7]

El Instituto Nacional de Antropología e Historia (INAH)—the National Institute of Anthropology and History—founded in 1939, was driven by the principal objective of shaping and presenting Mexico's heritage, history, and culture for scholarly, political, and tourist purposes. Significantly, it was placed under the auspices of the Secretariat of Education and given an overtly pedagogical and didactic role. Much of INAH's work involved research projects relating to indigenous issues and locations, including the construction of concepts of pre-Hispanic Mexico, which was undertaken through rhetoric and also tangibly with stone in the form of archeological sites and artifacts.

Instrumental in indigenous representation was el Instituto Nacional Indigenista (INI)—the National Indigenist Institute—which was created in 1948, with a base in Mexico City and with regional centers in diverse areas of the country. INI performed a crucial role in shaping formulations of, and relationships with and toward indigenous peoples, involving many of the contradictions and dichotomies inherent in discourse, ideology, and politics. These contradictions included a confused rhetoric that pronounced the desire to preserve, protect, and rescue practices (and in so doing, to reify and separate them out), yet at the same time professed the intention of integration, assimilation, and modernization, thus improving the lives of the indigenous peoples (as well as the economy of the country as a whole). Through INI and SEP, cultural policies were formulated and actioned in such as way that enabled indigenous peoples to access financial resources and to develop their sense of ethnic cultural practices, while also constructing a public image and concept of both indigenousness and folklore. A major element of INI's agenda was the involvement of anthropologists and folklorists in producing publications and recordings, all of whom adopted and projected ideological positions. In relation to music and dance practices, INI performed a complicated role, encompassing the dichotomy of supporting local activities of indigenous communities even as the practices were being appropriated and transformed into national public spectacle and cultural patrimony. Until its closure in 2003, INI funded many projects in the Lake Pátzcuaro region, particularly festivals and events involving *The Old Men* and *Night of the Dead*.

By way of an illustration, a widely disseminated INI publication of 1951, entitled *Cantos indígenas de México* (Indigenous songs of Mexico) (Michel 1951), delineated a clear ideological position regarding ethnicity, indigenous peoples, and music and dance. Comprising a selection of transcribed songs from various peoples throughout Mexico, including P'urhépecha, the book opened with an introductory text, authored by INI official Alfonso Pruneda, which created a framework for the whole collection. The text incorporated notions of nationality, authentic Mexicanness, folklore, indigenous culture, indigenous music and dance, and mestizaje. As with other writing concerning indigenous music and dance, a sense of romantic valorization infused the piece, alongside notions of primitive, emotional, and simple peoples. Indigenous culture was essentialized through the use of the singular "culture" to represent the diverse peoples and practices of Mexico, whose song lyrics were characterized as being "full of emotion and, not on rare occasions, also philosophy" (Pruneda 1951:7). Music and dance were given the special role of transmitter of the indigenous essence, thus "we can savor the emotion of indigenous music which, despite the primitive forms of expression, reveals the sentiments of those who lived a long time ago and which, through a special immortality, survive through the songs and dances, out of which shines the indigenous sensibility" (ibid.).

Indigenous peoples were portrayed as Mexican national cultural heritage and classified as "our indigenous." There was a clear delineation of us and them, such that "their music" provides the Mexican nation with "our folklore" as embodied in "our ancestors." The idea of possession, ownership, and paternity in reference to indigenous peoples and practices permeated much of the text, and indeed, Michel's whole collection was presented as a way of understanding "OUR MEXICO" (upper case in original). Crucially, Pruneda propounds notions of authentic Mexicanness and nationality as formed from "the fruit of the union between two groups of humans, the Spanish and the indigenous," resulting in mestizaje. Therefore, although the indigenous peoples and practices were distinguishable, valuable, and useful for providing the roots and heart of Mexicanness, the transformation toward a mestizo ethnicity was the objective. However, one purported function of the publication was to preserve indigenous customs "from disappearing through foreign influences" (Pruneda 1951:8), engaging with an overtly indigenista position of valuing indigenous practices for the good of the nation. Pruneda concluded the piece with a romantic valorization of indigenous peoples, summarizing "our folklore" as "the value of the indigenous culture, the beauty of the music, the tenderness of their traditions, the expression of their dances and fiestas and the other innumerable footprints of the soul of our ancestors, whose descendants are our contemporaries which is our good fortune" (ibid.).

As state-sanctioned pronouncements published by INI, the very institute whose primary role was to deal with indigenous issues, these concepts in Michel's book are vital in understanding how P'urhépecha dance, music, and ritual practices were framed, received, and interpreted. In general terms, state policies regarding indigenismo, indigenous peoples, assimilation, and folklore were formulated and disseminated through the work of numerous state institutions, creating the context within which the *Dance of the Old Men* and *Night of the Dead* could be further deployed by the state within nationalist and tourist agendas.

Gazing on Lake Pátzcuaro

In the Lake Pátzcuaro region large-scale, centralized official government research and educational projects were maintained. The objective of such projects was the development and integration of the local people into national society through intervention. The tone of much of the documentation and the titles of projects refer to "developing" the indigenous communities so that they could progress.[8] "The Tarascan Project," begun in 1936 (and interrupted during World War II), was continued in 1945 under the joint auspices of the Institute of Social Anthropology at the Smithsonian Institute of Washington, D.C. in the United States, and the National School of Anthropology in Mexico (Reyes Rocha 1991:33). The project included a series of ethnological, economic, and historical studies in the Lake

Pátzcuaro region. One of the team, U.S. anthropologist George M. Foster, who carried out fieldwork in the Lake Pátzcuaro region between 1944 and 1946, referred to both *The Old Men* and *Night of the Dead* in his seminal 1948 publication on Tzintzuntzan. As I noted previously, in reference to *Night of the Dead* on Janitzio, Foster observed that this ceremony "has become one of the most famous spectacles of Mexican indigenous life…Great crowds of tourists have come, and the Tarascan women show no hesitancy in talking with them" (1948:220–21).[9]

Of great significance for the dissemination of *The Old Men* and *Night of the Dead*, and for the development of the Lake Pátzcuaro region as a focus of study, was the founding, in 1951, of el Centro Regional de Educación Fundamental para la América Latina (CREFAL)—the Regional Center for Basic Education in Latin America (Medina 1986). Located in the home of former president Lázaro Cárdenas on the edge of Lake Pátzcuaro, this influential continent-wide educational institute attracted governmental representatives, pedagogues, and students from many Latin American countries, all of whom converged on the Lake Pátzcuaro area to study and carry out research. As a result the Lake Pátzcuaro region became a "zone of experimentation," incorporating many development programs, including an initiative in Jarácuaro to "better the school" (Vargas Tentori 1952:140) and ethnographic studies of the islands (Ballesteros 1958). There were also collaborations between the Cultural Missions, CREFAL, and INI involving pedagogical and indigenista transformation programs (Zantwijk 1974). Inherent in all the research and development activities and programs was an objectification of the peoples, practices, and locations of Lake Pátzcuaro. A spotlight was constantly on them as the subjects and objects of ethnological, pedagogical, sociological, and archeological research. Crucially, the research and development projects in the Lake Pátzcuaro area coincided and merged with the increased tourist activities in the region and with nationalist folkloric promotion.

Tourist activity in the Lake Pátzcuaro region continued to increase substantially, particularly as there was a surge nationally in tourist numbers from 1940 onward, due to the low price of Mexican currency and the "virtual closure of European countries" during the years of World War II (Caso 1942:25). In 1941, the government undertook a large-scale campaign to market Mexico to U.S. tourists, and subsequently, under the aegis of President Alemán (1946–1952), the tourist policy was further consolidated. In 1948 the National Tourism Commission was set up followed by the creation of the Secretariat of Tourism. Cultural and ethnic tourism were identified as particularly lucrative and efficacious resources, and a representation of Mexico created from the past continued to be promoted through official institutions, even though President Alemán attempted to refashion the image to a more modern, metropolitan, and businesslike one. Contemporary advertisements presented impressions of a romantic, mystical, and traditional Mexico, with "colorful" folkloric practices. During this time the draw of the folkloric was an essential aspect that was unabashedly utilized in advertising (Zolov 2001). Imaging Mexico for mid-century tourists engaged sets of binary concepts and images: indigenous, premodern, and backwardness with modern; the past with the present; and the folkloric and rural with the cosmopolitan. From the end of the 1950s onward, after the formation of the Ballet Folklórico company in Mexico City, dance was used in advertising campaigns, with images of the dance ensemble in colorful costumes featured prominently in promotional material. In this era, there was an important shift in the U.S. reception of Mexican nationalism that regarded Mexico as no longer barbaric but instead relied upon a more romanticized and nostalgic view (Delpar 1992).

During the 1950s and 1960s, by means of government initiatives, Acapulco grew from a small town into a major international resort, and Cancún was selected to become the ultimate in government-formed tourist locations. As I discussed in previous chapters, the Lake Pátzcuaro region had already been singled out for governmental attention back in the postrevolutionary era, marked through the constructing of the huge statue of Morelos in the center of the diminutive island of Janitzio. From the initial promotion of Lake Pátzcuaro and Janitzio as tourist attractions in the 1930s, the subsequent decades saw the island of Janitzio develop into an international tourist destination, principally through the actions of official governmental organizations and media (including INI and SEP), often in collaboration with local P'urhépecha initiatives. Images of Lake Pátzcuaro, Janitzio, *Night of the Dead*, *The Old Men*, and local P'urhépecha people undertaking quotidian activities were reproduced and circulated through major films and publications. In particular, men fishing with butterfly nets on Lake Pátzcuaro formed an important recurring image. As an example, in 1943 advertisements for the English-language magazine *Mexican Life*, produced for U.S. tourists, deployed black-and-white line drawings of fishermen in their canoes on Lake Pátzcuaro, specified with the words "Lake Pátzcuaro," juxtaposed with illustrations of: the snow-capped volcano Popocatéptl; the pyramid of Chichén Itzá in the Yucatán peninsula; and the Palace of Fine Arts in Mexico City. In an overt exhortation to U.S. tourists to buy a subscription to the magazine, the advertisement declared "Visitors in Mexico, carry back with you the most memorable souvenir of your Mexican Visit. Subscribe to *Mexican Life*, Mexico's Monthly Review in English" (1943, Vol. 19).

A central element of the attraction of Janitzio involved *Night of the Dead*, which was endorsed as a fundamental aspect of the character of the island and its inhabitants. In conjunction with this, *The Old Men* was promoted as an authentic local dance. Processes of site sacralization continued to reify Janitzio, *Night of the Dead*, and the *Dance of the Old Men*, particularly through visual imagery in guide books. Numerous marketing and promotional strategies and activities continued to perform roles in presenting Janitzio to national and increasingly international audiences, through leaflets, songs, films, magazines, newspapers, journal articles, and photojournalism, all of which were instrumental in developing a network of concepts and attributes associated with Janitzio, *Night of the Dead*, *The Old Men*, Lake Pátzcuaro, and the P'urhépecha people of the region. The perceived uniqueness and backwardness of the traditional way of life was an attraction in ethnographic and touristic terms, even as it was regarded as an obstacle in nationalist modernization terms. In the 1940s, two films—*The Three Caballeros* and *Maclovia*—and a book—*A Treasury of Mexican Folkways*—were particularly influential in circulating and disseminating images of the Lake Pátzcuaro region and P'urhépecha peoples to national and international audiences.

Donald Duck and Disney Adventures in Lake Pátzcuaro

The Disney film *The Three Caballeros* was released in 1944 and included explicit representations of the Lake Pátzcuaro region, depicting images of the island of Janitzio, men fishing with butterfly nets, and supposedly Janitzio islanders dancing in their village.[10] The film was produced by the Disney Corporation at the behest of the U.S. Department of State, and the motivation for making the film came within the context of World War II, which was becoming an increasingly global war. South America was drawn into the theater-of-war through a Nazi presence in Paraguay and through U.S. military links with Brazil. As unlikely as it may seem with a film staring an animated duck, *The Three Caballeros* was actually conceived primarily as a teaching tool, for an English-speaking U.S. audience, aimed at familiarizing military forces and the general public with aspects of the land, life, and peoples of South America and Mexico.

The film uses a deliberate touristic and journeying theme, with many "bird's eye views." The premise of the movie is that Donald Duck is given the gift of visiting various Latin American countries, including Mexico, Brazil, and Argentina. Donald takes a "fantastic journey through these colorful lands with his friends, Joe Carioca and Panchito...With lighthearted dance and lively music, it's a celebration the whole family will enjoy!" (*The Three Caballeros* DVD cover: 2008). Viewers are exhorted to "say 'Adios!' to the U.S. to explore the heart and soul of Latin America" (ibid.). In these brief phrases, ideas of Mexicans as exotic Others, and Mexico as a land in which music and dance are the heart and soul of life frame the reception. Throughout the film, cartoon animation and live sequences are blended together, with underscoring of music and explicitly musical "numbers" (both diegetic and non-diegetic) that serve to embed visual images of Mexico in sonic environments.

Pátzcuaro is one of four specific locations in Mexico chosen for depiction. The other three are: the seaside resort of Acapulco (where a beach full of young bathing-suit-clad women play ball with one of the animated cartoon characters); the seaport of Veracruz (famous for jarocho music, represented with live footage of a dance troupe performing in an obviously staged setting); and Mexico City (depicting the central plaza or Zócalo, and Xochimilco, the "floating gardens" to the south of Mexico City). The section focusing on Pátzcuaro is preceded by a series of vivid-colored animated drawings of romanticized scenes of Mexico, accompanied by a rendition in English of the song "México," in the crooning-style typical of the period. The penultimate image of the sequence depicts men in canoes fishing with butterfly nets, with the iconic conical form of the island of Janitzio silhouetted in the background.

In the Pátzcuaro section, three modes are intermingled: cartoon animation, live footage of places and people as ethnographic subjects, and live footage of a folkloric ensemble performing music and dance.[11] The third element is blended and edited with the "real" material to create a continuation of subjectivity, generating a framing of the scene as "real" and not "staged by actors" for the film, engaging a blurring of boundaries between real people and enactors, which leads to a reading of authenticity. The sequence starts with the animated figures of Donald and his two companions climbing aboard the colorful "magic sarape (poncho)" and flying away from Mexico City, over mountains, towns, and villages, until they reach Lake Pátzcuaro, identified simply as "Pátzcuaro" in the voice-over narration. Just prior to the views of Lake Pátzcuaro, 1940s black cars are depicted traveling along country roads, surrounded by green fields and wooded hills, endorsing and promoting Mexico as eminently suitable for road trips for U.S. visitors.

A remarkable succession of aerial shots captures Lake Pátzcuaro, the islands in the lake, the surrounding hills, a close-up of the statue of Morelos on Janitzio, and adobe houses perched on the sides of the island with their red-tiled roofs. In the foreground, fishermen paddle across the lake in their wooden canoes, clothed in straw hats and linen shirts, using butterfly nets. The live shots are overlaid with images of the animated characters on their magic flying sarape. As the ethnographic shot of the fishermen fills the whole screen, so then it is shrunk to the center of the image and enclosed within a cartoon animation of a photograph album standing upright on a shelf, reminding viewers that this is just a travelogue to fantastic lands. The three cartoon characters view the "photograph" in the album. The moving photograph depicts the live and moving fishermen paddling across the lake, in what might be described as a living diorama. For film viewers this shot creates a double-gaze through the framing of the photo in the album, which is inside the frame of the film. Then once again the narrative moves toward an ethnographic portrayal of purportedly traditional life on the island of Janitzio, in a close-up of a scene outside a house, which is actually a set inside a studio. The "traditional scene" includes: a cut-off wooden canoe with a fisherman seated inside (complete with paddle); the patio of a house with a red-tiled roof; a woman sitting on the ground cooking tortillas on a *comal* (a large pottery plate) over an open fire; and a butterfly fishing net leaning against an adobe wall. In this setting an ensemble of musicians (two violinists and guitarist) accompanies a group of men and women dressed in "typical" P'urhépecha and even pan-indigenous clothes (of linen shirt and trousers with poncho for men, and long skirt, apron, embroidered blouse, and blue-striped rebozo for the women) who are dancing. The whole context presents an impression that this takes place at the end of a normal working day, as villagers gather round to dance and make music together. (In actuality, communal dancing on Janitzio, and other Lake Pátzcuaro villages, only took place within the context of a fiesta, and the dance depicted was not part of a P'urhépecha repertoire, nor was it danced on Janitzio or any other Lake Pátzcuaro islands or villages.)

The scene closes with a shot of a map of Mexico, on which just a few locations in the whole country have been specified. A blue shape representing Lake Pátzcuaro is clearly marked. However, it is identified not in English but Spanish: "lago de Pátzcuaro." The only other identified places in the region are "Pátzcuaro" and "Morelia." In juxtaposition with the scenes of Acapulco and Mexico City, the Pátzcuaro section demarcates the place and peoples as traditional, folkloric, in the past, and indigenous, where music and dance are part of everyday life. Despite the fictionalization, the ethnographic framing and footage of genuine locations creates a seal of authenticity on the setting, displaying a romanticization and quaintness of Lake Pátzcuaro island life and creating a gaze on the real. When screened in the 1940s these images contributed to the dissemination and circulation of the network of associations at the heart of this study: Lake Pátzcuaro, Janitzio, local indigenous peoples, music and dance, and fishing with butterfly nets.

Maclovia and *A Treasury of Mexican Folkways*

From the 1930s onward Mexican cinema played an important role in disseminating images and concepts of rurality and indigeneity to both national and international audiences. Following the highly localized images of Lake Pátzcuaro and P'urhépecha peoples presented in the film *Janitzio* (1935), similar scenes were disseminated to a wider audience with *Maclovia* (1948), which made Janitzio an international spectacle (García Canclini 1985:58–59). In *Maclovia* romantic images of Lake Pátzcuaro depicted a traditional and indigenous way of life, which included fishing and, most importantly, the ceremony of *Night of the Dead*. Set on the island of Janitzio, the film tells the story of two young lovers, the beautiful Maclovia, played by top Mexican actress María Félix, and the poverty-stricken José María, who educates himself in order to earn enough money to buy his own fishing boat, which, he hopes, will win Maclovia's father's consent for marriage. An indigenous and traditional way of life is thoroughly embedded in the narrative, presented as a life in which outsiders are disdained and regarded with suspicion. In the final climax, the dramatic events take place during the *Night of the Dead*, thus constructing the intrinsic correlation between Janitzio and *Night of the Dead*, and propagating the network of images and concepts fundamental to both the touristic attraction and to the folkloric, nationalist imaging of lo mexicano.[12]

Whereas *The Three Caballeros* and *Maclovia* circulated moving photographic images, the populist book *A Treasury of Mexican Folkways* used still photography to disseminate visual representations of folkloric Mexico. As a result of the success of the bilingual magazine *Mexican Folkways*, editor Frances Toor produced *A Treasury of Mexican Folkways* in 1947 to provide an overview of "The Customs, Myths, Folklore, Traditions, Beliefs, Fiestas, Dances and Songs of the Mexican People" in the English language, aimed specifically at a U.S. readership.[13] With the postwar tourist boom, this publication presented enticing images of rural and indigenous Mexico that would appeal to those wishing to escape a modern, capitalist country in search of a traditional and indigenous past. A photo of *The Old Men* of Lake Pátzcuaro and of *Night of the Dead* on Janitzio were placed together on the same page, generating an associative reading of these two practices as indigenous and authentic P'urhépecha ritual activities (figure 1.14).[14] This publication contributed to framing and affirming the role and significance of *The Old Men* and *Night of the Dead* as important attractions of Michoacán and Lake Pátzcuaro. Placing these photographic images within the context of a selection of national practices and artifacts further constructed the notion of "most representative" within the nation of Mexico.

Tellingly, Toor's description of *Night of the Dead* on Janitzio contained a revealing reference to the practice and use of photography, perpetuating and confirming the activity of photographing the peoples and practices of Janitzio and Lake Pátzcuaro. Toor observed that "before dawn so many candles are lit that it is possible to take pictures" (1947:244). "Taking pictures" was therefore presented as a viable and acceptable activity for visitors to the ceremony and the cemetery. Through the action of capturing the P'urhépecha women in photographic images, notions of cultural heritage, patrimony of the state, and public tourist attraction were further validated as acceptable and intrinsic elements of the occasion as a tourist spectacle, and moved on from earlier experiences when tourists with cameras were at risk of being thrown into the lake. In her depiction of the dance of "the little old men" Toor placed it within a P'urhépecha framework, stating that it was danced in many villages "on secular occasions but chiefly during religious fiestas" (1947:356–57). Through this account Toor presented *The Old Men* as a form of religious ritual, even though the published photograph portrayed a political and state organized enactment. She also made an unambiguous link with pre-Hispanic origins by including the description of sixteenth-century priest Father Durán (cited at the opening of Chapter 1). As a contextualizing factor, it is also valuable to note Toor's formulation of ethnic identity: "It has been customary to speak of the population living in a folkloric way as 'Indian,' but that is no longer possible because many of the so-called Indians have adopted modern ways of living. Since there are no exclusive terms with which to designate folkloric peoples, I am using racial names, 'native' and 'folk,' to distinguish them from the modernized ones, to whom I refer as 'mestizo,' 'ladino,' or 'citified'" (1947: viii). The correlation between premodern, folk, and native (with an implication of "rural") is striking when placed in opposition to modernized, mestizo, and urban, and fitted entirely with placing the peoples and practices of Lake Pátzcuaro "in the past."

Transitory Tourism and Dancing in Hotels

Guided and enticed by photographic images and narrative descriptions in films, books, tourist guides and magazines, both Mexican middle-class tourists and foreign visitors, particularly from the United States, were attracted to the Lake Pátzcuaro region by the lure of authentic indigenous practices and lifestyles. For Mexican sightseers, the visit to Janitzio and Pátzcuaro enabled confirmation of their sense of a pre-Hispanic and rural element of their own modernizing Mexicanness. For most middle-class urban Mexicans, rural lifestyles were alien and "different" to their own. A visit to Lake Pátzcuaro to see the P'urhépecha peoples and their way of life therefore fitted the touristic notion of difference, even if the Mexican visitors lived as close to the area as Morelia. Lake Pátzcuaro also catered for the two "types" of U.S. tourists who were attracted to Mexico: official tourists who sought after the folkloric; and the beatniks and hippies ("unofficial tourism") (Zolov 2001). In both mainstream and hippy tourism, notions of authenticity and indigenousness were central to the success of the travel experiences, although in differing ways. From the late 1950s mainstream U.S. tourists visiting Mexico City were able to have certain expectations satisfied by attending performances of the Ballet Folklórico in the Palace of Fine Arts, where they could view "Mexico" in a comfortable and dioramic manner, through representational staged events that placed rural, indigenous, and traditional Mexico in a theater, purportedly capturing the essential qualities of the nation. Meanwhile, U.S. hippie travelers who sought a more "authentic" experience were able to go in search of the "real Mexico" in the villages and rural areas.

For both groups of U.S. tourists, a visit to Lake Pátzcuaro and Janitzio fulfilled their requirements. For hippies, the island setting was sufficiently authentic and included all the requisite elements of a real indigenous and rural lifestyle, with no perceptible elements of rehearsal, staging, and reenactment; and for mainstream travelers, the defined and framed experience of a hotel in Pátzcuaro and a short launch ride to Janitzio enabled this attraction to be adequately safe and bounded. Visiting the island of Janitzio combined experiences of culture and nature, through a journey across water in a motor launch to a small island in a lake where indigenous inhabitants went about their normal business of everyday life. On the island sightseers ate local fish and handmade tortillas in one of the small restaurants; perused the souvenir stalls; and walked to the top of the island to view the towering statue of Morelos. For those with sufficient energy, climbing up inside the statue via a winding staircase to emerge out of Morelos's wrist topped the experience, enabling a bird's eye view of the island, lake, and surrounding hills. From this vantage point, visitors could be assured of their sense of having journeyed to another place and even time. For those who visited Janitzio for *Night of the Dead*, both groups of tourists were similarly effectively catered for. The experience fulfilled the hippie agenda, with the visceral nature of the celebration, and the perceived mysticism of an island environment filled with the aromas of flowers and breads, and lit by the gentle glow of candles. For more mainstream tourists the event was carefully managed and later festivalized to enable an experience of controlled exoticism.

As tourism in the Lake Pátzcuaro area increased, opportunities to provide entertainment for the visitors grew, and hotels and restaurants became recognized venues for performances of *The Old Men*. Performances in hotels framed and confirmed *The Old Men* as an unambiguous spectacle for tourist entertainment, further validating this dance as *the* most representative of the region. The most prominent hotel in Pátzcuaro was, and remains, La Posada de Don Vasco, located on a tree-lined street that runs between the town of Pátzcuaro and the dockside where motor launches transport locals and tourists to Janitzio.[15] La Posada de Don Vasco mostly hosted transitory visitors who included Pátzcuaro and Janitzio on their itinerary of important attractions on their travels through Mexico. In contrast to the type of tourism in resorts such as Acapulco and Cancún, these tourists stayed for one or two nights to get a flavor of the region, and their experience, therefore, consisted of a "taste" of what was selected and promoted as most representative. For U.S. tourists, journeys to Mexico generally entailed very long road trips, involving huge distances by car, crossing the Mexico-U.S. border, and then traveling from the north of Mexico hundreds of miles on newly made-up roads, passing through many "destinations" and "attractions" on their route[16] (14 ◉).

In the setting of the hotel La Posada de Don Vasco, one man from Jarácuaro, Gervasio López, established performances of *The Old Men* with his family ensemble of four dancers and three musicians. As I discuss presently, this one islander from Jarácuaro became prominent and specifically associated with *The Old Men* from this time onwards. In the hotel setting of La Posada de Don Vasco, performances of *The Old Men* took place inside the restaurant area, where tourists could eat their meal after a visit to Janitzio and take in a performance of authentic indigenous music and dance. Once the hotel became a significant venue for performances of *The Old Men*, ensembles from Jarácuaro continued to dance there on a twice-weekly basis right through to the twenty-first century. In the 1980s, postcards depicting *The Old Men* performed by López and his ensemble in the grounds of La Posada de Don Vasco were produced. In the twenty-first century, these same postcards are still being sold (figure 1.2) (08 ◉).

With the transformation of *The Old Men* from local activity to tourist spectacle, the notion of exchange value became an integral element of the context. Musicians and dancers were paid for their performances, undertaking to perform on a regular basis at nominated times. From the perspective of López and his family, regular performances in the hotel enabled them to earn a little extra money, in addition to their income from hat-making. Similarly, items of costume were transformed into objects for sale. The advent of teachers at the institute of CREFAL at the beginning of the 1950s had boosted the market for the sale of Old Man masks, with these artifacts becoming a commodity as the teachers regarded the masks as "art." Prior to this, Old Man masks were mostly only sold to those participating in the dance. For the mask-maker in the Lake Pátzcuaro village of Tócuaro there was a notable change as the masks became objects with an exchange value within a much wider market (García Canclini 1985:21).

After the initial appropriation and public display of *The Old Men* in the post-revolutionary years, local ensembles in the Lake Pátzcuaro region continued to develop their performances of the dance. Groups from the villages of Santa Fe and Cucuchucho and the islands of Jarácuaro and Urandén participated in local competitions and festivals, and performed for private local fiestas and for the burgeoning tourist market in hotels in Pátzcuaro. On the island of Jarácuaro transmission through families continued to take place in a musical environment where ensembles formed and were disbanded as members came and went, and as opportunities for performance presented themselves. Many villagers played instrumental music for fiestas and for their own entertainment, also serenading sweethearts with *pirekuas* (songs in the P'urhépecha language). In this context Gervasio López made his mark as a musician and promoter of *The Old Men*. As a child López was taught by the musicians Nicolás Bartolo Juárez and Aurelio Calderón, playing violin in the musical ensemble of a *mariochada* (a form of mariachi ensemble) and with the *Orquesta Juárez*, the chamber ensemble of the Bartolo Juárez family. López danced *The Old Men* for local events, including visits of the state governor, Lázaro Cárdenas, to the island of Jarácuaro. By the 1950s López directed his own ensemble of *The Old Men* and was the first to undertake enactments of the dance in a hotel context in Pátzcuaro, initiating the trajectory that continues to this day. Significantly, López's role in relation to *The Old Men* gradually developed as he became the state-sanctioned "representative" of this dance. In the same way that the initial appropriation and transformation of *The Old Men* involved government-sponsored actions incorporating one Jarácuaro islander, namely Nicolás Bartolo Juárez, so from the 1950s onward, this trajectory was again pursued through Gervasio López. As I discuss further presently, López was increasingly given the role of national icon as the authentic and principal exponent of *The Old Men*. Curiously, through López *The Old Men* was assigned a level of personalization that was often at odds with the concept of anonymous folklore, encapsulating the ambivalence and contradictions inherent in characterizing folklore with anonymity and communality of creativity, while simultaneously utilizing a nameable individual to signify the authenticity of the practice.

As López and others villagers developed their ensembles on Jarácuaro, on the nearby island village of Urandén, two families (Gabriel and Camilo) also initiated groups of Old Men dancers, particularly influenced by Bartolo Juárez. The two families continue to vie for "ownership" of the dance, each setting out a narrative for their own processes of instigation, which indicates how the aura around this dance is sufficiently noteworthy to make it important for the families to stake a claim for tenure. According to the Camilo family, *The Old Men* was started on the island in 1935, after Dimas Camilo borrowed masks from Bartolo Juárez. According to Evaristo Gabriel Cortés, *The Old Men* on Urandén was initiated in 1948 by Evaristo's father, Rufino. It was performed in Pátzcuaro for the fiesta of 8 December and on Urandén for *Noche Buena* (Christmas Eve). Both families continue to perform into the twenty-first century in events in the Pátzcuaro region and in Mexico City (figures 1.10, 10.1, and cover) (25, 31–34 ◐).

During the 1940s and 1950s local contests, organized by SEP and the Cultural Missions, provided a context in which the Lake Pátzcuaro ensembles danced, with groups from Urandén, Jarácuaro, Cucuchucho, and Santa Fe participating. Increasingly, ensembles from Jarácuaro also enacted a version of *The Old Men* in local fiestas, most notably for 22 January in their home village and in the mestizo highland town of Carácuaro, for a celebration in honor of Christ of Carácuaro (28–30 ◐). For both events López and others directed large numbers of dancers, mostly boys rather than men, sometimes accompanying them with just the jarana, and at other times forming a trio of violin, vihuela, and bass. In a very different context, in the late 1950s, the Gabriel family from Urandén deployed *The Old Men* as form of political demonstration. As the little island of Urandén did not have electricity, the islanders decided to take a petition to the governor of Michoacán. A deputation of islanders made their way to the capital city of Morelia, and as they handed in their request, they also performed *The Old Men* as a means of drawing attention to their uniqueness.

As villagers performed *The Old Men* in local contests and fiestas, overtly regionalist and nationalist events continued to take place in the Lake Pátzcuaro region, deploying *The Old Men* as an obvious symbol of local tradition, further establishing it as an iconic and representative dance within a national and international framework. Three events at, and connected with, the continent-wide pedagogical institute CREFAL serve to illustrate such uses. In 1951, *The Old Men* was performed at the inauguration ceremony of CREFAL.[17] Political and pedagogical representatives from all Latin American countries were present, as were top-level Mexican politicians and governmental representatives, including former President Cárdenas. A wooden platform was erected in the grounds of the CREFAL campus, on which music and dances were performed for the official opening. Villagers from Cucuchucho performed *The Old Men*, accompanied by a single musician, Antonio Pablo. The event also included the *Dance of the Moors* and *Las Canacuas*, in which P'urhépecha women presented gifts to Cárdenas, perpetuating the "suite" of P'urhépecha rituals and dances established in the 1920s.

With a less global audience, in 1954 *The Old Men* was performed at another event held at CREFAL in celebration of the 28th anniversary of the formation of municipalities of Michoacán. Again, Lázaro Cárdenas attended the proceedings, along with serving governmental and institutional officials. However, on this occasion the dancers were not inhabitants from the Lake Pátzcuaro communities but children and young adults from across the whole state, with each municipality presenting a group of Old Men dancers. In this instance, *The Old Men* was transformed into a folkloric and civic activity, performed by non-P'urhépecha Mexican citizens in a state-organized event, in an endeavor that subsequently became a frequent facet of school and civic occasions.

Also in 1954, a Festival of Song and Dance (*Festival de Canto y Danza*) took place in May, in the central plaza in Pátzcuaro, organized to celebrate the 3rd Anniversary of CREFAL. The event was promoted in the newspaper *Heraldo Michoacano* by the state tourist office (Dirección Estatal de Turismo). The advertisment for one part of the whole occasion, the Fiesta of Song and Dance (*Fiesta de la Canción y de la Danza*), clearly demonstrates the differentiation of participants and practices.

The participants are:
Distinguished performers from the Mexican Institute of Dance of the National Institute of Fine Arts who will present three 'ballets' that were part of the final season of Modern Dance in the Capital of the Republic;

Los Niños Cantores (the Boy Singers) of Morelia, under the directorship of the professor Romano Picutti, who will perform works by Mexican composers;

Groups of dancers (*Las cuadrillas de danzantes*) from the communities of San Pedro Pareo and Cucuchucho, who will dance, respectively, *Los Matlachines*' (sic) and *Los Viejitos*;

The State Band.
  (*Festival de Canto y Danza* 1954)

An article in the same newspaper two days later captured key elements of the occasion, noting the presence of the top politicians (including Governor of Michoacán, Dámaso Cárdenas) and using poetic and florid language to describe qualities of the event:

> Thousands of people of all social conditions came to admire...the most beautiful, regal and vibrant of the art, music and dance of the Tarascan peoples (*los pueblos tarascos*)....From an early hour the great the plaza of San Francisco served as an authentic open air theater (*teatro al aire libre*)...the dancers displayed rhythms and emotions whose essence and artistic virtues were strongly applauded by the people (*el pueblo*).
>
> (*Magno Festival en el CREFAL* 1954)

Tarascan Rituals: Real Life and Reenactment

In 1961 another film, entitled *Rituales Tarascos* (Tarascan Rituals), was screened in cinemas throughout Mexico, disseminating images and ideas about Lake Pátzcuaro, *Night of the Dead*, *The Old Men*, and P'urhépecha peoples. Whereas the films *Janitzio* and *Maclovia* were purportedly narrative, fictional productions, *Rituales Tarascos* followed more in the vein of the "Pátzcuaro" sequence of *The Three Caballeros*, in that the content regarding the activities of the inhabitants of Lake Pátzcuaro was presented as ethnographic reality,[18] yet the production was imbued with a blurring of real life and dramatization, mixing fictional events with enacted presentations. *Rituales Tarascos* was created locally for a wide audience in both Mexico and Latin America and was produced by the cinematic news company Noticiario Mexicano in collaboration with CREFAL. This combination of a news company and a state pedagogical institution indicates the framing of this film as ethnographic documentary, in which the lives and rituals of indigenous P'urhépecha islanders were presented as factual. The film was intended for the general public who attended cinemas throughout the country, and the performed "message" was that of an active and participatory community of P'urhépecha islanders, continuing to undertake their traditional celebrations (Rodríguez Yerena: personal communication).

However, the material of the film also concerned visitors and tourism, documenting the presence of outsiders on the island of Janitzio for *Night of the Dead*, and showing obviously staged, theatricalized, and dramatized enactments taking place on the basketball court. Although not billed as such, this staged event for outsiders was the first of the Festivals of Music and Dance that have been an essential element of *Night of the Dead* on Janitzio since the 1960s. Middle-class, urban audience members were invited to attend this special occasion. As clearly visible in the film, the majority of the audience were attired in 1960s-style urban clothing (men in city suits and ladies in dresses and high-heeled shoes) in contrast to the clothes of the P'urhépecha islanders. Significantly, the live event shown in the film was organized by Janitzio islanders in cooperation with the Council of Pátzcuaro, presenting a model that has been replicated ever since.

With a program of dramatic scenes, dances, and music, the live event followed a format combining cuadros costumbristas (theatricalized scenes of customs), staged representations of pre-Hispanic narratives and rituals, and the dance contests and festivals organized by the Cultural Missions and schools. The basketball court served as the stage area, with a tiered wooden structure for seating the audience. Very large *chinchorro* fishing nets were hung up around the space as scenery and a backdrop. The main element of the staged event was a depiction of the pre-Hispanic origin of the festival in honor of the dead, through the dramatization of a legend acted by Janitzio islanders. Reenactments of the ceremony for *Night of the Dead* in the cemetery were also staged, in conjunction with a performance of *The Old Men* by Jarácuaro villagers. The film captured the distinctive sound of the dance, with the precise rhythmic footwork accompanied by a single jarana.

Two sets of representations and frames were present: shots of the Lake Pátzcuaro region and shots of the staged event on the basketball court. These distinct elements were edited in such a way that they seemed to merge into one another. Indecidability of interpretation imbues the film, merging the boundaries between live display, real life, and make believe, bringing into play questions concerning the efficacy of bodies as authentic. For cinema audiences *Rituales Tarascos* created a collective gaze that encapsulated an image of an authentic and indigenous Mexico, in which both *Night of the Dead* and the *Dance of the Old Men* were central to the imaging of Mexicanness. Placing these two activities within the same interpretive and representative frame perpetuated the association of one with the other. The documentary context, depicting P'urhépecha people carrying out everyday and ritual activities, alongside dances, music, and dramatizations, engendered notions of indigenous people and practices as an attraction for consumption and utilization in both nationalistic and touristic contexts.

Particularly poignant in terms of exhibiting everyday life was the use of the large chinchorro fishing nets as scenery for the spectated event. Hanging up nets as scenographic objects effected the transformation of the utilitarian objects that were vital to the lives of the islanders into decorative artifacts for visitor and tourist consumption, clearly evidencing processes of refunctionalization, commodification, and commoditization. As fishing was the central activity of the region for centuries, both for personal consumption and trade, so fishing nets had been the essential piece of equipment for sustaining lives. Hanging up fishing nets was a key element of the practice of fishing, both for drying and mending purposes. In the postrevolutionary period, this very activity had been captured photographically by Carlos González (1928b) and Frederick Starr (1928:5), and disseminated through *Mexican Folkways*. The photos depicted Janitzio fishermen standing by their drying nets, undertaking an everyday work act.[19] In a private ritual, once a year on Janitzio nets were also hung up in a symbolic rather than utilitarian act, as they were carried through the island and displayed around the church for the celebration of Corpus Christi, a ceremony of thanksgiving for the continued source of their livelihood. In contrast, the act of hanging the nets as symbolic and performative objects to decorate the area of staged spectacle for non-Janitzio spectators radically altered the function of the object. This element of presenting everyday work objects and activities within a symbolic tourist frame became increasingly important with the escalating tourist numbers visiting Janitzio.

Entertaining the Crowds: the Night of the Dead Festival of Music and Dance

By 1964 visitor numbers for *Night of the Dead* on Janitzio had increased to such an extent that an official Festival of Music and Dance was instigated to provide entertainment for the sightseers. The cemetery on Janitzio was tiny and the ceremony of *Night of the Dead* centered upon sitting around the graveside of deceased loved ones throughout the night until dawn broke. Not only was it impossible for the mass of visitors to observe this, but also the hours of such "inactivity" were not sufficient to keep the crowds entertained throughout the cold night. Using the model of the staged event filmed for *Rituales Tarascos*, a Festival of Music and Dance was initiated, which consisted of short music and dance pieces and scenes of local life, usually performed by villagers from the Lake Pátzcuaro region. As previously, tiered seating was erected around the basketball court and the display area was dressed with fishing nets and the distinctive, orange-colored *cempasuchitl* flowers. Stalls were set up selling hot drinks, food, and souvenirs. *Ofrendas* to the dead, decorated with flowers, bread and sugar shapes, were created and placed on display as exhibits for the tourists. As each year went by, these were larger and more elaborate, often utilizing national symbols such as an eagle devouring a snake (García Canclini 1985:58–9).

These Festivals of Music and Dance were complex events in ideological terms. Organized locally by a committee from Janitzio, they were given financial support by governmental bodies such as the Michoacán Tourist Board and INI, ultimately benefiting both the local community and tourist industry businesses in the area. Musicians and dancers were either paid to perform or they competed for prize money. Some dances, such as *la Danza del Pescado* (The Dance of the Fish), were originally performed because the participants "owed" a *manda* (a promise). However, by the 1980s, the idea of performing such dances for a religious obligation had been replaced by the notion of performing for recognition from visitors, and receiving financial remuneration from governmental sources. As seen in *Rituales Tarascos*, *The Old Men* was included as an essential element of the festival from the beginning, whereas other dances were newly created. Janitzio-born musician and teacher Aurelio de la Cruz directed a group of young performers for whom he created new choreography that was purposely aimed at tourists. Under de la Cruz's direction, the group subsequently traveled to various places in Michoacán, Mexico City, and even Spain to perform. P'urhépecha villagers from many communities formed small groups specifically for the festival, creating short staged pieces either based on existing dances, music, and ritual or using local work activities as the movement vocabulary (fishing: *Pescado, Pescador Navegante, Chinchorros, Mariposas*; sowing: *Sembradores*; and transporting pottery: *Huacaleros*) (25 and 40 ⬤). The Festival of Music and Dance on Janitzio therefore encouraged and supported creativity through the composition of new dances and music expressly for the event; however, despite the variety of music and dance presented, *The Old Men* continued to be promoted as *the* most representative dance.

Regional Dances of Mexico: Fixing, Notating, and Publishing

As the uses of *The Old Men* by Lake Pátzcuaro villagers proliferated in tourist and political events, in a national arena the teaching and dissemination of *The Old Men* continued apace, alongside other Mexican Regional Dances in school and pedagogical contexts. By the late 1930s a repertoire or collection of regional dances was already formulated using the model of the costumbrista exhibitions and as displayed in *Danzas Auténticas Mexicanas* in Mexico City. The repertoire included dances framed as indigenous and others which were presented as mestizo and urban. In the vein of the didactic publication by Johnston (1935) discussed in the previous chapter, books and leaflets were produced that included ostensibly factual notation and descriptions in order to teach the dance. Each dance was purportedly appropriated from its ritual and local setting and adapted to be performed by a group of children or adults in folkloric ensembles, with elements of choreography, floor patterns, duration, and proxemics altered to suit festival occasions. All schools and pedagogical institutions directed through SEP were instrumental in organizing festivals and contests for regional dances. Boarding schools were particularly important in the transmission process, with the staging of contests and the production of audio recordings and descriptive documentation (see, for example, Castro Agúndez 1958, Hellmer 1963). Published descriptions had the effect of "fixing" the origins and meanings of dances, and of disseminating a unified and often invented tradition for the purposes of folkloric nationalism. Notions of shared practice, cultural patrimony, ownership for all, and national unity were propagated and embodied in these processes and practices.

In order to illustrate the nature and format of didactic and folkloric publications that circulated in Mexico and abroad during the 1940s and 1950s, here I use four exemplars. Firstly, in 1947 Robert Riveroll produced a striking book in the English language, but published in Mexico, entitled *Mexican Dances*. Details of twelve dances were beautifully documented through exquisite paintings, movement notation, musical transcription, and textual description. For *Los Viejitos* floor patterns, line drawings of bodily positions, detailed descriptions, musical notation, and a color illustration of the costume were given, with textual and choreographic descriptions undertaken by L. Felipe Obregón, the teacher of the Cultural Missions who had documented *The Old Men* in Tzintzuntzan with the ensemble of Nicolás Bartolo Juárez in 1931.

Secondly, *Dances of Mexico*, produced in 1954 in English by Guillermina Dickens, was published in Great Britain rather than Mexico or the United States.[20] The book included three regional dances, one of which was *Los Viejitos*, for which descriptions, choreographic and musical notation and drawings were given. It was intended as a didactic and instructional resource for schools of dance, and is a good illustration of how a repertoire of just three Mexican dances was disseminated beyond Mexico. As this publication is one of the series of books on "Traditional Dances of Latin America" and also linked with a series of "Handbooks of European National Dances," the inclusion of *The Old Men* as one of only three "Dances of Mexico" places it decisively into the category of most representative. As was common practice in schools of dance, the musical accompaniment was played on a piano, so Dickens includes a music transcription for piano, with bar numbers linking in with the choreological details, along with very comprehensive description of the dance steps and patterns (1954:22–29). Although the music was transcribed for piano, the arrangement maintains a sense of a chordal, strummed accompaniment, however, pianistic embellishments and arpeggiated chords, especially in the bass, were also included.

Thirdly, in 1958 SEP published a book encompassing narrative descriptions, musical notation, and drawings of a selection of dances performed for contests in state-run boarding schools between 1953 and 1958 (Castro Agúndez). An account of *Los Viejitos* is included as one of the dances. Although Castro Agúndez does identify this dance as P'urhépecha and acknowledges the prominent place of this dance in programs of costumbrista exhibitions, he does not mention the island of Jarácuaro, preferring to frame this dance in terms of specific Roman Catholic celebratory days and periods (Patron Saint, the Santa Cruz, Christmas, the anniversary of the birth of the Holy Child, and 8 December in homage to the Virgin of la Salud) (1958:39–40). Fourthly, Luis Bruno Ruíz's book entitled *Breve historia de la danza en México* (Brief History of Dance in Mexico), published in about 1956, includes references to *Los Viejitos*, presenting it as a folkloric and regional dance and associating it with Michoacán and with pre-Hispanic roots, through citing part of the reference by the sixteenth-century priest Durán (no date: 51).[21]

Alongside dissemination in books, other media such as journals, magazines, and newspapers also included articles describing and referring to *The Old Men*. In the intercontinental journal *América*, published in Cuba, within a section entitled "La Danza en México" (Dance in Mexico) both indigenous dance in general, and *The Old Men* of Michoacán in particular were represented as part of a premodern configuration. Francisco Frola, the author, essentialized indigenous dances and people by associating them very specifically with a state of mystical adoration and surrealism which was alcohol and drug induced, stating that "the indigenous people dance without ceasing, to the music of their primitive instruments" (Frola 1942:68). Even the briefest descriptions that encompassed such characterization performed a potent role in perpetuating the notion of *The Old Men* and indigenous dance and people as situated thoroughly in the past.

Through multiple didactic and populist publications, the *Dance of the Old Men* was fixed choreographically and given a permanent place in the repertoire of representative Mexican dances. Each publication contributed to the essentialization process, defining meanings and significations, and consolidating the role of dance as an efficacious corporeal medium for creating a shared sense of belonging, and for shaping a notion of Mexicanness in international contexts.

The Ballet Folklórico de México

Alongside books and magazines, another major activity that fixed a staged folkloric version of *The Old Men* and embedded it within a set of Mexican Regional Dances was the formation of the profoundly influential Ballet Folklórico de México (the Folkloric Ballet of Mexico) in 1959 in Mexico City. As a highly trained, professional company, this ensemble became more famous than any other dance company in Mexico and had a significant impact both in Mexico and the United States. In tourism terms, the company was, and still is, used as a marketing image, and in nationalistic terms, the company was highly influential in providing a model for the formation of Ballet Folklórico companies, amateur and professional, throughout Mexico and in the United States.

As with other worldwide national folkloric dance companies, the Ballet Folklórico de México was fundamentally concerned with the representation of a nation-state, encompassing and embodying notions of ethnicity and race on both a national and global stage. From its inception, the Ballet Folklórico fulfilled a signifying role for the dual and yet interfacing elements of Mexican nationalism, and national and international tourism, and the dances that formed the repertoire ostensibly symbolized the nation's essence and provided "a coherent, exportable picture of Mexican Otherness…packaged for tourist consumption" (Zolov 2001:242). Tourist audiences formed an impression and view of the country through the performance. For audiences of Mexicans in Mexico City, the performance had to both appeal to, and be acceptable to an audience of upper-middle-class elites, with whom political and economic benefits were associated (Shay 2002:89). In creating the repertoire, choreographic choices and strategies designed for specific visions of national representation were crucial, and although this process had started many decades prior to the establishment of the Ballet Folklórico, the high profile of the new company meant that the nature of the representation of Mexico through dance would be more influential than any other in Mexico.

The founder and director of the Ballet Folklórico de México, Amalia Hernández, was central to the creative decision-making processes, and her sense of dance aesthetics, theatricalization, and folklore were of utmost importance.[22] It is therefore significant that Hernández specialized in Mexican art (with Miguel Covarrubias) at the National School of Anthropology, and also danced in the Mexican Academy of Dance. In 1952 she formed the Modern Ballet of Mexico, which transformed into the Ballet Folklórico of the Palace of Fine Arts, and subsequently became the Ballet Folklórico de México.[23] In 1952, under the sponsorship of the powerful mass media magnate Emilio Azcárraga Milmo she created choreography for television programs known as "Gala Performances," which were folklore programs designed specifically for television. A representation of Michoacán, entitled *Sones de Michoacán*, was one of her first choreographies, encompassing an aesthetic presentation not dissimilar to the theatricalized cuadros costumbristas of the 1920s and 1930s. In 1959 her ensemble represented Mexico in the Panamerican Games in Chicago, and by presidential order, the Ballet Folklórico was made into an official national company, under the auspices of the National Institute of Fine Arts (INBA), and was promoted through the Department of Tourism. Although the company was privatized in 1964, state sponsorship (both "artistic" and touristic), along with the support of large corporations, has been fundamental to the company's promotion. As the government-run Palace of Fine Arts continued to be the base for the Ballet Folklórico, the performances maintained a role as state-approved dance and music representations of Mexico, appropriate for ideological purposes, both nationally and internationally. From its inception, the Ballet Folklórico was used as a major part of advertising campaigns in tourism, shaping and reinforcing the concept of folkloric performance as a central component of the tourist experience.

Dance Aesthetics: Ballet/Folk and Centers/Peripheries

The Ballet Folklórico de México relied upon a romanticized and virtuosic aesthetic, utilizing a large company of highly trained dancers, competent in a range of techniques, who filled the vast stage of the Palace of Fine Arts with intricate, geometric, and often symmetrical patterns to form a spectacle of color and sound, along with many musicians who accompanied the pieces who were also often on stage. A variety of dance styles was incorporated, including dances that were either drawn from the repertoire shaped through the 1920s onward, or, ostensibly, "collected" from villages and adapted for the stage.[24] In addition to these set dance pieces, Hernández also created "choreography with an argument," which were "suites that have story lines" (Shay 2002:99). For this Hernández developed a story using a series of songs and dances that reflected the traditions and nature of a region, for example, *The Tarascans* (ibid.). Although not acknowledged as such, these suites drew directly on the model developed in the 1920s and 1930s in which cuadros custombristas exhibited everyday life on stage.

Engaging the term "ballet" in the name of the company was significant for the way in which it invoked ideological notions of dance aesthetics that had their roots in the immediate postrevolutionary years. Ballet was highly regarded in Mexico City in the nineteenth century, and took on a new dimension in the early twentieth century through performances of the Ballet Russes, and in particular with Anna Pavlova, whose performance of the vernacular *jarabe tapatío* en pointe generated a new fusion and concept of dance. Back in 1921, when creating *Noche Mexicana* in Mexico City, Adolfo Best Maugard had classified the vernacular and rural dances as "ballet," which set up a tension between forms, because using the term "ballet" engendered a certain perception, and so, as López has commented, the audience expected more than folk dances could deliver (López 2006:28). In that postrevolutionary period, one school of thought considered the intervention of cultured artists to be necessary in order to place vernacular and popular art in front of a public audience, engaging a distinction between aesthetics of dance performance. In the 1950s, therefore, naming the company Ballet Folklórico perpetuated that discourse and practice, implying that "ballet folklórico" was a theatricalized version of a vernacular style that existed somewhere else in Mexico, performed by authentic indigenous and rural peoples. Notably, Miguel Covarrubias (artist, ethnologist, and art historian) and Vincente T. Mendoza (music folklorist) suggested that in appropriating dance, the characteristics remained the same, while the traditions of the people were enriched (Covarrubias and Mendoza 1967).[25] As the Palace of Fine Arts was the most prestigious venue in Mexico, hosting mostly opera, classical music, modern dance, and ballet, so deploying the same stage for the professional Ballet Folklórico created a place and status for the professionalization of dance labeled folkloric, which comprised vernacular dances transformed by trained professionals.

The choreography for *The Old Men* as performed by the Ballet Folklórico de México drew directly on the versions danced in the early 1920s by the Orozcos and Bartolo Juárez of Jarácuaro, and by Antonio Pablo and his family of Cucuchucho, using the theatricalized Mexico City events and the Lake Pátzcuaro Cultural Missions contests as models. Therefore, the form danced by most Ballet Folklórico ensembles, both in Mexico and the United States, traces directly to these families of Lake Pátzcuaro. However, with the Ballet Folklórico the form was commodified to become more showy, with an emphasis upon the speed and intricacy of the footwork; exaggeration of characterization; and precision of the floor patterns and proxemic relations, which gave the whole dance a more "spectacular" feel. Curiously, U.S. scholar Janet Brody Esser, in her work on P'urhépecha masks, states that the version performed by dancers from Jarácuaro in the 1970s was influenced by the Ballet Folklórico de México, suggesting that the Jarácuaro version was "inauthentic" because of this possible influence by a folkloric company and performances for tourists (Brody Esser 1984:107). With the influence of the Ballet Folklórico, a network of Ballet Folklórico ensembles was established throughout the country, further perpetuating the divide between authentic and inauthentic bodies, movements, and displays. I discuss further ramifications and consequences of the influence of the Ballet Folklórico de México in subsequent chapters.

The End of an Era: the Massacre and the Olympics

Through the Golden Age of the 1940s and 1950s, and into the 1960s, *The Old Men* and *Night of the Dead* were promoted as icons of Mexicanness and lo mexicano, circulating through multiple representational modes, including films, guide books, marketing materials, and newspaper articles. Crowds of tourists, Mexican and international, flocked to Lake Pátzcuaro and Janitzio to witness and experience *Night of the Dead* and *The Old Men*. The dance was fixed as an inherent element in the repertoire of Mexican regional dances and disseminated through schools and folkloric ensembles and through performances by the Ballet Folklórico de México. In the late 1960s, *The Old Men* was chosen to be performed at a Boy Scout Reunion in France as a presentation of "the essence of [Mexican] nationality" (Ibargüengoitia 1998:69).[26]

In 1968, as professional staged reenactments of *The Old Men* were taking place in the Palace of Fine Arts in the heart of Mexico City, on the island of Jarácuaro the ensemble of Gervasio López was rehearsing the dance for a performance at the Olympic Games in Mexico City. Just days before the Olympics started, a massacre took place in Mexico City that had repercussions for the representational role of *The Old Men*. In the following chapter, I turn to the post-1968 events, discussing how, in an attempt to reconstruct a national and shared sense of belonging after the devastating massacre, the government turned to populism, engaging a form of folkloric nationalism that had its roots in the postrevolutionary years, and deploying *The Old Men* and performers from Jarácuaro as an overt icon of national unity.

CHAPTER 8

Experiencing *Night of the Dead*

Festivals, Contests, and Souvenirs

AFTER THE IDEALISTIC postrevolutionary era of the 1920s and 1930s, and the Golden Age of the 1940s and 1950s, by the 1960s Mexico was moving into a troubled period economically and politically. Societal values and attitudes toward the ruling regime were changing, with public and political problems festering away. Certain dramatic and tragic events that happened in 1968 can be seen as the grounds for the close of Mexico's Golden Age.[1] On 2 October 1968 in *La Plaza de las Tres Culturas* (Plaza of the Three Cultures), Tlatelolco, Mexico City, a massacre of students and workers took place, just ten days before the opening of the Olympic Games in the same city. The shooting, shrouded in mystery at the time, but later revealed to have been carried out by the Mexican Army, rocked the nation.[2] The year 1968 therefore marked a transformative moment in Mexican history, in which a sense of national belonging was shattered. Not only were Mexicans shocked and shaken by affair, the event resonated globally due to Mexico's role in the spotlight as the host of the Olympic Games, the first time in a Latin American country.

In the wake of these events, and in the subsequent decades, the *Dance of the Old Men* and *Night of the Dead* were promoted and disseminated even more vigorously for nationalistic and touristic agendas. Indigenous representation and politics figured on the political agenda as an ongoing inherent factor. In this and the following chapter, I discuss the ever-increasing contexts in which *The Old Men* and *Night of the Dead* were deployed after 1968, and the consolidation of their roles as embodiments of Mexico. In the first part of this chapter, I give a brief overview of central political strategies and governmental institutions, relating particularly to: indigenous politics; music and dance; European tours and Mexico City performance events; and radio and education. In the second part of this chapter, I concentrate on tourism and tourist initiatives, discussing the development of *The Old Men* in Morelia and Lake Pátzcuaro, and then focusing on *Night of the Dead* in Lake Pátzcuaro, with a particular emphasis on Festivals of Music and Dance, and the experiential encounter on Janitzio.

National Fragmentation and Indigenous Politics

After the 1968 massacre, the political response was to turn, or return, to populism as a means of uniting the nation and regaining political control. Reconstructing a shared national identity and renewing a sense of an imagined national community and belonging was paramount. One element of the populist style of governance instigated by President Luis Echeverría Álvarez (1970–1976) drew upon a folkloric nationalism that had its roots in the postrevolutionary years, deploying a gentle, colorful, and rural folkloric and indigenous image as a means of projecting Mexico to national and international audiences.[3] The period from 1982 onward is best characterized as one of great hardship for most Mexicans. A debt crisis hit Mexico in 1982, marking the end of the successful and prosperous post-1940 economic system. The political and economic disaster was compounded in 1985 as Mexico City was rocked by a huge earthquake, one of the most devastating quakes in the history of the Americas. By the late 1980s and into the 1990s, the overriding political discourse and ideology was one of neoliberalism, which led to fragmentation, corruption, struggle, and an ever-widening gap between rich and poor. This was fueled by the signing of the *Tratado de Libre Comercio de América del Norte*, TLCAN (North American Free Trade Agreement, NAFTA) in 1993 (which ostensibly strengthened trade relations with the United States and Canada), and Mexico again suffered a massive debt crisis, with the devaluation of the peso in 1994, severely impacting upon virtually all Mexicans.

Also in 1994, the indigenous rights campaign movement of the *Ejército Zapatista de Liberación Nacional*, EZLN (Zapatista Army of National Liberation) in Chiapas, fronted by the masked Subcomandante Marcos, was significant for its impact upon national indigenous politics, and for the increasing militarism which ensued. The EZLN sought, and continues to seek, recognition of indigenous rights. As the new millennium commenced, many in Mexico were optimistic for the dawning of a new era, with the end of one-party rule, and the election of Vicente Fox as president. However, this hope turned to disappointment as levels of governmental corruption and economic disparity continued unabated. In the twenty-first century, Mexico—as nation and peoples—continues on its path of complexity, richness, disparity, and diversity.

Through the last three decades of the twentieth century and into the twenty-first century changes were made to government policy regarding the representation of indigenous peoples. Following an important critique of indigenismo, anthropologists, and the role of the National Indigenist Institute (INI) (Warman 1970, Bonfil Batalla 1970, Nolasco 1970), by the 1980s government terminology was altered to include the concept of multiculturalism. However, the government still maintained an objective of acculturation to Eurocentric goals, despite the change in rhetoric, with the alteration of the language simply giving the impression of progress (Bartolomé 1994, Nash 1997, 2001). INI continued to engage in dichotomous practices, with the two-fold aims of promoting distinctive cultural practices to a wider public (Mexican and foreign), and conserving and rescuing cultures within a community to ensure the healthy future of the traditions (see

Stavenhagen 1979). In the P'urhépecha region, many projects were supported by financial resources channeled through INI (regional branches), with cultural events organized by INI taking place in the Pátzcuaro area, including staged events and festivals for *Night of the Dead* incorporating *The Old Men*.

In 2003, INI was disbanded and a new body, *La Comisión Nacional para el Desarrollo de los Pueblos Indígenas*, CDI (the National Commission for the Development of Indigenous Peoples) was put in its place. The new organization aims to be much more concerned with the rights of peoples and communities, and seeks to respect the pluricultural and multiethnic character of the nation. The move toward the repositioning of indigenous politics was particularly driven by the actions and rhetoric of the uprising in 1994 and the continuous protest and presence of the EZLN, with demands for: local autonomy; an end to racism; a respect for indigenous traditions and customs; and the right to educate children in their native language. Historic questions about the role of the peoples designated as indigenous in the nation's identity and the importance of national unity in pursuing the nation's interests remain wholly central. The peoples of Lake Pátzcuaro and the practices of the *Dance of the Old Men* and *Night of the Dead* are inherently part of the construct.[4]

Music and Dance Research Centers, European Tours, and a Folklore Colloquium

In the wake of the 1968 massacre it was crucial that the government was seen to be performing a unifying role, renewing a sense of an imagined national community and belonging, and enabling participation, thereby regaining political control. President Echeverría strategically attempted to reshape and reformulate a sense of national identity through a populist style of governance, establishing numerous state-run art institutions, and also reforming those already in existence, in order to mold perceptions of indigenousness, Mexicanness, and folklore for the agenda of nationalism and also tourism. Intellectuals and artists continued to be influential in processes of collecting, documenting, publishing, and disseminating practices and artifacts. Both institutional bodies of INBA (the National Institute of Fine Arts) and INAH (the National Institute of Anthropology and History) performed significant roles in "conserving cultural patrimony" (Davis 2007). Under the auspices of the newly inaugurated National Center for the Arts (CENART), two other centers—the National Center for Musical Research, Documentation and Information (CENIDIM), and the National Center for the Development of Dance (also called the National Dance Collection) (FONADAN)—played instrumental roles in developing research and dissemination of national and popular music and dance.[5] Significantly, the director of FONADAN, eminent dancer and choreographer Josefina Lavalle, was directly involved with promoting performances of the *Dance of the Old Men*. FONADAN was also concerned with disseminating nationalistic dance and music through Radio Educación, a governmental radio station that transmitted to Mexico City and the surrounding areas.

In October 1968, even as the country was reeling from news of the massacres, the ensemble of Gervasio López of Jarácuaro performed *The Old Men* in Mexico City in front of an international audience, as part of the nationalistic displays for the Olympic Games.[6] In the early 1970s, as part of President Echeverría's populist strategizing, López's ensemble was again deployed in high-profile, politically charged performances of *The Old Men*—firstly, in state-sponsored tours to Europe, and subsequently in staged events in Mexico City. Both events featured as elements of governmental policy to reunite the nation and to present Mexico in a positive light to the world. In 1974, the European tour lasted twenty-two days, during which time the company of musicians and dancers visited various cities, including Bucharest and Paris, with performances taking place inside theaters and in front of museums. The tour took place under the auspices of FONADAN, and was organized by Josefina Lavalle (director of FONADAN), and her husband, Mario Kuri-Aldana (a researcher with FONADAN and a prominent musician and composer). Ideologically, politically, and aesthetically the tour performed a role both in a transnational context, through the actual presence of the Mexican performers in European cities, and also in a national context, through reporting of the event in the Mexican media.

On the return from Europe, representatives of FONADAN issued a press release that circulated predominantly in Mexico City. This account had two objectives: to announce and publicize the beneficial work of President Echeverría and his government; and secondly, as a means of advertising the imminent staged events of *The Old Men* in Mexico. As with other documentation, the text of the press release performed an overt role in framing the dance, the people of Lake Pátzcuaro, and the position of the state, and here I replicate an extract of the narrative as a valuable source of contextualization:

> One of the *costumbrista* activities which best characterizes the lake region of Michoacán, is, without doubt, the dance of "THE OLD MEN," which best emphasizes the rhythmic sensibility of the indigenous tarascans who participate in religious fiestas. The version from Jarácuaro is accompanied by jaranita, violin, bass guitar and vihuela. The performers successfully participated in the Folklore Colloquium in Bucharest, Republic of Romania...[they] took part by Presidential order through FONADAN...[Performances of the Dance of the Old Men] will be presented on 8 September 1974 as part of the program "Art in the City" in the Plaza of the Three Cultures and in the left hand patio of the National Museum of Anthropology.
>
> (*Los Viejitos* Press Release FONADAN 1974)

Presented as a costumbrista activity, or scene of authentic custom, *The Old Men* was unequivocally depicted as wholly part of a traditional Lake Pátzcuaro context, associated specifically with the indigenous P'urhépecha (tarascan) peoples, and framed in relation to religious fiestas. Characterizing indigenous musical aesthetics by invoking rhythmic sensibility and referencing the term "folklore" located this practice in opposition to art, while simultaneously engaging a position of indigenismo through the utilization of an overtly indigenous practice. By highlighting the successful participation in a European context, the *Dance of the Old Men* and the P'urhépecha musicians and dancers were given a place on the world stage as iconic embodiments of Mexico, benevolently enabled through the *order* of the president of the nation.

Following their return from the European tour, López's ensemble performed *The Old Men* in two events in Mexico City, both of which were staged in deeply significant and poignant sites: the Plaza of the Three Cultures, Tlatelolco, and the National Museum of Anthropology. The Plaza of the Three Cultures was a place of profound ideological and political resonance, both as the site of the state-engineered massacre just a few years earlier, and as the marked location of the initiation of mestizo Mexico. A plaque in the plaza elucidates the central issue concerning ethnicity and race in Mexico: "On the 13th of August 1521, heroically defended by Cuauhtémoc, Tlatelolco fell into the hands of Hernán Cortés. It was not a triumph, nor a defeat. It was the painful birth of the mestizo people that is Mexico today."

The National Museum of Anthropology also dealt with weighty issues of ethnicity, race, and pre/postincursion peoples. Founded in 1964 under the auspices of the National Institute of Anthropology and History (INAH), the National Museum of Anthropology had performed an overt role exhibiting indigenous cultures since its instigation. A major intention of the founder, Ignacio Bernal, was to represent homogeneity, which was very much part of the centralist project (García Canclini 1995:123).[7] Embodied and contained within the single edifice of the museum was an exhibition of indigenousness and Mexicanness. Educational dioramas depicting pre-Hispanic life, and displays of artifacts of indigenous peoples were central aspects of the museum, presenting a purportedly enlightening show for visitors. However, the concept of "indigenous" only engaged with the past, for, as Zolov has noted, "the Indian present was virtually absent; dioramas instead focused on an imagined ideal existence before the time of the Spanish Conquest. Moreover, the sheer number of rooms and artifacts tended to have the effect of blurring an understanding of the historical differentiation between the cultures represented; in the vastness of their display, they all became 'Mexican'" (Zolov 2001:244). As the museum became a tourist destination, this allowed both national and international visitors to get a taste of perceived authenticity by viewing real indigenous objects (Lomnitz 2001:133).

Enacting *The Old Men* with dancers and musicians from Lake Pátzcuaro within this ideologically potent space framed practice, people, and artifacts (costumes and props) as objects of display for study and ethnographic gazing. The interface between the inanimate objects in glass cases and dioramic displays, and the live bodies of villagers from Lake Pátzcuaro set up complex resonances. In order to create a scene of authentic custom—a costumbrista activity—local food from the Lake Pátzcuaro area was also prepared and served, including *atole* (a hot maize drink) and *charales* (small white fried fish). In this setting, the P'urhépecha dancers and musicians participated in a staged re-creation of what was portrayed as their traditional lifestyle. The context was one of governmental exhibition of ethnicity, using live models as a living diorama in an ethnographic display within a pan-indigenous framework.

As these two performance events in Mexico City were managed and organized by FONADAN, deploying *The Old Men* as an indigenous traditional practice, and engaging P'urhépecha people to perform in these significant settings enacted a form of indigenismo and state-controlled folkloric cultural heritage. As with the overtly ideologically framed and officially sanctioned staged events of *Hamarándecua* and *Danzas Auténticas Mexicanas* in Mexico City in the 1930s, *The Old Men* was again used in the heart of Mexico City by the president of the nation for a manifestly nationalist and populist agenda. The overriding objectives involved engendering a sense of Mexicanness, reconstructing shared belonging, and creating unification through reference to a pre-Hispanic past, potently and poignantly embodied in the figures of living peoples, relying on notions of authenticity, tradition, ritual, and ethnicity.

In the year following the European tour and enactments of *The Old Men* in Mexico City, a team of researchers working for FONADAN produced an audio recording and information booklet entitled *Danzas de la región lacustre del Estado de Michoacán* (Dances of the Lake Region of Michoacán) (1975). The team included Josefina Lavalle, Mario Kuri-Aldana, and Marcelo Torreblanca, the former young student who, back in 1924, had danced the very first version of *The Old Men* in a national context, as taught by Nicolás Bartolo Juárez. Expressing the populist agenda of the Echeverría era, Kuri-Aldana noted that the publication was "not an academic work, but a popular publication to be owned by libraries and the general public with an interest in such matters" (1975). Information was presented with a quality of authority and stated as "factual," with references to *The Old Men* characterizing it as pre-Hispanic ("it is one of the few popular dances of Mexico that we are certain was danced from the pre-hispanic era") while also suggesting that it had been modified substantially over the centuries (ibid.).

These populist activities of the Echeverría six-year term were efficacious in reinforcing icons of Mexicanness through a form of indigenismo by engaging *The Old Men* and Lake Pátzcuaro performers as a major signifier. Although a governmental control element was openly present in these activities, the impact of these actions and strategies must also be viewed in relation to the experiences of the many musicians and dancers of the Lake Pátzcuaro region who were engaged in the tours and centralist events. Their experience was one of opportunity, widening participation, and state-backing, and as one prominent musician from Janitzio, Aurelio de la Cruz, remarked, "A time when I strongly felt the support of the government was in the period of Don Luis Echeverría" (de la Cruz: personal communication). Even as the European tours and Mexico City enactments involved elements of governmental management, indigenismo, and folkloric nationalism, so these events were also celebratory and affirmative in terms of giving value to P'urhépecha actions and peoples. For local musicians and dancers, these were occasions for travel and participation in national activities.

Folklorists, Ethnomusicologists, and Radio Educación

Many of the same musicians and dancers from the Lake Pátzcuaro region were also involved in state-sponsored radio programs in Mexico City. As part of the broad brief of Radio Educación, numerous programs in the 1970s and early 1980s were produced by the Department of Ethnomusicology within CENART. In these programs, musicians and dancers from many regions of the country were interviewed by respected governmental music and dance researchers, including Mario Kuri-Aldana and Marcelo Torreblanca. A number of ensembles from the Lake Pátzcuaro region were invited to appear in these programs, playing music and talking about their music and lives. As Kuri-Aldana observed, series such as programs on "Popular Composers of Michoacán" and "Music of the Traditional Dances of Mexico" were recorded in order to disseminate these practices (Radio Educación C-752). In these programs there was a strong focus upon nationalism, presenting styles of music and dance as authentically Mexican, and constructing a discourse concerning the attributes and characteristics of music and dance that were considered to be useful in shaping a populist sense of belonging. Torreblanca was engaged as interviewer and presenter for a selection of programs, including those involving musicians and dancers of *The Old Men* from Jarácuaro. In those interviews Torreblanca recalled and reflected upon his own process of learning the dance in the 1920s from Bartolo Juárez, particularly expressing a sense of deep respect for the Jarácuaro villagers, acknowledging them as authentic and indigenous peoples.[8]

Dancing in Schools and Folkloric Ballet Ensembles

Educational strategies for disseminating dance and music also continued apace throughout the state school system and in the context of other state-run institutions, within a populist ideological framework of national identity. A repertoire of national dances was taught in schools, which included *The Old Men* of Lake Pátzcuaro as an integral component. Throughout Mexico, school festivals of regional dance, summer courses, and Diplomas in Folkloric Dance continued to include *The Old Men* and promote the importance of this dance as representative of Michoacán (Torreblanca 1980). Live diffusion of *The Old Men* also took place through numerous Ballet Folklórico ensembles that were established throughout the country, particularly in cities and within university environments, some modeled on the Ballet Folklórico in Mexico City, and others coming out of earlier models of regional dance groups. In Morelia, for example, the Folkloric Ballet of the University of Michoacán (UMSNH) had an important didactic and cultural role from the 1970s onward, and was directed by Sálvador Próspero Román, a musician and teacher from the P'urhépecha region, who engaged Gervasio López of Jarácuaro to teach *The Old Men*.[9]

In 1988, Josefina Lavalle, in her role as director of FONADAN, published a book on the jarabe, in which she included discussions that are highly pertinent to this study, concerning notions of Mexicanness, folkloric and touristic dance, and national identity. As Lavalle had been involved with *The Old Men*, specifically organizing the European tour and staged costumbrista events in Mexico City, her understanding and analysis of the role of popular dance was shaped in part by those experiences. In relation to the dance education system, Lavalle questioned the notion of defining what the "cultural values of each community" are, claiming that a "false, arbitrary, superficial and 'touristic' image of our identity is used in education" (1988:14). Lavalle went on to describe how she regretted "the irresponsibility and ignorance with which the concepts of 'mexicanness' and 'national identity' are used in artistic education, and the indiscriminate use of dances [*danzas y bailes*] which are supposedly folkloric,... [and which are] frequently valued by the commercial television and the State, unfortunately without the explicit warning 'this product can be damaging to mental health and to the destruction of our cultures.' The confusion that exists in the field of theatrical 'folkloric dance' between teachers, students, and directors of groups of dance is a reality" (ibid.). She underlined the importance of dance in society, as "a tool for teachers who wish to understand the complex development of dance as a human activity, in all its forms and derivations" and she regreted the fact that the jarabe, one of the important genres of popular dance, "finished as an official symbol of 'mexicanness' in school fiestas" (ibid.). Significantly, Lavalle continued to be involved in the field of dance research and education for many years, and was influential in developing a more rigorous approach to dance scholarship, distancing herself from didactic, folkloric contexts.

Tourism, Weekendismo, and Souvenirs

Throughout the second half of the twentieth century and into the twenty-first century, tourism continued to form a central element in the economic development policy of the Mexican government, with vigorous strategizing and marketing to promote both the nation of Mexico and specific locations within Mexico. Internal Mexican national tourism consisted mostly of visits to: beach resorts; preincursion archeological sites, such as Chichén Itzá (a reconstructed Mayan archeological site) and Lake Pátzcuaro; and colonial cities such as Morelia, Guadalajara, and Guanajuato. International tourism also centered on these locations as the principal destinations and attractions; however, visits to Mexico City and to villages designated as indigenous within an ethnic-tourism and ecotourism framework also featured heavily.

Whereas Pátzcuaro and Morelia continued to be the principal sites for staged performances of the *Dance of the Old Men* with musicians and dancers from Lake Pátzcuaro, a few major beach resorts frequented by Mexicans and international tourists were also prominent in terms of tourist displays. Acapulco, Cancún, and Puerto Vallarta in particular have all played host to performances of *The Old Men* as part of national folkloric dance entertainment by professional dance ensembles. In Mexico City, the Ballet Folklórico represented the height of virtuosic, professional folkloric representation of the *Dance of the Old Men*, attracting international audiences to the Palace of Fine Arts.

The government, through the centralized Mexican Tourist Board, continued to perform a major role in developing policies, and in shaping sites/sights and attractions for the tourist industry. In conjunction with the nationwide organization, each individual state also had their own regional tourist board. In the late twentieth century, *The Old Men* played a leading role in the State of Michoacán Plan for Tourist Development as developed by the Michoacán State Secretary of Tourism. According to one state official, the plan involved the dissemination of the practices of the culture of Michoacán and "regional folklore...particularly music and dance" (Bosco Castro: personal communication).[10] Marketing campaigns continued to utilize a repertoire of folkloric and indigenous images to promote specific regions and to advertise Mexico. For *The Old Men* this process reached its apogee in 2006 when a photograph of an Old Man dancer from Jarácuaro was given center place in the three-image poster of the Mexican Tourist Board advertising campaign in Europe, marketing Mexico on the global stage (see chapter 12 for an analysis of these photographic images) (figure 1.8).

Although the Lake Pátzcuaro region was the "home" setting and principal location for tourist performances of the *Dance of the Old Men*, Morelia became the second site of importance. As Morelia developed as a destination for both national and international visitors, promoted by state-run and private businesses, so openings for visitor entertainment increased, with touristic uses interfacing and merging with staged events for local and political agendas. In Morelia each staged and representational occasion encompassing *The Old Men* performed a role in shaping the tourist gaze, reinforcing the importance of this dance as a "must-see" aspect of the visit, and generating further opportunities for display. A range of privately owned enterprises utilized *The Old Men* to attract clients, including the Hotel Misión de Calle Real, the Rincón Tarasca (which later became the Peña Colibrí), and the Hotel Alameda. Ensembles from Jarácuaro were contracted to perform on a regular weekly basis, with enactments of *The Old Men* functioning as an authentic indigenous display, attracting both national and international tourists, and also local middle-class clients. The Friday and Saturday night performances in the Peña Colibrí (described in chapter 1) exemplify this mix, with a clientele comprising national and international tourists, and also local Moreliana/os and Michoacana/os who regard *The Old Men* as an element of their local and regional identity. It has been a common practice for citizens of Morelia to take visiting friends and family members to the Peña Colibrí to see *The Old Men* as a form of demonstration of their own cultural patrimony, local heritage, identity, and traditions[11] (00–07 ◑).

Other staged events in Morelia encompassed a wide range of venues and functions, including entertainment at conferences, opening ceremonies, private socioreligious celebrations and fiestas, political campaigning, state-run festivals, and museum performances. In one noteworthy and illustrative event in the 1990s, a performance was staged in the Michoacán State Museum, attracting an audience of local Moreliana/os, and national and international visitors. *The Old Men* was performed by young boys from Santa Fe de la Laguna (the village where, in the

1920s, the Orozco brothers of Jarácuaro witnessed a dance of old men which they replicated in their own village). It was directed and accompanied by Juan Hernández, then in his eighties, who had been directing *The Old Men* for decades. Presenting a complex ideological, political, and aesthetic context, the event framed the dancers, musician, and the practice as living, cultural heritage, located within the walls of the state museum, alongside artifacts and texts of the Michoacán past. Simultaneously, the event also celebrated the work of these performers, affirming their place in the history of the state and nation (22 ●).

In the Lake Pátzcuaro region, the trend of ever-increasing numbers of both Mexican and international visitors continued, fostered by multiple promotional activities of national and worldwide tourist organizations, and state-run and private enterprises. Back-packing visitors, mostly from Europe and the United States, were attracted to the area by the perceived "unspoiled" indigenous and colonial experience, and were accommodated in the growing number of small local lodgings. Catering to a different market, package tours were arranged through transnational corporations that worked with large Pátzcuaro hotels, notably La Posada de Don Vasco and El Mesón del Gallo, taking busloads of tourists to the area. These large groups would generally stay for a day or two, or simply pass through, stopping only to visit Janitzio and eat (14 ●). As Morelia became increasingly important as a tourist destination, and as the road links between Morelia and Lake Pátzcuaro improved, so day visits were far more feasible than previously. Many tourists, national and international, spent a long weekend (weekendismo)[17] or week in Morelia, and made a day trip to Pátzcuaro. As a consequence, the majority of the tourists viewed a selected part of the local life, and the residents of the region had limited contact with the tourists. For most visitors to the Lake Pátzcuaro region, the itinerary usually included two main components: a journey to the island of Janitzio and a stroll around the town of Pátzcuaro. While Pátzcuaro encompassed all the elements of colonial and mestizo Mexico, Janitzio represented all things indigenous, pre-Hispanic, and other.

In Pátzcuaro, as tourist numbers grew so opportunities arose for villagers from Jarácuaro to perform the *Dance of the Old Men* in hotels, restaurants, and festivals. After the first performances in the hotel La Posada de Don Vasco by the López ensemble, the venue continued to be the most important site for *The Old Men* in Pátzcuaro. A succession of groups from Jarácuaro performed there twice weekly from the early 1960s onward, and performances of the *Dance of the Old Men* continue there in the twenty-first century. Performances took place in two restaurant areas: in one restaurant, the walls were decorated with masks of the Old Man, generating an impression of the integral nature of the dance to the area, and boosting sales of Old Men masks as tourist souvenirs; the second restaurant was located in an outside patio area, where a raised platform was erected and tables and chairs were arranged around it to create a focal point. For this event, clients booked a place in the restaurant, with the entertainment of the *Dance of the Old Men* and P'urhépecha music as the principal attraction (08, 14 ●).

Other hotels, restaurants, and locations also provided suitable venues for the dance. The ensemble of Abel Orozco of Jarácuaro regularly performed in the small

Restaurant El Patio, and played in more informal locations, such as La Casa de los Once Patios (the House of Eleven Patios), a sixteenth-century ex-convent and location of numerous craft shops and workshops. This well-known tourist location was noted in many tourist guide books, and was particularly suitable for performances of the dance because one of the eleven patios was surrounded by balconies, enabling visitors to stop and spectate for a while (figure 1.9). Other ensembles from Jarácuaro also sought out informal locations where tourists gathered and passed by, and where they were able to request money in return for their performance. Two frequently-used locations were the expansive Plaza Vasco de Quiroga in the heart of Pátzcuaro, and the main dockside by the lake where visitors embarked and disembarked for their trip to Janitzio. On the dockside, visitors milled around, purchasing tickets for their journey, perusing the souvenir stalls, and eating at the many little restaurants and food stands that lined the pier. There was no obvious space for the ensemble to dance, with people moving around as they explored what the jetty-area had to offer, so the performers chose a place by the side of the ticket office. In recent years, groups have also begun to enact *The Old Men* on the island of Janitzio itself, at the base of the statue of Morelos. In each setting, the musicians and dancers adapted to the space available, dancing for as long or short a time as spectators were present, and quite literally passing the hat around to appeal for payment. With fluctuating tourist seasons, however, there has been no guarantee of any monetary income (09–13 🕭). In addition to hotels, restaurants, and informal sites, other performances of the *Dance of the Old Men* in Pátzcuaro took place within festival settings and in the Teatro Caltzontzín in Pátzcuaro, as part of events organized through official institutions, such as the local tourist board, INI, and the Pátzcuaro town committee.

The presence of the *Dance of the Old Men* in the Lake Pátzcuaro region existed not only through live display, but also in the network of artifacts and images circulating in the area. Old Men masks hung on restaurant walls, and countless souvenirs made use of a range of Old Man images: T-shirts (depicting dancers against a backdrop of a colonial building in Pátzcuaro; an embroidered skeleton Old Man dancer with hat and cane; and humorous caricatures featuring the Old Man figure); mugs and key rings; body-shaped pens painted with an Old Man costume complete with beribboned hat; souvenir bottles of *charanda* (a local cane alcohol) decorated with a miniature fabric costume of the Old Man with diminutive wooden mask and straw hat atop the bottle; embroidered wall-hangings; bookmarks; postcards; full-size and miniature Old Man masks and hats; and costumed Old Man wooden figures with tiny straw hats and colorful ribbons. The wooden figures were usually carved and costumed by villagers from Jarácuaro, whose expertise in hat-making enabled them to create perfect miniature replicas (figure 1.1). Promotional flyers, publicity material, tourist magazines, and guides incorporated both literary references to the dance and also photographic images of the mask and dancing figure. Two examples illustrate such uses: firstly, a publicity poster, produced by the Michoacán Secretariat of Tourism, utilized a photograph of two Old Men dancers in an explicit promotion of the state of Michoacán. The word "Michoacán" figured as the main image on the poster, with each letter being formed from a single photographic image. The "M" of Michoacán was created from a photo of two Old Men dancers (identifiable to me as dancers from Juan Francisco's group when performing in the Hotel Alameda, in Morelia). This application gave the *Dance of the Old Men* the role of forming the initial letter of the state;[13] secondly, a glossy tourist magazine—*Michoacán cómo y dónde* (Michoacán Where and How)—included photographs and narrative references to *The Old Men* (2000). Within a section entitled "Michoacán and Popular Culture" two photos, one depicting an Old Man dancer and one of a souvenir mug with the Old Man dancer image, were accompanied by text stating that "The dance of the Old Men is one of the most traditional of the state" (ibid.: no page).[14] Countless recurring references and images such as these reinforced and reified the role of *The Old Men* as an essential element of the Lake Pátzcuaro experience. Whether or not visitors had seen the dance embodied in a live show, they departed with a memory that included *The Old Men* as an iconic referent of Mexicanness, indigenousness, and authentic tradition.

Experiencing "P'urhépecha World," Festivals, and TV Crews

For most visitors to Lake Pátzcuaro the collective tourist gaze was directed toward Janitzio as the most important sight/site, and an essential objective was therefore a visit to the island. In the immediate aftermath of the massacre and the Olympic Games in Mexico City in 1968, promoting Janitzio as an international tourist attraction continued apace. As an illustration, under the banner headline "An unforgettable visit: Janitzio wows journalists," a photomontage article was published in a Michoacán newspaper (*Un recorrido inolvidable* 1968). The article specifically endorsed Janitzio as a worldwide tourist destination, reporting on the visit of a party of foreign journalists to the island. Together, the photos and captions created a tableau that depicted a city dweller's visit to an Othered destination. One photo captured a group of business-suited men, with collared shirts and ties, sitting in a launch, arriving at the island Janitzio, with the towering body of the statue of Morelos in the background. Three further illustrations showed: a mini-skirted woman journalist holding a souvenir butterfly fishing net; a souvenir stall with journalists purchasing articles; and a crowd of visitors on the island with the houses of Janitzio in the background. Finally, one shot enabled the viewer of the newspaper photo to place themselves in the role of visitor to Janitzio, gazing over the shoulder of two other visitors, who themselves are captured gazing at the island.

For tourists visiting Janitzio, both the journey to the island and the encounter with people in their home village enabled the often enacted "pursuit for otherness and difference" to be fulfilled (MacCannell 2001:381). Not only did the trip allow direct contact with real lives, as distinct from a display or a living museum, but it also encompassed an experiential and sensorial element. The journey to the island and the activity of "getting there" created a very specific experience of both temporal and spatial separation, traveling and "being transported" to another place and time.[15] Piloted by local residents the launches departed from the dockside to journey to island, leaving one world behind and entering another, a notion reinforced through an awareness of separation by a body of water.[16] The importance of a boat journey across water enabled a corporeal and sensorial experience. Sightseers could sense the undulations of the lake and feel the spray on their faces (23 ●). On board the launches, sweet-sellers sold local candies from large baskets beautifully decorated with banana leaves, while musicians serenaded the passengers.[17] The feeling and understanding of journeying to "another world" relied upon associations with an indigenous lifestyle and past traditions. As the launch neared the island, fishermen in small canoes could be seen fishing with their butterfly nets, a sight familiar to visitors from photographs in guide books, marketing brochures, and postcards. Once the fishing display was over the fishermen approached the launches, reaching across to the visitors with their fishing nets to request payment for their performance, capitalizing on the opportunity of performing-fishing. Close by, other fishermen were using their large multiperson *chinchorro* nets to catch fish to be eaten by their families and to sell. In this setting, a complex interplay of real life and displaying real life was present, generating and reinforcing notions of a premodern and unspoiled world.

A romanticized and authenticated experience continued once the visitors disembarked on the island. With no entrance barrier or "pay to view" encounters, sightseers were free to wander through the narrow streets, to peak through open doors and windows, to purchase food and souvenirs from the many stalls and shops, and to walk to the top of the island to look down on the surrounding water and the ring of hills encircling the lake. For those who climbed up the staircase inside the statue of Morelos and peered out of his wrist, an aeriel view allowed a sensation of observing a living diorama, consisting of roof tops, winding lanes, P'urhépecha men and women going about their daily lives, and fishermen on the lake. The only intrusion in the scene of everyday P'urhépecha island life was the presence of other tourists.

Island-hopping for *Night of the Dead*

Whereas both Pátzcuaro and Janitzio acted as tourist attractions throughout the year, the whole Lake Pátzcuaro area transformed into a visitor attraction for one week of each year for the celebrations of *Night of the Dead*. As with general tourism to the Lake Pátzcuaro area, visitor numbers increased with each passing year, and the huge influx of visitors for the few days of events was good for the business of hotels, restaurants, and shops. Most visitors stayed in Pátzcuaro itself, and the whole town swarmed with people as hotels became fully booked (and charged double their usual rate) and restaurants were crowded. The Secretariat of Tourism and the Michoacán Tourist Board both encouraged and made the most of the massive incursion of visitors the Lake Pátzcuaro region by organizing a whole week of cultural events as entertainment for the tourists. Overall, the visitor experience centered on a complex and contradictory mix of overt and covert display and exhibition, relying on a network of associations engaging notions of indigenousness, ancient tradition, authenticity, mysticism, pre-Catholic, and premodern activities.

A major feature of the organized cultural events were Festivals and Contests of Music and Dance. After establishing the Festival of Music and Dance for *Night of the Dead* on Janitzio in the 1960s, more and more festivals and contests were organized, generally in collaboration with state tourist institutions. Festivals took place in the obvious locations of Pátzcuaro and Janitzio, and also in other communities of the lake, including the islands of Urandén, Jarácuaro, Pacanda and Yunuén, and the lakeside settlement of Tzintzuntzan. Some events were very low key, while others had a much higher profile, involving tens of thousands of audience members. Depending upon the location and timing of events, some were attended by mostly local audience members (for example the Festival on Urandén) whereas others drew a mixture of national and international visitors. In Pátzcuaro, a number of large staged folkloric performances were organized by the Secretariat of Tourism, with a stage being erected in the central plaza and chairs provided for audience members, affording a comfortable environment in which to spectate the range of entertainment on offer. Financial support for the festivals came from various state organizations, including the Tourist Board and INI (before its closure in 2003). In the 1990s, government funding for *Night of the Dead* events was distributed to groups in all six islands (Jarácuaro, Janitzio, Tecuena, Urandén, Yunuén, Pacanda) and to the lakeside villages of Ucasanástacua, Tzintzuntzan, Ihuatzio, and Tzurumútaro. Some events were in the form of contests involving a panel of judges who adjudicated and the awarding of money prizes. Other events were by invitation only, with each performing ensemble being paid for their participation. Festivals and contests involved themes of *Danzas Tradicionales* (Traditional Dances), *Ofrendas y Artesanias* (Altars and Crafts), *Danza, Pirekuas y Orquesta* (Dance, P'urhépecha Songs and Ensembles), and *Traje Tradicional* (Traditional Clothes and Costumes).

Whereas Pátzcuaro was the hub of the tourist gathering, and Janitzio the "must see" for most visitors, the lakeside community of Tzintzuntzan became a principal location for festivities and events, promoted for its significance and resonance as the former capital of the P'urhépecha empire, complete with an authenticating preinvasion site/sight, albeit reconstructed, of the yácatas (ceremonial constructions), providing a tangible and visible link to the indigenous past. Whereas Janitzio could only be reached by boarding a boat, Tzintzuntzan was accessible by road, so tourists could come and go as they pleased. Tzintzuntzan hosted various Festivals of P'urhépecha music, dance and traditional clothing-costume, and also an Arts and Craft Week. Within the entries representations of the *Dance of the Old Men* were often created, for example, as small straw figures of dancers and musicians (figure 8.1). For spectated events, a stage was set up in the grounds of the yácatas, providing an authenticating backdrop. Participants were generally people from the surrounding region who competed to gain recognition and prize money, or who were invited to perform and were remunerated financially for their participation. As part of the festivals, many performances of the *Dance of the Old Men*

Figure 8.1 A scene of small straw figures representing P'urhépecha activities that was entered into the Arts and Craft Contest for the events of *Night of the Dead*, Tzintzuntzan, 1997. The figures depict an amalgam of practices and clothes, blurring distinctions between costume and everyday clothing, and between *The Old Men*, the *Dance of the Fish*, and women undertaking quotidian work practices. An ensemble of musicians forms the back of the scene (19–21, 24–25, 40 🔊).
Photo by Ruth Hellier-Tinoco.

took place, enacted mostly by groups from Jarácuaro (creating a link back to the contests of the Cultural Missions in 1931 in Tzintzuntzan) (19–20 🔊).

Since the 1960s the island of Jarácuaro has also hosted a Contest or Festival of Music and Dance, which has taken place during the night of 1 November. In Jarácuaro the inhabitants would communally undertake their vigil and ceremony in the cemetery during the day of 2 November, therefore the music and dance festival preceded the ceremony. Organized by village officials and with support from the tourist board and INI, the festival comprised a series of short dance and music pieces performed on a rough wooden stage erected in the atrium (as described in the opening of chapter 1). In this setting the *Dance of the Old Men* was performed many times over, as each ensemble in the village presented their version of the dance, with some participants working on a performance solely for the festival. Unlike the audiences for the festivals on Janitzio and in Tzintzuntzan and Pátzcuaro, which comprised almost entirely national and international visitors, the majority of spectators for the festival on Jarácuaro were villagers from that same village and nearby communities, creating an atmosphere of celebration and validation.

On the island of Urandén, a Festival of Music and Dance has been staged on the basketball court during the night of 31 October each year since the 1980s. This event is particularly noteworthy because of the large number of local participants who have been involved over the years. Urandén islanders perform the *Dance of the Old Men* and the *Dance of the Butterfly Nets*, alongside both new and older dance and music pieces.[18] Similarly, from the 1980s onward a Festival of Music and Dance has also been staged on the island of Yunuén. As with Urandén, the event, located on the basketball court, consisted of a succession of short pieces of music and dance performed by local people mostly from the nearby islands and villages. One objective of this festival has been to draw attention to the island in order to attract more visitors, thus generating a financial income. Yunuén residents have also undertaken other initiatives to attract tourists to the island on a year-round basis, including constructing a cluster of wooden self-catering chalets on one end of the island in the 1990s, an action given the support of the local tourist board (21 ◑).

The once-yearly festival on Yunuén draws a small number of national and international visitors to the island, and has also attracted media interest. An occurrence in the 1998 festival involving a group of residents from the neighboring island of Pacanda provides a good illustration of how these events have been utilized by national and international media companies, encapsulating a prevailing attitude toward performances and performers designated as traditional and indigenous. In the 1990s, the Alejo Reynoso family of Pacanda formed a small musical ensemble, and one brother, Pablo, taught his two young daughters, Zintlali and Yvon, to dance in the local style. Breaking with normal convention, Zintlali learned to execute zapateado, the fast rhythmic footwork usually only undertaken by boys and men. Pablo created a dance piece for his daughters to perform at festivals, in which they enacted a scenario involving a P'urhépecha fisherman going to work and his wife taking him food and then receiving the catch. Accompanied by the family music ensemble, the two girls expertly performed this dance-drama piece as part of the Festival of Music and Dance on the basketball court on Yunuén. Once they had finished, the crew of a television company requested that they go to the atrium of the church to perform the dance for a recording. Zintlali, Yvon, and the ensemble of musicians were asked to perform again and again so that the presenter, director, and producer could capture the shots that they desired. No payment was offered and no permissions were sought. According to the TV company, these musicians and dancers were simply local P'urhépecha people carrying out their normal activities and therefore they would neither expect nor be given any form of recompense (personal communication). The images were later used by the celebrated Mexican singer Juan Gabriel in one of his videos, and were also broadcast in the United States in a Spanish-language program reporting on *Night of the Dead* in Lake Pátzcuaro (figure 8.2). From the perspective of the Alejo Reynoso family, the episode was one in which they felt utilized and exploited in an inappropriate manner (personal communication) (38 ◑).

On the island of Pacanda, a Festival of Music and Dance was initiated in the 1990s attracting a small number of visitors. In a context similar to that on the

Figure 8.2 A TV crew filming the musical ensemble of the Alejo Reynoso family (of the island of Pacanda) during the Festival of Music and Dance for *Night of the Dead* on the neighboring island of Yunuén, 1998. This filming took place *after* the ensemble had finished their festival performance, on a different part of the island, where they were asked to repeat their performance multiple times. A well-known U.S./Mexican TV company later screened these shots in prominent programs. No financial remuneration was given to the musicians and dancers (38 ◓).
Photo by Ruth Hellier-Tinoco.

island of Yunuén, the residents of Pacanda were involved in promotional activities to attract visitors to the island. A restaurant was constructed on the island in the 1990s, but little used. Pacanda has, until recently, been the most difficult to reach by launch, being farthest from the Pátzcuaro dock. By the end of the 1990s, plans were underway to convert part of the local school building in the centre of island into a small hotel, particularly to enable people to stay on the island for the duration of *Night of the Dead*, and to attend and witness the events in the cemetery. This proposition caused controversy among the islanders, with half the inhabitants in favor of the plan, desiring economic development, and half against, wishing to maintain their privacy and seclusion. After long deliberations the conversion took place in 2007 and a new launch service from the nearby shoreside village of Ucasanástacua was established to facilitate visitors with their visit to the island. With these new initiatives, the festival on Pacanda reaches a wider audience.[19]

Clothes, Costumes, and Cultural Heritage

In all of these island and village contexts, the Festivals of Music and Dance for *Night of the Dead* have equally sustained existing practices and enabled the creation of new work. Some of these occasions, particularly the nighttime festival on the island of Urandén, have provided contexts in which local P'urhépecha people come together from different villages to share their practices. Yet for tourists to the region, the Festivals of Music and Dance created environments in which the staged displays by P'urhépecha residents were viewed with an ethnographic and othering gaze, as the performances and practices were framed and interpreted as features of everyday P'urhépecha life, much as in the Disney film, *The Three Caballeros*. Ideas of indigenousness and authenticity were integral to these occasions, and the blurring of boundaries between everyday life and rehearsed enactment generated a context of P'urhépecha people as artifacts on display, and a heightened reading of national cultural heritage.

In a similar vein the Contests of Costume and Regional Clothing held in Tzintzuntzan and Pátzcuaro engendered an even more complex reception environment for audiences. Staged dance and music events inherently encompassed a display of local clothes and costumes, creating contexts in which P'urhépecha women wore their everyday clothes, and P'urhépecha men and boys wore a costume that was read as everyday clothes. In the most overt example, the costume for the *Dance of the Old Men* was a slightly modified version of early twentieth-century men's P'urhépecha clothes (which was also framed as pan-indigenous clothing), and when placed in contexts of normal life (for example, on Janitzio), caused a phenomenon of indecidability concerning real life or reenactment. However, creating an overt and deliberate exhibition of P'urhépecha clothing worn by and modeled on *any body*, as happened in the contests, placed the focus on the artifacts themselves as a form of cultural heritage. Competitions and events in which non-P'urhépecha people wore P'urhépecha clothing became a frequently used form of embodying a sense of nostalgia, and expressing an idea of *raíz Michoacana* (Michoacán roots).[20] The core of the issue is neatly encapsulated in the words of the governor of Michoacán, Cuauhtémoc Cárdenas Solórzano (1980–1986) (son of Lázaro Cárdenas), in a state publication documenting P'urhépecha clothing (1986). He dedicated the work to "the indigenous communities who have known how to protect and preserve their traditional clothes," going on to emphasize the importance of reviving, conserving, and disseminating those clothes as cultural heritage (1986:1). Through the contests in Tzintzuntzan and Pátzcuaro, staged as part of the *Night of the Dead* events, garments worn by local Lake Pátzcuaro residents were placed into both an ethnographic and an entertainment frame, performing as cultural heritage and a referent of tradition and authenticity.

Pilgrimage to Janitzio: Circulating Poetic and Premodern Images

As the ultimate environment of authenticity and cultural heritage, *Night of the Dead* on Janitzio remained the highlight for most visitors, with their overall objective being to attend the ceremony on the island. Each year the occasion comprised the same activities: throughout the evening a flotilla of boats, piloted by men from Janitzio and other islands, transported a constant stream of visitors to the island. Once on Janitzio, the tens of thousands of visitors were free to view the cemetery, to buy food, drink and souvenirs, and to be entertained by the Festival of Music and Dance that continued throughout the night on the basketball court. The festival changed little from the 1960s onward, incorporating a succession of local groups of musicians and dancers performing P'urhépecha pieces, and a repertoire comprising older works and newly created pieces (often based on themes of everyday life and work).

Desires for the experience of *Night of the Dead* on Janitzio were generated by photographic images and literary descriptions, setting up expectations of difference, exoticism, pilgrimage, and spirituality, and encompassing a magical and mystical dimension, allowing visitors to immerse themselves in a total experience. The journey to Janitzio and the encounter on the island enabled a fulfillment of certain anticipated desires. Unlike the journey to the island throughout the remainder of the year, for that one night the voyage took place in darkness, adding a distinct air of remoteness and dislocation. As the boats chugged through the water, the travelers passed candlelit canoes, eventually viewing the island emerging out of the dimness and mist, lit by thousands of candles. Visitors disembarked into another world—a world of the past and of difference, where women wore their traditional clothes and knelt by gravesides, surrounded by flowers and food. All the senses were engaged with the feel of the cold, damp mist; the pungent smell of incense and flowers; the sweet taste of *ponche* (hot fruit punch); the distant sound of music drifting through the air; the soft vision of shadowy figures in the graveyard; and the dazzling sight of brightly lit dancers and musicians performing on the basketball court. The one intrusion in the sense of total immersion in authentic ritual was the presence of tens of thousands of other visitors, who functioned as a constant reminder that this was very much a spectator occasion. Departing the island in the early hours of the morning, visitors journeyed back to their hotels and lodgings in Pátzcuaro leaving behind Janitzio, *Night of the Dead*, and the islanders in their separate and unique world.

In this setting representations of ethnicity, and notions of merging of real life/ reenactment, life/death, and an ethnographic/entertainment gaze were selectively shaped and promoted by the Michoacán Tourist Board, by state organizations (such as INI), and by private enterprise, including businesses and individuals of the Lake Pátzcuaro region. Images and literary texts performed potent roles in molding and constructing notions of tradition, indigenousness, and authenticity, circulating ideological and aesthetic concepts through tourist guidebooks and leaflets, postcards, posters, magazines, and newspapers. Embodied imagery most frequently replicated two iconic corporeal figures: women kneeling by gravesides, surrounded by candles and flowers; and men in canoes with butterfly nets, often lit by moonlight, with the island of Janitzio silhouetted in the background.

Each year the official printed program for *Night of the Dead*, published by the Michoacán Secretariat of Tourism, performed a profoundly influential role in shaping reception and interpretation of activities, peoples, and locations. The freely available and readily circulating trilingual publication (Spanish, French, English) engaged a form of language and imagery very similar to that used in the 1920s and 1930s in printed materials, such as the magazine *Mexican Folkways*, the academic journal *Ethnos*, and the theater program for *Hamarándecua*. Poetic descriptions were blended with purportedly factual information to give an impression that visitors were somehow simply eavesdropping on occurrences that would be taking place even if tourists were not present. Descriptions emphasized the authenticity of the region and inhabitants in terms of an unbroken bloodline to the pre-Hispanic era. In relation to Jarácuaro, the accounts described how the island was populated from ancient times, and emphasized the point that the islanders resisted the chichimeca conquistadores (a preincursion civilization), managing to preserve the traditions within an atmosphere of great purity (*Noche de Muertos* 2000: 15). Contextualization of the Festival of Music and Dance on Jarácuaro presented the activities as wholly embedded in village life, stating that "in the little plaza of the village, a place is given to all the groups of dancers from the village who show off their skills and virtuosity, because Jarácuaro, more than all the other villages of the region, is distinctive for the love that the inhabitants have for dance, song and for the extraordinary flautists. Jarácuaro has notable composers and choreographers" (ibid. orig.). Significantly, a photo of Gervasio López was also included in the brochure, yet rather than naming him, he was left as an anonymous face, and indeed was unpaid for the use of his image in this tourist guide (personal communication). In the 2007 brochure, dancing was framed as an inherent element of the *Night of the Dead* ceremony on Jarácuaro, with the statement that "this ancient town has conserved its tradition with a more pure atmosphere. The ceremony begins with the placement of large archways....Then groups of dancers perform in the plaza demonstrating their virtuosity as they execute beautiful pieces. Jarácuaro is famous for its musicians and dancers" (*Noche de Muertos* 2007:29 orig.).

On a national and international basis, Web sites and newspaper articles have been instrumental in propagating and perpetuating prescribed representation. One English-language tourist Web site refers to Janitzio as "quaint," noting the accessibility of the island—"located only 20 minutes away from Patzcuaro's dock"—and characterizing the activities as ancient— "The native communities who inhabit this beautiful place still preserve their ancient customs" (www.best-day.com). The performance by the men in their canoes is represented as part of the traditional ceremony of *Night of the Dead*—"One of the most famous customs is the Night of the Dead; during this celebration all the fishermen sail out with their butterfly-shaped nets and decorate their boats with candles" (ibid.). In another example, from the organization Inside Mexico, the description acknowledges the presence of tourists and folkloric dance, yet still uses potent language to reference preinvasion custom:

On the even of El Día de Muertos, the boats are loaded with people that are very busy taking the flowers and essential articles for the celebrations. The island is dressing up with beauty and mysticism! On the lake, one can also see the fishermen with their traditional nets that grace the view. They are called Butterfly Nets. Watching the fishermen go out in groups is a bewitching spectacle...The people of Janitzio have conserved this form of fishing, as well as other millenarian customs and traditions that are part of the enchantment of this island. Especially distinctive is the way in which the women dress, and their methods of cooking...It is surprising how in such a little island, thousands and thousands of visitors will arrive in order to witness this beautiful rite. In the preceding hours, the carpenters laboriously work to set a stage for the folkloric dances that will be performed as part of the celebrations. At night, with everything ready, the dances begin. The Danza de los Viejitos, Dance of the Old Men, is representative of this region. In pre-Hispanic times this dance was performed as a ritual honoring the Sun.

(Herz n.d. English original)

Even more fantastical, a description of Day of the Dead in Latin America on Wikipedia states that "At midnight on November 2, the people light candles and ride winged boats called mariposas (Spanish for 'butterflies') to Janitzio, an island in the middle of the lake where there is a cemetery, to honor and celebrate the lives of the dead there" (en.wikipedia.org).

In another striking illustration, a newspaper article documenting the event on Janitzio in 2007 engaged a form of poetic and myth-making language to describe the occasion, in a form very similar to that of the 1920s. A few examples of the text will serve to exemplify some of the key issues.

With devotion and faith, true to their traditions and customs, hundreds of indigenous P'urhépecha from the Lake Pátzcuaro region relived the ritual pagan-religious tradition Night of the Dead, whose ceremonies have lasted as a mark of their genuine nature and identity.

Neither the intense cold nor the delicate economic situation in which they live stopped the indigenous people from venerating their dead ancestors...

The spectacle of these pagan-religious celebrations of Night of the Dead in Michoacán has become famous internationally. (Roque 2007)

The journalist goes on to describe the women and children of Janitzio as being like "phantasmagorical figures, full of love and piety, bringing fruit and flowers, who sit by the graveside, with resignation and crying" (ibid.). By way of the passive description that the event "has become famous internationally," Roque chose to portray the process as a spontaneous one, not one which had been deliberately promoted and marketed with specific economic, political, and ideological goals in mind. The event was configured as a pagan-religious ritual, therefore characterizing it clearly as not Roman Catholic, and making associations with pre-Hispanic eras. In a similar vein, not only are the women framed as specifically in the past, in other words they are not "real" but phantasmagorical figures, but they are also denied their modernity in terms of their place in the economic world. Roque suggested that the "delicate economic situation in which they live [has not] stopped the indigenous people from venerating their dead ancestors," yet it was precisely the economic situation in which they lived that encouraged them to perpetuate a spectacle for the tens of thousands of visitors. The women and children had to perform for the multitudes of tourists, either inside or outside the cemetery, because of their marginalized economic situation. As the biggest money-making event of the year, the complex visitor attraction of *Night of the Dead* on Janitzio generated a utilitarian response in which the islanders would utilize the situation in whichever way they saw fit. Even as Roque refused to view the economic element for the Janitzio residents, he specifically dealt with financial issues in relation to businesses in Pátzcuaro noting that the hotels in Pátzcuaro were at full capacity, hosting about one hundred thousand Mexican and international tourists, going on to list the various countries from which visitors had come (England, the United States, Norway, Italy, Switzerland, Germany, France, Canada, and Cuba) (ibid.). Even as these Mexican and global visitors and the Pátzcuaro business owners were encompassed in a modern, and even postmodern economic world, the Janitzio residents were placed outside of this arrangement. Their lives and actions were interpreted as being of the past, propagating their function as iconic referents of authentic indigenousness.[21]

Exhibiting the *Soul of Mexico* in 3D

Perpetuating the role as spectator event, initiated in the 1920s with the visit of outsiders to Janitzio to witness *Night of the Dead*, so in the twenty-first century, the live occasion continues to attract vast crowds. Whereas the *Dance of the Old Men* circulates as a live spectacle in multiple contexts, both in Mexico and beyond (performed by P'urhépecha performers, school children, and Ballet Folklórico ensembles in Mexico and the United States), after the costumbrista theater performances of the 1930s, viewing *Night of the Dead* as a live event has required spectators to go to one unique location to observe the Janitzio islanders in situ and to experience the authentic, ancient ritual undertaken by authentic indigenous peoples. As journalist Roque noted in his newspaper article, Europeans journeyed to Janitzio and Pátzcuaro for the one special occasion. In 2000, however, the ritual of *Night of the Dead* on Janitzio, as enacted by the islanders, was transported to Europe as *Soul of Mexico*, with the promise that viewers and onlookers could experience the authentic ritual "as if they were there" (Hanover 2000, press release and www. mexico21.org.mx). Capturing the Janitzio residents undertaking *Night of the Dead*, *Soul of Mexico* was a filmic exhibition of *Night of the Dead* on Janitzio that was screened in Germany. The exhibition was staged in the Mexican Pavilion at *Expo 2000*, the World's Fair in Hannover, using footage that was filmed over a thirty-six-hour period on the island of Janitzio in 1999. Using large screens and a walk-through gallery, images of the activities in the cemetery on Janitzio were projected on both sides, creating an interactive experience. By wearing special glasses, visitors could view the figures of women and children as a "living diorama" in 3D (ibid.). Yet the presence of the tens of thousands of visitors on the island was absent from the display (see chapter 12 for detailed analysis). With this filmic exhibition, *Night of the Dead* on Janitzio was deployed as a representation of Mexico on the world stage, with the embodied activities of the P'urhépecha women were projected in an authentic and preinvasion ritual. In a trajectory leading from the earliest visit of state officials, from the initial photographic reproductions of the women in their cemetery captured by Carlos González, and from the staged theatrical representations in the postrevolutionary era, *Soul of Mexico* epitomized the profound signification of this embodied icon.

CHAPTER 9

Disseminating *The Old Men*

Mexico City, Europe, the World

THROUGHOUT THE LAST three decades of the twentieth century and during the first years of the twenty-first century, performism processes invoking and evoking *The Old Men* burgeoned in national and international contexts. Tours and staged events inside Mexican borders, in Europe, and in the United States incorporated *The Old Men*, and countless articles and publications included references to and descriptions of the dance. Television and radio programmes involving and referencing *The Old Men* were influential in the early 1980s, as part of the populist drive for national unity; and audio recordings of the music for *The Old Men* circulated in vinyl, cassette, and later CD form, particularly being used by folkloric dance ensembles throughout Mexico and the United States. With motivations ranging from the ideological and the political to the economic, a diverse range of people was involved in representational and dissemination processes, including state-sponsored and state-employed intellectuals, artists, and officials; individuals in autonomous private organizations and cultural associations; entrepreneurs; and independent artists. State-produced and state-endorsed outputs and events continued the trajectory of government-based scholars and artists disseminating representations of indigenous peoples and practices. In addition, private sector organizational deployment and usage proliferated. In virtually all cases, the representations of *The Old Men* perpetuated the network of signification established in the postrevolutionary era, invoking and alluding to notions of authenticity, origins, and othered peoples and bodies, and continuing to frame the dance as part of traditional village life. These images and portrayals often displayed an overtly ideological position, particularly taking an ethnographic and cultural heritage stance.

In this chapter my aim is to provide a sense of the multifarious forms and contexts of presentation that proliferated. In chapter 1 I documented exemplars of contemporary uses of *The Old Men* and here I offer a further small selection. These illustrations are each presented as short paragraphs that provide brief snapshots and glimpses of the wide range of circulating practices. The chapter deals with material chosen from a plethora of cases, firstly, staged events (live and recorded); and secondly, publications (encompassing literary and photographic texts). In chapters 10 and 12 I analyze further contemporary occurrences (including post-cards, tourist illustrations, and the European advertising poster). I conclude this chapter with a more developed example of the proliferation of Mexican Folkloric Dance ensembles across the border in the United States.

Staged Events: Live and Recorded

Arturo Macías, a prominent architect and sculptor from the Michoacán town of Uruapan, organized and managed a tour to Spain and Morocco in the early 1970s that lasted for just over two months, comprising ensembles from Michoacán (forty-five people in all), including *The Old Men* from Jarácuaro (with López and Francisco); the Bautista brothers from Paracho (performing as "Erandi"); and the Pulidos sisters from Uruapan. Just prior to this, Macías had produced an audio recording entitled *Música Indígena P'urhépecha* (P'urhépecha indigenous music), as part of a series of recordings *Maestros del Folklore Michoacano* (Masters of Michoacán folklore) (1973).

In 1985, after a huge earthquake had struck and caused devastation in Mexico City, officials engaged a P'urhépecha ensemble that was already living in the city to per-form *The Old Men* and P'urhépecha musical selections in parks and gardens every Sunday. The ensemble, *Los Nietos del Lago* (the Grandsons of the Lake) was that of the Gabriel family of the island of Urandén, Lake Pátzcuaro, who had migrated to the capital in the 1960s (cover photo). The strategy was a populist governmental gesture toward community consolidation and solidarity. Even as the city had been fragmented physically through the destruction of the earthquake, enacting *The Old Men* represented an embodied Mexican national spirit, enabling a sense of shared belonging and cohesion.

During the 1980s, Cuauhtémoc Cárdenas, governor of Michoacán, organized a series of tours and events encompassing music and dance, including *Fiesta Michoacana*, a staged occasion in Mexico City that comprised dances, music, and food, in much the same way that the FONADAN concerts in the National Museum of Anthropology had done in the 1970s, with *The Old Men* being featured as an integral element. Cárdenas was interested in promoting all things Michoacano, and an important aspect involved activities from the Lake Pátzcuaro region, where he had spent time as child, and which had therefore shaped his childhood. With *Fiesta Michoacana* there was an element of demarcation between authentic and folkloric performances and performers, made tangible through the notion of indigenous performers. As part of the event, Amalia Hernández, director of the Ballet Folklórico de México, was booked to give a class to some of the dancers, a method that Janitzio musician Moisés de la Cruz considered to be inappropriate, for, as he commented, "Her way of preserving the traditions isn't correct" (personal communication).

Television programs aired performances of music and dance designated as indigenous, gaining viewing figures of millions. In 1986 Gervasio López of Jarácuaro appeared on *Hoy Mismo* (Televisa); musicians from Janitzio performed on the variety show *Siempre en Domingo* with Raul Velasco; and an ensemble from Jarácuaro performed on *Vida Diaria*. For each appearance, musicians and dancers were given money for accommodation, food, and travel, but no wage.

An ensemble of *The Old Men* from Jarácuaro calling themselves *Los Nietos de los Viejitos* (the Grandsons of the Old Men), directed by Oliberto Matías, toured to Austria in the 1980s. They visited Spain, France, Germany and Italy, and danced as a form of publicity and campaigning to reclaim the pre-Hispanic feathered headdress or Penacho of Moctezuma.

Moisés Felipe, principal organizer of the Civil Association for the Promotion of P'urhépecha Culture in Mexico City, arranged and directed performances and tours incorporating *The Old Men* during the 1980s and 1990s. An objective of the P'urhépecha association was to publicize P'urhépecha practices to both P'urhépecha and non-P'urhépecha audiences in the capital. For the many P'urhépecha people who had migrated to Mexico City, this association enabled them to participate in their traditional festivals and to therefore pass on their traditions to their children (Nava 1998:27). Demonstrating collaboration between an autonomous association and state institutions, in 1989 Felipe was the principal organizer of a large event held in the National Auditorium in Mexico City, entitled *Fiesta P'urhépecha*, which was supported by the government of Michoacán, particularly through the endorsement of the governor of Michoacán, Genovevo Figueroa, and the director of the Michoacán Cultural Institute, P'urhépecha intellectual Ireneo Rojas Hernández. Felipe also took *The Old Men* on tour, both nationally and internationally, as part of an event in the vein of *costumbrista* performances comprising a repertoire of dances from Michoacán. Both the Gabriel family (of Urandén, but living in Mexico City (cover photo)) and López's ensemble (of Jarácuaro) participated with *The Old Men*. One staged performance took place in San Antonio, Texas, for the inauguration and closing ceremony of an event of traders and craftworkers of which Felipe was president. Another performance in Mexico City was organized in order to receive the wife of President Salinas de Gortari. Felipe also recorded many P'urhépecha musical ensembles in Mexico City.[1]

Pedro Dimas, originally from the Lake Pátzcuaro village of Ichupio, and also a long-time resident of Morelia, made various trips to California between 1980 and the early twenty-first century. With his family ensemble, he performed both *The Old Men*, and music and dances composed and created by himself. Such excursions involved transporting costumes of *The Old Men* to the United States for use by folkloric dance ensembles.

The directors of Discos Corasón, a renowned recording company based in Mexico City, invited López and his ensemble to perform *The Old Men* for a concert of P'urhépecha music in London, England, in 1994.[2] Discos Corasón had already produced recordings of the López musical ensemble "Amanecer" and of other P'urhépecha musical groups (see *Dalia Tsïtsïki*), so they wanted to provide an opportunity for López's group to perform in Europe. However, López declined to go, feeling that the fee was not sufficient and that he was therefore being exploited (personal communication). The musical group "Erandi" (the Bautista family from the highland town of Paracho) went in their place.[3]

The Michoacán State Tourist Board organized, and continues to organize, many tours and events in the United States (particularly the southwestern states), throughout Mexico, and within the state of Michoacán, incorporating *The Old Men* and engaging musicians and dancers from Jarácuaro. As an official, state-sponsored iconic representation of the state of Michoacán, *The Old Men* plays a leading role within the Michoacán State Plan for Tourist Development. According to one state official, the principal objective is to disseminate "the values of our culture [and] our folklore [through the presentation of] indigenous music and dance groups from the region in national and international events" (Bosco Castro: personal communication). Embodying these qualities and attributes, both *The Old Men* of Jarácuaro and the musicians and dancers from Jarácuaro have frequently been used as artifacts of cultural heritage and "our folklore."

An event entitled *Fiesta Purépecha* was organized and hosted by the National Museum of Popular Cultures in Coyoacán, Mexico City, in 2001. Three other governmental organizations also contributed to the occasion: the Michoacán Cultural Institute; the College of Michoacán (a graduate college in Zacapu, Michoacán); and the Program for Support of the Municipal and Community Cultures.[4] In addition to a program of P'urhépecha music played by el Grupo Purépecha de Charapan and the launch of a scholarly book on Michoacán songs published by the College of Michoacán (Ochoa and Pérez 2001), *The Old Men* was danced by P'urhépecha residents of Mexico City, fulfilling its role as the most representative P'urhépecha dance.

Publications

In 1972, an article published in the 1920s that included references to *The Old Men*, the island of Jarácuaro, and Nicolás Bartolo Juárez, was reprinted in the national newspaper *El Sol de México*. The author was renowned theater director and writer Rafael M. Saavedra, who, along with Carlos González, Francisco Domínguez, and Rubén M. Campos, had been influential in instigating the postrevolutionary state-sponsored theater movements under the auspices of SEP (see Bullé Goyri 2003). In the article, which appeared in a section entitled "Our Mexico," Saavedra characterized *The Old Men* as an overtly ritualistic and indigenous practice, describing indigenous peoples as "our Indians," and referring specifically to Bartolo Juárez as an "indian of pure race (*indio de raza pura*), who, in addition to composing, directs a quartet of dancers who dance 'The Old Men' for religious fiestas.... From the door of the church come 'the old men' formed in a line" (1972). Despite being a recirculation of ideas from the 1920s, the piece in the 1970s context was not reframed or positioned as an historic document, but was presented as entirely relevant to the contemporary environment.

Francisco J. Bravo Ramírez published a book documenting the economic, political, and social aspects of Michoacán (1975). The book included a full-page photo of *The Old Men*, with the accompanying caption "La Danza de los Viejitos, Pátzcuaro, Michoacán" (1975:61). Although not named, the ensemble depicted is that of López from Jarácuaro (with Gervasio López on vihuela and Felix Francisco on violin). In close proximity to the photo, just a few pages away within a section on "Indigenismo," Bravo Ramírez refers to "the indigenous problem," characterizing the population as "our indigenous," and stating that "the Government of Mexico has followed a policy of help, in every way possible, for our indigenous; however, their integration into the progress which the country has been achieving has still not been managed" (1975:67). The juxtaposition of the photographic image of the iconic dance and the overt ideological reference to the indigenous problem highlights the continuing dichotomous usage of *The Old Men* and the Lake Pátzcuaro performers as simultaneously valorized and backward.

A book entitled *Mexican Native Dances: Regional Dances of Mexico* (n.d.), by Luis Covarrubias (published in English and Spanish in Mexico City), comprised a short descriptive text and colored illustrations of fourteen dances, including *The Old Men*.[5] The tone of the description was factual, emphasizing the ritualistic nature of the dance and analyzing it in reference to a P'urhépecha pre-Hispanic past. Colored drawings of *The Old Men* depicted two masked dancers (one playing a jarana with six strings). Of particular note is the contrast between the brown-skinned hands with the pink of the masks (n.p.). Covarrubias's account has been frequently recycled in later documents.

U.S. scholar Janet Brody Esser referred to the *Dance of the Old Men* of Jarácuaro in her book on the ceremonial masks of the P'urhépecha highlands, published by INI (1984). She dismissed the version from Jarácuaro as inauthentic, due to a perceived influence of the Ballet Folklórico of Mexico City, commenting that "the group does not perform in their birthplace, where there is no dance of *Los Viejos*, but they are contracted to dance in neighboring villages and in the most expensive tourist hotels in Pátzcuaro" (1984:107).

Néstor García Canclini, scholar of Mexican popular culture, made various references to *The Old Men* is his publication *Notas sobre las máscaras, danzas y fiestas de
Michoacán* (Notes about masks, dances, and fiestas of Michoacán), published by
the government of Michoacán (1985). He detailed aspects of the lives of the musicians and dancers of Jarácuaro, particularly in terms of capitalist modernization
(see chapter 13 for further discussion). Notably, when García Canclini undertook
the research for this book he was near the beginning of his academic career. As he
went on to become an internationally renowned scholar, famous for his seminal
works on popular culture, hybridity, and modernity, it is significant that one of the
formational and foundational experiences encompassed *The Old Men* and the
Lake Pátzcuaro context.

The *Católogo de danzas y fiestas de Michoacán* (catalogue of dances and fiestas of
Michoacán), published by the government of Michoacán, documented dozens of
practices, itemizing each in terms of location, uses, and age (García Contreras
1986). The itemization for *The Old Men* of Jarácuaro noted that it was danced on
22 January and 25 December, was more than one hundred years old, and was
known as "the most representative demonstration of the folklore of Michoacán"
(ibid.: n.p.).

Musical transcriptions of Gervasio López's compositions for *The Old Men* were
reproduced within a didactic book for learning to play the violin, published by two
governmental institutions: the National Institute of Fine Arts (INBA) and the
National Center for Musical Research, Documentation and Information
(CENIDIM) (Hernández and Dordelly 1986). Entitled *Sones para violín*, the
teaching material encompassed short musical pieces from a selection of regional
dances and ballroom dances. López was named as the composer, and "Jarácuaro"
given as the location.

An elaborate book entitled *Tradiciones mexicanas* (Mexican Traditions) included a
description of *The Old Men* and full-page color photo of four musicians and four
dancers from Jarácuaro posing in Morelia in front of the fountain of *Las Tarascas*
(the P'urhépecha Women) (Vertí 1991: between 272 & 273, 387)(46 ◉). The dancers
and musicians in the photo are unnamed, however, they are the ensemble of Juan
González and Juan and Felix Francisco from Jarácuaro. The performers were not
aware that the photograph had been published and did not receive any form of
remuneration for this. Although not credited as such, the text is an exact copy of
that published by Nestor García Canclini (1985:40). (For a discussion of this photo
and the fountain see chapter 12).

Circulating internationally, and aimed particularly at back-packing tourists, the
guidebook *Lonely Planet Mexico* referred to *The Old Men* of Pátzcuaro within a
section entitled "Indian Dance" (Noble 1995:51). Similarly, the *American Automobile
Association Travel Guide to Mexico* noted that "many of the colorful native dances
performed throughout Mexico originated here [Pátzcuaro]. One of the most

widely known is 'Los Viejitos' (the little old men), a witty commentary on the manners and foibles of age" (1990:104)

The *Eyewitness Guide: Dance*, an English-language publication for children, with a readership predominantly in the United States, Europe, and Australasia, included *The Old Men* of Jarácuaro (Grau 1998:32). Within a section entitled "Behind a Mask," a photo of two masked Old Men dancers from Lake Pátzcuaro are juxtaposed with four other masks from around the globe (Papua New Guinea, Borneo, Himalayas, Côte d'Ivoire) (ibid.). A brief textual reference serves to contextualize the Old Man mask and dance: "Little Old Men dance masks, Mexico. Clown-like figures are part of many mask traditions. In the Mexican state of Michoacán, wooden masks painted pink represent the Viejito, or Little Old Man, a grandfather cavorting around in a humorous manner" (ibid.).

More Border Crossings: U.S. Ballet Folklórico Ensembles and the Chicano Movement

Returning the focus to the United States, from the 1960s onward *The Old Men* played a significant role as an iconic referent and marker of Mexicanness in the context of Ballet Folklórico Ensembles. In the early 1960s, the professional ensemble of the Ballet Folklórico de México traveled to the United States, performing a repertoire that included *The Old Men*.[6] The tours had a great impact upon Mexican-American audiences, particularly of the Southwest, influencing the course of Mexican dance in the United States through the formation of numerous Ballet Folklórico ensembles and setting in motion a potent poetic and artistic movement with considerable political implications. The tours took place precisely at the time when the Chicano movement was developing and were therefore efficacious as a highly visual and replicable form of Mexicanness. Rooted in civil rights, the Chicano movement dealt with the political and ideological shaping of a newly evolving Chicano identity, in other words, a Mexican-American identity in the United States. With the performances of the Ballet Folklórico, the iconic dances provided a tangible form for expression of heritage and tradition, and created a sense of pride and ethnic awareness in the Mexican-American/Chicano community. In the wake of the tour by the Ballet Folklórico de México, scores of similar dance companies were created at universities, colleges, and high schools throughout the Southwest by students of Mexican heritage, soon forming what became the Ballet Folklorico Mexicano[7] organization. From the outset the Folklorico Movement took an ideological stance and engaged with the ongoing political situation and struggle. As a form of resistance to the domination of the U.S. racist policies and practices toward Mexicans, the Folklorico Movement of ensembles emerged as a resistant, creative, and self-assertive force. In one instance, students of Mexican heritage throughout the Southwest held demonstrations demanding funding, teachers, and classes to establish the dance organizations (Shay 2002).

The aesthetic model for most ensembles and dances was drawn directly from the Ballet Folklórico de México, for the newly formed companies wanted to recreate "the authenticity, *espectáculo*, and pride in heritage and ethnicity created by Amalia Hernández" and were "not interested in recreating authentic dances from obscure villages" (ibid.:87).[8] *The Old Men*, as performed by many Mexican Folklórico companies, did indeed draw upon the spectacular and virtuosic nature of the Ballet Folklórico de México version, a practice that continues into the twenty-first century. Thus, as *The Old Men* formed part of the repertoire of the Ballet Folklórico, so it became a fundamental element of the repertoire of the Folklórico ensembles in the United States. *The Old Men* was further commodified, with a heightening of the exaggerated and virtuosic elements, and an increase in the number of participants, often through the inclusion of many dancers. Curiously, the long line of dancers was closer to that deployed for the nonpublic uses of Old Men dances in the P'urhépecha region. Costumes and masks for the dance were ordered from the Lake Pátzcuaro area, and any people who made a journey to the region was charged with carrying back items. Although the folkloric and theatricalized form of *The Old Men* was a dance for men only, a role was also created for women, with extended lines of dancers wearing the costume of *uarhecitas* (P'urhépecha young women), dancing bare-foot, swaying gently, and holding brightly colored painted *jícaras*, the P'urhépecha utilitarian object used as scenographic imagery in 1919 in *Fantasia Mexicana* and in 1921 in *Noche Mexicana* (42 ◉).

In summary, by the end of the twentieth century, through these multiple forms of communication, *The Old Men* of Jarácuaro was thoroughly embedded in myriad modes as an efficacious icon of Mexico. In the twenty-first century, processes of performism ensure that representational transmission and circulation of the *Dance of the Old Men* of Jarácuaro continues in manifold contexts both in Mexico, the United States, and internationally. From the initial staged theatricalization of *The Old Men* in the postrevolutionary years of the early 1920s, when Nicolás Bartolo Juárez taught the dance to a group of student teachers in Mexico City, the trajectory of deployment as an iconic, embodiment of Mexico has been maintained and perpetuated. In the twenty-first century, individual musicians and dancers from the village of Jarácuaro still perform the dance, and continue to be captured and reproduced in photographic form in the distinctive linen costume, grinning mask, and beribboned hat.

CHAPTER 10

Keeping It Local

Reappropriation, Migration, and the Zacán Festival

EVER SINCE THE early 1920s, residents of Lake Pátzcuaro communities have been essential to transmission processes of *The Old Men*, as teachers, dancers, musicians, organizers, costume-makers, and mask-makers, undertaking roles which continue through to the twenty-first century. Yet even as the *Dance of the Old Men* was circulating in national and international environments, people in both the Lake Pátzcuaro area and also the wider P'urhépecha region used and reappropriated the dance for local contexts, particularly socioreligious occasions and festivals. Having reviewed examples of multifarious dissemination cases in national, U.S., and international contexts in the previous chapters, here I turn the focus back on the Lake Pátzcuaro and P'urhépecha region. Firstly, I discuss processes of transmission and family involvement, including the experience of Gervasio López of Jarácuaro, and the migration of the Gabriel family of Urandén to Mexico City to create a mariachi ensemble.[1] Secondly, I address issues of reappropriation and revitalization of P'urhépecha cultural practices, noting uses of *The Old Men* in local events and fiestas, and initiatives in the P'urhépecha region connected to political autonomy movements. Within this context I analyze the P'urhépecha Artistic Festival of Zacán, an event that was initiated in the 1970s as a low-key local fiesta, and was transformed into an international spectacle, in which performances of *The Old Men* by P'urhépecha and folkloric ensembles form an integral part.[2] Finally, I reflect upon my own presence and impact as a musician and researcher, particularly related to the making of an audio recording of compositions by Nicolás Bartolo Juárez, among others, with musicians from Jarácuaro, and the consequences of this for one member of the Bartolo Juárez family.

From Father to Son: Family Transmission in Lake Pátzcuaro

From the postrevolutionary years onward, ensembles of Old Men dancers and musicians from Jarácuaro have been the principal source for regional, national, and even international events. In addition, there have been significant ensembles on the island of Urandén, and in the lakeside villages of Cucuchucho, Santa Fe, and Ichupio. Family groupings, both blood relations and *compadrazgo* (godparent relations), in combination with the concept of passing on the tradition have been important elements in the formation and maintenance of these groups, engaging a principal and practice of transmission of responsibility which usually relates to socioreligious contexts. A *carguero* (person in charge) has the obligation of organizing a fiesta or religious celebration for one year, and then transfers this duty to another person for the following year. On Jarácuaro various ensembles of *The Old Men* have formed, disintegrated, merged, and reformed over the decades, and processes of transmission through a family line have persisted, with fathers and uncles conveying and handing on their skills and knowledge to their sons and nephews, incorporating them into an ensemble at a young age. *The Old Men* on Jarácuaro is a cottage industry, in much the same way as hat production. It is part of the fabric of life and an activity in which many family members have been engaged in some way, forming a significant element in the collective identity of the community. Although most musicians and dancers undertake hat-making as their main source of income, *The Old Men* can provide a supplement to this, as some performers actively seek out venues and events at which to perform, although the amounts earned are usually small.

In terms of transmission patterns, the legacy of Nicolás Bartolo Juárez is significant because, although no family members directly related to Bartolo Juárez continued with the dance, many villagers who were taught by him subsequently formed their own ensembles and continued to pass on *The Old Men* through family lines.[3] In the 1930s, Gervasio López, Braulio González, and Felix Francisco, among others, were taught by Bartolo Juárez, and all went on to teach the dance and music to their sons (Atilano and Pedro; Juan; and Juan, respectively), who similarly taught their sons. As migration has had a great impact upon the lives of many Jarácuaro residents, so in some cases the familial transmission patterns associated with *The Old Men* have been interrupted by migratory activities. As boys have become young men, so they have chosen to migrate (either within Mexico or to the United States) on a permanent or transitory basis. In the late-1990s, at the age of seventeen, Miguel and Israel, the oldest sons of both Juan González and Juan Francisco, who danced in the Peña Colibrí in Morelia as children, migrated to the United States.[4]

With regard to the other originating family, the Orozcos, it was not until many decades later that members of the Orozco family renewed an interest in the dance. In 1986 through an initiative of Abel Orozco (a great-nephew of Simón and Andrés Orozco) the ensemble Los Artesanos was formed with various family members. At first there was minimal interest, with the group coming together just for sporadic events. However, by the mid-1990s Abel had composed a collection of pieces and organized more opportunities for performances, particularly in tourist locations in Pátzcuaro (figure 1.9). Abel's daughters, as well as his sons, perform as musicians in the ensemble, an aspect that is still little repeated.

In the formation of an ensemble various motivations came into play, such as the desire to perform for a special event (for example the Festival on Jarácuaro for *Night of the Dead*) or the possibility of earning some money. One ensemble, "Alegrir de Vivir" (Joy of Living), took shape following the death of a fellow islander through alcoholism. Coming together through Alcoholics Anonymous on the island, the group desired to celebrate their own lives by dancing *The Old Men*. Processes of transmission and teaching have generally been informal, with the learning of both music and choreography taking place through listening and watching. Groups get together in a house or in one of the performance venues to go over the steps and to make adjustments to the music. From the 1960s onward, recordings of the music for *The Old Men* of Lake Pátzcuaro circulated in the form of LPs, cassettes, and later CDs, so musicians also learned by listening and playing along. Many local ensembles made recordings of their music for the dance in small, commercially run studios, either in Mexico City or the Michoacán town of Uruapan. One company, Alborada Records of Uruapan, ran a system which enabled musicians to easily and cheaply make a recording, by providing a studio, recording facilities, and technical staff. Once the recording was completed, Alborada kept the master recording and made copies for trade, which then circulated throughout the central Michoacán region. These recordings have particularly been distributed in the P'urhépecha region, and have also been used by school and adult folkloric ensembles in Mexico and the United States as the accompaniment for performances of *The Old Men* (figure 1.7) (48 ◓).

Of all the individuals, groups, and families connected with *The Old Men*, Gervasio López has been the one person represented as synonymous with the dance. It seems remarkable that thousands of Mexicans, particularly in Michoacán, but also in other states, knew the name "Tata Gervasio," and associated it specifically with *The Old Men* and with Jarácuaro. As I noted in chapter 7 López grew up on Jarácuaro, where, under the tutelage of Bartolo Juárez, he was involved with *The Old Men* from an early age. In the mid-1950s, he formed his own ensemble and from then until his death in November 1999 he performed in countless venues throughout Mexico, and in Europe and the United States. López was frequently promoted through governmental agencies as an authentic representative of the P'urhépecha people. His embodied, photographed image, along with that of his ensemble of musicians and dancers, appeared on postcards, tourist guides, and publicity material, and continues to circulate even after his death (see chapter 12 for a discussion of postcards using López's image). He was represented as an object of cultural patrimony that belonged to the nation as an artifact of public property. The official projected image of López characterized him as a creative individual who was indigenous, rural, poor, and self-taught, who fished in the lake, and who wove hats for a living. As a musician he was portrayed as having an unsophisticated and "natural" performance style that "reflected" his lifestyle. He was glorified and valued, but only in a prescribed manner, and was therefore constrained to the role assigned to him by others. Although he attempted to make the most of opportunities that were presented to him, he was frequently caught in a context of reconstructed ethnicity that therefore required a utilitarian response. In other words, he lived up to the role of indigenous P'urhépecha villager, in the expectation that he would at least receive a worthwhile financial remuneration. López, and also his sons, were acutely aware of the sense of fame, glorification, and romanticization that surrounded them, and despite the numerous state-organized events in which they performed (for which they were generally paid only token fees), they remained financially poor, causing bitterness, frustration and a impression of having been exploited (personal communication).

After López died in 1999, his death was capitalized upon much as was his life. *La Voz de Michoacán*, a daily newspaper with a wide readership in Mexico and the United States, ran a front-page article on him ("Murió Tata Gervasio" 1999). In the article, music for *The Old Men* and other compositions by López were described as "symbols of the P'urhépecha musical culture," and associated very specifically with the term "folklore" and the Lake Pátzcuaro region (ibid.). The iconic status of the *Dance of the Old Men* of Jarácuaro was affirmed through the declaration that it had been presented around the world, further solidifying its place in the imaging of Mexicanness through indigenous practice in a global arena. Continuing the dichotomous construction of anonymous folklore and newly created tradition—a construction from the 1920s—at least López was afforded a position as "the creator of the traditional Dance of 'the Viejitos'" (ibid.). López's legacy as the principal representative of *The Old Men* also lives on at the yearly P'urhépecha Artistic Festival of Zacán. In 2000, an award dedicated to the memory of López was created, and each year since that time, ensembles from the P'urhépecha region and from folkloric organizations have performed *The Old Men* in a bid to win the prize (discussed later in this chapter) (17–18 ⬤).

Migration, Mexico City, and Mariachi

During the twentieth century, ensembles of *The Old Men* were formed in the Lake Pátzcuaro communities of Santa Fe, Cucuchucho, Ichupio, and Urandén. In the village of Santa Fe, the dance was perpetuated by Juan Hernández, who played for the Ballet Folklórico of the Michoacán Cultural Institute in Morelia in the 1980s and 1990s, which involved tours to Europe. Hernández continued to direct groups of children from Santa Fe for performances in folkloric festivals and state events, including an enactment in the Michoacán State Museum in Morelia (22 ⬤). Up until the 1960s, musicians and dancers from the lakeside community of Cucuchucho played a prominent role, with one particular ensemble participating in many national and regional events predominantly in the 1930s and 1940s. In 1963, a version of *The Old Men* was recorded by folklorist José Raul Hellmer, in which musician José Pablo of Cucuchucho accompanied the dancers with a small guitar with metal strings (*La Música Tradicional en Michoacán* 1990). During the latter years of the twentieth century, as dancers and musicians of *The Old Men* in Cucuchucho died or migrated, it was no longer practiced in the village. However, in the 1990s school-teacher Pablo Alejo Reynoso, from the island of Pacanda, taught *The Old Men* to his pupils, resulting in performances in the village again.

Pedro Dimas, who grew up in Ichupio and migrated to Morelia for work pur-poses, formed a family-based ensemble which enacted *The Old Men* in juxtaposition with Dimas's own choreographic piece, *La Danza de los Tumbís*, which he specifically created for display at the tourist-oriented Festivals of Music and Dance for *Night of the Dead* in Lake Pátzcuaro. In creating his dance, Dimas specifically aimed to pro-vide a point of comparison and contrast with *The Old Men*, so he invented *Los Tumbís*—the young ones (personal communication and Vázquez 1986: L9) (39 ◑). As Dimas's ensemble was permanently based in Morelia, they were frequently con-tracted to perform *The Old Men* for commercial and folkloric events.

On the island of Urandén, following the death of Rufino Gabriel in 1958, the responsibility of being *a cargo de* (in charge of) *The Old Men* went to his oldest son, Esteban, until he emigrated from the island to look for work in Mexico City in 1963. Esteban's brothers, José Fausto and Evaristo, continued to rehearse and perform *The Old Men* on Urandén, until they too left their island for Mexico City in 1967. At this point Evaristo's brother-in-law, Genaro Camilo, continued *The Old Men* on Urandén, with his own sons Simón and Elías and other family members participating. When Genaro's own sons also migrated (to Mexico City and Guadalajara) Genaro kept the group going, relying on musical support from the members of the family when they returned to the island for special events, particularly the celebration of *Night of the Dead* (figure 10.1) (21 ◑). For the Gabriel family in Mexico City, the *Dance of the Old Men* remained an important aspect of their lives. Although their principal source of earnings was, and continues to be, as mariachi musicians, with their own family-based ensemble Mariachi Juvenil, the family has continued to perform *The Old Men*. They have taught the music and dance to their children, all of whom were born and brought up in Mexico City. Unlike the majority of the ensembles in the Lake Pátzcuaro region, in which only men and boys participated, three girls of the Gabriel family in Mexico City (Verónica, Teresa, and Fabiola) performed *The Old Men*, learning the music and choreography from an early age. These girls also performed with the mariachi ensemble, with Verónica as vocalist, and Teresa and Fabiola as vio-linists. In Mexico City, the principal audiences for *The Old Men* have been P'urhépecha and Michoacán migrants (for whom *The Old Men* acts as a potent signifier of *home*), and residents and tourists attending folkloric events. Taking their lead from a finan-cial consideration, the priority of the Gabriel family is to perform as a mariachi ensemble, which often entails having to turn down work performing *The Old Men* and other P'urhépecha music in order to take mariachi contracts. Although they have not produced any audio recordings of their mariachi ensemble, they have made numerous recordings of their own P'urhépecha music compositions, including music for *The Old Men*, which they sell both in Mexico City and in the Lake Pátzcuaro region.[5] Even though Mexico City has been their place of residence for many decades, they have maintained close ties with Urandén, returning to their island for special dates, and performing *The Old Men* locally for festivals (Hellier 2001b) (Cover photo: the Gabriel family.) (31–37 ◑).

Figure 10.1 An all-day event entitled *P'urhépecha Festival* organized by, and held in the grounds of the Instituto Nacional Indigenista (INI) (National Indigenist Institute), Pátzcuaro, in 1998. Arranged solely for P'urhépecha participants and spectators rather than tourists and visitors the occasion encompassed food, crafts, music, and dance. The music and dance contest was held on the basketball court, decorated with a painted backdrop depicting the island of Janitzio, P'urhépecha residents, and the *Dance of the Fish* (Pescado). A *chinchorro* fishing net, usually deployed on the nearby lake, was strung up over the performance area as a scenographic feature. In the photo, the Genaro Camilo family of the island of Urandén perform the *Dance of the Old Men* (24–25 ◉).
Photo by Ruth Hellier-Tinoco.

Old Men Dancing in the Church

The dance of old men that the Orozco brothers and Bartolo Juárez enacted in Jarácuaro in the 1920s was a durational, non-fixed form that they danced in the streets, particularly during the Christmas and New Year festivities. Even as this form was commodified and fixed to become the *Dance of the Old Men* in national and international contexts, so dances of old men continued to circulate in Lake Pátzcuaro villages throughout the twentieth century, being developed and reappropriated for local contexts, as part of socioreligious events, and for festivals and competitions, particularly from the 1970s onward. Touristic, political, and local settings interfaced, and at times amalgamated, as the fixed form so familiar in appropriated contexts became just another element in private fiestas. In some instances, all dramaturgical elements of *The Old Men* as enacted in folkloric and touristic contexts have been engaged, whereas for other occasions only certain components have been deployed. For example, within one group of dancers a range of different masks of old men may be used, some of which are those worn specifically for touristic, folkloric events, while others are only utilized for non-public occasions. Similarly, the music may be that which is played for tourist audiences, even as the choreography differs considerably. Notably, as the dancers on Jarácuaro have developed a more virtuosic zapateado style for public audiences, this alteration has also been incorporated into local performances.

One of the main occasions for which *The Old Men* is danced locally is the celebration of *Nuestro Señor Cristo de Carácuaro*, Our Lord of Carácuaro. Each year this occasion is marked with two events by people from Jarácuaro: a local fiesta in Jarácuaro, and a pilgrimage to the village of Carácuaro in the Tierra Caliente (which is not part of the P'urhépecha region). In both locations *The Old Men* is enacted in the atrium of the church, and danced as a ceremonial and ritual act (28–30 ◑). Similarly, forms of dances of old men and *The Old Men* have also been used on Jarácuaro for celebrations of *Señor de la Misericordia* (Lord of Mercy) on 22 January, and to mark the feast of *San Pedro* (Saint Peter), the Patron Saint of the village, on 29 June. Boys and girls dance on these occasions, with the girls costumed as a *uarhecita* (P'urhépecha young woman) in full P'urhépecha dress, while the boys wear the *traje de manta* (linen suit), with hat and mask. Throughout the day a dance of old men is danced inside the church, outside in the atrium, and in the courtyards of the houses of the *cargueros* (those in charge). *The Old Men* in its folkloric form has also been used on Jarácuaro, and by Jarácuaro residents away from their village, as entertainment for celebrations such as baptisms and weddings.

In various communities of the Lake Pátzcuaro region, forms of masked old men dances are enacted during the season of Christmas, New Year, and Kings' Day (6 January). Celebratory dances take place inside the church in front of the altar (sometimes with no congregation present) and then continue throughout the day along the streets and around the village (26–27 ◑). In the community of Ichupio dances of old men take place on 25 and 26 December and 6 and 7 January, organized by Pedro Dimas. Dimas's *Dance of the Tumbís*, created specifically for the tourist Festivals of *Night of the Dead* (mentioned above), has also been drawn into the local calendar and is performed on 24 December for a pilgrimage from the hamlet of Ojo de Agua to the church of Tzintzuntzan.

Continuation, Revitalization, and Reclaiming Janitzio

Quite apart from the many dances using old men figures, a diversity of other dance and musical practices are enacted throughout the year for local socioreligious occasions in the Lake Pátzcuaro region. Even on the island of Janitzio, although visitors are present in the village for most days of the year with huge influxes of tourists for *Night of the Dead* and during seasonal vacation periods, the principal socioreligious calendared occasions have continued to be celebrated as local festive events, with a richness of practices that reveals the importance of music and dance as key elements in ongoing fiestas. For example, Corpus Christi is celebrated with masked dances, musical ensembles, processions through the island, and durational rituals, involving all the residents. As Corpus Christi is a celebration of thanksgiving with specific reference to trades, crafts, and occupations that have sustained each family throughout the year, villagers create representations of their vocations (such as model launches hung around their bodies), processing and dancing with these to the temple. Some families are still sustained by fishing, so large replicas of fish are danced through the streets, with masked characters carrying fishing nets. Inside and over the entrance to the church, fishing nets are strung and draped as forms of decoration, tying in with the scenographic and performative uses of fishing nets for the Festivals of Music and Dance for *Night of the Dead* and for the tourist displays in canoes for visitors to the island. However, for this one occasion of Corpus Christi the nets perform a symbolic act in a private ritual of thanksgiving for Janitzio islanders (40–41 ◗).

In the mid-1980s, Mexican ethnomusicologist Arturo Chamorro stated that "tradition has been sacrificed" to the demands of tourists and tourism, characterizing the situation as one in which tourism demands spectacle in return for money exchanged during the visitors' stay, therefore leading to sacrificing the tradition (1983a:3). Chamorro noted that the east side of the lake had been transformed more than the west side, due to the influx and presence of tourists (ibid). In a similar vein, Fernando Nava, scholar of P'urhépecha culture, asserted that "national society is increasingly suffocating [P'urhépecha] indigenous culture" (1998:24). Taking a different position, P'urhépecha anthropologist and priest Agustín Jacinto Zavala suggested that national culture can enable the P'urhépecha people to survive and flourish by "selecting those parts or aspects of the national culture which will strengthen the revitalization of the [P'urhépecha] culture" (1988:134).[6] Throughout this study I have documented processes by which two specific elements of music, dance, and ritual of Lake Pátzcuaro were commodified and promoted by governmental agents and institutions within nationalistic and touristic agendas. Here, addressing the observations of Chamorro, Nava, and Jacinto Zavala, I turn my attention to activities in the P'urhépecha region that have involved often rather complex collaborative ventures. I particularly relate this to the idea that cultural revitalization movements among various ethnic groups in the last hundred years or so have led to self-conscious efforts to preserve their heritage of folk music and dance (see Rosenberg 1993). Although this principle is applicable in certain ways to the P'urhépecha context, the situation has mainly been complex and contradictory. Processes of appropriation, reappropriation, representation, and revitalization have interfaced and blended together, often taking place through composite sets of connections between organizational bodies and individuals. Whereas many aspects of P'urhépecha culture have indeed been altered and transformed throughout the twentieth century, the circumstances resulting in such changes are multifaceted and paradoxical. New possibilities have opened up and fresh elements of P'urhépecha culture have been created, even as other components have fallen into disuse. The nationalistic and touristic promotional activities of *The Old Men*, and the Festivals of Music and Dance for *Night of the Dead* on Lake Pátzcuaro have led to contexts for original compositions and choreography, and to revitalization and reappropriation for enactment at local socioreligious occasions.

In the main there have been three overarching organizational agents and processes: firstly, state led and controlled; secondly, P'urhépecha led and controlled; thirdly, individual enterprises (such as the tours in the 1970s and recordings by nongovernmental production companies). In many instances, these agents have worked in combination and collaboration. However, from the second half of the twentieth century onward there were also self-conscious efforts for local revitalization. As Chamorro commented, "Groups of intellectual natives have also emerged, including some musicians and writers who have been well recognized for their work and labor of promoting the P'urhépecha culture" (1994:82). Throughout the 1980s and 1990s, events, projects, and investigations relating to P'urhépecha culture took place that were either wholly or partially conceived, instigated, and undertaken by P'urhépecha people. However, these activities did not just promote P'urhépecha culture, as Chamorro suggested, but, as with all other dissemination processes, also *shaped* it through choices concerning which material to endorse. It is notable that many of those who became the most prominent P'urhépecha activists were those who had moved away from their home village in the P'urhépecha region to urban areas of Mexico (particularly Morelia and Mexico City) or to Europe and the United States. Their political and aesthetic positions were therefore often fashioned by viewing their home context from outside. Therefore, the cultural revitalization and politicization processes in the P'urhépecha region were frequently linked with a movement calling for P'urhépecha autonomy.

The most well-publicized and overtly political event undertaken entirely through nonofficial channels is the (re-)invented tradition of the P'urhépecha New Year, held in February annually, since 1982. Agustín García Alcaraz initiated the celebration as a festival "whose express purpose is to reclaim ethnic identity in the context of a search for ideological, political, and economic autonomy" (Nava 1998:25). Each February the P'urhépecha New Year celebration is held in a different location, with thousands of people gathering for a day of ritual festivities from all areas of the P'urhépecha region. In 1998 the celebration was held on Janitzio in an overt act of marking the island as a P'urhépecha cultural location. The island swarmed with hoards of people, but on that occasion they were local P'urhépecha visitors, rather than international and Mexican tourists.[7]

Additionally, since the 1960s, there has been an ongoing interface between governmental institutional activities and local P'urhépecha-led activities, involving the promotion and preservation of music and dance. In Morelia, the Center for Research into P'urhépecha Culture (CICP), directed by P'urhépecha scholar, Ireneo Rojas Hernández, was established at the University of Michoacán (UMSNH), becoming an important organization for the dissemination of transcribed and recorded P'urhépecha music.[8] One publication included biographical details and transcribed compositions of Nicolás Bartolo Juárez (Barrero Próspero and Grandos Hurtado 1991). Numerous governmental initiatives were implemented with the aim of supporting and developing local projects that promoted and disseminated P'urhépecha music and dance, often providing financial aid in the form of monetary prizes and funding for costumes and instruments. SEP (through the General Direction of Popular Cultures) and INI (through the program of Funds for Indigenous Culture) oversaw many projects with the specific objectives of rescuing, preserving, registering, and promoting cultural patrimony. As with the Festivals for *Night of the Dead*, the initiatives often served a local agenda and also performed a role in developing the tourist destination, with many festivals and competitions being planned through an alliance of government money and P'urhépecha organization. Government-funded music and dance contests were particularly popular in the Lake Pátzcuaro region in the 1980s (Chamorro 1983a: 3) and many formed part of a process of reactivating what were regarded as traditional sites of competition (Chamorro 1994).

One specific annual event is noteworthy because it was wholly state-organized and funded and took the format of folkloric and touristic spectator occasions, yet was entirely staged for P'urhépecha participants and spectators. Billed as a *P'urhépecha Festival* and marking la Día de la Raza (12 October), the local Pátzcuaro branch of INI organized a whole-day event each year involving food, crafts, music, and dance. The event was held in the grounds of the INI premises in Pátzcuaro, with the music and dance spectacles taking place on the basketball court, in front of a painted backcloth depicting Lake Pátzcuaro and local men and women (figure 10.1). Stalls serving food and displaying craft work from many areas of the P'urhépecha region were set out nearby. In stark contrast to *Noche Mexicana* in 1921, in which elite Mexicans served P'urhépecha food, for these occasions P'urhépecha women cooked and gave out their own produce, circulating their recipes amongst the other P'urhépecha attendees. All participants were given funding by INI to support their involvement, so the food was free to all who attended. Throughout the day, musicians and dancers performed and competed within formal categories, with money prizes being awarded according to the decisions of a panel of judges. Musical groupings included *bandas* (brass and wind bands), *orquestas* (mixed string, wind, and brass ensembles), *conjuntos* (string groups), and *pireris* (singers with guitar). Dances included *Los Paloteros* from the highlands; the *Huacaleros* from Santa Fe, the *K'urpitis* from the Sierra, and various ensembles performing *The Old Men*. In a context reminiscent of the contests in the early 1930s, *Old Men* ensembles from Urandén and Jarácuaro competed against each other. All the commentary was given primarily in the P'urhépecha language, with translations into Spanish, marking the event as by and for local peoples, yet still functioning within a governmental framework. Despite the close proximity to the tourist gaze of the visitors in Pátzcuaro and Janitzio, within the privacy of the INI compound *The Old Men* functioned as an activity entirely for local P'urhépecha spectators[9] (24–25 🔊).

From Local to Global in Thirty-seven Years: The Artistic Festival of P'urhépecha People

In contrast to the INI-sponsored *P'urhépecha Festival*, another festival was organized entirely outside of governmental domains by a group of P'urhépecha professionals. In considering issues of revitalization, reappropriation, and P'urhépecha-organized events, the *Festival Artístico de la Raza Purépecha* (The Artistic Festival of the P'urhépecha People[10]) stands out as a unique occasion that encompasses many of the complex and paradoxical aspects of folkloric display, indigenous objectification, globalization, and reappropriation, particularly in relation to *The Old Men*. Certain aspects of the event appear to conform to state folkloric festival frameworks, instigated and promoted as governmental cultural patrimony (for example, the choice of repertoire), while other elements demonstrate resistance and cultural creativity (for example, the self-directed role of the P'urhépecha organizers). The festival takes place each year in the P'urhépecha highland town of Zacán. *The Old Men* of Jarácuaro has a prominent place in two major ways: firstly, it is performed numerous times during the course of the festival both by P'urhépecha and non-P'urhépecha groups; and secondly, a prize is dedicated to the memory of Tata Gervasio López, to commemorate his life-long role in promoting *The Old Men* and acting as a representative of indigenous peoples. Since its inception in 1971, the festival has gradually been transformed from a local celebration into an international extravaganza, generating comparisons with the Guelaguetza festival in Oaxaca. Yet the festival offers an alternative position to the state-run festivals so prevalent in the region, representing an overtly P'urhépecha-led and P'urhépecha-managed staged event.

Zacán is a small village in the P'urhépecha sierra located in the folds of volcano Paricutín. In 1943 Paricutín erupted, as a result of which local people lost terrain. Traditional fiestas of the villages in the vicinity were affected when people moved away from the area to look for land and work elsewhere. In 1971 a group of professionals from Zacán (The Association of Zacán Professionals), all of whom had left the region at a very young age, initiated the Zacán Festival. Having returned to their home village they sensed an uncertainty of identity among the young P'urhépecha people and perceived that their traditions were being replaced by non-P'urhépecha music and dance. They therefore decided to recultivate and "rescue" certain customs by reinstating a traditional fiesta. Choosing the dates of the celebration of Saint Lucas, the patron saint of the village for the occasion (17 and 18 October), they established the Artistic Festival of the P'urhépecha People and modeled the event on usual practices for Saints' Days. At first it was to be an occasion solely for the people of Zacán and other local communities, particularly as the location up in the mountains made the event comparatively inaccessible. Music, dance, food, and fireworks were all important elements of the festivities, and, as with most traditional fiestas, a music and dance *serenata* (serenade), *concurso* (contest), or *competéncia* (competition) was also a fundamental feature, with participants competing for prestige and prize money. Local groups performed one after the other in front of a small community audience on the basketball court. The event was not part of any governmental or touristic framework, but instead served as a point of reunion and cohesion for the local community members.

Even as the festival strove to remain unconnected to officialdom, the state became involved through the publication of a book in 1985 entitled *Zacán: renacimiento de una tradición* (Zacán: Rebirth of a Tradition), which was published by the Michoacán State Government and included a foreword by Cuauhtémoc Cárdenas Solórzano, governor of Michoacán (Cárdenas Solórzano 1985, Bugarini 1985). Taking the form of a photo-ethnography, with minimal literary textual sections to frame the photographs, the book presents the Zacán Festival within an ideological, anthropological, and ethnographic framework. Significantly, anthropologist Andrés Medina from the National Autonomous University of Mexico (UNAM) in Mexico City was central to the production of the book, indicating the continued focus on P'urhépecha peoples and practices as objects of anthropological study. The writing employed a romanticized and ethnographic tone, while the photographic imagery (black and white), generated a similarly nostalgic and ephemeral quality, reminiscent of the photographs of *Night of the Dead* on Janitzio by Carlos González of the 1920s. One half of the photographs depicted a regular village patron-saint fiesta, with illustrations of *bandas* promenading in the streets, saints' images, candles, and food. Other photos illustrated the competition element, showing dance and music groups performing on the basketball court. In the prologue, by government official Leonor Ortiz Monasterio, the stated objective of the Zacán Festival was that of rescuing the values of the P'urhépecha race ahead of the avalanche of values completely foreign to indigenous idiosyncrasy (1985:8). This sentiment set up the indigenous difference factor, which was then directly connected to the *Dance of the Old Men* through a specific mention with the observation that "there is a great variety of dances in the P'urhépecha culture. Perhaps the most well-known is 'La Danza de los Viejitos' which is accompanied by simple music with a marked rhythm; generally it is one of the dancers who strums the guitar. The dancers, disguised as *viejitos* with funny masks, dance with backs bent over supporting themselves on a stick; the loud and lively *zapateo* contrasts with the apparent frailty of the old men" (ibid.:9). It was López's ensemble from Jarácuaro that performed *The Old Men* at the Zacán Festival at this time, therefore it was the folkloric, touristic version of the dance that Monasterio was referring to as "traditional custom." These observations concerning *The Old Men* are particularly striking given the context of Monasterio's narratives in which she attempted to prove the importance of indigenous music, dance, and people, argued predominantly by distinguishing between what was and was not indigenous, through comparison with European practices (ibid.:10). In this context, *The Old Men* and Lake Pátzcuaro peoples were characterized as innately indigenous, through separation from European features and characteristics.

During the period when the book was published, the festival was still a comparatively local occasion, with a few hundred people in attendance mostly from the closest communities. As the years passed by, other villages were gradually involved, leading to the presence of people from all the sectors of the P'urhépecha region including the area of Lake Pátzcuaro. Groups from further a field were particularly attracted by the prospect of larger prize money, for by the mid-1990s funding from governmental organizations was used to sponsor elements of the event in a similar manner to many of the Festivals for the *Night of the Dead* in the Lake Pátzcuaro region. However, despite the relatively close geographic proximity to towns such as Uruapan and Pátzcuaro, the location was still comparatively inaccessible due to the unmade roads. Musicians and dancers who made the journey from Lake Pátzcuaro incurred considerable costs.

After initially positioning the music and dance competition on the basketball court, by the mid-1980s numbers had increased, so a small stage was erected. This was followed in the 1990s by a larger stage within an auditorium that was capable of accommodating a substantial crowd of people. By the late 1990s, the festival was still a gathering of mainly P'urhépecha performers, with a few folklórico groups also participating. The audience comprised people from the P'urhépecha region, with just a handful of the judges and audience members who were state dignitaries and workers from Morelia. The contest itself used the format of many previous festivals and contests, with ensembles performing a set piece or series of pieces according to certain categories, as a panel of judges awarded marks. P'urhépecha music, dance, and ritual practices were presented in a theatricalized form, drawing on a repertoire of music heard only in local contexts, and also overtly staged P'urhépecha folkloric dance, as shaped and promoted within the nationalistic framework in Mexico City and further developed in the Lake Pátzcuaro region, particularly using new compositions and dances created for the Festivals for *Night of the Dead* (18 ●).

With the inclusion and involvement of non-P'urhépecha ballet folklórico ensembles in the 1990s, this altered the nature of the event considerably, transforming it from an occasion with, by, and for local peoples of the region, to one of a folkloric show, in which community cohesion and sharing of practices was still central, but which was simultaneously dissipated by the presence of other concerns. For example, in 1998, *The Old Men* was performed by Gervasio López and his ensemble from Jarácuaro, and on the same stage the Ballet Folklórico of Michoacán (a non-P'urhépecha group from Uruapan) performed *La Danza de los Enguangochados*, a dance created in the village of Jarácuaro. The inclusion of both groups fashioned a context for engaging with issues of authenticity, overtly highlighting difference in a context where previously such notions had been irrelevant. Relatedly, the practices themselves were also regarded as authentic or inauthentic. As a requirement of the contest, dances and rituals had to be described and categorized in terms of their place in the traditional village setting, therefore establishing them as authentic custom. Thus, for each dance an announcement had to be made indicating: the place of origin; the motive for dancing it; the date on which it is performed; and the saint or divinity to whom it is dedicated. Purportedly newly created dances were not part of the contest. As with the Festivals for *Night of the Dead*, performances involved reenactments of village celebrations and rituals that were placed on stage in a theatricalized format in much same way as the cuadros costumbristas of the 1920s and 1930s. Many ritualistic acts were reenacted and exhibited, even though no longer practiced in the village (such as the *torrito* of *Carnaval* (the little bull) of Jarácuaro) while *The Old Men* in its folkloric, touristic form was displayed as inherently part of village life. The situation with musical ensembles was somewhat different, for in contrast to the dance section, for which no purportedly new choreographic practices were valid, the requirement for bandas included pieces that were specifically newly composed (in addition to an overture and a regional *son* or *abajeño*). In this way, newly generated P'urhépecha compositions became a fundamentally important element of the Festival of Zacán, continuing the usual practice of serenatas of village fiestas from decades earlier.

Since the inception of the festival, *The Old Men* has had a prominent role as a representative traditional P'urhépecha practice, being enacted by ensembles from the P'urhépecha region and later by ballet folklórico ensembles. In 2000, both *The Old Men* and Gervasio López were given even greater prominence and a permanent place within the Zacán Festival. After the death of López in 1999, a special prize was established, named "La Danza de Los Viejitos, de Jarácuaro," to honor López's memory (see "Homenaje al creador" 2000). To compete for the prize, one of three dances has to be performed: the *Kúrpites of San Juan Nuevo*; the *Kúrpites of Caltzontzín*; or the *Old Men of Jarácuaro*. The monetary reward is significant (approximately $1,000 in 2005), marking the importance of both *The Old Men* and the figure of Gervasio López within the P'urhépecha-directed Zacán Festival.

By 2005 the festival had been transformed considerably from the original shape of 1971. There were one thousand artists participating, including P'urhépecha and non-P'urhépecha folkloric ensembles (forty-five bandas, thirty orquestas, ninety pireris, and sixty dance groups). A large, new, permanent, concrete auditorium was inaugurated (the Cultural Auditorium of the P'urhépecha People) and government representatives of the very highest level were present, in the form of Martha Sahagún de Fox, the wife of President Vicente Fox, and Lázaro Cárdenas Batela, governor of Michoacán (grandson of Lázaro Cárdenas). Other dignitaries included directors of governmental departments such as the director of Support for Indigenous Peoples, the director of the National Advisory Department for Culture and the Arts, the rector of the University of Michoacán and sixteen municipal presidents of the region. Media representatives from Michoacán, from Mexico, and from foreign organizations were also present. The audience was no longer principally local villagers, but consisted of national and international spectators. Financially, the event was supported by many government bodies, including the Mexican Tourist Board and the Cultural Department. The festival was promoted heavily through television and other media, and the event itself was also broadcast on television. As a representative of the State of Michoacán, the director of the Commission for Fairs, Exhibitions and Events in Michoacán, speaking at a press conference to publicize the Zacán Festival, recognized the impact of the festival in attracting national and international tourist attention (*Listo, Festival de la Raza P'urhépecha* 2008). At the same time, maintaining the festival as a P'urhépecha-managed and organized event has been a crucial aspect of the ongoing changes, with the P'urhépecha-led Organizing Committee protecting and structuring the complexities and dichotomies of the festival context. Jorge Morales Campos, president of the Organizing Committee in 2008, expressed the importance of the festival in terms of cultural revitalization, noting that "the competition has enabled the strengthening of the creation, performance and diffusion of the cultural richness of the diverse expressions of the P'urhépecha people" (ibid.).

Centers and Peripheries

In the space of just thirty-seven years the Artistic Festival of P'urhépecha People was transformed from a local fiesta into an international festival for global audiences, through processes and practices that generate and constitute a notion of festivalization. In some ways it would seem that the festival has become just another folkloric spectacle in which P'urhépecha people have again become incorporated into both national and global networks, reenacting bygone activities, and embodying indigenous Mexico. Yet the Festival of Zacán encompasses many intensely complex and contradictory elements regarding indigenous participation and representation in Mexico, a context in which *The Old Men* of Jarácuaro is inherently implicated. According to Sayer, "Individuals and groups may creatively adapt and use forms through which, on another level, they are confined and constrained," noting that "when we are dealing with issues of power and resistance, then we are in the presence of something that is deeply and eternally contradictory" (1994:376). The Festival of Zacán, the role of *The Old Men* of Jarácuaro, and even the figure of Gervasio López present many forms of resistance and reappropriation. Concepts of centers and peripheries are also useful in this context, particularly in relation to inclusion and exclusion, integration and incorporation, power relations and agency, and self-determination and plurality. All these factors are applicable in terms of geography, ideology, and ethnicity, and relate specifically to the processes of folkloricization and festivalization encompassing *The Old Men* and the Zacán Festival. The repertoire for the Zacán Festival recreates and perpetuates a form of traditional local repertoire, yet much of this had been generated for national integrationary, indigenismo, and tourism agendas. The festival encompasses a notion of contemporary indigenismo, relying heavily on institutional and governmental frameworks, in terms of notions of value, cultural heritage, national patrimony, and folkloric constructions, perpetuating the iconic images from the officially constructed and sanctioned governmental events. As nonlocal performers from folklórico dance ensembles participate alongside local performers, often enacting the same dance form, such as *The Old Men*, so notions of corporeal authenticity are brought into play, overtly framing indigenous bodies alongside nonindigenous bodies. For a large portion of the audience, both Mexicans and non-Mexicans, the experience of the Festival of Zacán revolves around concepts and perceptions of authenticity, otherness, and foreignness. Even the journey to Zacán engages a sensory experience of moving from modernity to the preindustrial, traveling along bumpy roads into an environment of wooden houses and smoky air from open wood fires. The activities offstage cohere with those onstage, creating a generalized atmosphere of everyday indigenous life. In this context, ethnicity still seems to be reduced to external, essentialized folkloristic forms, and romantic valorization appears to remain the order of the day.

Yet the Zacán Festival has been deeply significant in terms of self-determination and indigenous politics, signaled through the location and organization. Even in the twenty-first century, Zacán (and the highland region) remains as an area of limited accessibility in terms of roads. This area therefore encompasses the notion of a periphery and remoteness in geographical terms, and also in temporal and ideological terms. With the location of the event in the mountains in a P'urhépecha village there are certain points of comparison to be made with the Zapatista Army of National Liberation (EZLN) up in the mountains in Chiapas, in terms of agency and carving out a space for rights of indigenous peoples. It is highly significant that hundreds of people from outside the P'urhépecha region make the journey to Zacán for this event—whatever their motivations, they travel to a still fairly inaccessible place, to experience live performances of P'urhépecha music and dance. Associated with this is the attendance of very high-profile politicians, at the invitation of the organizing committee, again reversing previous configurations of power relations, in terms of centers and peripheries. These city-based, elite figures of power travel to the P'urhépecha region to an event arranged by nongovernmental, local organizers. In terms of the managerial role of P'urhépecha leaders, despite governmental involvement through funding, other decisions, specifically artistic and directorial, are fundamentally P'urhépecha-led. Not only was the event instigated by P'urhépecha locals, but the executive role has also continued that way throughout all the transformations from local event to international extravaganza. In relation to the twentieth-century trajectory and history of indigenismo and hegemonic folkloricization processes, this act of agency by P'urhépecha leaders is profoundly significant.

The deployment of the very icons and symbols that are used in national and international constructions of Mexicanness, as generated and shaped by hegemonic processes of state projects, is paradoxical. Utilizing *The Old Men* within the Zacán Festival in the highland village performs roles of reappropriation, de-centering, self-legitimation, and self-assertion. Although using such an iconic practice engages with essentialist classification, such categorization can be efficacious for establishing rights, presence, and territory (including ideological territory) through self-representation. The Zacán Festival legitimizes and endorses practices and peoples, and acts as a context for creativity. Labeling and naming the event as *artistic* escapes the folkloric, performing an act of agency by reclassifying and redefining these practices as artistic in an historical trajectory which has framed them primarily as folkloric and traditional. *The Old Men* is at the heart of these processes, enacting a provocative role that obfuscates and complicates issues of the designation and practice of indigenous peoples and indigenismo in twenty-first century Mexico. With the instigation of the award "La Danza de Los Viejitos, de Jarácuaro," in memory of López, both *The Old Men* and the person of Gervasio López, utilized so successfully within national governmental structures, have been reappropriated and reclaimed within a locally organized P'urhépecha framework.

Placing Myself in the Frame: Connections and Responsibility

Furthering the discussion of centers and peripheries, my own involvement with local contexts and with scholarly and populist dissemination is relevant,[11] particularly in terms of my impact as a researcher and musician in processes of transmission and representation related to *The Old Men* and the music of Nicolás Bartolo Juárez. As with the Zacán Festival, the situation is complex and contradictory. Here, I reflect upon a few of the most salient elements, although I recognize that this brief discussion only begins to touch on some of the multifarious issues. Two central aspects, both involving relationships of power, concern the actions and activities of scholars and academics, and issues of representation. As one of the central aims of this study is an analysis of processes of appropriation and representation surrounding *The Old Men* and *Night of the Dead*, I acknowledge that as a non-P'urhépecha middle-class musician and scholar, I am implicated in the very history and trajectory that I am critiquing.

As an embodiment of a European colonizing country, I represent a complex reality in relation to certain issues of presence and representation, yet throughout my years in Mexico this has been tempered by my close family ties in Morelia through marriage. Initially, the presumption of many people was that I was a *gringa*, from el norte (in other words, a citizen of the United States). An understanding that I was not from the United States but from England altered the perception, for, despite the history of European colonization, my Europeanness removed me the current sociopolitical tensions between the United States and Mexico. Being married to a Mexican man also impacted upon my relationships, generating certain notions of *insider*. However, as the relationships that I formed had aspects of otherness and difference bound up with them, encompassing an array of ethical issues, I was cognizant of notions of responsibility and reciprocity at all times (Hellier-Tinoco 2003a, 2005). My presence in Lake Pátzcuaro villages as a participant in numerous fiestas and events, and my role as violinist with the ensemble of Juan Francisco in the Hotel Alameda, the Peña Colibrí, and other venues in Morelia, both have their repercussions.

Concerning the politics and poetics of representation, Steven Loza has raised the issue of intellectual capitalism and academic hegemony, particularly in terms of the relationship between U.S. and Mexican scholars and scholarship (2006:361),[12] while Joseph et al. have discussed the issue of self-conscious outsiders as a recurring element of artists and scholars working in Mexico (2001). Placing myself in this framework and aware of my complex positioning as self-conscious outsider yet integrated into Mexican cultural practices through marriage,[13] I chose to interrogate the processes at work in twentieth-century cultural politics, which encompassed my analyzing of ethnographic representations of music and dance in the Lake Pátzcuaro region, rather than presenting an ethnography. However, I acknowledge that in this chapter particularly, my discussions have encompassed aspects that draw directly on my experiences of, and research in, the P'urhépecha region of Michoacán, which I rationalize by suggesting that this is necessary to create understanding in relation to wider processes of nationalism and tourism. I am also mindful of the fact that in seeking to justify my own research and situation, I am perpetuating the position of previous academics and artists discussed in this study, such as Nicolás León, Rubén M. Campos, Francisco Domínguez, and Carlos González, all of whom sought to rationalize their representational modes through reference to a wider good.

In this study, my approach has been to draw attention to political, ideological, and epistemological issues concerning knowledge bases, subjectivities, and processual modes of knowledge, closely connecting personal, political, and representational processes. One of my interests lies in tracing the lives and consequences of individuals – of tracing threads in a complex and constantly being woven tapestry. I am interested in the value of connections, networks, and fragmented narratives, of the relationship between the micro and the macro, exploring how these fragmented narratives play out in the macro contexts of twentieth- and twenty-first century Mexican nationalism and tourism. As one of the individuals in the narrative, I am aware of the traces of my own "shadows in the field" (Barz and Cooley 2008). In concluding this chapter, I mention five of these traces and connections.

Trace One: In the mid-1990s as I sat in Morelia and read the classic postrevolutionary work *Folklore and Mexican Music* by Rubén M. Campos, I was particularly drawn to the photo of a man leaning against a tree, with a poncho slung over his shoulder, looking wistfully into the distance, captioned as "the composer Nicolás Bartolo Juárez" (1928: 86). Soon after that occasion my connections to Nicolás Bartolo Juárez became tangible when I met villagers on the island of Jarácuaro, including members of his family. Simultaneously, I began playing violin with an ensemble of musicians from Jarácuaro for performances of *The Old Men* in Morelia every weekend. The ensemble of four became a group of five for the years during which I lived in Morelia. My presence as a performer with the ensemble presented certain multifaceted aspects, for I embodied a form of *difference* which set the ensemble apart from others, and which therefore led to a certain amount of recognition for the group as the one with "la inglesa" (the Englishwoman), yet sonically, the ensemble only altered through the addition of another violin line. When in Jarácuaro and other Lake Pátzcuaro villages, I performed for local events and tourist occasions, playing violin not only with Juan Francisco's ensemble, but also with other groups.

Trace Two: In 1998 with the ensemble of Juan Francisco, I participated in making an audio recording of P'urhépecha pieces that came out of particular series of events. Soon after gazing upon Nicolás Bartolo Juárez's photo in Campos's book, I met his daughter, Adelaida, who owned a copy of Campos's publication with her father's image and transcriptions. She knew some of her father's pieces because they were still played by local ensembles; however, other pieces she was only aware of in transcribed form. I therefore proposed making an audio recording for Adelaida so that she could hear her father's compositions. As the older villagers and musicians of Jarácuaro were keen to bring these compositions back into circulation, this scheme came to fruition.[14] I played the pieces from Campos's transcriptions and after having made a rough recording, the ensemble then decided to make a professional recording using the services of the company Alborada Records. The final recordings included compositions by Nicolás Bartolo Juárez and also other pieces in the group's repertoire, including the music for *The Old Men*, compositions by Juan Francisco, and one of my own P'urhépecha sones. This recording was issued as a cassette and CD, *Los P'urépechas de Jarácuaro* (1999 and 2000),[15] and was sold mostly in the Lake Pátzcuaro region and Morelia (see figure 1.7).

As with my presence in the live ensemble, my photographic representation on the cover of the cassette and CD also functioned through an embodied framing of ethnicity. The images performed in a dichotomous manner similar to that of my live body, being paradoxically both problematic and also efficacious. I appear in both photographs—a white-skinned woman violinist, with a group of dark-skinned male musicians and dancers. On the cassette cover, I am wearing the traditional Lake Pátzcuaro P'urhépecha women's clothes (blouse, skirt, apron, braided hair decorated with woolen braids and ribbons—mostly given to me Doña Maria, Juan's mother). I sit on the ground in front of Francisco, Esteban, Ramírez, and Matías, all of whom wear their costume of poncho, hat, and embroidered shirt and trousers. Each of us holds our instrument as we pose very obviously for the camera. The image is one of a traditional P'urhépecha setting, disrupted by my body—a white-skinned woman's body in a brown-skinned men's context.

The photograph for the CD cover depicts the interior of the colonial Hotel Alameda in Morelia, with stone steps providing a suitable raked platform for the ensemble of musicians and dancers, and archway above affording a sympathetic frame. Nine bodies make up the image—five musicians and four dancers. I stand in the center of the line with the other four musicians, while the dancers pose in their Old Man stereotypical positions in front, but with their masks removed. In the line of musicians, each of us holds our instrument as if playing. I am clothed in a white P'urhépecha blouse, and only my head, shoulders, and arms are visible. In both these images the concept of difference is established through juxtaposing both skin color and gender. These elements enabled my presence to be utilized as a differentiating and generally efficacious marketing tool, drawing attention to these particular recordings amidst many others. Yet simultaneously I embody a form that highlights the notion of indigenous bodies and peoples, perpetuating the essentialist and delimiting framework constructed in the postrevolutionary years (see chapter 13 for a discussion of the dichotomous consequences of essentialization in symbolic and economic structures).

Trace Three: After making the audio recording I gave a copy of the CD to Leobardo Ramos Bartolo[16] in Mexico City, who in 2007 gave a copy to another family member, Gilberto Cázares Ponce, grandnephew of Nicolás Bartolo Juárez, who in turn was motivated to reconnect with his family on Jarácuaro and record his own CD of his family's compositions. Growing up in Mexico City, Cázares Ponce took little interest in his family on Jarácuaro and rarely visited, even though his mother, Enedina, made frequent journeys between Mexico City and Jarácuaro. As the daughter of Alejandro Bartolo Juárez, (Nicolás's brother) Enedina was very aware of her family's musical legacy. Her two brothers, Rafael and Bonfilio, both had musical careers, although much of their time was spent away from Jarácuaro. Cázares Ponce was conscious of some musical connections in his family; however, although his career in Mexico City was that of a musician and choir director, he had not played any of his family's music. When he received the CD *Los P'urépechas de Jarácuaro*, he was simultaneously surprised that a foreigner knew more of his family and his family's music than he did, and inspired to get to know and record his own family's compositions. Within a short time, Cázares Ponce initiated his process of recordings, and with his mother singing in P'urhépecha, and he himself accompanying on synthesizer, he recorded *Los Grandes Compositores de la Isla de Jarácuaro, Michoacán (Great Composers of the Island of Jarácuaro, Michoacán)*. Cázares Ponce's CD includes compositions by his grandfather Alejandro, granduncle Nicolás, and his uncles Bonfilio and Rafael. Cázares Ponce reproduced a photo of each composer for the cover image, and in reference to his mother as the *pireri* (P'urhépecha singer) he names her as "Aunt Nina, Voice of the P'urhépecha Soul."

Trace Four: In 2007, two days following my meeting with Cázares Ponce in Mexico City, after listening to his beautifully produced CD and gazing at the photos of his family, I was able to travel back to the village of Jarácuaro where I visited his uncle, Rafael, then eighty-seven years old. Amidst hats and strands of woven straw, with a sewing machine standing nearby, and a trombone hanging on a wall, Rafael shuffled into an adjoining room and returned with a dusty violin case. I gently removed his violin from the case and played a P'urhépecha *son*, as the maestro leaned toward me, listening intently. I passed his violin to him and, with fingers bent with age, he grasped the bow, placed his left hand under the neck, and tenderly formed a tune. By my side sat Enedina (Rafael's sister and Gilberto's mother), listening intently to her brother play tunes that were so familiar. In that moment, I was aware of a great connection with the first moments of the transformation of *The Old Men* in the years immediately following the revolution. In that very place, Nicolás Bartolo Juárez, with Rafael present as a little boy, had strummed the jaranita and placed a mask of an Old Man over his face. Even as we sat there, dancers in folklórico ensembles in Mexico and the United States were placing Old Man masks over their faces, and potential tourists in European cities were glancing at the Old Man mask emblazoned in photographic form on the Mexican Tourist Board advertisements.

Trace Five: To bring this course of connections and events up-to-date, on May 15 2010, a 50-minute radio program entitled "Los Grandes Compositores de la Isla de Xarakuaru Michoacán" (Great Composers of the Island of Jarácuaro), compiled by Gilberto Cázares Ponce, was transmitted in the village of Jarácuaro. Comprising a combination of compositions by Nicolás Bartolo Juárez and his family, and drawing on aspects of my research and Cázares Ponces's experiences, this programme returned life-stories and music to their village of origin.

PART III

Embodiment, Photographs, and Economics

CHAPTER 11

In the Body

Indigenous Corporeality, Work, and Interpretation

Janitzio
Preparation for the commemoration of the Wake for the Dead begins the night of the 1st on this picturesque island in lago de Pátzcuaro... women and children go to the cemetery in silence.... The candles that are lit in the cemetery illuminate the faces which, on that night, will depart with the dead. A bell hanging in the archway leading into the cemetery tolls all night to evoke the spirits of the departed.

Jarácuaro
This ancient town has conserved its tradition with a more pure atmosphere. The ceremony begins with the placement of large arches... in the atrium of the church.... Then groups of dancers perform in the plaza demonstrating their virtuosity as they execute beautiful pieces. Jarácuaro is famous for its musicians and dancers.

Noche de Muertos 2007, original in English

Inscribed and printed in the twenty-first century in a Michoacán state-produced tourist guide, and available free to visitors to the Lake Pátzcuaro region for *Night of the Dead,* the texts quoted above express a romanticized and essentialized view of the people of Janitzio and Jarácuaro as they perform *Night of the Dead* and the *Dance of the Old Men,* placing them together in one frame; authenticating the practices and peoples; valorizing them for their ephemeralness and virtuosity; and displaying them as embodiments of an indigenous, traditional, and ancient Mexico. Performing a role in constructions of indigenousness, the narrative guides the gaze of the thousands of tourists who look on as the people of Janitzio and Jarácuaro enact their activities. Hundreds of thousands of pesos and dollars change hands in this setting as the visitors perform economic transactions. In a global marketplace these P'urhépecha individuals are valuable corporeal actualities, representations, and iconic referents of Mexico. Forming strands in a complex twenty-first century tapestry of Mexicanness, and embodying Mexico in a web of considerable intricacy whose reach, use, and efficacy extends far beyond the geopolitical terrain of Mexico, these people and enactments perform as icons of the nation.

In part III, the final section of this book, I move away from a chronological approach, and engage a more theoretical and discursive style, while also undertaking detailed dramaturgical analyses of specific exemplars. I particularly relate these discussions back to the frameworks introduced at the beginning of this study and implemented throughout the chronological account in discussing the processes of performism. Dividing this section into three chapters enables broad consideration of major issues inherent in the ninety-year trajectory of the public uses of *The Old Men* and *Night of the Dead* of Lake Pátzcuaro. In chapter 11 I consider issues of reception, interpretation, signification, and embodiment; in chapter 12 I examine and analyze visual images, particularly photographic media; and in chapter 13 I conclude with a discussion concerning indigenous and folkloric representation; symbolic and economic production; and relationships of power.

At the heart of the success of the iconicity of the *Dance of the Old Men* and *Night of the Dead* lies a web of communicative significances. From the incipient uses in the early 1920s, both activities have proven to be potent sites for signification. Meanings have been generated through networks of representations that have been selected, shaped, circulated, and reproduced for their efficacy in molding perceptions of indigenous, authentic, and different people and practices. These meanings rely on associations, both implicit and explicit, with locations, landscapes, histories, corporeal activities, and somatic types. As an integral element of performism processes surrounding *The Old Men* and *Night of the Dead*, creating and sustaining an officially sanctioned lattice of ideas and imagery formed an essential strand of activities in the postrevolutionary era, and has continued ever since. Through this study I have traced the trajectory from the 1920s and discussed a range of exemplary cases through to the twenty-first century, encompassing printed material, live events, audio and video documents, and souvenir objects. At the heart of the matter are issues of indigenousness. Whereas the practices and bodies have been classified as inherently indigenous through the reasoning that the people *are* P'urhépecha (and *are* indigenous), such a designation relied upon cyclical and reinforcing processes of performism that shaped notions of indigenous bodies/people.

In the twenty-first century, displaying a depiction of an Old Man dancer as the centerpiece in the 2006 European promotional campaign for the Mexican Tourist Board reveals the importance of this iconic body in signifying Mexico and in making an embodied declaration that "this is Mexico." Correspondingly, exhibiting moving images of the women on Janitzio undertaking *Night of the Dead* as a 3D photographic show at the World's Fair in Germany engaged these representative bodies as intrinsically Mexican. In both cases the Mexico on display through these embodied performances is that of an indigenous, preinvasion, traditional, rural, and authentic Mexico. Two sets of bodies—masked Old Men dancers, and women kneeling at gravesides with candles and flowers—were configured to reinforce notions of indigenousness cultivated in postrevolutionary Mexico, perpetuating and maintaining a form of indigenismo.

In this chapter I turn my attention to analysis of interpretations and significations of *The Old Men* and *Night of the Dead*. Firstly, I outline theoretical issues of reception, signification, and communication; secondly, I discuss concepts of embodiment, and the constructed nature of the human body as signifier in relation to indigenousness and the people of Lake Pátzcuaro; thirdly, I examine the network of ideas associated with Lake Pátzcuaro, preincursion ancestry, and the display of work and everyday life; and finally, I analyze specific dramaturgical elements of both *Night of the Dead* and *The Old Men*.

Processes of Signification and Interpretation: Shaping a Network of Ideas

When dealing with the issues of signification, communication, and meaning in multiple contexts an important question must be "meaning for whom?" Spectators, audiences, viewers, and readers of representations of *The Old Men* and *Night of the Dead* have included a diverse assortment of people, including Mexican school children; urban, middle-class adults; foreign dignitaries; international tourists; hippy travelers; pilgrims; and Mexican migrants in the United States. Although theories of reception offer that multiple interpretations are possible (Fish 1980, Jauss 1982, Rabkin 1985), my contention is that, despite the scope, multiplicity, and diversity of readers and viewers, interpretations in disparate contexts have been remarkably similar, even when the motives and objectives differed, due predominantly to a consistency of processes of shaping and active framing surrounding the practices. Delimiting frames were consciously created and adopted, leading to unconsciously used conceptual scaffolds or networks of ideas that more or less fixed interpretations and created a collective gaze. In many cases, the frames themselves became so "natural" that the framing was ignored or regarded as being "how it is." Particular elements were presented and reinforced to signify and "mean" something very specific, producing unquestioned acceptance.[1] Each representation offered, encouraged, and imposed particular explanations, and each occurrence contributed to the shaping of the reception of performance as meanings were perpetuated and recycled from one context to another.

The projected set of meanings and significations was founded upon constructs or subjective notions generated through complex chaining processes. With the presence of one assumed notion, so others fell into place. These were often formulated around a concept of oppositional binaries (traditional-modern; spontaneous-composed; body-mind; rural-urban; there-here; past-present; them-us). Meaning is ultimately created though differences. One term of the two in the opposition is always privileged, and by identifying the privileged concepts in the pairs, the ideology operative in the event, performance, or documentation can be revealed and examined (Derrida 1998 and 2001). Through juxtapositions and careful placing, concepts and images cohered and merged, with one reinforcing another, functioning as shorthand for places and peoples, often perpetuating myths and expectations. Generating both a tourist gaze and populist, nationalist gaze through processes of performism (which included reification and site sacralization) created a perception and assumption that specific places (Lake Pátzcuaro and Janitzio), practices (the *Dance of the Old Men* and *Night of the Dead*), and peoples (P'urhépecha islanders) were significant, representative, and worthy of attention. As a result, viewers searched for possible symbolic denotation and simultaneously made assumptions about significance, thereby fulfilling a need and desire to *find* meaning. With *The Old Men* and *Night of the Dead* two essential concepts contributed to these interpretive and chaining processes: *ritual* and *indigenous*. Interpretations of *The Old Men* always led back to a categorization of the practice as a ritual dance (in opposition to a social or theater dance), and *Night of the Dead* was known simply as a ritual. Both practices were regarded as indigenous through location, enactors, and historical contextualization. Both attributes contributed intensely to a compelling necessity to uncover and know inherent meaning and signification.

Embodiment: Constructing and Shaping Useful Indigenous Bodies

Concepts of embodiment are fundamentally appropriate for engaging with the nationalistic and touristic uses of *The Old Men* and *Night of the Dead* due to the centrality of human bodies as primary signifiers. In each context of display and representation, live bodies and mediated/inscribed bodies (moving/still bodies in photos, drawings, and models; and written accounts) were viewed, read, and interpreted. In order to analyze the potency and efficacy of the body in these representational practices, I engage with the concept of embodiment using three interrelated definitions, as outlined in chapter 2. Firstly, I use the notion of being *in the body* and *taking form in human flesh*, specifically referring to the materiality of the body to examine how a human being becomes classified; how people/bodies are designated as indigenous (through external designation or self-designation); and how somatic traits (and therefore ultimately human beings) are labeled as indigenous. At the heart of this study is an exploration of ways in which an officially sanctioned essence of Mexico was given human form through bodies/human beings on display. The second definition relates to representing, standing for, and symbolizing an idea; making an idea actual or discernible; and expressing something abstract in tangible, material form. Thus, the ideological concepts of lo mexicano, Mexicanness, and an essence of Mexico were given tangible form through the practices of *The Old Men* and *Night of the Dead*. Thirdly, embodiment indicates notions of making something part of a system or whole. This definition is wholly germane in terms of indigenous incorporation for national development. Thus, the people/human bodies undertaking *Night of the Dead* and *The Old Men* were incorporated and integrated into the nation of Mexico, even as *The Old Men* as embodied practice became an integral element in the set of Mexican Regional Dances, and *Night of the Dead* was ultimately included in the select body of activities identified as World Heritage. Significantly, all three designations of embodiment are pertinent and applicable to the context under scrutiny, and all three theorizations and characterizations merge and intersect even as they are discrete.

Concepts of indigenous people and indigenousness were central to nationalist and tourist agendas, functioning in overlapping and interfacing areas. For nationalism these concerned both nationalist incorporation (and mestizaje) and indigenismo; and for tourism these related to forms of ethnic-tourism. To summarize some brief details, nationalist strategies of incorporation and mestizaje necessitated acts of identifying and classifying bodies/people as indigenous in order to incorporate thousands of disparate communities of peoples into the national body thereby facilitating economic development and state control. Simultaneously, mestizaje required the modification of each individual into a mestizo, effectively seeking to "whiten" people in order to create a newly authentic Mexican nation—an inherently corporeal and body-centered act. Such a transformation signaled the incompatibility of "indigenous" bodies in the modernizing future, so despite the purported benevolence of incorporation and mixing, mestizaje encompassed a notion of false inclusiveness that functioned as a mechanism of exclusion, thereby actualizing a colonial legacy (Miller 2004).[2]

The ideology of indigenismo also necessitated the identification and classification of bodies/people as indigenous but romanticized and valorized them as useful to the formulation and construction of the Mexican nation through their purported intrinsic worth as authentically of the past. Indigenismo relied upon an assembly of materials presented as from the past but designed for usefulness in the future. Whereas previous indigenismo had looked for vestiges of the past in myths, in the stones of pyramids, and in archeological remains of pottery, postrevolutionary indigenismo sought presences in the bodies (and embodied practices) of living indigenous peoples in a re-membering and re-presentation of history. In considering the writing of history, Peggy Phelan has characterized it as a process in which "one engages in a restaging of the disappeared," suggesting that "historians offer their writing as compensation for that loss. Words can be accepted as substitutes for missing bodies because words are themselves the shells of missing bodies. What they convey is the disappearance of the thing they re-present" (1995:205). Taking this idea a step further, deploying *The Old Men* and *Night of the Dead* enacted a form of writing history through the body, for as words act as substitutes for missing bodies, then even more potent is the idea of a live body substituting for missing bodies. These live bodies stand in for lost bodies of the past, which are then rendered as exotic and even backward bodies. In *The Old Men* and *Night of the Dead* the participants were interpreted as re-membering and em-bodying the preinvasion past.

In a highly potent correlation, the bodies/people provided a link from bodies of the past, to the present, to living bodies of the future, through a (real or perceived) direct unbroken bond, a continuation of life, a bloodline, and a living, life-giving, breathing body. Whereas archeological explorations revealed inanimate artifacts from the preinvasion past; and historical and anthropological documents recreated bodies from the past in words; and monuments restaged significant pre-Conquest bodies in larger-than-life yet motionless bronze and stone sculptures; the bodies of living people provided flesh and blood models as living artifacts with a real or imagined direct linkage to previous civilizations. These were historical and archeological bodies, yet they were also animate, sentient, living bodies, offering multiple possibilities for the future even as they provided deep resonances with the past. Thus, the "authentic body" took center stage, charged with re-creating, re-embodying, and restaging the past.[3]

In terms of tourist agendas, indigenous bodies were also extremely valuable for contexts in which ideas of the indigenous past and the indigenous present were promoted as attractions. As tourism advocates the restoration, preservation, and re-creation of ethnic attributes (MacCannell 1992:168), therefore cultivating and shaping tangible features of indigenous locations, practices, and peoples was capitalized upon. In locations perceived as indigenous, cohering with stones and artifacts from pre-Hispanic eras, live human bodies undertaking corporeal activities framed as traditional acted both as exhibitions of the past and as material for staged authenticity, providing a vital attraction for both Mexican and foreign tourists.

Although the notion that the body acts as the central element may appear somewhat obvious, the idea of "naturalness" can lead to overlooking the complexities and constructed nature of the communicating factors and the signifying power of the concrete body (Butler 1993). In many contexts, the body generates a metalanguage for communication, with physical traits and phenotypic characteristics providing signifying elements. Divisions of race, cultural identity, and gender are often founded upon the body as a material sign of social difference, and the body itself, as a physical entity, acts as "the ultimate signifier of identity and the final authenticator" (Desmond 1999: xiv–xv). A form of "physical foundationalism" has a structuring function in social classification, such that "in numerous realms of thought…bodies are the epistemological equivalent of 'the buck stops here'" (ibid.). This epistemological function of the authenticating power of bodies was central to the "construction" of bodies as signifying entities in processes of nationalism and tourism in twentieth-century Mexico, encompassing the peoples of Lake Pátzcuaro undertaking *Night of the Dead* and *The Old Men*. "Embodied difference" was codified through a historical trajectory based upon physical foundationalism, traceable to a nineteenth-century model that was thoroughly embedded in postrevolutionary intellectual research and display projects. As a mode of knowledge, physical foundationalism encompassed the idea that difference was represented by, and understandable through, direct observation of "specimens," together with a conceptual system that mapped species, people, and races into typologies based on bodily difference, such as skin color, eye form, stature, and type of hair.[4]

In postrevolutionary Mexico the flesh and blood body *did* matter, with ever present presumptions and constructions, overt and covert, subtle and inescapable. Difference was codified in bodies; bodies framed and read as "indigenous" equated with the idea of an authentic body through an innate and unquestioned correlation.[5] Notions of race and ethnicity as formulated through skin color and physiognomy were, and continue to be, a central element in Mexican politics, ideologies, and ontologies. Over the centuries processes of othering have taken place through shaping perceptions and constructions of bodily difference. Yet in postrevolutionary Mexico, the status of people categorized as indigenous and mestizo was of a highly subjective nature, depending as it did on "a range of perceived characteristics, rather than on any immutable and innate attributes" (Knight 1990:74). After four centuries of miscegenation, racial strains had become thoroughly mixed, and divisions were there mostly ethnic, rather than racial. As a fascinating and potent illustration, anthropologist and government official Manuel Gamio, a key individual in shaping racial and ethnic ideology, moved from a biological to a cultural definition of race (following the model of his mentor Franz Boas) for the reason that "in his fieldwork, [Gamio] encountered fluidity and hybridity in both cultural and somatic traits" (Vaughan and Lewis 2006:11). In much documentation of the period, there is conflation of, and a slip between, somatic and cultural traits. This factor is crucial in understanding the efficacy of the iconic nature of *The Old Men* and *Night of the Dead*, for bodies were both *interpreted* as indigenous, and *classified* and *designated* as indigenous, with codified traits reinforcing one another.

Despite Gamio's move toward a cultural definition of race, the prevalent formulation was one that referenced somatic aspects in combination with home location and perceived heritage, resulting in selected peoples being framed and represented as indigenous (as opposed to mestizo). Such peoples were characterized as having an authentic or pure body, and were utilized for display as specimens, for, as Desmond has observed, "it is the physical presence of *some* bodies, not others, which functions as the ultimate grounding for these notions of the 'authentic' " (1999: xix). Engaging with the current understanding that authenticity is a socially constructed concept concerned with the negotiation of meaning and that its social connotation is therefore not given but negotiable, so these bodies/people were given the label of "authentic" through processes of performism. It is these processes, which led to and enabled particular bodies to be read, interpreted, and accepted as "authentic" bodies, that are key to this analysis.

To accomplish Gamio's intent to "forge an Indian soul," "Indians" had to be distinguishable from other Mexican citizens, hence the implementation of processes that sought to represent and classify difference and otherness, engaging strategies for constructing and shaping the concept of "indigenous bodies." As in other world contexts, such processes and constructions reached back "to the late nineteenth century (with antecedents much earlier) when a nexus of visual representation, popular performance, anthropology and bodily 'sciences' like craniology came together to produce a popular 'scientific' ethnographic gaze" (Desmond 1999: xiii–xiv). In Mexico, during the postrevolutionary era, this popular scientific ethnographic gaze, which focused on those designated as indigenous peoples, was central to nation-building strategies. The investigation of the "Indian [by] skilled and sympathetic intellectuals, ethnographers and anthropologists" (Knight 1990:94–95) formed a vital core in processes of codifying indigenous bodies. The subject matter of the studies was human beings who were reified as they undertook everyday activities. The very normalcy of such bodies in action—often depicted standing, harvesting, fishing, and weaving—highlighted their purported difference as indigenous. Data concerning these bodies was classified, presented, framed, and received as factual and objective rather than fluid and subjective, with the very practices of representation (photographic and literary documentation, and live display), and the specificity of their placing (scholarly publications and museums) creating the context for their reception and interpretation. As scientific and academic enquiries were state-driven and state-funded, they were inextricably linked with official representations.[6] Even as these bodies were constructed for nationalist agendas, simultaneously they were taken up and utilized within touristic settings.

Authenticating Indigenous Bodies of Lake Pátzcuaro

Moving from the general to the specific, I reiterate that the usefulness and success of both *The Old Men* and *Night of the Dead* as embodied practices was predicated upon their signification as featuring indigenous, authentic, and different bodies. As I have documented in the course of this study, from the 1920s to the present day, through a multiplicity of representational processes of performism, both practices and associated bodies/people were presented as indigenous, and more specifically, P'urhépecha. In conjunction with the designation of these people *as* P'urhépecha, a network of attributes and associations was invoked to authenticate the bodies as indigenous, and to perpetuate useful notions of indigenousness. These centered upon five authenticating concepts: a pre-Conquest configuration; physiognomy; location; cultural practices; and quotidian activities.

Pre-Conquest Configuration

The pre-Conquest relationship centered on the location of Tzintzuntzan as the former capital of the P'urhépecha people, and the Lake Pátzcuaro region as the site of a great pre-Hispanic empire. In the postrevolutionary epoch, the classification "P'urhépecha" (or Tarascan) was able to signify more than a generalized pre-Hispanic construction. Part of the doctrine of the indigenismo movement delineated that the focus should be upon indigenous peoples whose cultures could be linked to "a glorious pre-Columbian past" (Dawson 1998:283). Such linkage was eminently possible with the P'urhépecha people, and details of this illustrious past was disseminated in ethnographies and histories.[7] Tangible demonstrations of connections with the preincursion past were strengthened from the 1930s onward when archeological explorations at Tzintzuntzan and the nearby village of Ihuatzio began. These sites were excavated and restored, revealing stones and objects from the pre-Conquest era.

Physiognomy

In terms of physiognomy, a number of traits were delineated which were used to classify the bodies/people as indigenous, engaging specifically with "the intractability of the notion of the 'body' as that which is really 'real', a repository of truth"

(Desmond 1999: xiv–xv). The practice of identifying phenotypic traits of peoples designated as indigenous in the early twentieth century formed a vital element in anthropological research, dissemination, and classification, connecting with ideas of appearance (*physis*) being used to interpret (*gnomon*) qualities of character, temperament, and mind. Describing somatic traits was very much evident in the work numerous scholars. Nicolás León, for example, in his 1934 ethnography, stated that "the tarascos of Lake Pátzcuaro, [have] dark skin,... wide face and nose,... mongoloid eyes, well separated, thick lips, turned up. Black, straight hair..." (1934:163), and Carlos Basauri, in his seminal 1940 publication on the indigenous people of Mexico, gave a short description of P'urhépecha male physical features in the following manner: "color of skin, dark brown; hair black and straight; eyes quite far apart and often 'mongoloid'" (1990 [1940]:498). By means of associated endorsing and reinforcing actions, physiognomy was used to interpret and label the bodies/people as indigenous and P'urhépecha, simultaneously ascribing them with character traits and attributes, such as innate creativity, simplicity, and spontaneity.

Skin color, in particular, was an important and contentious distinguishing feature and marker of identity. Despite being an ambivalent and ambiguous feature (Henson 1999), the construction of status around skin color has formed a central element in Mexican racial and ethnic ideology since the Spanish incursion. In the colonial era, categorization was implemented for the various permutations of mixing, typically related to skin color and perceived racial traits. Notwithstanding the intervening years, one element of postrevolutionary ideology specifically focused upon skin color, as mestizaje sought to whiten people. In this configuration, and engaging a binary notion and hierarchical vocabulary, white was placed against non-white or brown.[8] Brown skin was therefore a seal of authenticity in terms of indigenousness in Mexico, being regarded both as a problem (for the modernizing project) and an asset (for indigenismo and tourist projects). Skin color played a part in these doctrines, and was a feature within policies of change and transformation.

It is, of course, significant that Mexico's most omnipresent and enduring national icon is "La Virgen Morena"—The Brown-Skinned Virgin (The Virgin of Guadalupe). Since her origination, the color of The Virgin of Guadalupe's skin has been the most important and distinctive somatic signifying element. In other mass-circulating contexts allusions to skin color are frequent in popular cultural forms, including songs, which have continued to include references to *la morena*, the brown-skinned woman or girl. In the twenty-first century, although not often a focus of overt discussion, skin color in Mexico *is* important. One only has to peruse the television, magazines, newspapers, and advertisements to see that whiteness is a marker of a status of difference, and that this status is predominantly associated with attributes such as affluence and intelligence.

Location

The site and sight of Pátzcuaro, with its lake and island communities, has been eminently important in designations, readings, and interpretations of the bodies of the peoples of Lake Pátzcuaro as indigenous and authentic. The lake environment, with villages on the shores of the lake and island settlements within the waters, combined with preincursion history and bloodline, permitted a network of associations particularly referencing a folk society construction, encompassing a pristine, traditional way of life. As one of the most iconic and oft-reproduced geographical features in Mexico, the island of Janitzio, a landmass that both rises out of the water and is incorporated into the body of water, has been used to signify a place and peoples protected and preserved since time immemorial.[9]

Cultural Practices

The configuration and qualities of the "The Folk Society" (Redfield 1942), encompassing ideas drawn directly from European formulations of folk, were disseminated within Mexican intellectual circles, and applied to rural and indigenous communities. The well-preserved folk-society model that was applied to the peoples of Lake Pátzcuaro covered notions and attributes of premodern, preindustrial, natural, unspoiled, simple, utopian, isolated, illiterate, and homogenous peoples, with innate creativity and natural inspiration, engaging in noncommerical activities. Concepts of utopia, traditional occupations, and preindustrial methods were explicitly associated with Pátzcuaro and villages of the Lake Pátzcuaro region (particularly Santa Fe de la Laguna and Tzintzuntzan) through a very specific historical relationship with the sixteenth-century priest, Vasco de Quiroga. Tata Vasco, as he was affectionately called, worked with local peoples to create utopian communities (Warren 1963) and his legacy particularly lay in the craftwork undertaken in many villages (for example, hat-making in Jarácuaro and pottery in Santa Fe) and the fabrication of the cotton fishing nets used on Lake Pátzcuaro (a practice instigated by Vasco de Quiroga).

In material ways, the peoples of the Lake Pátzcuaro region retained their small rural communities, with traditional occupations and forms of agriculture, fishing, and artisanal labor, representations of which were exposed and disseminated through *Mexican Folkways* and many other publications.[10] Processes of production remained those of cottage industries, despite attempts by politicians such as Lázaro Cárdenas to transform them into more industrial units: villagers in Santa Fe continued to produce ceramics in family units, and in Jarácuaro hat production persisted as the mainstay of the community, with each family weaving and sewing their own batches of hats. Such traditional notions of the art and craft of indigenous peoples tied in with the attributes outlined by postrevolutionary intellectual, Dr. Atl (Gerardo Murillo) in his thesis on race, authenticity, and postrevolutionary populist nationalism, in which he emphasized Indianness, spontaneity, authenticity, the collective subconscious, manual industries, and premodernity (López 2006:35–6). Dr. Atl and others propounded the notion that racially indigenous and culturally pristine peoples possessed innate skills and used natural creativity, musicianship, and artistry. A nonprofessional status of musicians was stressed whilst the idea of agency of creators and performers was rejected. In numerous writings and images, these ideas have been promoted specifically in relation to the people of Lake Pátzcuaro, and associated with *The Old Men* and *Night of the Dead*. I have given some examples in previous chapters and here I offer a few further illustrations. Rubén M. Campos observed that "the musicians [Bartolo Juárez and family] from Jarácuaro don't know why they are poets" (1928:86), and Francisco Domínguez noted that they follow "traditional destiny" and "natural inspiration" (1941). Writing in the 1960s, folklorist José Raul Hellmer asserted that P'urhépecha musicians were unique in terms of their "musical sentiment and the indigenous aesthetic" emphasizing "their enormous creative ability, their closeness to nature, their innate refinement and distance from vulgarity, [all of which] are clearly perceptible" (1990:64). In radio programs produced by Radio Educación in the 1980s, interviews with musicians and dancers from the Lake Pátzcuaro region focused upon notions of spontaneity and authenticity, and in the 1990s, musician and teacher Sálvador Próspero Román noted that "our musicians didn't imitate the false commercial music...they earned money for their performances, but in a way that was justifiable and honest" (1987b). In the late twentieth century, groups of P'urhépecha musicians and dancers were still presented using similar associations: groups who performed at the government-run *Centro Cultural* (Cultural Center) in Morelia in weekly events of *Domingos Familiares* (*Family Sundays*) were often introduced with the words "they are not professional, they are indigenous; they don't have the same discipline, they come with their families."

Quotidian Activities

Interpreting bodies as authentically indigenous was also engendered through the configuration of activities being enacted, and by indexing the home setting and everyday lives (in conjunction with all the attributes discussed above). Studying people carrying out quotidian activities formed a fundamental aspect of anthropological and ethnographic domains, and was thoroughly entrenched in a Darwinian focus upon humans as specimens. In the 1920s and 1930s, a key element of the study of P'urhépecha peoples involved the documentation of their everyday lives, which for the islanders of Lake Pátzcuaro centered on fishing, agriculture, and craftwork. In an associated postrevolutionary activity, representing and enacting indigenous and rural daily life formed the core of the costumbrista movement: a scene of trading in a P'urhépecha market was placed on stages in Mexico City, alongside reenactments of *Night of the Dead* and *The Old Men*, and formed one of the scenes to be enacted in the United States by Spanish-language students (Johnston 1935) (see chapter 6). Within this framework, distinguishing between different forms of activities (work, everyday life, ritual, social dance, folkloric show) was rendered particularly complex. Bodies/people were presented as specimens by sheer dint of their designation as indigenous. In 1928, González's photos of women on Janitzio simply standing facing the camera were integrated into Toor's article documenting *Night of the Dead* on Janitzio (1928a:68–69).

Observing work and everyday life within an ethnographic framework cohered with a similar focus within tourist frameworks where such pursuits acted as potent attractions as tourists escaped their own work for leisure activities that involved watching the display of work by others. Observing the display of work enables visitors to feel as though they can get to "know the life of the native peoples as it is actually lived" (MacCannell 2001:383–4). Bodies/people undertaking certain corporeal activities are transformed into objects of display through processes of objectification, as the presence of a particular gaze of an onlooker shapes and reinforces notions of authentic indigenous bodies, invoking ideas of a folkloric, rural idyll. The tourist experience on Janitzio encompassed such ideas, transforming the normal, natural, and working bodies of the inhabitants into objects for the pleasure and leisure of visitors. Thus, "the whole scene becomes an object of touristic consumption to be taken in as an example of *the picturesque* with a message: work is *natural;* work is *beautiful; work is picturesque*" (ibid. italics in original). Since the 1980s, postcards of the Lake Pátzcuaro region have included numerous images of work activities (weaving, fishing, pottery-making) alongside depictions of *The Old Men* and *Night of the Dead* (see following chapter for analysis). Concomitantly, live displays for Festivals of Music and Dance have often used work activities as the material for newly created dance. In many of the dances, participants have replicated an aspect of life, work, and ritual that ceased to exist many years previously, although this point of fact has not been made evident to the visitors.

Of all the work and way-of-life activities represented, fishing has been the most ubiquitous and iconic. Reenacted in live displays, danced in festival performances, reproduced as and on tourist souvenirs, and replicated in countless photographs, fishing on Lake Pátzcuaro is an essential embodied activity signifying P'urhépecha indigenous life. For visitors to Janitzio, fish is served as the main foodstuff in restaurants and food stalls on the dockside. In a self-perpetuating cycle, each representation and signifying activity reinforces the notion of fishing on Lake Pátzcuaro as a preindustrialized method of work that enables the sustenance and continuity of life. Fishing with a butterfly-shaped net controlled by individual fishermen in small canoes was discontinued in the second half of the twentieth century, however, as the activity of butterfly-net fishing declined, the fishermen capitalized on the notion of the performance of fishing, continuing to practice the work activity for survival by transforming it into an exhibition to entertain visitors and thereby generate some income. As tourists make the journey across the water to Janitzio by launch the fishermen enact their fishing activity—a scene involving real water, real nets and canoes, with fake (or already dead) fish. Once the performance is over, the islanders draw close to the launch to request payment for their work.

Further blurring the boundaries between authenticity, work, ritual, and representation, Janitzio islanders have also used their butterfly nets and canoes as part of the *Night of the Dead* celebrations in an endeavor to provide an interesting experience for tourists. The image has been reproduced in words and photographs in countless tourist guides, giving an impression that this is an intrinsic element of an ancient custom. One tourist Web site notes that "One of the most famous customs is the Night of the Dead [on Janitzio]; during this celebration all the fishermen sail out with their butterfly-shaped nets and decorate their boats with candles" (www.bestday.com). In a similar vein, *National Geographic Traveler: Mexico* includes a highly romanticized photographic image depicting five fishermen with their butterfly nets sitting in their canoes (in the foreground), which draws the gaze of the viewer to the island of Janitzio (in the background), shrouded in mist, in the low light of dusk, dotted with small points of light. The whole photo is tinged with a pinky, purple hue, creating an aura of mysticism and ritual (Onstott 2001 and 2006:162). In an insightful and revealing piece of editing, the one-sentence caption for this photo in the 2001 and 2006 editions of this publication generates two different interpretations for its readers. Although the photo is identical, the caption in the 2001 edition states: "Purépecha Indians fish in the traditional way on Lago de Pátzcuaro." By 2006, this has been replaced with: "Fishing with traditional butterfly nets is now done mainly for tourists." The second text demonstrates and communicates recognition that this fishing-activity is a reenactment.[11] The distinction between the two frames of reference and reading (real-life activity and tourist-display) remains problematic, as the necessity for interpretation as real is inherently part of the Janitzio experience.

Overt, conventional staged performances on Janitzio and in the Lake Pátzcuaro region have engaged fishing as a major theme, particularly for the Festivals of Music and Dance for *Night of the Dead*. *The Dance of the Butterfly Nets* (*Las Mariposas*) is standard alongside *The Old Men* in festivals on the islands (25 ●). With these framed events, the proximity of the bodies/people engaged in re-presenting fishing to those fishing on the lake, both as a display for tourists and to catch food for their livelihood, renders the interpretation complex by setting up an ethnographic-gaze and an iconic juxtaposition. As real fishing nets are utilized as scenographic elements by being draped around the enactment area, so their function significantly alters, yet the realness in relation to an indigenous work activity remains. Although fishing constituted the most-often represented work activity, as Festivals of Music and Dance for *Night of the Dead* proliferated, villagers from the Lake Pátzcuaro region created dances drawing on other work activities connected with their own lives and those of their predecessors. So, for example, the Dance of the *Huacaleros* simulated the transportation of *huacales* (wooden crates), containing heavy pottery items made in Santa Fe; and Gervasio López and his sons created *La Danza de los Sembradores* (*The Dance of the Sowers*), in which they choreographed and theatricalized their own agricultural activity.[12] With the interface of real life and reenactment, reading the corporeal movements and the bodies undertaking the movements as indigenous and authentic relied upon complex framing processes in which the observer's desires and expectations had to be met.

In a rather pertinent and weighty example of the need to maintain and perform indigenous and traditional-looking ways of work and everyday life in order to satisfy the desires and expectations of tourists (entailing the perpetuation of the construct of authentic indigenous bodies), the performance of preparing tortillas became an essential element of the visitor experience on Janitzio. As a quintessential Mexican foodstuff, tortillas have had their place at all levels of society, but they have had particularly strong associations both with pre-Hispanic Mexico and with contemporary indigenous peoples. In oft-reproduced images (for example those by postrevolutionary muralist Diego Rivera) a pan-indigenous woman is depicted in a kneeling position preparing tortillas. The process for making tortillas necessitated grinding maize entailing hours of back-breaking work kneeling on the ground in front of a *metate* (a slab of black stone near ground level). In the 1920s and 1930s, as traditional rural lifestyles gradually gave way to modern mass production (through processes that were actively encouraged by postrevolutionary governments [Pilcher 2001:75]), the mechanization and urban industrialization of food production transformed tortilla-making through the introduction of automatic tortilla makers and the use of *masa harina* (dehydrated tortilla flour) produced by the Maseca corporation. In 1936 women living near the shores of Lake Pátzcuaro asked President Lázaro Cárdenas "for help to obtain a mechanical mill to grind corn for making tortillas and in this way to liberate them from the 'bitter, black stone with three feet called the metate'" (Pilcher 2001:87). Assistance was forthcoming and for many P'urhépecha women, including most on Janitzio, grinding on the metate became an activity of the past. Yet the move toward mechanization in food preparation did not meet with tourist expectations and desires for authenticity, consequently, concealing and masking the mechanized processes, and performing tortilla-making in the pre-mechanized manner became an essential activity. In their performance for visitors, women on Janitzio created dough with Maseca-brand masa harina then reground it on the metate (with a full choreography of kneeling, pushing, and pulling), followed by patting out the tortillas by hand, rather than placing them in a wooden press. Undertaking the activity in this way enabled the women to be read as indigenous and authentic as they were ostensibly preparing tortillas in the pre-mechanized, traditional manner.

In these illustrations of corporeal work/life activities the matter of reading and interpreting bodies is central. Boundaries between real life and reenactment were blurred, as framing encouraged a literalism of interpretation and a desire to read the bodies as authentic specimens not enactors or actors taking on a role in display, thereby invoking an interplay of truth-fiction, real-fake, and fictional identities–real identities. Such a context produces an unsettling occurrence through the indecidability of whether one is dealing with reality or fiction (Lehmann 2006:101). An impression of unmediated encounter and realness is created through the notion that the activities are being done rather than represented (Kirshenblatt-Gimblett 1998:55). In such contexts, the notion of mimesis (in which there is a break between the real and its representation) tends to be merged with or surpassed by a notion of actuality, leading to a reading not of representations but of actualities and displays of the real, engaging a befuddled ethnographic-cum-touristic gaze (Urry 2002:3). This gaze frames and transforms the bodies into specimens, for "live exhibits tend to make people into artifacts because the ethnographic gaze objectifies" (Kirshenblatt-Gimblett 1998:55). In relation to *Night of the Dead* on Janitzio, the people engaged in both the activities in the cemetery and the activities on the basketball court were read as "real" bodies through the location in their site of home. In this context, the notion of naturalness or iconicity is central, for semiotically the bodies are both signs and signifiers of themselves. As the concept of iconity deals with this relationship between sign and signified, encompassing a perceived similarity or resemblance, so the bodies are signifying indigenous body and at the same time *are* (sign) indigenous body by designation, leading to a reading of "naturalness." On display, the bodies are not merely fulfilling the role of representing, nor are they simply a metaphor; rather, the bodies become signs and signifiers of themselves (MacCannell 1999:156; Kirshenblatt-Gimblett 1998:18). However, one additional crucial element is that "the performers become signs of what the tourist audience believes them to be" (Desmond 1999: xx). In this case, the "performers" are the inhabitants of Janitzio and Jarácuaro, going about their daily lives, enacting *The Old Men*, undertaking the ceremony of *Night of the Dead* in the cemetery, and creating scenes of work and life framed and perceived as indigenous, authentic, and traditional.

Constructions of Authenticity: Interpreting *Night of the Dead* and *The Old Men*

Turning to signification and meanings related to *The Old Men* and *Night of the Dead*, these two corporeal activities simultaneously encouraged interpretations and generated constructs of indigenousness and realness, through cyclical processes of affirmation and explanation. Specific elements of both practices engendered and reinforced ideas concerning the authenticity of these bodies as indigenous. With regard to *Night of the Dead*, the location in the cemetery particularly enabled readings of ritual and authenticity, because the transformation from private ritual to publicly witnessed occasion in situ did not appear to entail commodification of any elements, other than the accommodation of the bodies of spectators in the same shared cemetery space. Although in the cemetery the women have had to performatively reproduce the embodied activities and replicate the patterns of movement year after year, framing the activity as ritual always shifts the interpretation of the repetition into a different class of activity. Reinforcing the notion of authentic ritual, there is no spatial demarcation of the area, other than the walls of the cemetery, and temporally the only boundaries are set with the natural elements of night fall and day break.

In the cemetery the women of Janitzio wear their everyday clothes, comprising a rebozo (which covers or shrouds the head and encircles the face), embroidered blouse, and full skirt. The rebozo is, in essence, just a simple strip of cloth, yet it is a ubiquitous article of Mexican women's clothing, useful for its multifunctionality (such as carrying babies, firewood or vegetables; as protection from the cold and from the sun; as a covering for religious respect in churches; for hiding one's face in towns; and for wiping children's dirty faces). In the P'urhépecha region, rebozos are typically blue, usually with fine white and black stripes. Representations of P'urhépecha women undertaking *Night of the Dead* usually portray the rebozo encircling the face, creating associations with religious iconography and sacred figures.[13] Although the face is not actually covered, the rebozo acts as a form of mask or disguise, highlighting, framing, and transforming each face. In still images, each woman is characteristically depicted in a kneeling position, with her head bowed and hands (when visible) in prayer position, or holding a candle or bundle of flowers. As a live performance, the women's movements in the cemetery involve *normal* activities, such as walking, kneeling, laying flowers, and lighting candles. All the actions are fluid, gentle, slow, gliding, and floating. The sonic landscape is often silent and always hushed, with the women voicing sounds of muted whispering, weeping, soft praying, and gentle singing. All these dramaturgical components index a nurturing, motherly role, combined with notions of religiosity, reverence, fervency, subservience, and servitude.[14] As scenographic objects, the flowers, candles, and food also contribute to a reading of spirituality, protection, veneration, sustenance, compassion, and care. As the scene is lit only by the glow of candles and the radiance of the moon, there is a sense of attempting to peer through the darkness to make out the whereabouts and appearance of the women. As the candles flicker, so the light creates moving shadows, both of the women's bodies and the crosses on the graves. Dramaturgically, the combination of elements coheres to create a reading of indigenous authenticity, in which the realness of the event underpins and reinforces notions of indigenousness that are wholly intact in the twenty-first century.

Since the initial staged public uses, the *Dance of the Old Men* has also facilitated a reading of authentic indigenous practice and people, signified through the music, the costume of pan-indigenous everyday clothes, the superimposed mask, and the movement vocabulary. In terms of musical accompaniment, the instruments, playing style, and compositional elements all reference a folkloric Mexican construct. Although string instruments were not used in Mexico prior to the Spanish incursion, their development and ubiquity afforded easy linkage with the notion of being authentically Mexican, with Campos even describing the jaranita as "fundamentally Mexican" (1930:185). Similarly, the notion of *simplicity*, so crucial to the formulation of a folkloric construct, was indexed through the eight-bar repeated phrases; the regular rhythm patterns; the I, IV, V harmonic patterns played as a plucked bass line and strummed chordal sequence on jaranita or vihuela; and the formulaic, motif-based melodic lines with small pitch range.

The costume of hat, shirt, trousers, poncho, and sandals worn both by dancers and by musicians has formed a central signifier, with much of the connotation resting on the usage of a costume that was, in effect, not a costume, but rather the everyday clothes of many indigenous and rural men. The costume was therefore not a fanciful disguise that marked the event as "theatricalized rehearsed event" but rather signaled "display of real life," generated through the distinctiveness and ubiquity of the clothes as pan-indigenous. Carlos Basauri, in his 1940 ethnographic account of the indigenous population, described how "the men wear unbleached linen or cotton shirt and pants [*traje de manta*], fastened at the waist with a cummerbund or belt of wool or cotton, of bright colors; straw hats of different shapes and styles; ponchos of wool...and a neckscarf" (1990 [1940]:518–20). Although this description exactly matches the costume of *The Old Men*, Basauri was, in fact, describing the everyday clothes of P'urhépecha men. Only two items were omitted—the ribbons and the mask. These clothes

were not only worn by P'urhépecha men but were also ubiquitous as the garments of indigenous and rural males throughout Mexico. Norwegian explorer
and ethnographer Carl Lumholtz, documenting his experience in Mexico during the last years of the nineteenth century, noted the "use of *sarapes* [ponchos]
in the whole state by *indios* and working class Mexicans" (1945:353). President
Porfirio Diaz, during his tenure in the late nineteenth and early twentieth centuries, banned the wearing of traditional white cotton clothes worn by indigenous peoples within the boundaries of Mexico City, for he regarded the
"'backward' Indian" as a blemish (Krauze 1997:39).

By the 1920s and 1930s, the omnipresent indigenous clothes were the focal
point for various discussions. Writing in the 1930s, Samuel Ramos (philosopher
and author) denounced the stereotypical use of the image of "the 'Indians' with
their *traje de manta* " (1998:90), while the Mexican consul in Berlin, commenting
on the world's fair in Seville in 1929, noted that he found it "'contradictory that
on the one hand we try to expunge the white cotton pants and leather sandals of
the Indians from our nation, while on the other we make an effort to exhibit these
articles in foreign countries'" (Tenorio-Trillo 1996:233). This attire was on display
at world's fairs as an artifact of everyday indigenous life, exhibited in both object-
form and through photographs, making its use as the costume for *The Old Men*
even more potent.[15] In the 1950s and 1960s, leather sandals and stereotypical
indigenous clothing (which included poncho and unbleached linen or cotton
shirt and pants) were appropriated by the countercultural beatniks and hippies
from the United States, who traveled to Mexico for an "authentic" experience
(Zolov 2001:255). This move in turn led to Mexican middle-class youth clothing
themselves in these indigenous garments, reinforcing the reading of the costume
of *The Old Men* as "non-costume." The ubiquity of these clothes is succinctly captured by anthropologist Anya Royce in her description of the Zapotec *son*: "The
man...is thoroughly Indian. His traditional costume of white cotton shirt and
baggy pants, sandals, sombrero, and red neckerchief, is like that of almost every
other Indian or peasant group in Mexico" (1977:169). The ordinariness of the Old
Man costume was even more apparent when juxtaposed with that of other dances,
and in particular with the *Dance of the Moors*, which was most often performed
with *The Old Men* in nationalistic and folkloric contexts of the 1920s and 1930s.
As the *Dance of the Moors* utilized an elaborate costume representative of a foreign
other, which included silk brocade, colored gauze to veil the face, a turban and
pearls, comparisons between the two dances led to an interpretation of *The Old
Men* as an enactment of real life.[16]

Other factors also indexed ideas of indigenousness and authenticity, particularly the use of natural and local fabrics and materials, such as the hats woven from
local plants, the unbleached linen or cotton pants and shirts, the woolen ponchos,
the wood and leather shoes, and the masks molded with clay or carved from wood
with hair formed from plants. In addition, the rough textures and the bright colors
formed part of an aesthetic preference for contemporary cultural rebirth in the
postrevolutionary era. Associated with this, the walking stick held by the dancers
evoked preincursion iconography and primitivism, for although it was simply an

upturned root, rather than being carved into a deliberate form, numerous accounts interpreted the shape as that of a deer's head.

Masking, Zapateado, and Posture

Of all the many elements comprising the *Dance of the Old Men*, the mask stands apart in terms of potent iconic usage and signification. In many instances, the disembodied mask has been deployed as the only signifier referencing *The Old Men* and peoples of Lake Pátzcuaro. As a generic object, the mask engages notions of ritual, disguise, and superimposition, associated particularly with hiding, transforming, and revealing identities. Octavio Paz, one of Mexico's most eminent philosophers and authors, explored the theme of "Mexican Masks" in his writings on Mexican identity, equally posing the elemental question: "What is behind the mask?" (Paz 1972 [1950]) and invoking the most fundamental feature of masking, namely superimposition.[17] The mask is superimposed over an already existing face, thereby provoking such queries as: what is the "real" face behind the mask? and who is the "real" person? The Old Man mask superimposes one self over another—old over young; mestizo over indigenous; white skin over brown skin. Significantly, both Mexico as a political entity, and Mexicans as peoples, may be regarded as products of superimposition; one identity over another, one culture over another, and one past over another.[18] In their writings on music, Gabriel Saldívar and Elisa Osorio Bolio characterized the situation as one in which mestizo culture was superimposed over the indigenous one, as the culture and music of the indigenous population "was covered by the imported one" (1934:160). It is the juxtaposition of the mask and "real" body beneath that gives potency to the masks in *The Old Men*. The superimposition of a whitish face over a brown face—the Old Man mask placed over a P'urhépecha face—was a powerful signifier of the ideological doctrine of mestizaje, even as it was also valuable in contexts of indigenismo.

In 1929 an edition of *Mexican Folkways* was dedicated entirely to the theme of Mexican masks, particularly emphasizing indigenous and ritualistic uses. Significantly, all the contributors were major intellectuals, artists, and politicians of the era, demonstrating the role of agents of the state in constructing and shaping notions of indigenousness specifically associated with ritual and dance. Three authors in particular expressly engaged with the concept of transformation: Alfonso Caso (archeologist and anthropologist) indicated that masks "convert those who use them into new beings and produce by imitation that which is desired" (1929:111), while Miguel Covarrubias (painter, ethnologist, and art historian) proposed that masks "possess a very real magic in that they have the power to transform both the actor and the audience" (1929:116). Adolfo Best Maugard (painter, film director, screenwriter, SEP worker) suggested that a mask "transforms and protects us, gives us other personalities and preserves our own hidden self behind the mask" (1929:126).[19]

Interpreting the Old Man mask as mestizo and nonindigenous relied on referencing certain facial features, and in particular skin color. Phenotypic descriptions, such as those of León and Basauri (cited above), and photographic images created a context in which contrasts between the Old Man mask and P'urhépecha features were apparent. Skin color was the most obvious point of difference, juxtaposing white with brown (and in black and white photographs, pale with dark). In actuality, the color of the masks varied according to the materials from which they were made and the place of production. Masks for use in the Lake Pátzcuaro region were initially made from clay in the lakeside village of Santa Fe, where the pigmentation tended to be bright pink or red. Although these clay masks continued to be used by villagers from Santa Fe, due to their fragility, most other dancers of *The Old Men* changed to using wooden masks, carved in the lakeside village of Tócuaro near Jarácuaro. For these masks, the face was coated with a pale pink- or peach-colored paint. The U.S. anthropologist Ralph Beals, who worked in the P'urhépecha region in the early 1940s, described the Old Man mask of the upland region as indicating a "Caucasian racial type" (1946:149). When these masks were carved from wood this job was undertaken by the *santeros*—those who sculpted images of saints for the churches—and it was for this reason that many masks had the faces of saints, particularly in terms of coloring (Brody Esser 1984:131, Ogazon 1981:13). Normally, saints images were sculpted with "European" features and a given a very pale, almost white skin. The brown face of the image of the Virgin of Guadalupe is, of course, an exception. In all cases, Old Men masks were pale "skinned," which particularly contrasted with the visible body parts on show during the dance, notably the hands of the dancers, and the faces of the unmasked musicians. Even when *The Old Men* was performed by ballet folklórico ensembles, the pink skin of the mask continued to reference the brown skin of the "original" Lake Pátzcuaro dancers. In postrevolutionary settings, the indexation of a mestizo face with the Old Man mask presented itself powerfully as an ambivalent signifier, with the potential to explore boundaries and to highlight the contradictions and dichotomies of the indigenista and mestizaje ideologies. In more contemporary events a similar ambivalence continues to generate questions about skin color and status.[20]

In conjunction with the pan-indigenous costume and the pink-colored mask, corporeal postures and movements have been fundamental to interpretations of the bodies and the practice as indigenous, as features of both the body in motion and the body in inert positions are potent sites of interpretation and signification. *The Old Men* uses three vocabularies of movement: (1) everyday human movement; (2) mimetic movement; and (3) zapateado (rhythmic footwork), all of which are structured within short, repeated sections, and placed in a space with geometric figures. Movements involving walking and running are immediately recognizable and identifiable, and similarly, mimetic movements (for example bending the back and hobbling uneasily while leaning on the walking stick) are based on a normal bodily usage. The basic body position (captured and reproduced in still images) is curved forward with an exaggerated arch, as the torso gestures toward the earth in a downward motion. One or both hands grasp the walking stick firmly, as the stick takes the weight of the aged body. The stick, an upturned root, forms a connection with the earth. Such a stance contrasted with the erect form of classical dance (such as ballet) and "Spanish-heritage" dances, and was read as "typical of Mexican Indian dance" (Royce 1977:169).

The rhythmic footwork, or zapateado, also engendered associations with indigenousness. As both a generic term and a Mexican and pan–Latin American movement classification, zapateado holds connections with both social and ritual dance, and is particularly associated with Mexican popular dance. However, although zapateado refers to movements executed by the feet that are always rhythmic and include stamping and tapping, there are various modes of execution that therefore lead to distinctions between the differing styles consequently being labeled as "indigenous" or "Spanish." For example, in referring to the indigenous Zapotec *son* dance form, Royce observed that "[the dancer's] steps...are the typical modified zapateado found all over rural Mexico" (1977:169). Following a performance in 1962 of the Ballet Folklórico of Mexico in the United States, one reviewer related his comments specifically to a characterization of origins and nationality, observing that "in contrast to the Spanish—'who stamp in pride and arrogance'—the Mexicans came across as primitively charming: '[They] skip happily on bare feet or shuffle in sandals'" (Zolov 2001:243). The "shuffling in sandals" related to the zapateado utilized in dances regarded as indigenous, such as *The Old Men*. Engaging a form in which the back is bent over, executed by leaning forward, and in combination with a downward motion, the foot-stamping movement requires the weight of the body to be focused downward, using gravity to pull the dancer toward the ground. This movement indexes ideas of "earthy" (generated through associations with pounding the earth); "rurality" (linked with agricultural activities such as preparing the earth); and with rhythm as life force.[21] Over the decades of public use, of all the elements in the dance, commodification of the zapateado has moved toward a more spectacular and virtuosic style. A shift from single to double zapateado, the development of more intricate patterns, and the addition of wooden soles to the sandals all created a focus on the footwork, enabling audiences to be captivated and thrilled by the idea of the skill of the dancers (12 ◐).

Lastly, the element of humor has been of central importance in terms of signification, with the notion of "indigenous humor" often being referred to in characterizing *The Old Men* as P'urhépecha. Through the characterization of the "old man" who is barely able to stagger onto the stage and yet who can perform leaps and intricate footwork, the contradiction of appearance and action forms the essence of *The Old Men* in terms of humor and pleasure, drawing on genres of ritual and visual clowning so often associated with festival and carnival. Elements of humor based in contradictions and in sheer physical clowning are most evident (and often most exaggerated) in the section named *El Trenecito* (the Little Train). As the linked line of dancers travels around the performance area in train-like fashion, (each dancer connected by holding onto the stick of the dancer behind), and as the music increases in tempo, the effect of Old Men running fast and losing control of themselves, with one or more dancers from the end of the line becoming disconnected and disoriented, provides a stimulus for kinesthetic and sensory pleasure and laughter. Dancers engage with their audiences and play on this aspect, emphasizing the humor to elicit as much laughter as possible, through exaggeration and melodrama.

In combination with *The Old Men* as practice, documentation configuring the dance as pre-Hispanic, old, and with ritualistic meanings circulated throughout the twentieth century, presenting *The Old Men* and dancing bodies as indigenous and authentic. From the postrevolutionary era onward, dissemination both of records of Spanish chroniclers of the sixteenth century, and of the work of commentators, propounded the connection between indigenous dance and pre-Hispanic communities, characterizing dances as prolific in indigenous cultures and deeply part of religious ceremonies, often involving thousands of dancers (c.f. Covarrubias and Mendoza 1955). The sixteenth century account by Father Diego Durán, encompassing a very brief description of a dance of old men with similar attributes to the twentieth-century version of the Lake Pátzcuaro *Dance of the Old Men*, has been used repeatedly to prove that *The Old Men* from Lake Pátzcuaro is indeed a pre-Hispanic dance, and that by indexation, the dancers are also indigenous.[22] The notion of age, coupled with the concept of location of enactment, has frequently been invoked to determine authenticity. For example, as noted in chapter 9, in a comprehensive catalogue of Michoacán dances and fiestas, *The Old Men* of Jarácuaro was classified as being "more than 100 years" old, performed in the village on 22 January and 25 December, with the "original" practice having suffered as a result of external performances (García Contreras 1986).

The notion of "the real meanings" of *The Old Men* was often circulated through replication and recycling of purportedly factual information from one document to another, affirming the meaning of *The Old Men* in an objective manner. Descriptions in one source were identical to others in later documents, demonstrating the workings of processes of transmission and dissemination that perpetuate ideas once set in motion. All the documented meanings relate specifically to indigenous and religious contexts, often encompassing a strong magic and supernatural character and making associations with the sun and moon. Frequently, the figures of the Old Men are described as the Wise Men of the community, and the satirical and humorous nature is used to draw attention to a purported essence of the P'urhépecha character. The walking stick is described as a deer's head, and associated with authority and with cultivating the earth. One final recurring interpretation is linked to making fun of the Spanish invaders, as narrated succinctly in the tourist and backpackers guide series *Lonely Planet*: "The dance and costumes of Los Viejitos (The Old Men), which can be seen in Pátzcuaro, Michoacán, originated in mockery of the Spanish, whom the local Tarasco [*sic*] Indians thought aged very fast!" (Noble 1995:51). Even in this brief explanation, *The Old Men* is connected with indigenous P'urhépecha peoples and with the location of Lake Pátzcuaro, setting up an interpretation juxtaposing colonial Spaniards with a pre-Hispanic population.[23]

Embodying Indigenous Gender

In concluding this discussion concerning shaping and constructing embodied notions of indigenous Mexico through bodies interpreted as indigenous, the pairing or binary of *The Old Men* and *Night of the Dead* is significant. In juxtaposition, the iconic woman's body of *Night of the Dead* and the iconic man's body of *The Old Men* act as referents of gendered indigenous bodies. Cultural ideologies of gender differences are reproduced, and distinctive and emblematic gendered roles are evident, maintaining and preserving the prescribed roles and identities of pan-indigenous women and men, and again reinforcing interpretations as indigenous bodies. Even in postrevolutionary staged events in Mexico City in the 1920s, both activities were enacted within the same frame and setting, and this pairing has continued ever since, as these practices are placed side-by-side in photographs in guide books and postcards, and are witnessed as live events in close proximity at Lake Pátzcuaro. As is common in many dance styles, movement vocabularies of men and women demonstrate the ideals of gendered difference in action (Reed 1998:516), a principle that is clearly evident with *Night of the Dead* and *The Old Men*. Whereas each practice is significant and powerful in its own right, the reception is even more potent when the bodies are compared and contrasted, generating associative pairings and binaries. Even in the most basic terms, the men's vocabulary involves fast, direct, strong, rhythmic, sudden, energetic, virtuosic, geometric, and complex movement, while the women's vocabulary encompasses slow, indirect, light, flowing, sustained, gentle, unskilled, free, and simple movement.[24]

Summarizing this chapter, through multiple processes of representation, the bodies of the women and men of Lake Pátzcuaro were molded and projected as indigenous, with qualities and traits that were presumed to reflect their innermost selves, maintaining their usefulness as iconic referents for touristic and nationalistic purposes. "Indigenous Mexico," as embodied in the women undertaking *Night of the Dead* and the men enacting the *Dance of the Old Men*, continues to be efficacious in multifarious contexts, within Mexico and beyond. Visual representations, particularly reproduced through photographic media, have been central to the effective deployment of *The Old Men* and *Night of the Dead* since the postrevolutionary era, capturing and directing attention to the iconic bodies.

CHAPTER 12

Capturing Bodies

Postcards, Advertising, and the World's Fair

REPRODUCED PHOTOGRAPHIC IMAGES have played a central role in processes of performism, circulating ideas about the *Dance of the Old Men* and *Night of the Dead* from the 1920s onward by engaging a highly potent form of visual and embodied representation. My focus in this chapter is on specific photographic reproductions current in the twenty-first century. Firstly, I discuss postcards circulating in the Lake Pátzcuaro and Morelia region; secondly, I briefly analyze two associated iconic images of P'urhépecha people/bodies in the form of Las Tarascas fountain in Morelia, and advertisements using fishermen on Lake Pátzcuaro; thirdly, I evaluate the marketing poster of the 2006 European campaign of the Mexican Tourist Board, discussing the design and photographing processes; and fourthly, I consider *Soul of Mexico*, the filmic exhibition of *Night of the Dead* on Janitzio at *Expo 2000*, the World's Fair, Germany.

Photographs have a particular value through iconicity, making them highly efficacious for imaging Mexico, shaping and directing the tourist gaze, and perpetuating networks of signification. Through ease of reproduction photographic media have circulated readily in local, regional, national, and international contexts, propagating an iconography of indigenismo that promotes the people and practices of Lake Pátzcuaro as *Mexico* to diverse audiences. Photographic images of *The Old Men* and *Night of the Dead*, and interrelated images of Janitzio and fishermen on Lake Pátzcuaro, have been replicated countless times in a plethora of contexts, from populist magazines to scholarly journals, from advertising brochures to marketing posters, and from postcards to books, reinforcing their representative value as sights of interest and bodies of difference, within nationalist and tourist agendas. Each instance of exposition contributes to the ongoing processes of authentication and traditionalization, functioning to shape interpretations of *The Old Men* and *Night of the Dead* in relation to notions of indigenousness and Mexico. Twenty-first-century postcard images of kneeling women celebrating

Night of the Dead on Janitzio, heads covered with a rebozo, and surrounded by candles and flowers, replicate those captured by González in the postrevolutionary nationalistic era of the early 1920s. In Germany in 2000, the same corporeal iconography—reproduced as digitalized, virtual-reality, life-size, and moving figures—was exhibited as the 3D filmic exhibition *Soul of Mexico* at the World's Fair.

When bodies/people framed and presented as indigenous and folkloric are the principal subject matter, the photographs invoke a sense of realness and authenticity, dealing directly with traces, memories, histories, and the past. As iconic likenesses, photographs have a distinctive potency because they generate a particular mode of viewing, transforming the subject into an object (Barthes 1984:13), capturing and displaying bodies as ethnographic and authentic specimens that are framed as different. Even as the people are engaged in embodied movement (dancing, playing music, fishing, kneeling), they are displayed as frozen-in-time, for, as Phelan has observed, "the photograph…shows us the moment that has faded, the death and disappearance of that particular configuration of subjectivity frozen by the camera.… No longer fluid and moving, the image 'dies' in order to be seen again" (1995:202). Notions of the past resonate inherently since the body reproduced in the photograph is already older, different, and transformed in some way. In certain striking cases, the person/body circulating as a postcard or tourist brochure image is no longer alive (two notable instances are with photographs of Gervasio López and Felix Francisco).

Illustrations that circulate in the twenty-first century have their roots in knowledge and imagery accumulated from many decades earlier, having been collected and captured by intellectuals, scientists, explorers, lithographers, painters, photographers, and foreign travelers from the eighteenth century onward. Perpetuating this iconography into the twenty-first century points toward a trajectory of performing ideas concerning indigenous people, places, and practices that has consequences for contemporary people invoked by such ideas and images. By discussing a small number of specific photographic reproductions current in the twenty-first century, my aim is to highlight issues of the politics and poetics of exhibiting bodies through photographic imagery.

Postcards: Performative and Authenticating Objects

As tiny yet ubiquitous paper artifacts of travel and tourism, and as essential elements of the fabric of tourist industries worldwide, postcards circulate not only regionally but globally, acting as minute performative objects, and the ultimate in framed, transportable evocations and representations of places, peoples, and histories. As the postcard is transported around the world on a global and unpredictable journey, so processes of viewing and reception are flexible. The image is observed in the place of sale, en-route, and at the destination (by the recipient and casual viewers when the postcard is displayed in a house or workplace). In the tourist site, the presence of the postcard acts as a validating and authenticating signifier, shaping the tourist gaze, framing what the tourist must seek out, and acting as a guide to what is essential to their experience of that place. Postcards are supreme examples of overt framing, in as much as frames encompass "principles of selection, emphasis and presentation composed of little tacit theories about what exists, what happens, and what matters" (Gitlin 1980:6). The postcards under scrutiny here encapsulate a brief snapshot of immense ideological framing, generating and shaping expectations based fundamentally on notions of ethnic and bodily difference.[1]

Postcards may utilize a single photo, often with a caption or place name to guide recognition and interpretation. Others are composites, created from more than one image yet bordered by one frame—the edge of the postcard. Pertinently, engaging the term "composites" draws attention to the finished product as engineered from two or more constituent materials with significantly different properties, which together form a complete and functional whole. Thus, the combination and juxtaposition of images create a single visual postcard object with considerable signifying and essentializing power. Postcard images often form networks of oppositions and correspondences, generating associations with other real or potential images. The choice of what *not* to represent is as significant as the chosen images themselves. The composition of each postcard suggests and creates a narrative that relies not only on the images within the frame, but also what is beyond and outside the frame—with what is presumed, imagined, or absent. Networks of signification are created not only through juxtaposition within the same postcard frame, but also through juxtaposition with other postcards placed in the vicinity, and with all the other paraphernalia of the tourist industry, such as souvenirs, brochures, and posters.

Postcards have performed a significant role in the tourist complex surrounding *Night of the Dead* and *The Old Men*, displaying traces of an event and acting as miniature synthetic performances, capturing and imitating snapshots of local P'urhépecha customs and everyday life, as did the theatrical cuadros costumbristas (scenes of customs) during the postrevolutionary period. As tourist numbers increased in the Lake Pátzcuaro region, so postcards proliferated, utilizing images that drew upon and encapsulated the attractions formulated in the postrevolutionary years associated specifically with rurality, indigenousness, tradition, preindustrial lifestyles, and ritual. Principal recurring images have included: *The Old Men*, *Night of the Dead*, the island of Janitzio (aerial view, profile and close-up of the statue of Morelos), men fishing with butterfly nets, women weaving, utilitarian pottery objects, colonial churches, Roman Catholic icons, and stone statues.

In the examples that I give below, and in the many other postcards on sale in Morelia and Pátzcuaro, photographic reproductions of *The Old Men* and *Night of the Dead* are juxtaposed with other sites, sights, and peoples generating significations and interpretations which form a relationship with a natural environment, a pre-Hispanic and a colonial past, ritual dance, religious practices (indigenous and Catholic), and premodern and backward work methods. Invoking the Lake Pátzcuaro natural environment indexes ideas of history, millennia, and permanence, and viewing the people within this natural environment creates associations with naturalness, engaging the culture/nature divide. Although the built environment is presented as essential to the context, all the *buildings of significance* are colonial churches. Providing place names as locational markers and adding short phrases on the reverse of the card guides and shapes interpretation. Notably, only four locations are named: Janitzio, Pátzcuaro, Michoacán, and Mexico. The place of Jarácuaro, home of the villagers in the photographs performing *The Old Men*, has no place in this configuration. Conversely, through the inclusion of the signifier *Mexico* these postcards of *The Old Men* are transformed into potent objects, representing Mexico on a global scale. Inert photographed motionless bodies of men and women realizing *Night of the Dead* and the *Dance of the Old Men* perform their role as efficacious signs of indigenous and folkloric Mexico as postcard exhibits in an international marketplace. These embodied images in postcard photographs suggest ideas of packaging people, as the bodies are frozen-in-time and reproduced for consumption. Notably, although the people in the photos often posed specifically for the photographs, they received little or no financial remuneration. Their expectation was that they would receive an economic compensation through performances in tourist locations, which, as I discuss in the following chapter, often did not happen as anticipated (Orozco and López: personal communication). In the vicinity of Lake Pátzcuaro, living people interface with their captured static photographed selves on postcards, and also flyers and posters.

For each postcard, a decision-making process has led to a selection of images according to their potential to fulfill a communicative function, invoking an essence of Lake Pátzcuaro. Here I give a brief description of a handful of postcards to illustrate some of the most salient aspects (see website for reproductions of all these postcards).

Postcard One: A single image postcard, utilizing a photograph taken in the late 1980s, depicts the ensemble of Gervasio López performing *The Old Men*. The three musicians and four dancers pose in front of colonial arches on a grassy lawn (the unnamed location is the hotel La Posada de Don Vasco in Pátzcuaro). The pink-skinned masked faces contrast with the brown-skinned musicians' faces, generating an overt somatic comparative locus. With the caption "Saludos desde Pátzcuaro" (Greetings from Pátzcuaro) *The Old Men* is linked directly with Pátzcuaro, rather than Jarácuaro, and the seven performers remain anonymous (postcard visible in figure 1.1, and see figure 1.2 in which the top right-hand photo is this same image).

Postcard Two: In another single-image postcard, using a photograph taken in the early twenty-first century, the ensemble of Abel Orozco of Jarácuaro (musicians and dancers) poses on the dockside by the edge of Lake Pátzcuaro, with the island of Janitzio in the background. The caption states "Pátzcuaro, Michoacán, Mexico." Again, *The Old Men* and performers are not associated with Jarácuaro, but instead are placed in the frame with Janitzio.[2]

Postcard Three: In a composite three-image postcard, with the caption "Saludos desde Janitzio" (Greetings from Janitzio) the photographs show (1) an aerial view of Janitzio; (2) a group of women kneeling inside a small room weaving a *faja* (cloth belt); and (3) *The Old Men* (the photograph as in Postcard One above). This photomontage is reinforced by the wording on the reverse which labels these images as "views of Janitzio," perpetuating the notion that *The Old Men* is wholly associated with Janitzio. With the aerial shot of Janitzio the viewers have a bird's eye view, enabling them to see the little island completely surrounded by water (as in the Disney film, *The Three Caballeros*), marking this as a site that is separate, cut-off, and different. Two groups of people in action are framed within this island-home: women carrying out what is presented as an everyday work-task of weaving belts (these women are depicted kneeling on the floor inside a very low-ceiled room, clothed in skirt and blouse with long braided hair); and men performing *The Old Men*. These two groups of bodies coalesce to generate a notion of *different* indigenous bodies undertaking real life activities (figure 1.2).

Postcard Four: In a composite card comprising four photographs, *Night of the Dead* and *The Old Men* appear side by side, along with a single fisherman on the lake, and a colonial church, all tied together with the locational marker "Pátzcuaro, Mexico" (visible in figure 1.1).

Placing *Night of the Dead* and *The Old Men* within one postcard explicitly frames these two practices together. Images of rurality cohere with a colonial past. Women kneeling in the darkness illuminated by candles and surrounded by flowers cohere with the masked figure of an Old Man dancer leaning on his stick.

Postcard Five: Another four-image composite depicts aspects of the town of Pátzcuaro and the Lake Pátzcuaro region. Each photograph includes a representation of a human body: in three images the bodies are modeled in wood and stone and in the fourth they are live performing bodies. One depicts a stone statue of sixteenth-century Spanish priest Vasco de Quiroga; another shows the stone statue of independence leader Morelos, in the center of the island of Janitzio; the third displays the lavish and grand interior of a Roman Catholic church, with a saint's icon contained inside a glass case; and the fourth represents *The Old Men*, again with performers from Jarácuaro. In the first three photographs, the bodily positions are upright and erect, whereas the bodies enacting *The Old Men* are held in downward positions. In these images the bodies of saints in glass cases interface with stone statues of heroes. These people, long since dead, are captured in stone and wood and rendered immortal. Their monumentalized bodies are placed alongside the still-living bodies of the *Dance of the Old Men* performers from Jarácuaro, who are transmuted through this framing into fixed, motionless, inanimate objects, and anonymized heroes (figure 1.3) (14 ◐).

Postcard Six: In one final example, a composite image with five aspects of Michoacán and the caption "Michoacán, Mexico" places *The Old Men* in a wider geographical and ideological frame. Two images depict colonial churches in the state capital Morelia (the Cathedral and the church of San Francisco); one shows fishermen on Lake Pátzcuaro with butterfly nets; another depicts *The Old Men*; and the fifth one portrays handcrafted pottery objects. With this juxtaposition *The*

Old Men performs as representative of the state of Michoacán and the nation of Mexico, and as an authentic, pre-modern, indigenous ritual.[3]

Bare-Breasted Women and Men with Butterfly Fishing Nets

Although *The Old Men* and *Night of the Dead* are the central focus of this study, in order to understand the potency of the reproduction of photographed images of essentialized and generic P'urhépecha bodies, two other examples are noteworthy for their role as frequently reproduced depictions: the fountain known as *Las Tarascas* (P'urhépecha Women); and fishermen with butterfly fishing nets on Lake Pátzcuaro. Both form essential threads in the tapestry of signification molding ideas about indigenousness and bodies encompassing *The Old Men* and *Night of the Dead*, and both are used on postcards, in tourist literature, as advertising material, and as souvenir objects (43 and 46 🌑).

Las Tarascas is a representation of three P'urhépecha women, however, unlike most other photographed P'urhépecha figures, the bodies are not living, breathing, flesh-and-blood, but crafted in stone. Las Tarascas is a fountain-statue located in the main street in the historic center of the city of Morelia. According to a popular English-language tourist Web site, Las Tarascas "represents the fertility of the state of Michoacan [sic]. It depicts three indigenous women holding up a traditional basket full of regional fruits. This fountain has become one of the main iconic symbols of the city" (www.bestday.com). Photographic reproductions of this incarnation of P'urhépecha women's bodies have been used frequently in nationalistic and touristic contexts. I suggest that the depiction of the women's bodies, overtly labeled as indigenous and P'urhépecha through the title Las Tarascas, is highly problematic for various reasons. Las Tarascas takes its place as an embodiment of a state-constructed, officially sanctioned image of P'urhépecha women that both essentializes P'urhépecha women, through the symbolic representation of three identical bodies, but also presents them as *of the past*, through the common function of monumentalization. As a strategy of unification, monumentalization was part of governmental policy, celebrating and re-membering iconic figures by creating very public artworks to shape a unified set of heroes, who were inherently dead and of the past, even as they were deployed in constructions of the present and future (for example, the statue of Morelos atop the island of Janitzio). In general terms, monuments are commonly public statements that create a link with a person assumed to be dead, therefore serving to celebrate and remember the past. Las Tarascas provokes questions concerning the interface between living and dead humans, representing P'urhépecha women as of and in the past.

These three stone women stand in the middle of a round fountain, with water falling around their feet and spurting up in jets by their sides. Unlike most nationalist and tourist representations of P'urhépecha women, generally depicted undertaking *Night of the Dead*, in this portrayal the women stand erect with their arms held high, supporting a basket among all three. Obvious interpretations are associated with strength, encapsulating the notion of P'urhépecha women as providers and nurturers. However, one deeply problematic aspect is to be found in the clothing. Whereas the three stone women are clothed in the traditional P'urhépecha full-pleated skirt and have the classic rebozo draped over their head and back, they have no blouse—they are bare-breasted or topless. Such a representation raises numerous issues concerning the notion of indigenous bodies as *different*, with nudity in such bodies as acceptable because they are *native*. Images of bare-breasted women are not commonplace in Morelia, or indeed in any other city in Mexico. The only other reproduced displays of partially naked women's bodies are located outside Men's Clubs, and even then, the women in those oversized photographic representations are not bare-breasted. A number of contemporary P'urhépecha women still dress in the full-pleated skirt and rebozo, and walk through the streets of Morelia wearing these garments, therefore setting up a juxtaposition and intertextual relationship between themselves and the bare-breasted stone bodies of their essentialized representation, affecting the gaze of others upon them, and also their own gaze upon the statue. While attempting to make lives for themselves in twenty-first century Mexico, living P'urhépecha women are constrained by portrayals that essentialize them, framing them as of the past and just a memory.

In one striking example, a photograph depicts an ensemble of musicians and dancers of *The Old Men* posing in front of Las Tarascas. The placing of this image within a book entitled *Tradiciones Mexicanas* (Mexican traditions) affirms the role of these bodies and *The Old Men* within a construction of indigenous Mexicanness (Vertí 1991). As I noted in Chapter 9, the ensemble, of four musicians and four dancers, is that directed by Juan Francisco and Juan González from Jarácuaro. They took up their stereotypical corporeal stance in front of Las Tarascas in order to create an interesting composition. Yet the juxtaposition of the two groups of bodies sets up a curious relationship between the living men's bodies and the stone women's bodies, such that the stone bodies interface with the live bodies, generating a sense of transmutation and transfer between living and not-living. Both sets of bodies are motionless in the photograph, and both encapsulate essentialized indigenous peoples indexing ideas of *the past*.

As Las Tarascas embodies P'urhépecha women engaged in an activity of providing food for daily life even as they are of the past, so images of P'urhépecha men fishing with butterfly nets on Lake Pátzcuaro corresponds and coheres with this. The men sit in their small, wooden canoes, holding simple and uncomplicated nets (distinguished as distinctively P'urhépecha through countless reproductions). They are depicted working to provide food for daily life, using a rudimentary method in a wholly natural environment. One particularly striking recent deployment of this image was within the advertising campaign of TelCel, Mexico's largest cell phone company. As part of a series of bold, photographic images plastered on buildings, billboards, and magazines, one photograph depicts a P'urhépecha man in the foreground, clothed in the traje de manta, complete with red sash, who sits in his canoe with his net in front of him, framed by the blue waters of Lake Pátzcuaro. In the background the island of Janitzio provides the locational marker of Lake Pátzcuaro. A large TelCel hot-air balloon floats above the water, with the marketing slogan "Todo México es Territorio" (All of Mexico is our territory; or more colloquially—We have Mexico covered). Encapsulated in the image are notions of connections between time and space, present and past, modernity and the preindustrial. A P'urhépecha man, undertaking a purportedly existing yet premodern daily work practice, is deployed to sell a product of the latest technology (figure 1.15).[4]

Perception Management and the Truth Well Told

In 2006, *The Old Men* of Jarácuaro was used to promote Mexico in an overt publicity campaign in an international market place. The larger-than-life body of a P'urhépecha man formed the central focus (figure 1.8). The Mexican Tourist Board used an image of a single Old Man dancer as the centerpiece in their European advertising campaign, imaging Mexico through the corporeal referent of an Old Man dancer, reaffirming the role of *The Old Men* as one of the most representative icons of Mexicanness, and simultaneously performing a perpetuation of a form of iconographic indigenismo. Sandwiched between a clichéd sweeping landscape of rolling mountains and tall cacti (with a verdant golf course in the foreground) on one side, and the magnificent colonial church of Cholula overshadowed by the towering iconic snowed-peaked mountain of Popocatéptl on the other side, the head and shoulders of a pink-hued Old Man masked dancer from Jarácuaro, with beribboned straw hat, bright red poncho, and gnarled stick, formed the central image. The slogan "Mexico: Beyond Your Expectations" tied together the composite image. This use of a single photographic image of an Old Man dancer from Jarácuaro formed a definitive point in the trajectory initiated in 1924, when Nicolás Bartolo Juárez was taken from the island of Jarácuaro to teach *The Old Men* in Mexico City for a performance in an officially sanctioned, staged, public, folkloric spectacle. It encapsulates both the core and the complexity of the multifaceted and multifarious uses of *The Old Men* in the twenty-first century, and draws attention to the potency of photographic images in constructing and perpetuating essentialist notions of Mexico and indigenous people, effecting a romantic and folkloric valorization through associations of culture, tradition, indigenous ritual, and the past.

The advertisement was displayed in numerous locations in European cities, including buses, advertising columns, billboards, and street boards.[5] Engaging potential tourists through provocative imagery is an essential element of the marketing process, for "the act of touristic travel begins with an image, a dream, or a memory in which the tourist places himself or herself at an attraction" (MacCannell 2001:383). Tourist publicity campaigns in which select images play a vital role are therefore a major strategy. In Mexico these campaigns are designed and planned by the Committee of Mexican Tourist Promotion (PROMOTUR), through comprehensive processes of research and selection, as described by a representative:

The campaigns are based on market research, analysis of use of the media by the target consumers, focus groups and evaluations of the impact of the messages. As a general line, the campaigns enhance the perception of Mexican tourist destinations and stimulate the intention to travel, and are accompanied by direct calls to action so that the potential tourist seeks out new products and destinations, and so that the travel agents are aware of the national diversity and quality.

(Bustani Moukarzel: personal communication)

For the 2006 European campaign the call to action was encapsulated in the slogan "Mexico: Beyond Your Expectations," engaging directly with notions of dreams and difference. At the heart of this campaign was the embodiment of indigenous, folkloric, colorful, ritualistic, and dancing Mexico, captured in the body of the Old Man. As a PROMOTUR representative explained, the choice of the Old Man dancer was "to illustrate Mexican culture and traditions. We know well that the European market is attracted by culture, and so we chose this photo" (Ruffini: personal communication). Behind the straightforward explanation for the choice of this one dancing body as emblematic of Mexican culture and tradition lies a complex network of imagery. The iconic Old Man dancer was juxtaposed with other images, all drawn from past formulations reaching back to the eighteenth century as depicted by artists, lithographers, travelers, and scholars, encapsulating notions of past-present. A brief overview of that trajectory highlights the constructions of ideas and the processes of authentication, traditionalization, and exoticization into which *The Old Men* and P'urhépecha people were incorporated.

By the late nineteenth century, essentialist promotional imagery was disseminated in an international arena at the world's fairs, with objectives of attracting investment, garnering international confidence, and encouraging emigration (Tenorio-Trillo 1996:114–5). In particular, the paintings of artist José Maria Velasco performed the role of publicity and marketing material, with depictions encompassing concepts of modernism, industrial transformation, and technological advances. Railroads in landscape paintings symbolized progress and the taming of wild nature, and these were placed alongside national symbols and icons of the official nationalist ideology, such as the eagle and nopal cactus, scenes of manners and customs, and tropical or exotic natural beauty (ibid.). At the turn of the century the use of photography proliferated and was put to use in creating images to attract commerce and investment and to appeal to tourists, with depictions of modernity, technologization, the nation's wealth and beauty, and "the Indian past of Mexico" (ibid.). By the 1920s cinematic photography became a hugely important medium for exhibition and promotion, portraying Mexico's beauty and progress as well as its exoticism (ibid.:233).

In the postrevolutionary period, the primary elements of promotional iconography encompassed four aspects of Mexico that were considered to be of interest to tourists, reproduced through governmental channels and in national newspapers. These were: (1) scenic beauty (from beaches to snowcapped volcanoes and the varied countryside in between); (2) the colonial Spanish heritage; (3) indigenous cultures of the past and present; and (4) the new, modern, and industrial infra-structure (Waters 2006:230). Crucially, the idea of past indigenous cultures was projected through pyramids of past civilizations, while the "living Indians became folkloric in their dress, dance, music, and artistic production" (ibid.). In the mid-century the permutation of modernity, nature, and exoticism was still very much the essence of the configuration, portrayed with slogans such as " 'so modern and yet so foreign' and 'so foreign... and yet so near' " (Zolov 2001:246–49). Yet there was a perception of the nation as dominated, amongst other things, by " 'straw sombreros [and] serape blankets' " (ibid.:240), which therefore needed to be coun-tered with representations of modernity. In the 1960s, images of high-rise modern block buildings formed a significant element, alongside "colorful people," (ibid.) and in an overt use of dancing bodies to attract tourists, the Ministry of Tourism began to utilize images of the professional Ballet Folklórico of Mexico as an effica-cious representation of Mexican Otherness, neatly contained inside the frame of the stage of the Palace of Fine Arts, yet still evoking the past.

In the twenty-first century, the Mexican Tourist Board still engages with a past-present continuum, using the slogan "Welcome to Mexico, the country that has it all!.... a modern country, yet full of customs and tradition" as their primary essentialist characterization (www.visitmexico.com). Significantly, in the 2006 Mexican Tourist Board campaign poster, three out of the four early twentieth-century elements were very much in evidence: the scenic beauty, depicted with the rolling hills and snow-capped volcano; the colonial heritage, represented with the church of Cholula; and indigenous cultures, embodied in the Old Man dancer. The "modern and industrial" aspect had been modified from technological and architectural images (railways and skyscrapers) to a concept of the modern as the leisure activity of golf. The straw sombreros and serape blankets were present in the form of the costume for *The Old Men*, creating a stereotypically colorful, folk-loric, and traditional image.

A brief analysis of the advertising photo-montage serves to elludicate the com-plexity and efficacy. In the right-hand photo, the iconic snow-capped towering mountain Popocatépetl signifies concepts of awe-inspiring nature—immoveable, timeless, and even exotic. It has been reproduced innumerable times since the nineteenth century as a potent signifier of Mexico. In 1921 a working model of Popocatépetl was used in a display of overt Mexicanness as part of the nationalistic folkloric event of *Noche Mexicana* in Mexico City, figuring alongside folkloric dancers and indigenous food served in P'urhépecha jícaras. In the 2006 European campaign poster, Popocatépetl is majestic on a grand scale and towers above the white colonial church of Cholula below. The church of Cholula acts as an icon of Spanish colonial heritage, indexing Catholic (therefore postincursion) Mexico, and a human-made artifact.

In contrast to the imposing landmass of Popocatépetl, the landscape of the mountain range and tall cacti generates another image of Mexico and nature. The vast mountains with the iconic cacti (ubiquitous shorthand for "Mexico," and particularly omnipresent in signage for Mexican restaurants throughout Europe) has been made familiar to European audiences through the "Western" film genre, in which lawless Mexican bandits roam around the wild countryside, accosting and robbing well-meaning U.S. citizens. Yet while retaining its vastness, this landscape has been tamed and contained, for in the place of dry scrubland is the lush, neatly manicured, green grass (kept "green" through copious irrigation) of golf fairways. In this scenario, diminutive human figures are seen to be engaged in the leisure activity of hitting small white balls into little holes in the ground. A montage effect is created through the superimposition of the golfers in front of the cacti and mountains. Even by the 1940s, golf courses were part of the touristic promotion of Mexico (Saragoza 2001:108), and this imagery had become ubiquitous by the late twentieth century. Through golf, a primary leisure activity principally undertaken by men, the familiar is placed into an unfamiliar and even exotic frame, providing a sense of comfort and home. With notions of leisure time and superimposition, the golf course has been used to tame the wilderness, in correspondence with the images of railways in paintings and photographs from the late nineteenth century, simultaneously providing a symbol of progress while enticing tourists to experience Mexico.

The central photograph captures a dancer in full flight, frozen in a moment of movement. A red poncho and straw hat stereotypically signify Mexico. The pink mask superimposes the brown-skinned face, which, although not visible, is present through the inclusion of a brown-skinned hand that clutches a walking stick, incorporated just inside the photographic frame. This inclusion of the hand is crucial, signifying indigenousness and authenticity, and allowing difference and otherness to be observed. The mask effaces the individual and creates a generic, essentialized, and folkloric body. One body stands in for the nation of Mexico: the body of the Old Man dancer *is* tradition and culture, juxtaposed with nature, colonial heritage, leisure, and modernity. Yet despite the aliveness of the body in motion, inanimate icons of pre-Hispanicity could also have played the same role. Analogous tourist marketing material often incorporates archeological sites/sights to signify indigenous, of–the-past Mexico, such as the pyramids of Chichén Itzá and Teotihuacán.

Despite the anonymity and emblematic body of the Old Man as nation, the dancer in the photograph is one specific man, Bulmaro Paleo, from the tiny island of Jarácuaro, Lake Pátzcuaro. Somewhat appropriately, the image of Paleo was captured by U.S. photographer Bruce Herman at a tourism convention in the celebrated tourist resort of Acapulco, many years ago. Once taken, Herman sold the photo, and the image became property of other organizations, functioning in multiple transactions for generating financial income at the micro and macro levels (Herman: personal communication).[6] When the photograph was deployed in the 2006 poster campaign, it was owned by the advertising agency Young and Rubicam who loaned it to the Mexican Tourist Board for approximately three years for use in their publicity (Flores: personal communication). In this discussion of issues concerning marketing the nation of Mexico to a global tourist audience, it is pertinent and revealing that the agency controlling the photograph overtly deals in "perception management and public relations, brand identity and design" (www.yr.com). In an equally weighty demonstration of intention, it is significant that the slogan and philosophy of the second advertising company involved in the poster campaign, McCann Erickson, is *Truth Well Told*, drawing attention to notions of narratives, constructions, and ideological management of images and bodies to create belief in authenticity (Alter 1994). *The Old Men*, embodied in and through the masked body of one dancer, played its role in creating a narrative of the real Mexico, inviting and attracting tourists to consume the experience.

Soul of Mexico: Real Mexico

In 2000, photographed bodies of women on Janitzio undertaking their communal celebration of *Night of the Dead*, captured the previous year in the cemetery on their island using a sophisticated arrangement of cameras, were transported to Europe and exhibited in a 3D virtual, interactive, real-time performance as an essence of real Mexico to an international audience. Inside the Mexican Pavilion at *Expo 2000* the World's Fair in Hannover, Germany, large screens displayed the film exhibition *Soul of Mexico* to communicate a quintessence of Mexico on a global platform, functioning in much the same way as the paintings of Velasco had done at world's fairs in the late nineteenth century. The live people/bodies were captured and treated to become digitized images in a twenty-first-century materialization of nation. The activities of just a few hundred women were used to embody and represent Mexico. Viewers of *Soul of Mexico* could ostensibly experience the ritual "as if they were there," and by wearing special glasses they could witness the 2D bodies transformed into "real" 3D bodies. Visitors could walk through the tunnel "as if" walking through the cemetery, observing the P'urhépecha women kneeling and praying, lighting candles and laying flowers at the "ancestral celebration," and experiencing a "living diorama" (Hanover 2000: Press Release and www.mexico21.org.mx). As the ultimate extension of the re-creations of *Night of the Dead* on Janitzio as postrevolutionary theatricalized cuadros costumbristas, *Soul of Mexico* presented a twenty-first century staged display of pseudo-ethnography and technological artistry using authentic islanders (figure 1).

World's fairs are perhaps the most clichéd and obvious examples of nations displaying essences of themselves to a global audience. These large expositions have been staged regularly since the mid-nineteenth century. Since the early twentieth-century tourism, mass consumption, corporate power, and purchased entertainments have formed the central features and functions of world's fairs (Tenorio-Triollo 1996:199). Each aspect on show, including the concept and design of the pavilion and exhibition itself, is read as a weighty signifier of a nation, and the display of artifacts and objects, including living people, has been an important element of world's fairs since their inception. Vast amounts of time and money are expended as national committees and consortia, comprising both official and private representatives, select what to put on display. Mexico has had a presence at world's fairs since their commencement, and, as I mentioned above, formulating and depicting an image of pre-Hispanic and indigenous Mexico alongside modernity and progress has always been an integral element, with perpetual debates surrounding issues of indigenous representation. In 1889 the Mexican pavilion was designed as an Aztec Palace, with images of Aztec gods, goddesses, and kings in the form of bronze statues, which made a "statement about Mexico's Indian legacy in an era of science and nationalism" (ibid. 81). In 2000 the Mexican Pavilion encompassed the design of a pre-Hispanic pyramid.

In the mid-nineteenth century, forming part of the trajectory that leads directly to *Soul of Mexico*, discourses of Mexican anthropology and ethnography were fundamentally part of the aesthetic and ideological selection processes concerning exhibits, with Darwinist beliefs playing an important role. In the late nineteenth century, living people were displayed as artifacts and specimens at world's fairs, connecting with other presentations and performances of exoticism (Kirshenblatt-Gimblett 1998). By the early twentieth century, world's fairs were conceptualized as entertainment and amusement, and the burgeoning trend of tourism partially altered the framing of indigenous artifacts and peoples from "simply" exotic evidence of a far-away country, to the very stuff of attraction (leading to financial returns through the tourist industry infrastructure).

Following the path of exhibiting humans at world's fairs, and maintaining the trajectory of indigenous representation as a fundamental aspect of the Mexican presence at world's fairs, *Soul of Mexico* encompassed the display of twenty-first century indigenous people, whose bodies were configured within a Darwinian system of genuine specimens, perpetuating an anthropological and ethnographic path of factual and objective reporting. *Soul of Mexico* used indigenous peoples as subject and object, and created a didactic role through framing. Following another path from previous decades, *Soul of Mexico* engaged the most advanced technology. In the 1920s technological advances and the developing film industry led to a move toward the use of cinema as an efficacious exhibitionary medium, a trend that has continued into the twenty-first century, with *Soul of Mexico* utilizing the latest technological filmic advances to situate Mexico within a global network of nations.

As a useful description of the exhibition, here I cite the narrative as posted on the official Web site and in a press release, which provides a succinct outline of the salient features and carefully summarizes principal technological, performative, and reception elements:

> The second attraction created in collaboration with the company Barco is an 'IMMERSIVE GALLERY': a unique 3-D effect structure! Visitors walk along a 12 metre gallery whose walls project 3-D images of the Night of the Dead, an ancestral celebration filmed three-dimensionally in Mexico for 36 hours non-stop by de pinxi. This 'immersive tunnel', which can be compared to a LIVING DIORAMA, uses total immersion techniques to plunge visitors into the heart of this celebration of the dead so that they feel 'as if they were there'. This experience, impossible until now, is a real technological breakthrough. Visitors are given lightweight (polarising) glasses which make it possible to see the 3-D effects....

de pinxi, the designer of the project for the Mexican consortium, has joined forces with Barco Projection Systems which has developed, manufactured and integrated this unique projection structure: 12 BarcoGraphics 808s projectors are hung behind the walls and project the 3-D images.

> (www.mexico21.org.mx, and Hanover 2000:
> Press Release, EMPHASIS in original)

Soul of Mexico was one of three exhibitions displayed in the Mexican Pavilion at *Expo 2000*, and, as with other representational media, interpretations of one exhibition are formed through juxtaposition with other images, both present or imagined. The international visitors viewing *Soul of Mexico* also experienced the other exhibitions and had an awareness of the overall concept for the Mexican Pavilion. The original press release encapsulated the key elements:

> The design, architecture and museography of the Mexican Pavilion is organised around the central theme of 'Mexico: a millennial construction'. Mexico is a modern country with very ancient roots, based on traditions and religions, while at the same time vigorously looking to the future.
>
> (Hanover 2000: Press Release)

Within this configuration, *Soul of Mexico* embodied "the ancient and indigenous past" (ibid.), even as it emphasized the realness of the islanders of Janitzio living in the twenty-first century, which allowed the Lake Pátzcuaro region to be publicized and promoted as a site/sight for twenty-first century tourists. A brief description of one of the other two exhibitions permits appreciation of the potency regarding the juxtaposition with *Soul of Mexico*. As the press release stated, "The first attraction invites visitors on an interactive journey through the history of Mexico.... Immersed in virtual worlds, visitors discover the life-size site of the main square in Mexico City, the Zocalo [sic], at three periods of its history" (ibid.). Viewers were able to engage with the past through "digitally reconstructed" (ibid.), computer-generated imagery of people/bodies and scenes from previous eras, namely, preinvasion Aztec lives and architecture; and eighteenth-century lives and architecture. People/bodies appeared real yet were created as virtual representations by deploying the most advanced technological tools. To experience the eighteenth century, visitors could take "an interactive journey in an anonymous painting, rendered three dimensional! Visitors 'inside the painting' find themselves on the Zocalo [sic] and can fully absorb the atmosphere of the time, as well as the thousands of details which belong to this scene of daily life" (ibid.). The third time period depicted was "current life," using contemporary images of recorded film and live streaming. In contrast to this arrangement, *Soul of Mexico* emphasized the ethnographic realness and aliveness of the people undertaking *Night of the Dead* on Janitzio, even as this was framed as an ancient ancestral celebration. Despite all the configurations of "realness," however, there was a sense in which the island-world might just be a virtual world, brought to life through technological wizardry.

As was the case for many other staged events discussed in this study, the printed program for *Expo 2000* acted as an explicit, albeit brief guide to interpretation and reception of *Soul of Mexico* (The EXPO-Guide 2000). An ethnographic frame was generated through a number of narrative elements, guiding viewers in their reception and interpretation. The program included an extended description explaining that throughout the night of 1 November 1999 the activities of the villagers undertaking the *Night of the Dead* celebrations in the cemetery on the island of Janitzio were filmed. Naming the place as "Janitzio Island in Lake Pátzcuaro" pinpointed a clearly delineated location, which was both very tiny and surrounded by water, thus creating obvious associations with isolation and pristine peoples. The factual, as opposed to fictional, geographical location indicated that the film was not an artist's impression nor an imaginary fantasy, but an objective documentary record of a real event. As with other uses of the conception of the "island surrounded by water in the middle of a lake," this idea generated notions of a small community of people undertaking an unadulterated ritual as practiced since time immemorial. This image also connected to the originating myth of the Aztec civilization (one of the general-knowledge-facts disseminated in connection with Mexico and indigenous peoples).[7] The exhibition deliberately moved between the macro and the micro, playing with an essentialized and generalized image of indigenous Mexico, yet specifying very particular individuals from an easily identifiable place, creating a personalized, ethnographic gaze. Emphasizing the contemporary connection by filming the Janitzio islanders just a few months before the exhibition was staged highlighted the potency of living people, existing in another place, yet wholly connected to the past.

Key to the whole exhibition was an essential notion of realness. Real people, moving in real time, and undertaking a real activity were captured, transported, and re-presented in another continent, not as artistic performing bodies, but as ethnological objects framed for observation and scrutiny, transmuted into exhibitionary artifacts. Commenting on the temporal durational element ("filmed over 36 hours") emphasized the liveness and realness, for rather than being structured as brief episodes with a clear beginning and end for theater purposes, the film encompassed thirty-six hours of real-time activities, signaling that the participants were not required to follow directorial orders, or play to the camera, but simply carry out the ceremony as they and their ancestors had done for centuries.

Shaping a particular gaze was a central element of the exhibition. Audiences were not only invited but instructed to be voyeurs as they put on glasses to see the real effect, transforming people/bodies from two-dimensional objects into three-dimensional realities: "a living diorama." Invoking the idea of a diorama related specifically to notions of ethnographic display and models of reality. As nineteenth-century theater devices, dioramas were used to view a landscape painting, the effect of which caused audiences to believe they were looking at a natural scene. They were also display apparati utilized with the intention of giving the impression of the real. Most commonly this was a three-dimensional model or a small representation of a scene with three-dimensional figures, which was usually enclosed in a glass showcase for a museum and viewed through a window, typically showing historical events, nature scenes, and cityscapes. When the National Museum of Anthropology in Mexico City opened in the mid-1960s, numerous static dioramas recreated scenes of Mexican life, although "the Indian present was virtually absent: dioramas instead focused on an imagined ideal existence before the time of the Spanish Conquest" (Zolov 2001:244). In a rather different conceptual form of performative diorama, the staged cuadros costumbristas of the postrevolutionary era recreated representational acts of indigenous life in a form of ethnographic performance, framed by theater stages, in which the activities of *Night of the Dead* on Janitzio were captured as a brief episode. Designating *Soul of Mexico* as a living diorama encapsulated elements of both postrevolutionary cuadros costumbristas and museum-oriented showcases, since the photographic images displayed live people undertaking activities in 1999. Labeling the film as a *living* diorama signaled that the bodies were to be read as real bodies, not actors, or model figures, or even "digitally reconstructed," and that the activities were being done not represented. Crucially, what the film did *not* capture was the presence of the hundreds of thousands of tourists on Janitzio filing through the cemetery and witnessing the activities taking place. These bodies were left outside of the frame. Only the women and children of Janitzio were incorporated within the boundary of the frame.

Implementing groundbreaking technological and scientific achievements was central to the efficacy of the exhibition, maintaining an essential ingredient of world's fairs since their foundation, namely, the display of a nation's development and progress. In *Soul of Mexico* such progress, "impossible until now," as the publicity material proclaimed, was the power to ostensibly reach through time to capture and contain life's eternal uncertainty, and to revive bodies and souls. The very juxtaposition of scientific advances to secure and control something so ephemeral, elusive, and ethereal and then relocate and regenerate it at will and on demand demonstrated both the containment of death and mortality, and a level of ownership on a global scale. Yet the ultimate experience enabled through the innovative technology was to be one of intimacy, realness, and Otherness, subtly engaging dichotomous categories (such as body/soul, real/false, living/dead) as hierarchical organizing realities. Engaging the cutting-edge technology that claimed to "plunge visitors into the heart of this celebration of the dead so that they feel 'as if they were there'" enabled ideas of staged authenticity and interactivity to be foregrounded. *Soul of Mexico* created an environment in which to experience authentic tradition, and to connect intimately with the women in the cemetery on Janitzio, even as the exhibition was a simulation of reality. With technological advances, audiences expect to be able to interact and be insiders, with museum exhibits needing to be more "technologically interactive, performative, and 'audience-friendly'" (Gómez Peña 2004:346). Crucially, the makers of *Soul of Mexico*, the artists of the Belgian company de pinxi, were renowned experts in producing interactive experiences that have particularly been utilized in amusement parks and museums. In creating *Soul of Mexico* their expertise in technologically advanced interactive museum displays came to the fore. Significantly, technology has also impacted in the domain of international travel and tourism, where experiences of virtuality have become more prevalent, and media images of otherness are recognized as often being superior to the actual experience (MacCannell 2001:388). *Soul of Mexico* engaged with both these elements, providing an interactive experience and purporting to enable a superior experience of otherness through the virtual digitalized representation. As artists of de pinxi themselves remarked in the concluding statement of the press release for the Mexican exhibition: "We pride ourselves on our ability to translate an idea or scenario into an *out of the ordinary* general public interactive experience" (Hanover 2000: Press Release, italics in original).

Describing the exhibition as an "immersive tunnel" directed people toward reception of this exhibition as a sensorial experience in which they could participate fully. The program provided a clear directive: "Thousands of candles light up the room. Experience how the Mexicans celebrate the 'Day of the Dead' on Janitzio Island in Lake Pátzcuaro" (The EXPO-Guide 2000:192). The implication was that thousands of candles were present in the space—candles that could be smelt and felt; that could be extinguished if blown upon; and that would burn the skin if touched. Yet the candles were only present as a photographic representation. It was not the candles that lit up the room, but the light emitted by the projections of the candles. By extension, as the candles purportedly existed in the space, so too other elements of the ceremony were also present, including the women undertaking their acts of remembrance. Yet there were no beating hearts—no smell, no touch, and no reciprocity. The Janitzio islanders were not living breathing humans but photographic, digitally reproduced virtual realities. Despite all suggestions of "being there," the women remained as distant objects on their island-home thousands of miles away, setting up a powerful signifier of the authentic reality as elsewhere.

In a rather remarkable point of comparison with an exhibition of Mexico in Europe almost 180 years previously, *Soul of Mexico* perpetuated an act of engaging live indigenous peoples in displays purporting to give an experience of "being there." In 1823, Englishman William Bullock traveled to Mexico and collected material for displays that he then utilized to re-create the places he had visited. "Returning from Mexico in 1823 with casts of ancient remains, ethnographic objects, specimens of plants and animals, and a Mexican Indian youth, Bullock designed an exhibition that would make visitors feel like they were in Mexico enjoying a panoramic view of Mexico City (painted on the wall) and intimate contact with its inhabitants" (Kirshenblatt-Gimblett 1998:44). With the life-size bodies of the women in *Soul of Mexico*, visitors could have a sense of being in intimate contact with them, yet unlike the 1823 exhibition, no live Mexican body was present. Instead, the virtual 3D bodies moving in the dark, lit by the flickering glow of the virtual candles, created an impression of phantasmagorical figures, ghosts, and souls, conjuring up images of ancient pasts. Curiously, viewing the images without the special glasses led to a distortion of the body-form so that they appeared to be indistinct, out of focus, fuzzy, without clear boundaries, and therefore ghostly. As with all photographs produced for viewing as 3D images, the photographs only appeared to be real and lifelike when observed through the filtering lenses of the special glasses. Without the glasses, the bodies were almost translucent, creating traces of movement across the screen. As the photographs taken by Carlos González captured and displayed the women of Janitzio in 1923 in their cemetery celebrating *Night of the Dead*, pertinently described by Frances Toor as "a scene of an unreal world" (1928:68–9), so *Soul of Mexico* in 2000 displayed almost identical images of women on Janitzio, generating a notion of virtual travel, of being transported back in time and space, and of a pilgrimage to another place, both mythical and mystical.

As with other representational depictions of P'urhépecha people discussed in this chapter, the women in *Soul of Mexico* indexed notions of the past. The images of bodies that were declared as being so lifelike were connected to death both through the focus of the ceremony (*Night of the Dead*) and the presumed unbroken link to ancient ancestors. These bodies were not only bodies of the present, but they were also constantly referencing bodies of the past. Life/death and presence/absence were held in the same frame, even as the living diorama encapsulated images of death.[8] Utilizing the term "soul" in the title of the exhibition evoked a powerful signifier with a particular set of resonances associated with notions of the past and the death-life continuum. "Soul" coheres with its oft-cited (yet discredited) binary opposite "body," leading to an interpretation of the women in the cemetery on Janitzio as soul not body, as "phantasmagorical figures," and nonbodies. There is an obvious paradox or poetic potency of a *living* diorama representing a soul. In relation to processes of postrevolutionary nationalism, indigenismo, and constructions of indigenousness, the concept of soul frequently figured as a common trope, characterizing indigenous peoples as objects of the past and cultural heritage, useful because they were the "soul of our ancestors" (Pruneda 1951:8). Categorizing the villagers of Janitzio as the soul of Mexico perpetuated the usage and construction from earlier decades.[9]

Soul also formed a binary with notions of modern, generating ideas of a global communion to recover the loss of soul through modern alienation. As world's fairs often invoke and explicitly utilize the concept of a global village, the depiction of an intimate and ancient ritual ceremony on a tiny island was a powerful one, engaging archetypal themes of immortality/mortality, and originary memory; of communing with souls; and of joining together in a collective global communion. *Soul of Mexico* performed the role of a giant, technological 3D memento mori, proving to be an efficacious provocation through which visitors could contemplate their own mortality and existence (Hellier-Tinoco 2010b). *Night of the Dead* as *Soul of Mexico* was useful to invoke notions of imagined communities and distant imagining, and the women in the cemetery on Janitzio were profoundly valuable for embodying Mexico in a global marketplace.

Recycling the Past

In reviewing and discussing particular uses of photographic reproductions of *Night of the Dead* and the *Dance of the Old Men* in the twenty-first century, what is striking is that many of the frameworks and associations used in the 1920s and

1930s to construct a sense of Mexicanness and national belonging and to cater to a burgeoning tourist industry, are still apparent decades later. Mechanical and technological reproduction and photographic imagery have not only maintained and perpetuated the constructions of indigenismo and an ethnographic framework but have also increased the circulation and reach of the iconic images under the spotlight. In the twenty-first century, *the past* remains as potent a notion as it did in the struggle for modernity in the postrevolutionary years, and photographed people/bodies engaged in *Night of the Dead* and the *Dance of the Old Men* continue to be efficacious in embodying Mexico in multiple contexts, repeating their performance of Mexico in regional, national, and worldwide arenas.

CHAPTER 13

Celebrating and Consuming Bodies

Economic and Symbolic Production

IN AN AGE of commoditization of bodies, of mass consumerism, and of technological and mechanical reproduction the performance goes on—Old Men hobble across stages before breaking into virtuosic footwork, and rebozo-shrouded women kneel serenely by gravesides, surrounded by glowing candles and golden flowers. In Morelia and around Lake Pátzcuaro, tourists perform an interpretive role as Juan González, Juan Francisco, Abel Orozco, and many other Jarácuaro residents enact the *Dance of the Old Men* for their gaze. Each November, Janitzio inhabitants receive crowds of visitors onto their island for *Night of the Dead*, presenting their remembrances for the reflection of others. Embodied representations of both practices appear in a whole host of tourist, nationalist, populist, and educational contexts, from postcards to tourist guides, from marketing material to school books, and from newspapers to Web sites. In Mexico and across the border in the United States, schoolchildren and ballet folklórico ensembles dance *The Old Men* for festivals and shows. Inside the ornate Palace of Fine Arts in Mexico City, dancers of the Ballet Folklórico rehearse the complex zapateado for *The Old Men*, ready to thrill the expectant audiences. Yet even as the liveness of the flesh-and-blood bodies marks a moment in the present, signaling a half-remembered past, questions abound as to possible futures. In postmodern contexts of fragmentation and multiplicity, of migrant circuits and identities, and of transnational mass media, a shared sense of imagined community becomes even more sought after. Community identity and a sense of belonging are profoundly important in twenty-first century contexts of dislocation and disjuncture. The call of the masked leader of the EZLN, *subcomandante* Marcos, is for "un México donde quepan todos" (a Mexico where everyone belongs). *The Old Men* and *Night of the Dead* continue to be efficacious iconic referents and embodiments of Mexico, functioning in manifold contexts ranging from the local to the transnational. My contention is that the trajectory of applications, frameworks, and interpretations of *The Old Men*,

Night of the Dead, and the people of Lake Pátzcuaro has been one of continuation. There are a striking number of features of equivalence to those of the postrevolutionary era. Presenting and interpreting *The Old Men* and *Night of the Dead* as displays of tradition, folklore, and indigenous life are as important in contemporary contexts as in the 1920s. The desire to read bodies designated as indigenous through a lens of authenticity is still central, and engaging a dance practice classified as traditional continues to unify and create communities.

In this final chapter, I gather together several of the threads that I have woven through this study while avoiding the urge to tidy up the fabric by tying up the loose ends. As the processes, policies, and activities under scrutiny cannot be placed into neat and tidy packages, I aim to highlight some of the inherent contradictions, dichotomies, and paradoxes rather than to reduce the complexities to simple theoretical equations. In referring to postrevolutionary Mexican state formation processes and projects, cultural historian Derek Sayer has noted that "if this project does confine, it does so in very complicated ways," going on to emphasize the "polysemic, ambiguous, contradictory quality of these putative state forms: even as they oppress, they also empower" (1994:369–79). These principles are highly pertinent not only to the postrevolutionary era but also to the longer time period and the wider range of processes that my study encompasses. As an obvious illustration, the designation of people involved in *The Old Men* and *Night of the Dead* as indigenous and folkloric has been a valuable commodity and resource, and also a cause for prejudicial treatment in local, national, and international arenas. Displays of *The Old Men* enable performers to be valued, even though paid minimally, while also being essentialized within a delimiting system. In the twenty-first century, folklore, tradition, and indigenousness are useful commodities that are part of a web that is both complex and firmly rooted and that serves the big institutions of state and tourism, while often continuing to maintain those people invoked by these designations in social and economic marginalized positions. My intention is to appraise the ninety-year processes and contexts of performism surrounding *The Old Men* and *Night of the Dead*, and to reflect upon some of the consequences of the trajectory, particularly in terms of essentialization, the construct of folklore, symbolic and economic production, and relationships of power. These issues are especially pertinent in light of the recent analysis of eminent scholar García Canclini in his work on the power of popular culture, who has declared that "folk culture is seen as what is representative of Mexico," going on to discuss certain implications of this for Mexicans in a range of spheres (2008). Such an essentialization has implications both for those people directly involved with *The Old Men* and *Night of the Dead*, and for all Mexicans implicated by the designation *folk culture*.

In undertaking this review I am aware that readings transform with time and that changing perspectives alter understandings of a given situation. Something seemingly affirmative in one moment can appear discouraging and deeply problematic in another, and vice versa. A momentous turn-of-the-century episode in Mexican politics encapsulates such complexities and provides a pertinent contextualization for this final chapter as a consideration of the milieu of twenty-first century Mexico. In 2000, deep significance lay in the end of one-party rule of the PRI, the ruling party since the revolution, performed by, and embodied in the newly elected president Vicente Fox of the PAN party. As distinguished Mexican writer and commentator Elena Poniatowska wrote at the time, "No matter what direction Mexico follows during the new administration, one has to underscore the political satisfaction of millions of Mexicans who voted against the official party, the PRI" (Poniatowska 2001:xiv). Yet in the months and years following the election, hope turned to anger and disillusionment, and satisfaction turned to profound resentment and cynicism, as the six-year term of President Fox exhibited even greater corruption and economic disparity than in previous governments.

With these provisos in mind, I turn to discuss certain salient and significant aspects of contemporary contexts, evaluated in terms of the legacy of postrevolutionary policies and strategies, drawing attention to implicit and explicit contexts of power relations, hierarchies, and inequities. Firstly, I begin with a brief overview of noteworthy aspects of postrevolutionary processes associated with the transformation of *The Old Men* and *Night of the Dead*, namely: issues of indigenousness; the concept of folklore, folklórico, and folk; essentialization; and economic and symbolic production. Secondly, I discuss these same elements in late-twentieth- and early twenty-first-century contexts, particularly moving between macro and micro situations, encompassing consequences and implications for Mexicans in global arenas, and for villagers of Janitzio, Jarácuaro, and other Lake Pátzcuaro communities. In addition to indigenismo and essentialization, I address: issues of otherness, difference, and traditionalization; Ballet Folklórico ensembles; and processes of self-designation and legitimization. Thirdly, I evaluate the impact of postrevolutionary strategies in the Lake Pátzcuaro region concerning economic production and exchange value, commoditization, and tourism. In the Epilogue, I conclude with an account of a 2009 performance of *The Old Men* in the United States which has a direct connection to the very first public staging of the *Dance of the Old Men* in Mexico City, as taught by Nicolás Bartolo Juárez of Jarácuaro in the 1920s.

Postrevolutionary Performism

In the wake of the revolutionary civil wars waged between 1910 and 1920, a dance of old men and Night of the Dead of Lake Pátzcuaro were appropriated, promoted, disseminated, commodified, and commoditized by the state within contexts of nationalism and burgeoning tourism. Through processes, and in contexts, of performism, these two activities were shaped as national performances and cultural practices. I have used the term "performism" to refer to the all-encompassing agendas, strategies, practices, and processes that entailed constructing and shaping concepts of peoples, bodies, activities, and places through display and reproduction. Issues of race and ethnicity were at the heart of postrevolutionary agendas of nation-building, and notions of folklore and folk culture, indigenous people, and indigenousness became central components of the rhetoric, policies, and ideologies, enacted through state-controlled delineations of otherness, and the reification of practices, peoples, and places. As in analogous worldwide occurrences, classifying and labeling particular peoples, bodies, and practices as folk, folklore, and folkloric was an ideologically driven strategy.[1] Within the terminology of postrevolutionary rhetoric, folklórico and folklore were significant elements of the official state policy of integrating indigenous and rural populations, and also of the ideological movement of indigenismo. The categorization of music, dance, and ritual practices and also people as folkloric was deemed useful for creating a new national order, for mobilizing the masses, and for integrating the rural peoples, therefore operating paradoxically for both unification and stratification.

I have described how the *Dance of the Old Men*, *Night of the Dead*, and the people of Lake Pátzcuaro came to be labeled as folkloric in the postrevolutionary era, tracing and analyzing processes undertaken by pedagogues, intellectuals, artists, and politicians, notably Carlos González, Francisco Domínguez, Rubén M. Campos, Lázaro Cárdenas, and Frances Toor. Inherent paradoxical elements of the processes and strategies of performism encompassed a concept of public display versus conversion, and of exoticism versus integrationism, which entailed valuing the practice as authentically Mexican, while regarding the people at the heart of the practices as in need of transformation. Indigenista activists and governmental tourist agents sought to maintain and reify practices such as *The Old Men* and *Night of the Dead*, whereas others called for the transformation of Lake Pátzcuaro customs and people. In shaping *The Old Men* and *Night of the Dead* as national icons and cultural practices, a particular set of meanings was molded through processes of essentialization and signification, meanings that were most prominently associated with the terms indigenous and folkloric. These interpretations centered on notions of authentic, in the past, traditional, backward, and premodern.

Throughout this study I have primarily focused on the cultural, ideological, and political aspects of the performism processes surrounding the public uses of *The Old Men* and *Night of the Dead*. I have mentioned economic factors in passing, but not overtly. However, economic issues were obviously embedded in the rhetoric, strategies, and policies of the postrevolutionary era. As García Canclini has observed, separating areas of culture and economics is a form of false divide, for "in reality, economy and culture march along intertwined with one another.... any cultural fact... always leads to an implicit socioeconomic level... [and] any practice is simultaneously economic and symbolic" (1993:11). Central features of nationalism and tourism involved capitalist development, modernization, and economic improvement. National interest concerned both the integration of indigenous people (regarded as the problem) for overall economic improvement, together with the utilization of indigenous practices as national symbols of unity for the greater good of the country leading to financial progress. *The Old Men* and *Night of the Dead* as *cultural* practices were modified, resignified, and deployed as commodities, with meanings and functions that were shaped and reorganized into a unified system of symbolic production and expression with an exchange value in a larger system (García Canclini 1993:viii and MacCannell 1992:168).[2] As features of the symbolic production of the country, both practices were intrinsically implicated in an economic framework. However, entrenched in postrevolutionary appropriation for nation-building was the paradoxical situation of the incorporation and modernization (for the benefit of the nation), and the simultaneous reification and valorization (as the authentic soul of Mexico) of the very people who the incorporation was intended to bring out of poverty. On a local level, the objective of postrevolutionary policies and strategies was the economic betterment of the inhabitants of the Lake Pátzcuaro region.

The state actions for incorporating *The Old Men*, *Night of the Dead*, and the peoples of Lake Pátzcuaro into a national framework should be understood within a dichotomous and complex context of constraint and enablement. The policies and activities which appear as utopian, dogmatic, and even authoritarian have many times been critiqued as technologies of power (Knight 1994b:415–16). The postrevolutionary socialist rhetoric gave the impression of munificence and benevolence on the part of those enabling the incorporation, often presented through the notion of the protective guise of *paternidad* (paternalism), in which the state acted as caring father to the vulnerable children of the nation. However, these processes involved the imposition of ideas, categories, and policies from outside, and were intrinsically connected with managing othered collections of people, encompassing an inherent hierarchical context. In the following discussions, I turn to consider these issues in the postrevolutionary era, and in contemporary contexts. In reflecting on the consequences and ramifications of the actions, policies, and strategies of the postrevolutionary era, it is clear that the impacts are equally dichotomous and complex.

Indigenousness, Essentialization, Folk Culture

Although each case study and illustration in this study could be analyzed for the symbolic, economic, and power structures encompassed within it, as this is a diachronic inquiry covering a ninety-year period I am focusing on exemplary and salient instances. Presently I turn to economic issues concerning the peoples of Lake Pátzcuaro, but before that I step forward to the late-twentieth and early twenty-first centuries, moving between discussions of the specifics of *The Old Men* and *Night of the Dead*, and broad national issues and repercussions. In terms of a general theme, designating and dealing with peoples and practices as indigenous and folkloric was perpetuated through the twentieth century and continues into the twenty-first century. Discourses, policies, and practices surrounding the concept of indigenous peoples and practices and their role in the nation have remained at the core of Mexican politics, and an ideology of indigenismo is still current. Ideas about indigenousness persist as permanent elements of touristic and nationalistic contexts as policies of integration and participation continue to be blurred, and the complex context of exoticism versus integrationism is ever present.

In recent decades the indigenista policy of the past has been critiqued by anthropologists and government officials, with the language changing from one of integration to one of participation. As I noted in chapter 8 the National Indigenist

Institute (INI) was disbanded in 2003, and the National Commission for the Development of Indigenous Peoples (CDI) was created to deal with issues of the pluricultural and multiethnic character of the nation, placing agency, self-determination, and self-assertion on the agenda. With calls for cultural pluralism (Schmidt 2001:51), the challenge for Mexico has been "to establish an historical project that integrates the wishes and yearnings of a plural nation instead of an exclusive and homogeneous State" (Florescano 1999: 66, see also de la Peña 2005). Such a challenge would turn the focus toward indigenous communities in terms of their own diversity for its own sake, not as the servant of some politician, institution, or powerful individual.[3] Yet even within a context of plurality, tensions are created by enacting dividing practices which sets one group of people apart from another, perpetuating situations of otherness, while also acknowledging and exhibiting a plural nation. Such enactments, often performed through folkloric and touristic events, maintain the hierarchical status created through indigenismo and folkloric practices. The use of phrases and sentiments of "our folklore" and "our indigenous" are still in play. There are voices calling for "indigenous culture" to be a basis of national identity, invoking notions of a national cultural heritage: "Now is the time to adopt indigenous culture (*la cultura indígena*), the living *indios*, as a fundamental motor of our identity" (del Val 1995:53). Yet in this dichotomous context, the view that indigenous peoples are a problem is perpetuated and verbalized through expressions such as "No seas indio" ("Don't be like an indigenous person"). Peoples categorized as indigenous are admired for being the real soul of Mexico, "living proof of Mexico's noble pre-Hispanic heritage" (Friedlander 1975: xvii), and simultaneously discriminated against and devalued for being indigenous, guilty of the backward state and failure of the country and the enemies of progress (Garza 2000).

Relating this to *The Old Men* and *Night of the Dead*, the frameworks for interpretations and representations of live events are still comparable to those of the postrevolutionary decades, with consequences particularly relating to indigenousness, indigenous politics, folklore, and essentialization. The complex context of exoticism versus integrationism is ever present, and the paradox of reifying practices such as *The Old Men* and *Night of the Dead* as patrimony of the nation, for political and touristic agendas, whilst regarding the people at the heart of the practices as in need of transformation, remains in place. Concerning incorporation and participation, the peoples of Lake Pátzcuaro continue to be symbolically incorporated into the nation through uses of *Night of the Dead* and *The Old Men*, yet such displays also present rather ambiguous "spectacles of participation" (Gómez-Peña 2004:347), in which an impression of being valued is staged, yet without any significant decision-making process that may effect social change. The inherent paradox of displaying these practices does not get any clearer with the passing of time, as the inequalities become more palpable and the economic gap widens.

The Old Men and *Night of the Dead* continue to be designated as indigenous and folkloric, and are still reified as patrimony of the nation. Musicians and dancers from Jarácuaro are fundamentally part of the Michoacán state tourism project, regarded as objects of cultural heritage, and possessed by the people as "our folklore." An indigenous past and present is still explicit in the Mexican Tourist Board's promotional material, directly incorporating and implicating *The Old Men* and peoples of Lake Pátzcuaro. The act of deploying *The Old Men* and *Night of the Dead* as valuable narratives of the nation's past continues to perform a hierarchical exercise. Framed as indigenous practices, both are thoroughly incorporated as icons of national memory and ownership. In 2003, for *Night of the Dead* this was extended to a worldwide context, as UNESCO named "the Indigenous Festivity Dedicated to the Dead" in Mexico as a Masterpiece of the Oral and Intangible Heritage of Humanity. As Janitzio is one of the principal sites encompassed by this designation, the practice was incorporated into an ever-wider sphere of custody and international memory.[4]

Essentialization remains an absolutely indispensable element of the promotional and signifying processes surrounding both *Night of the Dead* and *The Old Men*. In the Mexican Tourist Board campaign of 2006, Mexico was essentialized through an extremely limited set of characteristics in which *The Old Men* signified authentic, folkloric, exotic, traditional, premodern, colorful, and indigenous Mexico. As essentialization is accomplished in part through the invocation of a series of binaries, certain attributes of both practices and peoples become fixed. Binaries of past-present, authentic-inauthentic, traditional-modern, preindustrial-industrial, rural-urban, and different-normal invoked through *The Old Men* and *Night of the Dead* create a hierarchical vocabulary that produces commodities out of attributes. *Night of the Dead*, *The Old Men*, and Lake Pátzcuaro with its island villages and basic fishing methods still provide and indeed rely on an experience of otherness, representing an extraordinary and different other, separated off from modern and postmodern life. Designations such as authentic and different are valuable exchange attributes in a tourist setting, yet cause prejudice and discrimination in another. In the twenty-first century, the image of the traditional rural idyll shows no signs of losing its attraction, and indeed, in the face of globalization and transnationalism, romanticized rurality is promoted even more vigorously, underlining the potency of ongoing processes of traditionalization. Through active and continuous processes of selection and re-selection, ideological constructions in the form of embodied icons and images are perpetuated, maintaining hierarchies, perceptions, and prejudices that these essentializations produce. For every moment of display, even at the latest point in time, a specific choice has been made. Selecting the figure of the Old Man dancer to represent Mexico for the European promotional campaign was the result of specific decision-making processes. In a global context, continuing to foreground Mexico through images of *The Old Men* maintains a tension between tradition and modernity.

One of the consequences of the classificatory and essentialization processes has been the effect of establishing and perpetuating a pan-indigenous category, with implications of unified form, features, and stylistic attributes, which have reduced complexity and diversity to a restricted set of features. For example, the high-profile tourist company Lonely Planet has characterized Day of the Dead in Mexico as "a hoot" ("A country so lively that even the Day of the Dead is a hoot"), yet presents indigenous peoples in essentialist terms through associations with religious and spiritual practices: "In indigenous communities, most notably the Purépecha of Michoacán, Día de Muertos is still very much a religious and spiritual event" (www.lonelyplanet.com and Noble 2006:84). On a local scale, complexity has been reduced to just a few practices. Despite the great diversity of music, dance, and ritual practices in the Lake Pátzcuaro region, only a small collection became known outside the P'urhépecha region. The iconicity of a couple of practices leads to the assumption that this is all that happens, simultaneously creating a context of exoticism, exhibition, and cultural artifact. Entrenched in the possessive, cultural heritage notion is an epistemological framing in which the restricted set of dances, music, and ritual practices are regarded as representative of a whole way of life, and that by knowing and viewing these practices, onlookers have knowledge of the real lives of these people as exotic others. At the end of the nineteenth century, U.S. anthropologist Frederick Starr wrote of his admiration for the exotic peoples of Lake Pátzcuaro (Scharrer Tomm 1995:13), and in the burgeoning tourist environment of Lake Pátzcuaro in the 1930s, tourists were eager to "know the habits and customs and folklore" (En Pro 1938). These ideas resonate with notions concerning Mexicans in "backwards cultural stages" as set out by Manuel Gamio (1925:6–7). A significant aspect of contemporary Mexican essentializing processes is the continued usage of the terms "folklore," "folkloric," and "folk" as ideologically inscribed concepts that cannot escape the particularities of both Mexican and global connotations. Scholars have been complicit in perpetuating these frameworks, utilizing the terms "folklore" and "folk" in pedagogical and scholarly literature. Two exemplars relating to the macro context of Mexico serve to illustrate the point: Bruno Nettl described "Mexican folk song" as a "definable category" (1985:4–5), and Gerard Béhague began a brief analysis with the comment that "the most typical performance characteristics of Mexican folk music comprise..." (1973:202), going on to list the characteristics.[5] Given the paucity of English-language scholarly publication relating to Mexican musics, such references by these well-known scholars carry great weight.

Characterizing Mexico through an embodied notion of folk has profound ramifications in an international context. Bias and constraints of essentializing processes have an impact from local spheres of influence to the global, for all national images and ideologies operate within a global web of power. As I mentioned above, García Canclini, in his recent work on the power of popular culture, has observed that "Folk culture is seen as what is representative of Mexico" (2008). Such a perception has far-reaching consequences not only for the status of Mexico in global political, ideological, and artistic terms but also for individuals and groups who are constrained by such essentializing practices. At a recent event in the Museum of Anthropology and History in Mexico City that included a performance of the *Dance of the Old Men* and P'urhépecha music, P'urhépecha musician Eliseo Martínez proclaimed "Our music isn't folklore," expressing a frustration at the constructions and frameworks within which they work and live, and raising questions regarding how they can resist and struggle against the constraining agenda, and carve out spaces for their own cultural creativity.

García Canclini's own analysis relates to issues of essentializing countries by the value placed upon art, noting that "while Mexicans and Latin Americans in general come to the United States as the citadel of the most developed artistic and scientific positions, many United States citizens and institutions tend to admire Mexico's past but refuse to consider Mexico's art production as holding its own in the world today" (ibid.). This stands in contrast to the situation in the 1930s when Mexico was seen as a nation of culture instead of being a backward country full of bandits (Delpar 1992:146). Although in the twenty-first century Mexico is still regarded as a nation of culture, that culture is often placed in the category of *folk*, perpetuated through processes of traditionalization primarily undertaken by tourist boards and official governmental cultural departments, and also selectively capitalized upon by those invoked by the term, such as the residents of Janitizio. Pertinent questions arise around the issue of how to subvert the traditional-modern dichotomy (Lomnitz 2001:132) and "how to change this relegation of Mexico to the past and bring to the fore recent cultural creativity and research [for this] is a vital issue for overcoming prejudice and encouraging different national communities to gain deeper knowledge of one another" (García Canclini 2008). As evidenced by the *Expo 2000* exhibition and the European advertising poster, international representational activities imaging *The Old Men* and *Night of the Dead* contribute to the perception of Mexico and Mexicans as folkloric and of the past.

Ballet Folklórico: Team Mexico

Ballet folklórico ensembles are an obvious illustration of a representational dance form that engages the term *folklórico* in the title; that involves essentialization; and that also incorporates and embodies *The Old Men*. The professional Ballet Folklórico de México and the multiple folklórico dance ensembles that exist throughout Mexico and in the United States all comprise certain elements that perpetuate dichotomous significations. It is notable that in recent decades these ensembles have proliferated, performing locally, regionally, nationally, and internationally at festivals, concerts, and competitions. In many ways these companies fulfill the nationalist performism and folkloricization expectations of the postrevolutionary era, uniting and binding popular masses around a set of symbolic (dance) practices which could be identified as Mexican, enabling people to identify with the concept of lo mexicano, inculcating pride in the country and solidarity with the government and place. In this discourse of cultural belonging, folklórico dance ensembles participate in national and international festivals, traveling as *team Mexico*, a unified body, wearing a sports-style uniform emblazoned with the name of the ensemble and the Mexican flag.

The Ballet Folklórico de México continues to act as a state-approved dance statement of Mexico, reinforcing images and perceptions of indigenousness and utilizing them in their own representation of Mexico.[6] The company still makes an impact in the United States, performing at numerous venues, including on Broadway, where "after 50 years, South of the Border Company is still at the Top of its Tradition" (www.alegria.org). Significantly, sponsorship for the tours in the United States comes from a combination of governmental tourist and cultural departments (the Mexican Tourist Board, the Mexican National Institute for Fine Arts, and the National Advisory Body for Culture), and also from the national airline company, AeroMéxico. Over the course of its existence, the Ballet Folklórico de México has performed the role of tourist attraction for international visitors, and catalyst and role model for numerous similar ensembles and companies created by Mexican-Americans and Chicana/os in the United States. As *The Old Men* forms one of the core pieces in the repertoire of these folklórico ensembles in the United States, performances of this dance across the border in el norte act as powerful contemporary signifiers, shaping, representing, and embodying ideas of identity, and creating community cohesion.

Yet essentialization in the ballet folklórico ensembles remains a problematic issue, particularly in relation to a few companies in the United States. A recent case, exemplified by the Compañia Mazatlán Bellas Artes de Sacramento, California, United States (a company directly influenced by the original Ballet Folklórico repertoire of Amalia Hernández), encapsulates the principal areas. By self-designation they are "one of California's principal Mexican folk dance companies" (Curriculum Guide for Educators 2009), undertaking live performances and also taking an overtly didactic role by delivering lecture-demonstrations. In presenting their work, a range of issues are prominent, all of which draw directly on postrevolutionary constructions, relating specifically to dance aesthetics, essentialization, ethnicity, pedagogy, and definitions of *folk*. According to their own literature, their performances "illustrate the rich cultural heritage of native Mexico.... The show will be similar to that of a visual fairytale with vivid characters in lavishly colorful costumes flowing from one folk dance to the next in a single choreographic symphony.... While paying tribute to their remote homeland, this is no mere presentation of peasant dance as it infuses village ritual with modern technique" (ibid.). One of the proposed discussion questions asks: "What did you learn about the Mexican culture from watching and listening to the performance?" (ibid.). In these performances, "native Mexico" is on show in the twenty-first century in the United States, represented through dance. Yet the company is at pains to distinguish between modern technique and village ritual dance, locating their own work at a great distance from villages in Mexico, in other words, villages such as those of the Lake Pátzcuaro region, including Jarácuaro and Janitzio, and thus distinguishing themselves from the residents (or "peasants") of such faraway places south of the border. An essentialized Mexico is encompassed by the notion of "the Mexican culture" presented in the singular, as evident from the simple discussion question. As didactic shows, with associated discussion points, an ethnographic focus and gaze is shaped that merges Disney-style *Three Caballeros* make-believe with authentic embodied artifacts in the form of dance practices.

Affirmation, Self-Determination, Exchange Value, and Production

The issue of essentialization is complex. Even as it can be problematic by constraining and causing prejudice, it can also legitimize, authenticate, and give value to those invoked by the practices and to those performing. By using the term "performing" I specifically allude not only to the dancers, musicians, and those being viewed/listened to, but also to the spectators, costume-makers, organizers, and supporters. Correspondingly, this context encompasses not only the P'urhépecha peoples of Lake Pátzcuaro, but also Chicana/os and Mexican-Americans in the United States as they strive to carve out and negotiate their own place and identities in multifaceted environments. Paradoxically, essentialization can be useful for self-representation, to establish rights, and to express difference even as it effaces difference. When the National Commission for the Development of Indigenous Peoples (CDI) was created, issues of the pluricultural and multi-ethnic character of the nation, of agency, self-determination, and self-assertion were part of the agenda. One central matter was the need for equitable systems of representation and participation, enabling groups to self-designate. Essentialization and a universalizing discourse can be useful in cases where music and dance groups self-designate, as exemplified by ensembles such as "Los Purépechas de Jarácuaro," the group directed by Juan Francisco (figure 1.7). Naming a group in this way provides these musicians and dancers with a form of value and identity that allows them to reassert themselves. Within the context of nationhood and tourism, carving out and shaping a space for themselves, and being easily identifiable for marketing and audience purposes, enables them to have a presence in an otherwise anonymizing context. Utilizing the term "P'urhépecha" in the multifarious location of Mexico City, where so much diversity abounds, provides a form of self-identity that is both commercial and ideological. In these contexts the musicians and dancers struggle with the dichotomy that the situation presents, using the concept of authenticity to legitimate themselves. When the Gabriel family of Urandén enacts *The Old Men* in Mexico City, they are often performing in folkloric contexts, where their employment and display is legitimized by their presence in Mexico City as authentic P'urhépecha villagers (and their profession as mariachi musicians becomes unimportant).

In a similar way, issues of legitimization are particularly conspicuous in relation to Lake Pátzcuaro festivals, competitions, and recordings, serving as contexts for creativity and as endorsement for practices, musicians, and dancers. Tourist contexts can act as a form of cultural affirmation, and the many contests and festivals function to celebrate, value, and perpetuate certain aspects of music, dance, and craftwork of the region, albeit a very limited range of what exists. Even as the essentialization of practices leads visitors to believe that they are viewing and accessing the real lives of the Lake Pátzcuaro residents, and tourists willingly follow their expectations that they are experiencing an intimate part of the lives of the Janitzio residents, many practices and celebrations remain private. Whereas *Night of the Dead* attracts huge numbers of tourists, other local fiestas are not attended by visitors, maintaining multiple elements of local residents' lives as not "on show" to visitors. Paradoxically, essentialization enables Janitzio residents to live on their island through the income generated from tourism, even as they maintain much of their lives away from the gaze of tourists.

In these complex situations much is at stake, with recognition and the winning of prizes and diplomas being discussed by musicians, dancers and their families many decades after an event. Families from Jarácuaro and Cucuchucho still talk about contests involving the *Dance of the Old Men* from the 1930s. Rivalry, competition, and creativity have formed intrinsic elements of Lake Pátzcuaro fiestas for decades, being particularly prevalent in the form of the serenata, an event in which financially sponsored musical ensembles competed for prestige. In the 1920s the Bartolo Juárez family gained their reputation through triumphing in local serenatas, therefore earning not only respect for their musical production but also monetary rewards. In recent decades festivals have provided a forum for new works to be performed, while opportunities for producing recordings have enabled music to be heard around the region in ways that were previously impossible. Roads between the lake region and the sierra have been notoriously difficult to pass and therefore recordings have served as transportable modes of transmission, coupled with the possibility for broadcast through local radio stations (see Chamorro 1992a, b and 1994).[7] Yet such contexts and products have been perceived as inappropriate forms of commoditization and commodification. U.S. ethnomusicologist Thomas Turino observed that "a number of local.... Purepecha performers of what were previously non-professional, non-staged traditions in Mexico recently drew my attention to their own adequacy as 'informants' by the fact that they had L.P.s as well as diplomas and prizes from staged contests and concerts. The potency of musical-product orientation, a reification that I am suggesting here accompanies the incorporation of formerly differentiated peoples into the mindset of the Western nations, is becoming increasingly prominent" (Turino 1990: 409). However, I offer that Turino is engaging his own mind-set in relation to notions of "professional" and "musical-product" in order to assess the activities and values of the P'urhépecha musicians and their actions with regard to difference and incorporation. There is an indication that an audio recording transforms the music-act and the musician from one state (nonprofessional) into another, with the other state (or mind-set) being the domain of "Western nations." Yet audio recordings and prizes are manifestations of complex contexts in which there are no clear designations of professional and nonprofessional, but where judgments of value are enacted through the exchange of money, food and drink, a diploma, or the offer of a future contract for a fiesta. The overriding issue, therefore, is not that the product per se has altered by being made into an L.P. or placed on a stage, or that the musician has been incorporated into another mind-set, but rather centers on who the receiver, listener, spectator, and legitimator is, and therefore, what relationship of power and exchange value is being performed. The P'urhépecha musicians with audio recordings, diplomas, and prizes had always played their music with an audience in place, commonly either a whole village during a fiesta, representatives of various villages for serenatas or *competéncias* (competitions), or a few friends at the weekend. Competition and rivalry were an inherent element of many local musical events, the demise and then revival of which was documented by Mexican ethnomusicologist Arturo Chamorro (1994). For many staged contests, audiences continued to be comprised either wholly or principally of P'urhépecha people. Similarly, audio recordings (particularly those produced in the Alborado Records studios) circulated in the P'urhépecha region and were broadcast on the local P'urhépecha radio station. However, as I have documented throughout this study, certain activities and practices were transformed through the presence of non-P'urhépecha spectators and audiences (predominantly comprising tourists, intellectuals, folklorists, ethnomusicologists, artists, teachers, and politicians).[8] One issue, then, concerns processes of decision-making. In relation to audio recordings, two crucial aspects concern how far the musicians have chosen to be part of any context of representation, and that if they make recordings and expect payment, that they are afforded equal treatment within the marketplace, if that is what they desire. Many musicians from Lake Pátzcuaro islands and villages have made recordings of music of *The Old Men* and other self-created compositions, but many have not been able to enter the marketplace despite multiple endeavors.

Paradoxical Lake Pátzcuaro

Continuing the focus on monetary matters, some of the most intricate aspects relating to uses of *The Old Men* and *Night of the Dead* concern issues of economic production and exchange value. Engaging with systems of exchange has been an ongoing and absolutely central element in the lives of people of Lake Pátzcuaro for centuries, however, from the initial stages of postrevolutionary nationalist appropriation, the Lake Pátzcuaro area was regarded as potentially useful for touristic development, and the economic factor became inherently part of the local context and more overtly part of the national context in terms of generating revenue. Numerous schemes were planned and organized by a series of institutions, whose central objective was to "bring out of their backwardness" the residents of the lake region. Many state-funded, public researchers and pedagogues who worked in the region from the early 1920s onward were seen to be dedicating their lives to improving conditions of the indigenous communities (Presentación 1990:9–10). Throughout the postrevolutionary period, and particularly under the leadership of Lázaro Cárdenas, the belief that development would bring economic benefits to the region through behavioral modernization and changing the systems of commercialization was prevalent. On Jarácuaro, Cárdenas attempted to improve conditions through the introduction of electric machines and hat presses, endeavoring to transform the conditions of production of hat-making (the principal economic activity) from a cottage industry to a more systematic and mechanized process. On Janitzio, Cárdenas's initiative entailed transformation of the location, through the construction of the statue of Morelos in the center of the island. This visual attraction, along with promoting the *Night of the Dead* ceremony for visitors, was a deliberate strategy to encourage touristic development.

Over the decades transformations in the Lake Pátzcuaro region did take place, most of which were a direct result of promotional imaging of Janitzio and *Night of the Dead*, leading to an influx of finance through visitors. Comparisons between Janitzio and Jarácuaro provide an interesting contrast, in terms of government initiatives and development, for while both communities remain in conditions of relative economic poverty there are very clear differences, particularly encompassing those families directly involved with representational activities of *Night of the Dead* and *The Old Men*. In general terms, Jarácuaro did not develop a more systematic and mechanized approach to hat-making, although this remains the primary economic activity. Despite the prominent uses of *The Old Men*, opportunities for financial remuneration through performances of the dance have been fairly minimal, with no musicians and dancers earning much more than expense-money. Migration away from Jarácuaro, to cities and agricultural regions in Mexico and across the border to the United States, therefore became a normal practice. In contrast, on Janitzio tourism *did* develop, initially as a direct result of government strategies, and then through local initiatives. The income generated through the tourist industry has enabled the resident population to remain and to live a relatively secure lifestyle, despite the dwindling fish-stocks.

Whereas tourism is pervasive in the area, particularly in the town of Pátzcuaro and the island of Janitzio, the Lake Pátzcuaro region has not been converted into an all-encompassing attraction and has not been taken over by tourist industry agencies and infrastructure. Even in the last twenty years there have been few dramatic changes to the area, and although for the week of *Night of the Dead* there is an impact upon the local population, this is not comparable to the extreme transformations that have occurred in other areas of tourist development in Mexico. In the Yúcatan peninsula, for example, the massive infrastructure required for mass tourism has completely altered the location and ways of life, yet in the Lake Pátzcuaro region, although the dockside area and streets in Pátzcuaro have been modified to accommodate larger numbers of people and cars, little else has altered.[9] Certain peak holiday periods draw crowds of tourists to the area, but the week of festivities for *Night of the Dead* is the only big event. Following the post-revolutionary years, the local inhabitants were able to control the context to a considerable extent, and were therefore agents of their own futures. Residents of Janitzio have engaged with the business of tourism in a variety of ways, including developing and running two enterprises providing motor launch services to transport visitors to Janitzio; setting up restaurants and souvenir stalls; and performing fishing. Of the other islands, only Yunuén and Pacanda have engaged with the tourist industry in a year-long, sustainable, and business-led enterprise.

Two significant changes resulting from tourism concern integration into a capitalist system and the accompanying interaction and behavior of Janitzio residents with the visitors. As members of a fishing community, Janitzio inhabitants, particularly the women, had always undertaken commercial transactions as a normal element of everyday life, traveling to Pátzcuaro and sometimes further a field to Morelia to sell their catch. However, dealing with tourists on their home territory was quite another matter. As I previously noted, in the 1920s Francis Toor, after her visit to the island for *Night of the Dead*, observed that "at no time do these fishermen welcome visitors, and less for this special occasion" (1928:68). Yet within just a few years these same people were dealing with, and indeed welcoming, large numbers of visitors to their home community. These residents developed an understanding of what is required of them in order to attract tourists, and have maintained elements of their lifestyle for the visitors, as the lure of authenticity, remoteness, and difference remains a highly potent attraction.[10] The islanders know how to take advantage of the performance of authenticity through displays of fishing and tortilla-making, and have retained images of tradition (sometimes interpreted as backwardness) in order to maintain the flow of visitors. As a result of increased income from tourism, the most noticeable alterations have been to buildings and infrastructure, as islanders have modified their houses from the *quaint and traditional* adobe-walled, single-story style with red-tiled roofs to breeze block constructions, often with a second story and windows, a kitchen with a gas cooker and sanitation. Paradoxically, the changes to the architecture and structures of the houses have actually made them less unique and more homogeneous with many houses throughout Mexico, therefore postcard and guidebook images still depict the Janitzio of former years.

On Jarácuaro the situation has been rather different. Although many similar alterations have been undertaken on the houses, generally the changes were facilitated with money earned either in the United States or in agricultural areas of northern Mexico, as the lack of a sustainable lifestyle, and the expectation of a better life through material wealth caused migration away from Jarácuaro. In the past Jarácuaro islanders fished both as a means of subsistence and for economic return. As fish-stocks decreased, while residents of Janitzio turned to performing fishing as means of remaining on their island through tourist income, those on Jarácuaro have had to seek other means. For the dancers and musicians of *The Old Men*, opportunities for economic return through tourism and through local contracts have been minimal. All the principal families involved in *The Old Men* for the last few decades have either seen family members migrate or they themselves have traveled across the border in search of an income. Some families and individuals, such as the López family and Domínguez, have migrated and then returned to Jarácuaro after encountering an environment far less rewarding than anticipated.[11]

Exchange Value and Consuming Bodies

In each situation of display and performance, issues concerning exchange value, commoditization, and the perception of value come into play. Aspects of financial remuneration and payment for products (embodied enactments and objects) are often obfuscated, particularly when interrelated with those of cultural patrimony and national heritage. Recognition and acceptance of the intrinsic economic factor is often resisted by commentators and tourists alike as they choose to consider commoditization and professionalization both as an affront to access to national cultural heritage and also as an objectionable aspect of the premodern construct.

Expectations that the musicians and dancers will perform for small amounts of money and for the honor of performing because their rituals and traditions are part of the patrimony of the nation still prevail. In regarding commoditization as inherently part of an economic system, a level of bias enters the situation. One notable critic of processes of commoditization, García Canclini, has examined aspects of tourism in Mexico particularly from an economic perspective, discussing factors that include the incorporation of indigenous peoples into a capitalist market; low incomes in the countryside; private and state promotion of craft products; and the transformation of objects and practices from a ceremonial to mercantile use (1993). It is significant that his ideas were shaped in part by his experiences in the Lake Pátzcuaro region in the 1980s. In an earlier publication he describes associated notable events and incidents, including the transformation of masks of *The Old Men* into marketable products for sale to tourists. In his discussion of souvenirs, objects, and costume he commented on the "transformation of the object as used in the performance into a marketable and collectable item [with] reproduction of the object as solely a souvenir" (1985:21).[12] García Canclini seems to have been struck by the way in which performers from Jarácuaro (López, Francisco, and González) returned to the mask-maker for more masks because the dancers and musicians had sold their masks to visitors who wished to have ornaments to decorate their apartments (1993:vii). Even though masks for *The Old Men* were not usually part of a ritual event, García Canclini expresses unease at the production of such objects solely for their exchange value in monetary terms and the transformation of a purportedly ritual object into a decorative and souvenir object.

Relating these issues to dance and music practices, there is a concern that traditional practices should not be paid for and should not be part of an economic system. Again, García Canclini revealed anxiety over corruption of a traditional system, which he construed through the action of dancers of Cucuchucho no longer dancing for goodwill, but rather being paid for dancing. Receiving financial remuneration for a traditional performance was giving in to capitalist modernization (1985:37). This proposition that payment and monetary value represent a form of alteration from a traditional system resonates with the context that Turino encountered (mentioned above) concerning P'urhépecha musicians and their recordings and diplomas. While trade and exchange value per se have been regarded as problematic, the wider issues concern aspects of control and relationships of power, as I noted above. A pertinent question, and one frequently dealt with by Lake Pátzcuaro villagers performing *The Old Men* and by tourist-industry agents involved with *Night of the Dead*, is "what are the consequences of the exchange?" Commercialization is often characterized as inherently "bad," coupled with the notion that money corrupts. Yet commercial transactions and some sort of payment (monetary or in-kind) have always been part of local and regional systems, and villagers from Lake Pátzcuaro have constantly produced and provided products for trade. In terms of musical products, in the 1920s, Rafael Juárez played flute with his family's ensemble as a child and he was contracted and paid as a musician for participating in fiestas (figure 4.1).

García Canclini's disquiet relates to issues of imbalances of power, exploitation, representation, and a wider political and ideological impact. Associated with this is the language of consumerism and the matter of who has the power to consume and represent another culture, with these technologies of power often being regarded as a form of domination (Clifford and Marcus 1986, Foucault 1982, Said 2002). García Canclini problematizes the purchase of indigenous dances and ritual as trophies of travel, and thus as overt indications of domination and superiority of one society over another through their purchasing power (1993:vii). A central issue also concerns the question "what is being paid for?" There is an exchange of something for money, whether this is an object, a performance, a place, a body, or a notion of difference and exoticism. As exoticism and difference are basic commodities of tourism, so these are fundamental to the Lake Pátzcuaro tourist environment and to many contexts where *The Old Men* is performed. When the central feature of difference is a body, or collection of bodies, issues of objectification prevail. Bodies have different values in different contexts. Commodity-value is assigned to a particular body when it is promoted and framed as an authentic indigenous body. This is clearly an intrinsic element in situations of ethnic-tourism and indigenismo— although payment repeatedly goes to those organizing the display, rather than the person whose body is the attraction. *Mexico* is marketed to potential visitors through reproductions of bodies, including the Old Man dancer and Janitzio women enacting *Night of the Dead*. In live events of *Night of the Dead* and *The Old Men*, the live bodies are the central focus, with attendant heightened signification through the notion of difference. Yet, problematically, while the notion of consuming these bodies is present through processes of a touristic, voyeuristic, and ethnographic gaze, as a result of the perception of the people and activities as traditional and as cultural heritage there is a concurrent reluctance to pay in exchange for the right to look—or indeed, the right to capture the person/body in photographic form. Through visual consumption tourists believe that they have come to know something that they didn't before (Desmond 1999:xiii), yet the money exchanged to see bodies that are different from their own is often not paid directly to those whose bodies are the center of attention. However, these same bodies captured as photographic images on postcards, emblazoned on T-shirts, replicated as wooden figures, and painted on mugs as souvenir-objects have a monetary value for the producer and vendor. The matter of who has the right to capture the bodies in photographic form and display them to the world, in exchange for some sort of payment, raises complex questions of ownership, dominance, and commercialization. The performers of *The Old Men* were rarely paid for photographic images and women and men on Janitzio were never paid.[13]

Four illustrations involving musicians and dancers from Lake Pátzcuaro make clear some of the complexities concerning payment for performances: (1) Rafael Juárez recalled that in the 1920s and 1930s state-employed folklorists, artists, and pedagogues visited Jarácuaro where they recorded (in written form) the music that the Bartolo Juárez ensemble was studying and asked for the names of the pieces, yet in return they only gave a tip and nothing more. (2) On a

Saturday afternoon in 1996 in the Peña Colibrí, Morelia, the leader of a party of middle-class Mexican tourists from the city of Guadalajara, some 150 miles away, wrangled with Juan González, director of one ensemble of *The Old Men* from Jarácuaro. The tourist guide insisted that her group of tourists had a right to see *The Old Men* because it was part of their heritage and not a commodity to be haggled over, stating that it was unreasonable to pay the fee that González was asking (which was low by all standards). Her argument was that the tourists really *had* to see *The Old Men* to make their visit to the state of Michoacán complete. The only options left open to González were a resolution that involved complying with the tour leader and lowering the fee or not performing *The Old Men* and therefore receiving no additional income. (3) In 1999, during the Festival of Music and Dance for *Night of the Dead* on the Island of Yunuén, the Mexican television corporation Televisa recorded the music and dance performance of the ensemble of the Alejo Reynoso family of Pacanda. No money was offered in return and no permission was sought for use of the footage (38 ◐). (4) For over fifty years Gervasio López, principal exponent of *The Old Men*, participated in countless official representations as an icon of Mexico, Michoacán, and P'urhépecha/indigenous peoples, in national and international contexts, often with little or no payment. Up until the end of his life he was still performing for a few hours each Sunday in a restaurant in order to continue earning enough money to make ends meet (17 ◐). In the mid-1990s, he turned down an invitation to perform in London because he perceived that he was being exploited. According to his sons, López died in poverty, with a sense of having been taken advantage of, and even exploited financially, despite being given high status and utilized to the full by government agencies.

Utilitarian Response: Economic Investment

López's career and life-long dedication to music and dance highlight the issue of professionalization and exchange value in as much as the attitude to the professionalization of music-making and dancing in certain contexts is regarded as problematic because it detracts from the idea of authenticity, coupled with a perception that it is incongruous with the indigenous construct. The right to charge and benefit economically from performances is still considered to be an affront. This state of affairs is particularly dichotomous given certain strategies concerning economic development in the Lake Pátzcuaro region in the postrevolutionary era. One major area involved the push for transformation of the conditions of production from cottage industry to more professionalized systemic organizational units (including for hat-making). However, this did not transfer to the professionalization of performances of music and dance. This situation has not altered with the passing of many decades. In stark contrast to the situation of the musicians and dancers of Lake Pátzcuaro, the full-time professional dancers of the Ballet Folklórico in Mexico City are well paid to perform *The Old Men* in the Palace of Fine Arts. In a paradoxical set of circumstances, images of *The Old Men* as a traditional and indigenous practice are used to attract tourists to the Lake Pátzcuaro area, yet tourists' unwillingness to pay for performances of *The Old Men*, because they perceive it to be part of everyday life not a commodity with a monetary exchange value, diminishes a potential source of income for the musicians and dancers, who therefore migrate to urban centers to make a living.

As both *The Old Men* and *Night of the Dead* have functioned within paradigms of official indigenismo, ethnicity-for-tourism, and folkloric nationalism, so those involved in the performances have attempted to satisfy the touristic and nationalistic demand, engaging in the situation with a utilitarian response (Knight 1990:99–100). Agency is a central issue in relation to commoditization, consumption, and the Lake Pátzcuaro and Michoacán tourist environment. In many instances, the state (in the form of official bodies such as the Michoacán Tourist Board) organizes events, and for a lesser number of occasions private companies are the principal organizers (notably in restaurants and hotels). Over and above this, the residents of Lake Pátzcuaro are the principal agents, making decisions as to where and how to perform for economic return, operating within a difficult marketplace. While they are constrained by the limitations set by the context, their aim is to exploit opportunities and capitalize on the projected images and perceptions in order to fulfill tourist demand and meet expectations by putting on a performance for the visitors. Musicians and dancers actively seek out opportunities to perform *The Old Men*, utilizing essentialist conceptions and classifications, such as the terms "folklore" and "P'urhépecha" in their own publicity to promote their product (as I discussed above). As the name P'urhépecha has been marked, set apart, and promoted through multiple uses, it enables the performers to utilize this classification for recognition and economic return. Similarly, images on business cards and self-produced publicity material are those that also circulate on postcards and state-produced tourist literature: Old Men dancers; men with butterfly fishing nets; the island of Janitzio; and kneeling women.

Whereas *The Old Men* is a delimited performance event with clear borders, the matter of exchange value for *Night of the Dead* is more complicated. Visitors go to the island to witness a traditional commemoration and do not perceive of themselves as paying to see the women perform their ritual in the cemetery. Other than the price of the launch ticket to cross to the island, there is no fee involved. Unlike a theme park, there is no charge for entry and visitors are free to wander over the island knowing that no payment has been made to cross a boundary, thus fulfilling an expectation of authenticity. However, if the attraction of *Night of the Dead* is to be of economic benefit for those whose home the island is, they must find opportunities to generate an income. Their activities need to encompass services to be charged for, such as transportation, food, drink, and souvenirs. In order to perpetuate an image of difference and authenticity, configured as indigenous, premodern, and traditional, the islanders are required to undertake a performance of everyday life, encompassing fishing and tortilla-making in the expected manner, and must embody the space "as if" no onlookers were present.

The desire to interpret *Night of the Dead* as an authentic ritual and to read the islanders on Janitzio as authentic peoples, therefore viewing them as outside of a commercial, capitalist system, continues to be projected in the twenty-first century, even as tens of thousands of visitors attend the event. I reiterate the sentiment of a 2007 newspaper report to illustrate the point (discussed in chapter 8). Ignacio Roque characterized the overall Pátzcuaro context as that of a tourist event, referring specifically to economic aspects and noting that all the hotels were full. He stated that "hundreds of indigenous P'urhépecha from the Lake Pátzcuaro region relived the ritual pagan-religious tradition Night of the Dead," commenting that their "ceremonies have lasted as a mark of their genuine nature and identity." He emphasized the ritual objective of the event by remarking "neither the intense cold nor the delicate economic situation in which they live stopped the indigenous people from venerating their dead ancestors" (ibid.). Yet it is precisely the economic situation in which the islanders live that compels them to undertake the event as they do. The women and children perform, both inside and outside the cemetery, because of their marginalized economic situation. The men perform an overtly commercial and economic activity by piloting the constant stream of launches that ferry the tens of thousands of visitors back and forth to the island. All the islanders decorate the village, run the launches efficiently for the tourists, and carry out the ritual in the cemetery because this is a major source of income and the biggest money-making time of the year. It is a complex tourist attraction that requires a utilitarian response. Roque suggests that any monetary exchange would somehow sully the authenticity of the event and the people, because these people are different, and are not engaged with capitalist and consumerist society. As such they are denied their modernity and place in a complex and economic world. Echoing García Canclini's concern over the transformation from the ceremonial to the mercantile, through his writing Roque performs a containing act that keeps the Janitzio islanders in their premodern configuration, choosing to ignore the basic realities of the situation. The irony, or perhaps profound paradox, is that the transformation from ceremonial to mercantile, and from private ritual to public spectacle has been undertaken so successfully that the visitors still travel to Janitzio for *Night of the Dead* with the expectation of, and belief in, an authentic ritual. For most of the islanders, their own demarcation between private and public remains intact, albeit in altered ways. They continue on their home territory, relatively economically secure, yet able to maintain private spaces, sites, sights, and practices unseen by tourists.

In contrast to the in situ *Night of the Dead* production on Janitzio, the exhibition *Soul of Mexico* at *Expo 2000* seems to fit comfortably with García Canclini's critique in terms of capitalist modernization. Ultimately and fundamentally the exhibition and the World's Fair was concerned with attracting economic investment, through tourism and business. Although visitor numbers to Janitzio may have increased as a result of the film exhibition, producing a direct economic benefit for islanders, a much more significant impact was expected in terms of wider business dealings and tourism to other areas of Mexico more familiar to European travelers, such as Cancún, Acapulco, and Puerto Vallarta. There was no representation within the Mexican consortium of the Janitzio residents. In a similar way, the objective of utilizing the photograph of the Old Man dancer in the European marketing campaign was to increase the flow of tourists to major destinations and resorts, with only minimal expected increase in the Lake Pátzcuaro and Morelia areas, therefore impacting negligibly on the economic situation of the Jarácuaro and Janitzio residents. Issues of exchange value, symbolic production, and economic return are complex and multifaceted. Global movements and local contexts interface, and *The Old Men* and *Night of the Dead* will continue to perform their roles in generating reactions and experiences.[14]

Embodied Connections in the Twenty-First Century

¿Que hay detrás de la máscara, qué es aquello que anima al personaje?
What is behind the mask, what is it that gives life to the figure?

(*La Llama Doble*, Octavio Paz)

In drawing to a close these narratives and scenarios of circulating practices, bodies, images, and ideologies, I turn to three twenty-first-century manifestations of the *Dance of the Old Men* that act as powerful signifiers of Mexicanness in diverse contexts, demonstrating continuing processes of performism: a simple mask-and-hat sculpture in China; a child's costume in Mexico; and a ballet folklórico ensemble in the United States of America. Each in its own way exemplifies aspects of the ninety-year trajectory, illustrating profound elements of individual and personal connection, and gesturing towards potential uses of the dance in the future.

Shanghai, China: Paralleling the representation of *Night of the Dead* on Janitzio at the World's Fair, Germany in 2000, just ten years later in October 2010, a year of multiple celebrations for the bicentenary of Independence (the start of the Mexican nation) and the centenary of the Mexican Revolution, the *Dance of the Old Men* was put on display at the World's Fair in Shanghai, China, inside the Mexican Pavillion. Quite unlike the exhibition of authentic bodies in the 3D film *Soul of Mexico*, *The Old Men* was represented simply with the iconic mask and beribboned hat, half-suspended and half-atop a fine metal support, alongside thirty-nine other mask-depictions chosen for their symbolic significance evoking all that is quintessentially Mexican. Even with this minimal artistic sculptural exhibit, the *Dance of the Old Men* was given a prominent place as one of Mexico's most significant embodied figures, despite the absence of a body.

Toluca, Mexico: I was grocery shopping in the large, industrial city of Toluca at the U.S.-owned supermarket giant, Wal-Mart. I walked up and down aisles, passing stacks of Coca Cola and Pepsi Cola, and shelves full of Maseca masa harina for making tortillas, and the once-quintessentially Mexican chocolate drink *La Abuelita*, now owned by transnational mega-company Nestlé—all signs of a global marketplace and mass corporations. As I rounded a corner stacked with cell phones and iPods, something caught my eye—hanging on a rail of disguises and costumes for children's parties, alongside Superman and a Halloween witch, was the mask of the *Dance of the Old Men*, complete with full costume, and bar-coded for ease of purchase. The child-sized traje de manta had been created as an all-in-one outfit, with shirt and trousers joined at the waist. Intricate cross-stitching decorated the cuffs; however, despite the illusion of hours of expert hand-sewing, the pattern was machine-printed. The mask, made of papier-mâché and painted bright pink, dangled from the hanger. Even though the disguise hung lifeless on a coat hanger in a disembodied state with an absent body, the costume still inescapably indexed an original—a body of a dancer from Lake Pátzcuaro and an indigenous traditional way of life (figure 14.1).

Santa Barbara, United States of America: Enthusiastic children eagerly pull on embroidered trousers and shirts, and place Old Man masks over their faces in preparation to rehearse and perform the *Dance of the Old Men* in the Grupo de Danza Folklórica Quetzalcóatl, directed by Francisco Espinosa. Some of the children have never been across the border to Mexico; others journey there to visit their grandparents, aunts, and uncles; and others have recently migrated to the United States from Mexico with their families. Gathered alternatively in the Casa de la Raza, a community center for Mexican-based activities and events, or in the bilingual Franklin Elementary School, the children and their assembled families join together to engage in the activity of dance. Of all the dances in the repertoire, the *Dance of the Old Men* of Jarácuaro creates ripples of laughter as the boys hobble and stumble, and then skillfully execute the rhythmic zapateado. In this dance context, as with countless other groups throughout the United States, *The Old Men* plays a role in the formation of a sense of community identity and cohesion, and enables new generations to begin to shape and construct their own identities, histories, and memories. When Nicolás Bartolo Juárez of the island of Jarácuaro journeyed to Mexico City in 1924 to teach a dance of old men to a group of trainee teachers, he could not have imagined that in the twenty-first century thousands upon thousands of children would be dancing the dance on stages in schools and community centers not only in Mexico but also in the United States. In a similar way, perhaps, these children in the twenty-first century would not imagine that many decades ago, in the aftermath of the Mexican revolution, one man from a little island began the path of transmission (figure 1.11) (48 ◑).

Although the broad connections through the decades and across borders are weighty, there is one very direct link between Nicolás Bartolo Juárez and the dance group Quetzalcóatl, embodied in the form of the director, Francisco Espinosa. There is a path of direct transmission of *The Old Men* of Jarácuaro from Bartolo Juárez to Espinosa, poignantly exemplifying individual acts, and personal histories and connections within the macro contexts of national and cross-border narratives and scenarios. In 1924, Nicolás Bartolo Juárez taught the young student Marcelo Torreblanca in Mexico City. Torreblanca took Bartolo

Figure 14.1 A child's costume for the *Dance of the Old Men* of Jarácuaro hanging in Wal-Mart, the US-owned supermarket giant, in the Mexican city of Toluca. Here, the costume is an all-in-one piece, with cross-stitch embroidery replicated by a single print on the fabric.

Photo: Ruth Hellier-Tinoco, 2007.

Juárez's role in the dance, performing *The Old Men* in the first staged version. Profoundly inspired by this experience Torreblanca himself went on to teach many students in Mexico City, including one Encarnación Martínez. In his turn and inspired by Torreblanca, Martínez formed and directed the Grupo de Danza Marcelo Torreblanca (Dance Ensemble Marcelo Torreblanca), a government-sponsored youth organization in Mexico City. Each week, teenage city boys were taught regional dances, including *The Old Men* of Jarácuaro. In the 1980s, as a child growing up in Mexico City, Francisco Espinosa attended the Grupo de Danza, and learned the *Dance of the Old Men*.

In the late 1980s Espinosa migrated to the United States and settled in Santa Barbara, California, where he formed the Mexican folklórico dance ensemble

Quetzalcóatl. Since that time, within a context of community and family identity, he has taught many children to perform the *Dance of the Old Men*, forming another thread in the complex and intricate tapestry of performism.

Behind each mask of the Old Men is an individual—an individual who is carving out and negotiating his or her own life and space on local, national, and global stages, within multifaceted, complex, and contradictory contexts. As the *Night of the Dead* continues to attract large crowds of expectant tourists; as the *Dance of the Old Men* is enacted on multiple stages before multifarious audiences in Mexico, the United States, and beyond; as postcards, brochures, and tourist guides exhibit images of men fishing with butterfly nets; and as photographs of Janitzio project this tiny body of land as a site and sight of otherness, so Mexico continues to be constructed and shaped by all who participate in these performances, as creators, visitors, viewers, organizers, listeners, teachers, spectators, and enactors. Yet questions abound. How will the residents of Lake Pátzcuaro continue to be part of this performance? Where do *The Old Men* and *Night of the Dead* fit into national, pluriethnic, global, and transnational contexts? What roles should they play? Whose lives will they participate in and whose identities will they shape?

In the village of Jarácuaro, old men and women reminisce about performances of *Old Men*, looking back over the past and wondering about possible futures. Don Dimas, Don Atilano, Don Pedro, Don Rodríguez, Don Braulio, Doña Maria, Don Juan, and so many others recount their stories to their grandchildren who listen intently as they too prepare to become *Old Men*, placing one face over another face, performing Mexicanness, and embodying Mexico.

APPENDIX 1

The Dance of the Old Men: Choreology and Music

HERE I GIVE a brief account of salient elements of the *Dance of the Old Men* of Jarácuaro and Lake Pátzcuaro as pertinent to this study. My intention is not to analyze the elements per se, but to give details of the most relevant aspects. Obviously processes of commodification and adaptation for stage and as spectacle are inherently part of the context, a point that has been at the heart of this study. Versions of the dance from Jarácuaro and other Lake Pátzcuaro villages were notated in the 1930s (Gamboa el al.) and since that time, various forms have circulated, based on a more or less fixed core of choreological patterns and musical accompaniment. Through transmission by ballet folklórico ensembles and teachers of folkloric dance, these fixed forms became more prevalent than others. The version taught to Marcelo Torreblanca by Nicolás Bartolo Juárez in 1924 in Mexico City formed one core of the fixed form, and this cohered in the 1950s with the version directed by Gervasio López of Jarácuaro (which drew on that taught to him by Bartolo Juárez on Jarácuaro). López's form was frequently utilized as the true *Dance of the Old Men*, and recordings of the music composed by López have continued to be used by ballet folklórico groups in Mexico, the United States, and beyond.

Choreological Account

Since the 1950s the number of dancers participating has been more or less standardized to four. Prior to this, and tying in with local performances of dances for fiestas, numbers were often considerably greater. In the 1920s, local versions were durational, often lasting for many hours as the groups of dancers and musicians progressed around the village through the streets, dancing both outside houses and inside in the patios. During this same period, the form presented on stages in Mexico City and for competitions in the Lake Pátzcuaro region was adapted to suit the context of a succession of ensembles one after another. In terms of spatial orientation, if the theater or performance space had a definite "front" then the dancers oriented themselves toward this. Alternatively, more of an "in the round" setup was created if this was more appropriate to the setting. All versions of the dance have utilized a basic formation of a line of dancers, which moves as a single line and in pairs to create floor and proxemic figures, motifs, and patterns. Structurally, while the village dura-tional performances utilized the same motifs danced repeatedly for long time periods, for staged events these same figures were shortened into brief sections each lasting just a few minutes. Over the years, each ensemble has named the various sections (for example, *La Entrada* [the Entrance], *La Competencia* [the Contest], *La Despedida* [the Farewell]); how-ever, although sections may have the same name, the choreography varies from ensemble to ensemble as each group has created its own patterns and figures and musical accompani-ment. For each section the format is similar, comprising a series of repeated phrases and a single tempo. An exception to this is the number called *El Trenecito* (The Little Train), which is based around a gradually increasing tempo. This section is the only one danced by all groups who enact the *Dance of the Old Men*, regardless of location, context, or participants.

Three basic elements are central to the dance: bodily positions and characterization; footwork; and floor patterns and figures. By way of descriptions of body position and characterization I draw upon three accounts relating to performances from the 1920s and 1930s: "In one hand they hold a stick on which they support themselves frequently during the dance . . . [they are] bent over the stick turning around it in a very small space, simu-lating the real movements of old age" (Mendieta y Núñez 1940:174); "dancers advance . . . bent over their sticks feigning . . . senility" (*Hamarándecua* 1930:11); "the posi-tion of the body imitates an old man without being ridiculous. It doesn't use the 'trem-bling' that those who are not natives do exaggeratedly" (Torreblanca 1980). In the final example, Marcelo Torreblanca was making a distinction between the style taught by Nicolás Bartolo Juárez of Jarácuaro in 1924 and subsequent performances that developed over the years. As the dance became more prominent as a tourist and folkloric spectacle, so Lake Pátzcuaro dancers moved toward altering elements that seemed to entertain audience members the most, eliciting laughter and applause. One principal change over the decades has been the increased virtuosity of the zapateado, putting an emphasis on the speed of the footwork and the height of the leaps. Similarly, the characterization of the Old Man became more exaggerated. In a linking segment between the close of one section and the start of another, each dancer takes on a particular role as the character of an old man who has to recover his strength after strenuous activity, staggering around, falling on the ground, and gasping for breath. Such an overstated frailty created even more of a distinction between the extraordinary powers of the Old Man, contrasted with his ordinary self at other times.

The footwork, *zapateado*, or *zapateo* (a generic term used in Spain and Latin America for a range of movements executed by the feet) is always rhythmic and includes stamping and tapping. Many forms of zapateado are used throughout Mexico in both social and performance/ritual dances. The zapateado for *The Old Men* has been commodified con-siderably to become more reliant upon the spectacle of virtuosity. In the 1920s and 1930s in the Lake Pátzcuaro region the zapateado was quite gentle, and the forward and backward movement of each foot was carried out at a much slower pace. While Mendieta y Núñez observed that "the steps are simple, moving only the feet" (1940:174), the rhythmic element of the zapateado has always been a key feature, for as Gamboa and colleagues noted, in reference to the performances of Nicolás Bartolo Juárez in the 1920s and 1930s, "all the steps require great rhythmic precision" (n.d.). From a form of simple or single zapateado, a faster and more intricate double zapateado was developed. From the 1960s onward, the sonic element of the zapateado was given more emphasis through the addition of wooden soles to sandals, enabling the rhythmic patterns to be heard with more clarity and volume. However, shoes or boots are still worn by dancers from Santa Fe, and the form there remains less virtuosic. One form of the dance relied upon pure zapateado (in other words, just the foot movements with dancers equidistant in a single or double line), while in other versions movements and figures or floor patterns were introduced. These involved more complex proxemic relations between dancers, with individually based movements often being created around geometric patterns. One pattern, known as *la Cruz* (the Cross), involved each dancer "drawing" the figure of a cross on the floor surface with the foot and leg movements. In another section entitled *El Saludo* (The Greeting), dancers formed pairs and created interfacing patterns with their bodies and hats.

The Little Train

El Trenecito is highly distinctive both musically and choreographically, and is always requested when the *Dance of the Old Men* is performed. Considered to be the most humorous section of the dance, it elicits the greatest response and never fails to trigger laughter. It is based upon the simple concept of successive increases in speed of the musical accompaniment, requiring the dancers to dance faster and faster, until they can no longer sustain their correct positions. The dancers form a line in height order—tallest at the front, shortest at the back—each connected to another by holding canes, creating a train effect, with the engine at the front *pulling* a line of carriages. In this line they snake around the performance space (or between tables in a restaurant, for example) using a straightforward running movement, emulating the rhythm of a train. In the fastest section at least one of the dancers (usually the littlest one on the end) can no longer maintain contact and is left struggling to keep up. As the accompaniment slows down, the dancers regain control and form a single line facing the audience, concluding the piece with a virtuosic section of zapateado. Although *El Trenecito* is often attributed to Gervasio López, most villagers on Jarácuaro concur that Aurelio Calderón, who played viola with Bartolo Juárez, composed both the music and choreography.

Musical Accompaniment

In the 1920s the dance was accompanied by various forms of guitar-like instruments generally known as a *jarana* or *jaranita*, the details of which varied. Rafael Juárez described to me how his uncle, Nicolás, played the *jaranita*, "una guitarra chiquita," "a little tiny guitar," with four strings. In the same period, Simón and Andrés Orozco accompanied the dance with a *jarana* and a *sexta*—another guitar-like instrument with six strings—, and Juan Orozco portrayed the instrument as a *jaranita* with ten strings strung as doubles. Ten-string, large bodied jaranas were also used in the villages of Santa Fe and Cucuchucho. Even in the late twentieth century, Juan Hernández in Santa Fe and Antonio Pablo in Cucuchucho were still using these to accompany the dance. According to Rafael Juárez, at times the dance was accompanied by violin, guitar, and jarana, a similar instrumentation to that which later became wholly associated with the dance.

While later versions of the dance encompassed two separate groups of performers—dancers and musicians—the form that was initiated on Jarácuaro, as appropriated from Santa Fe, entailed the musician or jarana player leading the dance in full costume, which involved being masked (and this is the form that Marcelo Torreblanca was taught for the first staged performance in Mexico City in 1924). However, as the instrumentation altered, so the inclusion of the musician as a masked dancer was dropped. One reason given for not accompanying *The Old Men* with the jaranita was the increase in volume of the footwork (with wooden-soled sandals) that obscured the sound of the music. By mid-century the reasonably standardized ensemble for accompanying the dance comprised one or two violins, *vihuela* and either *tololoche* (double bass) or *guitarrón*.

With the initial accompaniment on jarana, the music focused on an even-tempo rhythmic chordal strumming, although a melody line was also woven into this if the musician was sufficiently accomplished. The pieces were based on *jarabes*, or *música zapateada*, allowing the dancers to perform the particular rhythmic footwork. The *jarabe* was a form of social dance, with accompanying music, which had been popularized during the nineteenth century, being danced and played at fiestas and public celebrations. Drawing on his own experiences of hearing the music performed by his uncle Nicolás, Rafael Juárez observed that "the music for the *jaranita* which accompanied the Dance was very simple, with just three chords or notes, 1st [I], 2nd [V] and 3rd [V], played with different rhythms." As an accomplished musician himself, who played and taught many styles of music for the Cultural Missions throughout Mexico, Juárez's characterization of this music as "simple" is significant.

As the instrumentation changed to include violin and bass, so too the music shifted toward incorporating elements of the *abajeño*, a genre that has its origins in the Tierra Caliente region of Michoacán (Chamorro 1983a:6, 1992b:52, Stanford 1972:68) and in the sugar region in the south of the state of Jalisco (Vázquez Valle 1976), and that was modified to become the "P'urhépecha style *abajeño*" (Chamorro 1983a:6). Various other musical styles throughout Mexico use similar structures, harmonies, rhythms, motifs, and textures. Some musicians and scholars have suggested that the P'urhépecha abajeño is distinctive through its particular use of a type of polyrhythm, the *sesquialtera* (alternating pulsations of two and three: 6/8 and 3/4), however this feature occurs in a range of Mexican *sones* and other musical forms in Mexico, such as the jarabe and *huapango*. For discussion of alternating rhythm see Chamorro 1992b:54, Vázquez Valle 1976, Stanford 1972, Fogelquist 1975, Slonimsky 1946:55.)

Using the abajeño form, and with the instrumentation of violin, vihuela, and double bass, the violin takes a clear melody line in 6/8 time (and often with an alternating rhythm of 3/4), while the vihuela takes a harmonic chordal line, and the bass a plucked lower line. Each piece has a formulaic binary structure, with each of the two sections consisting of short phrases of four to eight bars in duration, and each phrase containing brief repeated motifs. Harmonically, the music has retained the three chords (I, IV, V) from the earlier jaranita accompaniment. Each ensemble composes their own pieces and also, with permission, utilizes compositions by other musicians. Each piece or section is named with a descriptive title appropriate to the dance movements. With the circulation of music through audio recordings, so the compositions of Gervasio López became those most frequently utilized by ballet folklórico ensembles. *El Trenecito* is unlike all other sections choreographically, and also musically. Along with the changing tempo, *El Trenecito* also differs through the use of a 4/4 time signature for the majority of the sections, only moving into 6/8 for the concluding coda in which the dancers produce an exuberant display of rapid, on-the-spot zapateado.

Interviews, Personal Communication, and Institutional Support

ALL THE PEOPLE listed below have been influential in some way in relation to this study, many contributing information or assisting in gathering data and ideas. I undertook formal interviews with many, had informal conversations with others, and was guided to information and archives by yet others. I have grouped these people together in terms of location, although some have dual locations. I have not included dates of formal interviews. Names are not necessarily listed in alphabetical order so musical and dance groupings or familial groupings are recorded together. I take full responsibility for all omissions. This error is entirely my own. I have included institutional affiliation as appropriate, however, this is not necessarily a reflection of current affiliation. Finally, it is with profound sadness that I acknowledge that some of those listed below have passed on—Q.E.P.D. I have decided not to distinguish these individuals but instead simply record each name.

Islands of Lake Pátzcuaro

Janitzio: Aurelio de la Cruz Campos, Moisés de la Cruz Campos, Francisco López Fermín (Orquesta Xanichu), Guadalupe Gabriel Antonio, Salvador Justo, Cayetano Camilo Castillo, Feliciano Justo, Lorenzo Diego, Juan Gabriel, Antonio Domínguez, Cayetano Reyes, Raúl Domínguez, Rolando Reyes, Luis López, Eugenio Barajas, Víctor López, Antonio Cortés Alcantar, Eulogio Cortés Alcantar, Pedro Cortés Alcantar, Fernando Cortés Alcantar, Juan Cortés Alcantar, Ernesto Campos, Jerónimo Candelario López, Esperanza López, Victor López, César Guzmán Soto, Heliodoro Guzmán Soto, Simón de la Cruz Gabriel, Maria del Rosario, Maria de la Luz, Gaspar, Juanito, Pedrito, Isaias Jacobo Ojeda, Heliodoro Fouar Fermín.

Jarácuaro: Rafael Juárez, Adelaida Bartolo, Félix Francisco Hernández, Maria Luisa Calixto de Francisco, Juan Francisco Calixto, Mari Salvador, Israel Francisco Salvador, Javier, Marbella, Juan, Uriel, José Guadalupe, Cecilia, Lucia (Iovana, José Carlos, Elizabeth), Fidelina, Antonio, Juana. Hermilla Francisco Calixto, Dimas Esteban Mangato and family, Rodrigo Candelario Pantaleón, Raúl Candelario Salvador, Manuel Candelario Salvador,

Raúl Candelario Salvador, Carlos Candelario Salvador, Santiago Candelario Teodoro, Oliberto Matías Domínguez and family, Gervasio López Isidro, Atilano López Patricio, Pedro López Patricio, Atilano López Pichátaro, Roberto López Pichátaro, Armando López Pichátaro, Israel, José, Jaime Antonio de la Cruz, Pedro Antonio, Saturnino Bartolo, Abel Orozco Capilla (Orquesta y Danza de los Viejitos Artesanos de Jarácuaro), Juan Orozco, Manual Orozco, Jesús Orozco, Jesús Alberto, Isidro Ramírez Domínguez, Nicodemos Ramos Calvario, Felipe Ramos Santiago, Daniel Yucatas Cázares, Braulio González Villanueva, Juan González Ramos, Miguel González, and family, Zacarias and Carmen Ramos, Pedro Patricio, Enrique Patricio, Juan Ramírez González, Procopio Cázares Patricio (Tzipikua Los Viejos Alegres), Claudio Lemus Bernardino, Bautista Antonio Secundino, Rigoberto Patricio Antonio, Édgar Patricio Antonio, Miguel Ángel Patricio, César Yácuta Antonio, Julio Antonio, Pedro Antonio, Cruz Guadalupe, Nicolás Constantino de la Cruz, Ricardo Yácuta, Isauro Constantino, Hernán López Constantino, Yosio Constantino García, José Avisain López Constantino, Pablo Edwin Yacuta Domínguez, Jiovani Constantino Cortés, Juan Daniel Lemos, José Arcadio Alonso, Gustavo Orozco, Bernaldino Lemus, Francisco Lázaro, Salvador Santiago, Lorenzo Santiago, Jesús Teodoro, Atilano Cristobap.

Pacanda: Arsenio Alejo Reynoso, Pablo Alejo Reynoso, Rosa, Zintlali, Yvon, Gris, Sergio Alejo Reynoso, Consuelo, Mago, Jessica, Elsa, Jesús Alejo, Vidal Alejo Reynoso, Daniel Campos Flores, Melitón Guzmán, Salvador Campos, Adolfo Antonio, Nicodemus Reynoso Campos, Elizar Reynoso Campos, Juan Flores, Jesús Amescua, Florencio Campos, Cristina Campos, Gerardo Guzmán Campos, *su mamá y su hermana.*

Tecuena: Los hermanos Morales, Jesús Morales Reyes, Higinio, Demetrio, Eleazar, Fulgencio, Esteban, Federico.

Urandén: Cecilio Gabriel, Adela Alejo, Rosa, Guillermina, Yolanda, Nelida (Alonso) Armando, Ariel, Lupe, Ezequiel Camilo, Dimas Cayetano, José Maria Cayetano, Dimas Camilo Castillo, Jorge Camilo, Cecilio Gabriel, Rosendo Cristóbal Camilo, Gregorio Camilo, Eliseo Camilo, Lázaro Camilo, Alejandro Cristóbal, Gerardo Mendez Ramos, Adolfo Gabriel Castillo, Elizar Gabriel, Pedro Cristóbal, Juan Curino, Cypriano Gabriel, Guillermo León, Matías León, Gabino Cortés.

Urandén/México DF; Familia Gabriel, J. Evaristo Gabriel Cortés, José Fausto Gabriel, Elvira Cristóbal, Rigoberto, Luis Alberto, José Refugio, Jesús, José Alfredo, Verónica, Teresa, Fabiola, Simón Camilo Alfredo, Elías Camilo, Adelina Gabriel;

Yunuén: Ezequiel Diego, Andrés Menocal, Santiago Menocal, Jorge Morales, Raúl Diego, Lionél Diego, Salvador Guzmán, Salud Gabriel, Faustino Menocal, Isaac, Ernesto Morales, Benjamín Antonio, Vicente Antonio, Domingo Menocal, Andrés Guzmán, Cristobal Diego, Alfredo Menocal.

Lake Pátzcuaro Region

Ichupio: Pedro Dimas Aparicio, and family, Fidel Esteban Reyes, Maurilo Aparicio, Raul Aparacio, Hermenijildo Dimas.

Cucuchuchu: Antonio Pablo, Floriberto Pablo.

Ihuatzio: Ismael García Marcelina.

San Andres Tzirondaro: Osvaldo Méndez Agustin.

Santa Fe de la Laguna: José Dimas, Ángela Dimas, Néstor Dimas, Ma. Guadalupe Hernández Dimas (Organización Uarhi), Juan Hernández.

Ucasanástacua: Oscar Basilio.

Tzintzuntzan: Francisco Antonio Benítez Méndez.

Pátzcuaro: Carolina de Escudero Múgica, Gabriel Ramírez y Ramírez, Juan Rodríguez Yerena (CREFAL), Juan Ponce Guía (CREFAL), Ricardo Urrieta Paredes (CREFAL), Marina Montaño (CREFAL), Hortencia Calderón, Ruth Almazán Rueda (MCP, Pátzcuaro), Raymundo Campo (INI, Pátzcuaro), Carlos Federico (INI, Pátzcuaro), Leopoldo García (INI, Pátzcuaro), Dagoberto Ángel Urbina (INI, Pátzcuaro), Paulina Odilia Molina Capilla (INI, Pátzcuaro).

Michoacán

Angahuan: Valente Soso Bravo.
Cherán: Leticia Cervantes Naranja, Ignacio Marquéz.
Morelia/Paracho: Juan Bautista Ramírez.
Morelia: Carlos Bautista Ramírez, Javier Bautista Ramírez, Joaquín Bautista García, Joaquín Bautista Ramírez, Lorena Fagoaga Lavalle (Casa de las Artesanías), Javier Samano Chango (Centro de Video Indígena), José Luis Aguilera (DGCP), Catalina Blanco (DGCP), Francisca Maldonado de Próspero, Rocío Próspero Maldonado, Salvador Próspero Maldonado, Joel Torres Sánchez (Radio Nicolaita), Juan Carlos Hidalgo (DGCP), Gerardo Sánchez (UMSNH), Ireneo Rojas Hernández (UMSNH), Alfredo Barerro Próspero (UMSNH), Gilberto Jerónimo Matco (La Voz), Benedict Warren, Patricia Warren, Marina Rico Cano (IMC), Gabriel Rico Mora (IMC), J. Guadalupe Escamilla (IMC), Juan Manual Pérez Morelos (IMC), Jaime Hernández Díaz (IMC), Arturo Chávez Carmona (IMC), Juan Bosco Castro García (IMC, Secretaría de Turísmo), Maria Irma del Perral Martínez (IMC), Gerardo Méndez (Ballet Folklórico, IMC) Argimiro Cortez Esteban (INI), Raúl Izquierda (MC), Guillermo Gamez Jiménez (MC), Ma. Teresa Martínez Peñeloso (Museo del Estado), Marina Tinoco (Secretaría de Turismo), Luis Jaime Cortés (Las Rosas), J. Encarnación Hernández Flores (SEP), Alejandra Flores (Sec. De Turísmo), Santiago Lomelí G. and Silvia Lomelí (Peña Colibrí), Guillermo Ramos (Prensa del Gobierno), David Maciel M and Osvaldo Campos H (Dueto Zacan), Joaquin Panotja, Alejandro Pico, Roberto González Cruz (MC), Rogelio Duran Ibarra (MC), Delia Castro Huerta (MC), Javier Tavera, Marina Tinoco (Secretaría de Turísmo), Wicho, Guillermo Ramos (Prensa del Gobierno), Salvador y Chelo Ramírez (FIMAX);
    Santa Ana Chapitiro: Roberto González Cruz, Rogelio Durán Ibarra, Delia Castro Huerta;
    Uruapan: Arturo Macías, Pedro Victoriano Cruz (*Xiraŋhua*), Francisco Elizade (Discos Kustakua Phorhepecha), Librado Pérez (Banda de Zirahuen, Coro Zezengari);
    Zamora: Arturo Chamorro (COLMICH), Álvaro Ochoa Serrano (COLMICH), Herón Pérez (COLMICH), Francisco Elizade.

Mexico City: Leobardo Ramos Bartolo, Quetzalli Alitzel and Erandi Xiadani, Fermín, Diego and Diana, Gilberto Cázares Ponce, Enedina Bartolo, Eduardo Llerenas, Mary Farquharson (Discos Corasón), Rogelio Gutierrez, Ricardo Torres (DGCP), Modesto López (Discos Pentegrama), Ernesto Arturo Moreno Martínez, Thomas Stanford (ENAH), Carlos Ruiz (ENM), Miguel Moreno Franco FONOMEX, José Antonio Hellmer, René Villanueva, Mario Crispin Acerdo Andrade (INAH), Guillermo Santana (INAH), Benjamín Muratalla (INAH), Felipe Flores Dorantes (INAH), Sol Levin (INAH), Norberto Carrasco (INAH), Marina Alonso Bolaños (INAH), Consuelo Mendez (INAH), Claudia Gortez (INAH), Jose Antonio

Robles (CENIDIM), Hiram Dordelly (CENIDIM), Guillermo Contreras (CENIDIM), Joel Almazán (CENIDIM), Mario Godinez (CENIDIM), Patricia Ruíz Rivera (CENIDI Danza), Maya Ramos Smith (CENIDI Danza), Josefine Lavalle (CENIDI Danza), Noemí Marín (CENIDI Danza), Victor Montez (CENIDI Danza), Xochitl Medina (CENIDI Danza), Alejandra Medillín de la Piedra (CENIDI Danza), Elizabeth Cámara, Lin Durán, Amparo Sevilla, Guillermo Santana (INAH), Consuelo Mendez (INAH), Norberto C. Balestrini (CNBA), Janet Hernandez (INI), Jose Luis Sagredo (INI), Magdelena Espinosa (INI), Julio Herrera (INI), Antonieta Morena (Ballet Folklórico de México), Mario Kuri-Aldana, Eliseo Martínez Martinez, (de Charapan) y Florentino, Rigoberto, Alejo (San Felipe de los Hereros), Angel Mendoza, Roberto Velázquez, Fernando Nava (COLMEX), Ramírez Gil, Felipe (ENM), Amparo Sevilla, Artemio Alcanzar marcos, Pedro Corona Martinez, Jaime Alcantar Garcia, Ofelia Audry Sánchez, Ofelia Cavadonga Ayuso Audry, Elisa Lipkau Henríquez, Clarissa Malheiros, Juliana Faesler, Julieta Navarro López, Rosendo, Julieta, Horacio, Aida, Henrietta Yurchenco (whom I met in Mexico City).

APPENDIX 3

Governmental Institutions and Departments

THE FOLLOWING LIST comprises the governmental institutions and departments through which I accessed documents and information. I am extremely grateful to all the many individuals who were instrumental in assisting me.

Distrito Federal: Mexico City
Archivo General de la Nación
Centro Nacional de Bellas Artes (CNBA); Biblioteca de las Artes, Fondos Especiales
Centro Nacional de Investigación Documentación e Información de Danza (CENIDI Danza)
Centro Nacional de Investigación, Documentación e Información Musical (CENIDIM)
Centro de Investigación, Información y Documentación de Los Pueblos Indígenas de México (CIIDPM)
Comisión Nacional de Cultura Física y Deportes (CONADE)
Colegio de México (COLMEX) Hemeroteca del COLMEX
Consejo de Promoción Turística de México (PROMOTOR)
Dirección General de Culturas Populares (DGCP): Museo de Culturas Populares, Coyoacán, y Centro de Información y Documentación
Escuela Nacional de Antropología e Historia (ENAH)
Escuela Nacional de Música (ENM), Biblioteca de la Escuela Nacional de Musica
Instituto Nacional de Antropología e Historia (INAH), (fonoteca)
Instituto Nacional Indigenista (INI) (biblioteca y fonoteca)
Radio Educación (fonoteca)
Secretaría de Educación Pública (SEP) archivo general
Universidad Nacional Autónoma de México (UNAM) Biblioteca del Instituto de Investigaciones Antropológicas; Hemeroteca de la Biblioteca Central de la UNAM
Morelia, Michoacán
Archivo Histórico del Ejecutivo
Biblioteca y Archivo del H. Congreso del Estado de Michoacán
Casa de las Artesanías
Centro de Video Indígena

Conservatorio Las Rosas
Dirección General de Culturas Populares
Instituto Michoacano de Cultura (IMC), Ballet Folklórico del IMC
Instituto Nacional Indigenista (INI)
Misiones Culturales (MC)
Museo del Estado
Secretaría de Turismo, Michoacán
Universidad Michoacana de San Nicolás de Hidalgo (UMSNH): Hemeroteca; Instituto
de Investigaciones Históricas; Centro de Investigación de la Cultura P'urhépecha (CICP)
Pátzcuaro, Michoacán
Centro Regional de Educación Fundamental para la América Latina (CREFAL)
Instituto Nacional Indigenista (INI), Pátzcuaro
Museo de Culturas Populares,
Zamora, Michoacán
El Colegio de Michoacán (COLMICH)
Cherán, Michoacán
Radio Cherán (INI)

Notes

Chapter 1

1. "P'urhépecha" is the name given to, and used by inhabitants or descendants of inhabitants of a region in the state of Michoacán, some of whom speak the indigenous language P'urhépecha, and some of whom are classified as P'urhépecha by virtue of aspects of their lifestyle and location. The term "P'urhépecha" has generally replaced the term "tarascan" which denoted the same peoples and language (for a discussion of these terms see García Mora 1997:40–1, Warren 1997:27). In this study I will use the terms as utilized in the source texts. The orthography of the term P'urhépecha is changeable, and the version used in each source text will be preserved.
2. Jarácuaro was an island until the mid-1980s, when a causeway was constructed to allow a land crossing.
3. The suffix –*ito* indicates either a very small size or a sense of endearment and fondness toward the person. For example, when referring to one's grandfather (*abuelo*) the term *abuelito* is generally used to indicate fondness. "Viejo" translates as "old" and in the case of the dance indicates "old man," but the addition of "-ito" can indicate both "little old man" and also "dear old man."
4. All translations are my own, unless otherwise noted. Some documents published in Mexico include text in both Spanish and English. For these I use the original English, and indicate this through "orig" alongside the quotation.
5. I will often abbreviate the long title the *Dance of the Old Men* to *The Old Men* throughout the text.
6. Los Urandenes refers to a collection of islands, of which Urandén de Morelos, shortened to Urandén, is the largest.
7. The original name of the city of Morelia was Valladolid, but was renamed to commemorate a famous inhabitant of the city, José María Morelos y Pavón, leader of the independence movement in the early nineteenth century.
8. For further information on *pirekuas*, see Dimas 1995, Gómez Bravo et al. 1987. *Son* is a generic term encompassing a wide variety of musical forms. P'urhépecha *sones* are usually slow, in 3/8 time, and with a lyrical feel.
9. The dancer is Bulmaro Paleo.
10. *The Nutcracker*. Directors: Andrea Conger and Donald LaCourse; writer: Andrea Conger; choreographer: Jesse Bethke Gómez.
11. *¡Llegaron Los Camperos! – Concert Favorites of Nati Cano's Mariachi Los Camperos* (see Hellier-Tinoco 2003b and 2006).
12. This celebration is also called *Día de los Muertos* (Day of the Dead) and All Soul's Day. In some places the vigil in the cemetery takes place during the day (Jarácuaro) and in other places at night (Janitzio).

13. As noted above (note 2), the term "P'urhépecha" has generally replaced the term "tarascan" which denoted the same peoples and language.

14. Issues of race, ethnicity, and class are central to twentieth and twenty-first century Mexico and the construction, formulation, representation, and performance of the concept of "indigenous" in Mexico is a central concern of this study. This term and concept must therefore be understood as an analytical and political device and tool (see Banks 1996:6). Indigenous is a term applied to people by the state, or is a term of self-designation by people who are engaged in an often desperate struggle for land, for political rights, and for a place and space within a modern nation's economy and society. Identity and self-representation are vital elements of a political platform. Certain texts utilize the term *indio*, translated as "Indian," as being synonymous with "indigenous." I utilize the term "indigenous" but will use "Indian" when the source text does so. "Campesino" is the term applied to peasants, or poor rural dwellers, regardless of ethnic background. In postrevolutionary Mexico, while the majority of the campesino population was not classified as "indigenous," the greater part of the indigenous population was classified as "campesino" because the majority were indeed rural dwellers.

15. For an in-depth analysis of *La Danza de los Viejitos* in the context of the period between 1920 and 1940 see Hellier 2001a, and 2004.

16. See Hellier-Tinoco 2009a and forthcoming for a discussion of theater performance as cultural memory.

17. My own journey in Mexico, and Mexican histories and politics began in 1991 in my capacity as professional actress, musician, dancer, and creator in the Leicestershire Theatre-in-Education company in the UK. One project entailed devising a theater piece for children entitled *Aztec*. In order to create the performance we had to immerse ourselves in histories of the moment of incursion, reading, viewing, and embodying every document, account, and image that we could lay our hands on, and role-playing scene after scene, while collaboratively working on dramaturgical and scenographic ideas. We grappled with the complexities of the events of the sixteenth century, always attempting to create connections with both our own lives and those of the children for whom we would perform. We were overwhelmed by the magnitude and the intimacy of the actions—of that moment in which one small group of people journeyed far across an ocean in their fleet of boats and transformed a powerful and sophisticated civilization forever. My character roles in the theater piece encompassed both a Spanish conquistador and a Nahua (Mexican or Aztec) child. In one profound moment my Nahua-child character looked up the towering figure of Hernán Cortés—the man who directed the theater of war. I was aware of the extraordinary poignancy and complexity of the relationship, of the constitution of centers and peripheries, of marginality and significance. What were the relations between a group of Spanish soldiers and a whole civilization of peoples? How did one constitute the other? What was the role of a single child? How does one man lead a group of people and change the course of histories? (*Aztec* 1991).

18. Narratives of many residents of the Lake Pátzcuaro region thread their way through this book. Most of those with whom I undertook formal interviews and had informal discussions and conversations are named in appendix 2, however, any omissions are entirely my own. My interpretations and descriptions are informed by these multiple narratives of dozens of people in the Lake Pátzcuaro region, particularly on all the islands (Janitzio, Jarácuaro, Urandén, Tecuena, Yunuén, Pacanda), and in the communities of Cucuchucho, Ichupio, Ihuatzio, Santa Fe de la Laguna, Ucasanástacua, and Tzintzuntzan.

19. For further historical contextualization see Beezley 2008, Beezley et al. 1994, Chorba 2007, Joseph and Henderson 2002, Joseph and Nugent 1994, Joseph, Rubenstein, and Zolov 2001, Meyer, Sherman, and Deeds 1999, Vaughan and Lewis 2006.

Chapter 2

1. In the now classic conceptualizations of nationalism, Ernest Gellner claims that "nationalism is not the awakening of nations to self-consciousness: it invents nations where they do not exist" (1964:169); Benedict Anderson configures the importance of imagined communities: "the members of even the smallest nations will never know most of their fellow members, meet them, or even hear them, yet in the minds of each lives the image of their communion" (1983:16); and Anthony Giddens describes the distant imagining of nationalism (1990). (See also Gellner 1983 and Hobsbawn 1990).

2. I specifically engage the term "bodies" to draw attention to the material corporeal entity. However, I also add the term "people" to this (with use of a forward slash, thus "bodies/people" or vice versa), in order to return the focus to the person. It is worth noting that the Spanish term *cuerpo*, which was used by all the dancers in referring to their own moving bodies when discussing the dance, is translated as "body."

3. See Fall/Winter 2003 edition of *Latin American Music Review* (24:2) for articles on Nationalisms and Latin American Music.

4. While Hispanism was a central concern in Mexican contexts, it is beyond the scope of this study to deal with the complexities that this wide-ranging concept encompassed.

5. Notions such as fakelore (Dorson 1950 and 1976) and folklorism (*folklorismus*) (Moser 1962, 1964) are linked to commodification, both invoking the idea of an original. Fakelore overtly references an inauthentic practice, and folklorism encompasses uses of a practice outside of the cultural context in which it was created.

Chapter 3

1. He also called himself Hernán and Fernando.

2. For scholarly work on the Virgin of Guadalupe, see, for example, Pool 1995 and Brading 2001.

3. See Tenorio-Trillo 1996 for an excellent analysis of Mexican representation at world's fairs.

4. See, for example, Lumholtz 1904 and Starr 1908.

5. Scholars and commentators are in disagreement about many aspects of the postrevolutionary period. I have made selections on two main counts: I have used details upon which there is a general convergence of opinion and I have only included those aspects that are most relevant to this study.

6. See González Navarro 1970:154, Rowe and Schelling 1991:184, and Barre 1983:34, 61.

7. See also Aguirre Beltrán 1970, Anderson 1970, Basave Benítez 1992, Bigas Torres 1990, Brading 1985, 1988, 1992, Dawson 1998, 2004, González Navarro 1970, Gutiérrez 1999, Mörner 1970, O'Malley 1993, Rhodes 1999, and Vázquez León 1992.

8. José Vasconcelos (1881–1959), philosopher, revolutionary intellectual, and political activist, was secretary of education (1921–1924), director of the National University, and director of the Library of Mexico. The concept of the "cosmic race" was even present in food, with cookbooks identifying *mole poblano* (turkey with chile pepper sauce) as a symbol of national identity, and a culinary emblem of the mestizo cosmic race (Pilcher 2001:80).

9. Calles was president of Mexico from 1924 until 1928, but he continued to be the de facto ruler from 1928 to 1935.

10. Gamio also published on indigenous art (1924).

11. One element of archeology involved the reconstruction of sites for nationalist and tourist agendas. For a discussion concerning the reconstruction of the

famous pyramid at Chichén Iztá, one of Mexico's most significant tourist attractions and cultural heritage sites, see Castañeda 2001.

12. Manuel Gamio was the first Mexican to receive a doctorate in Anthropology outside Mexico, under Franz Boas at Columbia University. Gamio was undersecretary of education in 1925 and the director of the Interamerican Indigenista Institute in 1941.

13. "…incorporar a los indígenas a la nacionalidad mexicana" (Stavenhagen 1979:45).

14. The influence of SEP extended into the everyday lives of Mexican citizens through the airwaves, using its own radio station (XFX) as a means of shaping national culture and identity by broadcasting cultural programs aimed at building national unity (Hayes 2006:249).

15. See Brewster 2005 for a discussion of the role of sport.

16. For examples of "revolutionary school music" see Booth 1941:123–41.

17. In this publication Saldívar and Osorio Bolio include a section on the Tarascos, discussing pre-Hispanic instruments and music (Saldívar and Osorio Bolio 1934:65–69). They note that although the conquest destroyed the powerful tarascans, before eradicating the original cultural expressions, the indigenous people managed to keep something of their sentiment and uniqueness in the music, and that these could still be identified in the rhythms of the indigenous sones of Michoacán (1934:69).

18. Even during the 1930s and 1940s, similar research and collection was carried out by missions sent by SEP, the Department of Indigenous Affairs, and the National University (Mendoza 1956:17). In a recent publication entitled *La "invención" de la música indígena de México* (The "Invention" of Indigenous Music in Mexico), Marina Alonso Bolaños documents some of the institutional research and recording processes carried out in Mexico from the 1920s to the mid-1990s, drawing on Hobsbawns's classic delineation of invented traditions as the principal thread (2008). Although this study includes some valuable contextual material, political, ideological, aesthetic, ontological, and epistemological issues concerning constructions and designations of notions of "indigenous," particularly in relation to the role of ethnomusicologists and other academics, are not fully addressed. This is particularly noticeable through the focus on ethnomusicologists whose principal work has been the recording and labeling of music as "indigenous music." The notion that there are "indigenous societies" and therefore there is something that can be labeled as "indigenous music" (however diverse) remains at the core (136).

19. I suggest that the term and concept of expropriation is also relevant in the Mexican context relating specifically to taking possession for national use. In the 1930s, the idea of expropriation was established at a national level, as being both necessary and normal for Mexican nationalization. In 1936 under President Cárdenas, the "Law of Expropriation for the benefit of the Nation" was decreed, followed in 1938 by the most "visibly" significant act of expropriation of the petroleum industry, which played a major role in the nationalization process (Morris 1999). Although expropriation related specifically to industry, it had wider implications and applications in postrevolutionary Mexican contexts, particularly in terms of cultural practice and artifacts.

20. Theater and movies were popular in both urban and rural settings. According to the contemporaneous account of Frances Toor, editor of *Mexican Folkways*, "Secular entertainments have been introduced through the Federal Rural Schools, and some villages have open-air theatres and movies" (1929:127). It is also notable that Mexico created a strong national film industry in the 1930s.

21. According to Ralph Boggs, Frances Toor "organized the periodical, inspired the writing of many of its articles, saw them through the press, and mailed out the

finished copies to subscribers" (1939:159). Other publications by Toor (1890–1956) include *Frances Toor's Guide to Mexico: Compact and Up-to-date* (1938), *El cancionero mexicano* (1926), *New Guide to Mexico* (c. 1944), and *A Treasury of Mexican Folkways* (1947). For an overview of publications and a general trajectory of *Mexican Folkways* from 1920 to 1937 see Sandoval Pérez 1998.

22. *Au Mexique: Études, notes et renseignements utiles au capitalistes, à l'immigrant, et au touriste* (Gostkowski 1900, cited in Tenorio-Trillo 1996:59).

23. Of great importance for this study is the fact that almost identical imagery was exhibited in the European advertising campaign poster of the Mexican Tourist Board in 2006 in which the Old Man dancer of Jarácuaro was incorporated as the exotic other (see discussion in chapter 12).

24. See Charlot 1963 and Coffey 2002 for a discussion of muralism.

25. Although Revueltas did not use actual appropriated melodies in his music, he evoked regional tunes such as a P'urhépecha *son* and Michoacán *corrido* by modeling his melodies on their characteristic features, thus creating a Mexican nationalist music (Garland 1991:153, Cortés Zavala 1995:96; Mayer-Serra: 1941b and c). Composer Miguel Bernal Jiménez, born in Morelia in 1910, was most closely connected to the P'urhépecha region. For a musicological analysis of postrevolutionary nationalist art music see Madrid 2009.

26. See Bruno Ruíz for a mid-century perspective on dance in the Porfiriato (no date). In the postrevolutionary era, dance was validated and consolidated as an independent artistic field and made into a respectable profession within the State (Audiffred 2000, Tortajada Quiroz 2000). In 1932, a National School of Dance was created by Nellie and Gloria Campobello, who emerged as "major choreographers of a revolutionary, folkloric, and nationalist aesthetic" (López 2006:27).

27. Lake Chapultepec is still used as a performance venue. The highlight of the year is the ballet *Swan Lake*.

28. In a trajectory that leads directly to performances of *el Jarabe Tapatío* (the Mexican Hat Dance) as the archetypal Mexican national dance in staged folkloric events throughout the world in the twenty-first century, the appropriation and commodification of a style of dances known as los jarabes began in the eighteenth century. Even by 1790, a form of jarabe was danced on stage in Mexico City in the Teatro del Coliseo, along with performing acrobats and clowns. In 1858, a comic opera based on national customs was performed in Mexico City and included a type of jarabe (Lavalle 1988:52). In this context, the French Cancan and the jarabe were pitted against each other in the same performance—one representing the foreign and one the national dance. In 1919, Anna Pavlova, dancer and choreographer with the classical ballet company Ballets Russes, performed *Fantasía Mexicana* in New York City, Mexico City, and Puebla, dancing a modernized rendition of the jarabe tapatío en pointe. The jarabe tapatío was given the status of national and official representative, in accordance with the new ideas of nationalist education (Lavalle 1988:45), and under the educational reforms of Vasconcelos in the 1920s, the fixed version of the jarabe tapatío was taught to pupils, and used in primary schools and official fiestas. Writing in mid-century, Bruno Ruíz describes the "double life" of the jarabe tapatío, noting that it was both a regional dance and a Mexico City vaudeville act. He indicates that the theater version is "artificial" (Bruno Ruíz, no date: 47). The jarabe tapatío became the official jarabe, emblematic of Mexican folkloric music and dance, danced by Mexican children as a national icon as the supreme national and Mexican dance, accepted by the educational authorities of the country and used as didactic material (Saldívar 1937, Saragoza 2001, Lavalle 1988, Joseph et al. 2001, López 2006).

Chapter 4

1. See also Fernanado Nava's work on the P'urhépecha language, specifically in relation music (1991, 1993, 1999, 2004).
2. The Bracero Program (*brazo* meaning arm) was a series of laws and diplomatic agreements, initiated by an August 1942 exchange of diplomatic notes between the United States and Mexico, for the importation of temporary contract laborers from Mexico to the United States.
3. Dances using masks of old men exist in many parts of Mexico and the world. As an old man is an archetypal figure, the existence of such masks and dances is unsurprising. My study is not concerned with making connections and tracing perceived origins, but rather with focusing on the details of one particular dance of old men that became *The Dance of the Old Men* in Mexico.
4. See Michel 1932, Barlow 1948, and León and Contreras 1944.
5. Generally a jaranita is smaller than a jarana, although many sizes and tunings existed. The instrument used by Antonio Pablo of Cucuchucho to accompany the dance had a large body and twelve strings.
6. In the twenty-first century, an annual night-time event takes place in Santa Fe in which many dances are performed with only a minimal presence of audience members from outside the village, perpetuating forms from the late nineteenth and twentieth centuries.
7. The *Dance of the Apaches* was accompanied by guitarrón and violin, with dancers using a costume that included a turban with a feather, and wide-legged trousers. Whereas the *Dance of the Apaches* ceased to be enacted, a dance of Old Men continued.
8. My aim in this study is not to explore the multiplicity of ways in which these days are marked and celebrated, but to examine the processes surrounding the transformation of the event on the island of Janitzio. For research on Day of the Dead, see, for example, Brandes 2006, and Lomnitz 2005.
9. See Arts Council Collection 1995.
10. A year later, Modotti wrote an article for *Mexican Folkways* on the theme of photography, stating that her photography was not art, but was the objective documentation of life (1929).
11. Between 1932 and 1933 Sáenz undertook an experimental project in the P'urhépecha village of Carapan (1936).
12. González and Domínguez worked alongside Rafael M. Saavedra, Luis Quintanilla and others in founding the various theater movements (Regional, Indigenista, Sintético, Aire Libre). For the Teatro Sintético, Quintanilla took inspiration from the Russian cabaret theater, Nikita Baliev's *Chauve-souris* (The bat), and founded his own "Bat" Theater, the Teatro Mexicano del Murciélago (Londré and Watermeir.2000:331, Bullé Goyri 2003:76).
13. "Ideas from Our Futurist Theatre will be: *Synthetic*. That is, very brief. To compress into a few minutes, into a few words and gestures, innumerable situations, sensibilities, ideas, sensations, facts, and symbols" (Marinetti et al. 1995[1915]:19).
14. The date is disputed. Campos registers this as 1923 (1930:200).
15. The program included P'urhépecha songs (from a ceremony known as *Canácuas*) with "indigenous airs on the *chirimía*, *teponaztli* and *tambor*, played by three *indios*" and adaptations of Maya and Tehuano music (Campos 1930:200).
16. According to Campos, González "respected the tradition of the Michoacán *guaris* (P'urhépecha women) who wore blue-black skirts and embroidered blouses, and colored waist-bands and ribbons in their loose plaits" (1930:201).
17. It is worth noting that although the *Fiesta of Song and Dance* took place in the P'urhépecha highlands, subsequently, only the Lake Pátzcuaro region was promoted for nationalistic and touristic processes.

18. Curiously, Campos did this by recounting a history of Japan and suggesting that the P'urhépecha people originally came from that part of the world and were therefore connected to the Japanese (1928:95).

19. In an article on the "Esthetics of Indian Dance," published in *Mexican Folkways*, artist Jean Charlot made a similar observation comparing urban artistic expression and dance with indigenous contexts: "Considering the complete decadence of our own dances and the barbarous style of some ladies' dresses, we could study with great advantage the Indian taste in dress and dance" (1925:6).

20. Brief biographical details are included in Barrero Próspero and Granados Hurtado 1991, Campos 1928 and 1939, Domínguez 1925 and 1941, Hernández and Rojas 1982, and Próspero Román 1987a and b.

21. Múgica was a socialist, liberal leader and a leading radical and anticlerical (Boyer Múgica 1997, Guzmán 1985, and Knight 1994b:419). Múgica spelled with both a "g" and "j" in offficial publications.

22. In a moment of deepest pleasure, while sorting through piles of unarchived papers at Doña Carolina's house, I came across a beautiful, handwritten music manuscript, with a watercolor painting of a delicate pink flower on the front cover under which the name "Bartolo Juárez" was inscribed. This original composition was dedicated to Doña Carolina in 1930. Two other such compositions are: "*Carolina*" by Nicolás B. Juárez, dated 30 Jan. 1942, and "*Un Recuerdo*" by Alejandro B. Juárez dated 22 April 1942, both dedicated to Carolina Escudero Luján de Múgica (original copies held by the Carolina Escudero de Múgica estate). These original handwritten manuscripts of Nicolás and Alejandro Bartolo Juárez are held in the private collection of the late Carolina Escudero de Múgica. I am wholly grateful to Doña Carolina (Q.E.P.D.) for her wonderful hospitality (47 ●).

23. As a later form of intercontinental dissemination, Mexican musicologist Daniel Castañeda referred to Bartolo Juárez, noting that in 1925 "characteristic music ensembles (*orquestas típicas*) of the lake region" went to the Capital to play their "sentimental and romantic island *sones*" (Castañeda 1941:447).

Chapter 5

1. Starr also registered and described popular dances. See Scharrer Tomm 1995:17 and Rodríguez Peña 1988:336.

2. In the late nineteenth century León published scholarly work on the Tarascans, for example an 1890 article on the teeth of pre-Columbian Tarascans.

3. Mendieta y Núñez repeats the same idea twice, hence two pages are cited.

4. After joining the revolutionary forces in 1913, Cárdenas later served as governor of the state of Michoacán between 1928 and 1932, then in 1930 became chairman of the National Revolutionary Party (PNR), and from 1934 to 1940 was president of the Republic of Mexico.

5. I came across this correspondence serendipitously in the *Archivo General de la Nación* (General National Archive), a vast, secure depository for millions of government documents. I had gone to look, in the hope of finding something relating to Jarácuaro. My efforts were rewarded. Finding and reading the letters gave me one of the most extraordinary moments in my research processes, with the enormity and poignancy of a situation encapsulated in an instant. I held pieces of paper in my hands as tangible objects representative of the direct two-way communication between Nicolás Bartolo Juárez and Lázaro Cárdenas. In this correspondence, Bartolo Juárez made a request for money for transport to Mexico City for a concert of P'urhépecha *sones* after an invitation from the director of Bellas Artes. He also noted that he had published some of his compositions through the government institutions of the DAPP (1937), but that he had only received 134 copies, rather than the 2,000 as promised. He told Cárdenas that he had composed a piece in his honor and that he would like to

publish this with a portrait of Cárdenas on the cover. He made a request for uniforms for his musical ensemble *Benito Juárez*, and also appealed for a portable motor for his boat. Private correspondence, 8 Sep. 1939.

6. Composed in 1933 and revised 1936. See Garland 1991 for an analysis of *Janitzio*.

7. Another fascinating example is the film *Redes* (Nets) made in 1936, which, although not focused on Lake Pátzcuaro, projected romanticized images of indigenous peoples. As a production of SEP, the producers were preeminent nationalist composer Carlos Chávez, and director of SEP, Narciso Bassols, with music composed by Silvestre Revueltas. Much of the imagery depicts indigenous fishermen (on the Veracruz coast) in their *traje típico*, and women wrapped in rebozos.

Chapter 6

1. Romero Flores later published texts relating to the customs and legends of Michoacán (1936a & b, 1938).

2. Domínguez particularly emphasizes their pre-Hispanic roots (1930a), while Campos suggests that it was a chapel-master in Paracho in about 1870 "who composed and spread the beautiful melodies of the *Canacuas*" through a process of "reconstruction" (1928:82).

3. In the same edition of *Mexican Folkways*, the other articles covered themes of burials; the Cult of the Dead Among the Maya; and Ritual for a Little Angel (by U.S. scholar Elsie Clews Parsons).

4. For an excellent overview and annotated bibliography of visual artwork in the postrevolutionary period, including cover artwork for *Mexican Folkways*, see Adés and McClean 2009.

5. In a clear aesthetic and ideological statement, Frances Toor commented on Domínguez's role in transcribing P'urhépecha music: "Francisco Domínguez studied the dance [Canacuas] in various villages, and took down the music, which he harmonized for both piano and orchestra. The music had never been set down previously, and, of course, the harmonizations are something added to the simple melodies which retain their original purity" (Toor 1930:108).

6. The correct title for the event was *Danzas Auténtics Mexicanas*, although in one advertisement the words were transposed, appearing as *Danzas Mexicanas Auténtics* (figure 6.1).

7. This was set in sharp contrast to other events for which names of performers, creators and designers was given.

8. The glass curtain separating the stage from the auditorium depicts the iconic, snow-capped volcanic mountain Popocatépetl, deployed so frequently in marketing Mexico for tourists, and utilized alongside the image of the *Dance of the Old Men* of Jarácuaro in the 2006 Mexican Tourist Board promotional campaign. In advertisements for *Danzas Auténtics Mexicanas*, the display of the glass curtain is mentioned as part of the event. See also Madrid 2009 for a discussion of the Palace of Fine Arts.

9. The term *el pueblo* can be interpreted and utilized to signify both the notion of "the people" and "village." Here the usage appears deliberately ambiguous, signifying both the notion of village and also the nation/people of Mexico.

10. The two other pieces from Michoacán that were part of these events were "Festejo Las Canacuas, La Huerta, Mich." and "Los Negritos, Tzintzuntzan, Mich." A full analysis of these theatricalized events reveals many more complexities, however, this is beyond the scope of this study given the focus specifically on *The Old Men* and *Night of the Dead*.

11. In a line drawing, the English tourist is costumed in an outfit that includes a pith helmet (associated with explorers and also worn by tourists of the period in exotic locations) and buttoned shoes.

12. In 1929 official recognition was given to mark October 12 as Día de la Raza, a commemorative day for mestizaje (see de la Péña 2006). The Day of Race, sometimes called Columbus Day, marked the so-called discovery of the Americas by Columbus, and was both a highly significant and contentious celebration, intrinsically associated with ideas concerning territory, boundaries, and identities, which generally focused upon the mestizo or mixed nature of the populations. The term *raza* later developed other political connotations in the United States in the twentieth century, particularly as part of the Chicano movement of the 1960s.

13. In the early 1930s San Antonio had a Casa Mexicana de Música (Mexican Music Center) selling records, sheet music, orchestrations and manuscript (Johnston 1935:77).

14. There may be the occasional exception to this, however, such uses are rare.

Chapter 7

1. The Partido Nacional Revolucionario, PNR (National Revolutionary Party) of 1929 then became the Partido Revolucionario Mexicano, PRM (Mexican Revolutionary Party) in 1938 and the Partido Revolucionario Institucional, PRI (Institutional Revolutionary Party) in 1946. The PRI was finally removed from power in 2000 when Vincent Fox of the Partido Acción Nacional, PAN (National Action Party) was elected president.

2. However, "lo mexicano came to serve counterhegemonic impulses as well as regime projects" (Joseph, Rubenstein, and Zolov 2001:8).

3. Rowe and Schelling 1991:18 and Schmidt 2001:26; see also Barre 1983:34, 61, and Lewis 2006:192 for alternative perspectives.

4. After the first Inter-American Indigenist Congress, anthropologists Alfonso Caso, Gonzalo Aguirre Beltrán, and Julio de la Fuente, among others, worked in the field of indigenismo and initiated what has been called the "Mexican school of anthropology" (García Canclini 1993:24 and García Mora 1997). The very title of Beltran's 1952 publication *Problems of the Indigenous Population* is an indication of the positioning of intellectuals and politicians regarding indigenous peoples in the 1950s and 1960s.

5. A rich source of contemporaneous contextualization comes from the writing of Nicolás Slonimsky in his 1946 publication *Music of Latin America*, resulting from his "Pan-American fishing trip"(1946:6). In an insightful and detailed section entitled "Artless Folklore" he noted that "it is a paradox of spontaneous creative force that folk music should be, by definition, an anonymous art, originated by simple men and women without learning, and yet attaining the most perfect musical expression of the nation's collective soul.... Not all folk songs are collective creations. Melodies composed by individual authors may become folk songs when they attain the simplicity and perfection of spontaneous art" (1946:38–9). Slonimsky also discussed the idea of "nation" in a section entitled "Is Latin America Latin?" capturing the concept of nationalism as it was being constructed in the early 1940s and the "rising consciousness of national culture." He noted that "Carlos Chavez writes: 'The music of the Indians is Mexican music; and also Mexican is the art of Spanish extraction. It is fit and proper to regard as Mexican even the native operas in the Italian style, or the German-inspired Mexican symphonies. Naturally, the state of being Mexican does not qualify an art product esthetically. Only when Mexican music attains artistic quality does it become true national art'" (1946:64–5, see also 225 for another version of same quotation). At a somewhat later date, the Spanish translation of the work of Brazilian Paulo de Carvalho-Neto, entitled *Concept of Folklore* was also significant in shaping ideas in Mexico. According to Carvalho-Neto, "Folklore is the scientific study, part of cultural anthropology, which deals

with cultural acts of any peoples characterized, principally, by being anonymous and not institutionalized and, possibly, by being ancient, functional and prelogical" (1965:17).

6. Key musical folklorists of this era included Luis Sandi, Raúl Guerrero, Vicente T. Mendoza, Francisco Domínguez, and José Raul Hellmer (Slonimsky 1946:252) and U.S. radio presenter and folklorist Henrietta Yurchenco. According to Slonimsky, Luis Sandi's compositions were "permeated with Mexican folklore, based on indigenous melodies" (ibid.). INBA was founded in 1946. The first director of INBA was the renowned composer Carlos Chávez. At this time, other influential institutions included the Museum of Plastic Arts, and the National Museum of Popular Arts and Crafts.

7. Indigenous and folkloric themes were used as material to create dances for the Academy of Mexican Dance, for example, *Día de Difuntos* (1947) and *Sinfonía India* (1949).

8. Writing about the island of Yunuén, Coca Ballesteros outlines the "possible factors for the development and progress of the community of Yunuén" (1958: 51).

9. George Foster's publication *Empire's Children: The People of Tzintzuntzan* (1948) presented research undertaken as part of the Tarascan Project, and in reviewing this book, Charles Wagley noted that "when this body of research is all published, the Tarascan area will be the best studied region of Mexico, or of all of Middle America for that matter. The present study by Foster and his associates is a major contribution to this over-all program" (Wagley 1950:219). For other contemporaneous writing see Arriaga 1947, Beals 1946, Beals and Rubin 1940, Carrasco 1952, and West 1948. Later, Foster published another scholarly work on Tzintzuntzan (1967).

10. My thanks to ethnomusicologist Mark Slobin for bringing this film to my attention in connection with the representation of Mexican dances.

11. I am using the term "live" to refer to living humans, in opposition to animated cartoon images. I am also distinguishing between shots of Lake Pátzcuaro with men fishing on the lake, for example, and rehearsed scenes using actors enacting a staged scenario.

12. Another example is *Qué lindo es Michoacán* (1943) directed by Ismael Rodríguez.

13. The acknowledgments for Toor's book read like a "who's who" of Mexican and U.S. folklorists, anthropologists, archeologists, scholars, and artists. Of particular significance for this study is the inclusion of Francisco Domínguez, George Foster, and Henrietta Yurchenco, (1947:ix–x).

14. Photo numbers 85 and 86 (no page). The captions read "Los viejitos of Michoacán" and "The cemetery on the island of Janitzio, lake Pátzcuaro, Michoacán, after midnight on All Saints' Day" (figure 1.14).

15. In the 1990s, this changed from an independently run hotel to a Best Western, marking a shift into the global, corporate market place (figure 1.2, top right hand corner).

16. During an informal conversation, ethnomusicologist Mark Slobin told me about a road trip that he made as a child in 1951 from Detroit to the Mexican-U.S. border, and then on to Guadalajara and Mexico City, taking in Lake Pátzcuaro and Janitzio on the route. Slobin has memories of the "naturalness" of Mexico and also of the journey across the water of Lake Pátzcuaro to Janitzio (Slobin: personal communication).

17. "Inauguración del CREFAL, 9 May 1951" (Video).

18. In the Disney production, the framing of the narrative was overtly fictional and the characters cartoon animations, which heightened the notion of real life in the documentary sections.

19. It is noteworthy that the film *Rituales Tarascos* also included scenes of the yearly event of *cacería de los patos* (duck hunting), an activity that had featured in an article in *Ethnos* in 1925 (La cacería del pato en el lago de Pátzcuaro) and is still

featured as part of the attraction of *Night of the Dead* of Lake Pátzcuaro (see Noche de Muertos 2007, Michoacán Tourist Board, pamphlet).

20. Dickens was born in Pachuca, a city north of Mexico City with strong connections through the mining industry to Cornwall, England.

21. Although this book has no publication date, using contextual information as a guide it is most likely that this was published in the mid-1950s. Two further interesting references to *Los Viejitos* are in Llano and de Clerck 1939 and Ibara 1952.

22. For Ballet Folklórico de México and Amalia Hernández see Shay 2002: 91–3, Israde 2000, Saragoza 2001, and Zolov 2001.

23. Ballet Moderno de México and Ballet Folklórico de Bellas Artes.

24. According to Shay, Hernández mistrusted "the actual peasant taste and production and feels [felt] the need to 'improve' upon them" and therefore she did "not attempt to place actual folklore on the stage" (2002:51 & 92). Anthropologist Edward Spicer's 1965 account of the transformation of the Yaqui deer dance by the Ballet Folklórico corroborates this to some extent, noting that the company went to great lengths to understand the essence of the deer dance and to perform an authentic ethnographic version with the general plan of the ballet, but that "what ones sees with the Ballet Folklórico de México is a new creation, a synthesis of certain elements selected from the yaqui deer dance complex with elements of the western tradition of modern dance as staged art" (Spicer 1965:132–3). For example, the Ballet Folklórico de México's performance of the deer dance includes a section of the death of the deer, with a corporeal conception of the movements based upon the muscular contractions and spasms observed in deer. Spicer suggests that this idea links directly to the Dying Swan of Anna Pavlova (1965:137), which would have been familiar to audiences in Mexico City. Through his brief article, Spice documents the transcendency of the Deer dance in Mexican culture, mainly through the Ballet Folklórico de México, and describes the process of acculturation. Significantly, the article was published in *América Indígena*, "the journal of the Interamerican Indigenist Institute." In 1937, Francisco Domínguez had published an article in *Mexican Folkways* on Yaqui music.

25. Vicente T. Mendoza was the founder and first president of the Folklore Society of Mexico in 1938. Mendoza and Virginia Rodríguez Rivera (his wife) also established the first Mexican School of Folkloric Study (see Cortés 1993).

26. Renowned Mexican writer Jorge Ibarguengoitia made this comment in his collection of articles entitled *Instructions on How to Live in Mexico*. The other dance that he noted was the dance of the *Concheros*.

Chapter 8

1. See Joseph, Rubenstein, and Zolov 2001 for a thorough discussion of this period, and see Gledhill 1993 for a focus on Michoacán.

2. Uncovering the truth surrounding the massacre, and piecing together the details, has been an ongoing task since the day of the shooting. As Luis Echeverría Álvarez was interior minister when the Tlatelolco massacre took place, he was blamed for the atrocious events. See Poniatowska 2007.

3. Simultaneously, a rediscovery of indigenous roots was also the focus of a form of cultural rebellion, along with a rise in Mexican rock music and Latin American protest song (Zolov 1999:16).

4. For discourse on the later twentieth century, dealing with issues of identity, ethnicity, indigenous politics, memory, and popular culture, see, for example Bartra 1999, Florescano 1994, 2001a and 2001b, Garcia Canclini 1993, 1995, 1996, and Monsiváis 1995. See also *Memoria de Gestión* (n.d.) for an official governmental summary as published by SEP.

5. CENART—Centro Nacional de las Artes; CENIDIM—Centro Nacional de
    Investigación, Documentación y Información Musical; FONADAN—El Fondo
    Nacional de Danza, or El Fondo Nacional para el Desarrollo de la Danza
    Popular Mexicana. FONADAN was closed when Salinas de Gortari took up
    presidential office in 1988 and was replaced by CENIDI DANZA, the National
    Center for Research and Documentation of Dance.
      The principal task of CENDIM was musicological analysis of Mexican music,
    through recordings made in situ, and using diverse sources including written and
    archeological. Exemplifying the framework of research of that era, Ramírez Gil's
    article (n.d.) utilizes Charles Adams's (1976) work on "Melodic Contour
    Typology" to analyze the P'urhépecha *pirekua* (song) *El Chinchorro* performed by
    an ensemble on the island of Janitzio. Ramírez Gil's aim was to differentiate
    between the *pirekua* and other indigenous Mexican songs (1989). Key figures of
    the time included Felipe Ramírez Gil, Robert Stevenson, Thomas Stanford, Irene
    Vázquez, Mark Foguelquist, and Edwin Erickson (Chamorro 1981:98).
6. López's ensemble comprised four dancers and four musicians, including López
    as director (playing violin), Dimas Esteban on guitarrón, and Gervasio's sons,
    Atilano and Pedro, as dancers.
7. See Florescano 1993 for discussion of the National Museum of Anthropology.
8. Programs made by Radio Educación are archived at Radio Educación and DGCP.
9. After having left his village of Tingambato at a young age, Próspero Román
    became deeply involved with processes of awareness-raising and revitalization
    of P'urhépecha music and dance.
10. The plan was El Plan Estatal de Desarrollo Turístico del Estado de Michoacán.
11. In the late 1990s, the ensemble of Juan Francisco and Juan González from
    Jarácuaro, who had been performing regularly at the Peña Colibrí in Morelia for
    many years, were invited to live and perform in the international vacation resort
    of Puerto Vallarta, in the newly opened Peña Colibrí set up by the owner of the
    business in Morelia. This was a difficult time for the eight villagers from
    Jarácuaro, who were far from their families, and housed in very basic living
    conditions. The business was not a success and as the venture closed, the
    musicians and dancers returned to Michoacán and to the former venue
    in Morelia (00–07, 15–16 ◉).
12. In Mexico, state holidays usually enable a *puente*, or bridge, of four days away
    from work, allowing many people to travel to destinations in reach and stay for
    two or three nights. Credited as the first anthropological article relating to
    tourism, "Tourism, Tradition, and Acculturation: Weekendismo in a Mexican
    Village," by Theron Nuñez, engages with the issue of short visits to rural
    communities (1963).
13. The "i" and "o" were both sections of a guitar, the "c" a fish, the "h" the brass
    tubing of a tuba, the first "a" a monarch butterfly, the second "a" a wooden
    carving of a sun with a face, and the final "n" a carved image of a saint's face. As
    an example of intertextual image referencing, the wooden sun-carving is the
    same image that was used in *National Geographic, Travel Mexico* as the opening
    photo inside the front cover, with the caption "wooden mask: Tzintzuntzan"
    (Onstott 2006:5).
14. Another photo depicts P'urhépecha musician Joaquín Bautista of Paracho
    playing the guitar.
15. Before motor launches were in use, visitors traveled by wooden canoe, paddled
    by islanders, thus giving an even greater sensation of being transported and
    floating. Elements of this are captured in the experiences of folklorists and
    collectors, as described in previous chapters.
16. There are similarities with the "It's A Small World" exhibition in Disneyworld
    and Disneyland, in which daytrippers climb aboard little boats that transport
    them around "the world" to view dioramas of small groups of figures
    undertaking representations of everyday life. In the Yucatán Peninsula the

creation of the *Mundo Maya* or "Maya World" generated a network of significant attractions. Comparisons between tourism practices in the Lake Pátzcuaro region and Cancún in the Yucatán peninsula make clear the different notions and perceptions of authenticity and indigenous peoples. In Cancún, the void caused by the near-absence of a modern cultural heritage is filled with "concocted images of faked authenticity, including Caribbean adventures and countless designs vaguely attributable to the ancient Maya. Given this Disneyland-like version of the archeological past, foreign guests commonly believe that the Maya are 'extinct'" (Pi-Sunyer et al. 2001:130). In Lake Pátzcuaro, people live in the same villages that their ancestors inhabited many centuries earlier, therefore presenting an image of authenticity.

17. These were generally not P'urhépecha groups, but local duos and trios playing a repertoire of well-known Mexican ballads and nationalistic songs on request.

18. Another site of significance during the *Night of the Dead* week of activities is the lakeside village of Ihuatzio. Close to the village are the archeological remains of pre-Hispanic P'urhépecha buildings, managed by INAH. In the late 1970s, the *Dance of the Fish* was revived in Ihuatzio by fishermen, through the intervention and promotion of the tourist board in connection with Day of the Dead (García Canclini 1985:36).

19. It is important to note that education on the island was not affected by the building conversion, and indeed, the three brothers and one nephew comprising the Alejo Reynoso ensemble were all trained and experienced primary school teachers who worked in nearby villages.

20. As an example of a more national expression of *indigenous roots*, on 12 December children wear the *traje de manta* pan-indigenous clothes purportedly worn by Juan Diego in the sixteenth century when he witnessed the appearance of the Virgin of Guadalupe.

21. For further discussions of these issues see Hellier-Tinoco 2009a and 2010b.

Chapter 9

1. According to López's son, Atilano, Felipe's main purpose was to make money and he only paid a small amount to the musicians. While it is difficult to corroborate such an observation definitively, the sense of exploitation that López felt, which is reflected in his rejection of the invitation by the owners of Discos Corasón to tour to England, was shaped through the experience of many years performing and recording for public consumption, with little financial remuneration.

2. The directors of this highly acclaimed company are Mary Farquharson and Eduardo Llerenas.

3. Performing as Erandi, the Bautista family present an interesting aspect in terms of P'urhépecha musical representation. The Bautista brothers grew up in the P'urhépecha highland town of Paracho but went on to receive classical musical training. Javier trained in Paris and for many years led the Morelia Symphony Orchestra. When performing P'urhépecha music their technique differs greatly from that used by the majority of musicians in the P'urhépecha region, setting up a point of comparison and adding another element to a context of interpreting P'urhépecha performance techniques.

4. El Instituto Michoacano de Cultura, el Colegio de Michoacán y el Programa de Apoyo a las Culturas Municipales y Comunitarias (PACMyC).

5. Luis Covarrubias was the younger brother of celebrated artist Miguel Covarrubias. It is significant that Covarrubuis referred to the *Dance of the Moors and Christians* in association with Lake Pátzcuaro and thus linked it with *The Old Men* of Lake Pátzcuaro.

6. One performance was presented by The University Musical Society of the University of Michigan, on February 26 1969. The program comprised eight "numbers" one of which was: "DANCE OF THE OLD MEN FROM PATZCUARO, MICHOACAN (from "The Tarascans"). The Dance of the Old Men provides a scene of extreme senility and decrepitude that is amusingly belied by the vigor and agility of the dancers" (Ballet Folklorico de Mexico – Amalia Hernandez, Program 1969). [Note - no diacriticals were used in the typography.]

7. In the United States the term "folklorico" is sometimes spelled without a diacritical mark on the second "o."

8. The very title of an article in the Los Angeles Times in 1969 specifically includes the terms creativity and authenticity in relation to the Ballet Folklórico de México: "Ballet Folklorico de Mexico: Controlled Creativity, Styled Authenticity" (Carriaga 1969, cited in Shay 2002).

Chapter 10

1. I am aware of possible charges that I am involved with similar hierarchical activities of representation that I am critiquing. I made a decision not to undertake an ethnographic study but rather to analyze processes of representation from one-step removed. However, in order to explain some of the intricacies of the processes of performism, I too am engaged with descriptive documenting of the lives of particular villagers of Lake Pátzcuaro.

2. For further discussions of local P'urhépecha fiesta contexts see Brandes 1979 and 1988, Carrasco 1976 and 1986, Chamorro 1983a, 1983b, Sepúlveda 1974, and for further discussion of academic studies in the P'urhépecha region see de la Peña el al 1987. See also Jacinto Zavala and Ochoa 1995.

3. Although Rafael, Nicolás's nephew, performed in the Bartolo Juárez orquesta as a child, he then moved away from the island to follow a long career as a music teacher with the Department of Indigenous Affairs and the Cultural Missions, working in many schools in various states around the country (playing and teaching a range styles of music), returning to Jarácuaro in 1989. Nicolás had one son, Cesario, an accomplished musician on cello, violin, and bass, who performed in the Morelia Symphony Orchestra, but who tragically died in a car accident while still young. Another family member, Enrique Bartolo Juárez, played clarinet and composed P'urhépecha music, publishing a book of pirekuas, sones, and abajeños (1994).

4. See Pietri and Pietri 1976 and López Castro 1988 for analysis of migration in the Lake Pátzcuaro region.

5. One example of recording by the Gabriel family is: *Los Nietos del Lago y Grupo los Gallitos: La Danza de los Viejitos de Urandén*. Fono-México TAR-676.

6. See also Jacinto Zavala 1996 and Jacinto Zavala and Ochoa Serrano 1995.

7. The P'urhépecha language was used throughout the day for the ceremony and announcements as a gesture to claim the event and mark the day as P'urhépecha. However, in the Lake Pátzcuaro region, many villagers who self-designate as P'urhépecha do not speak the language, which sets up a complex and exclusionary environment.

8. El Centro de Investigación de la Cultura P'urhépecha (CICP), at La Universidad Michoacano de San Nicolás de Hidalgo (UMSNH).

9. I recognize that my presence, and that of a few other non-P'urhépecha participants and audience members, creates a context that is not wholly P'urhépecha.

10. The event has also been called the *Concurso* (Contest) *Artístico de la Raza Purépecha*.

11. I published many short articles and photographs in local newspapers and magazines (c.f. Hellier 1999a/b). I continue to be implicated through publication both scholarly (c.f. 2004) and educational (2009b).

12. See also Américo Paredes' critique of the interpretive, analytical divide between Chicano/Mexican and Anglo/American scholars (2001).

13. Dealing with the shift of positioning as my marriage to my former Mexican husband ended also encompassed a complex set of issues.

14. Although in the postrevolutionary years many musicians on Jarácuaro read from musical notation, by the mid-twentieth century, most had shifted to oral transmission. Nicolás Bartolo Juárez's nephew, Rafael, had returned to Jarácuaro by the 1990s, but he did not immerse himself in village life.

15. The orthography of P'urhépecha on the cassette and CD is another form (P'urépecha).

16. Leobardo Ramos Bartolo was born on the island of Jarácuaro, but migrated to Mexico City with his family in his youth, and has lived there ever since, returning to his birthplace for celebrations and special events. On my first visit to the island of Jarácuaro in 1995, for the celebration of *Night of the Dead*, I was invited by Leobardo and his family to stay with them. I offer my heartfelt gratitude to Leobardo Ramos Bartolo and his family for their immense hospitality, and for Leobardo's continued support during my stays in Mexico City and Lake Pátzcuaro.

Chapter 11

1. As an example, a British friend, who happened upon a performance of *The Old Men* in Pátzcuaro while traveling through Mexico, described the dance as "obviously indigenous." An idea such as this tends to be based upon a presumption of what an indigenous Mexican dance might look like, shaped through multiple experiences and expectations.

2. See Tenorio-Trillo 1996 for an excellent discussion of nineteenth-century and early twentieth-century processes concerning racial and ethnic delineation.

3. See also Foster 1995 in relation to notions of bodies and history.

4. A twenty-first-century scholarly publication on music in Latin America recently perpetuated the problematic approach of framing people in Latin America, including Mexico, as exotic others, classifying and labeling "type" with essentialist description and obsessive categorization (Kuss 2004). The most extreme example of objectivizing humans is found in Marina Alonso Bolaños's chapter on Mexico, in the form of a photo of a girl labeled as "Nahua child" (2004: 240). A single body is presented as a specimen and type, and reduced to the anonymity of an ethnic, indigenous somatic classification.

5. A particularly striking example of a performance context leading to a reading of bodies as real, indigenous, authentic Mexican bodies occurred in 1992, with the performance *Two Undiscovered Amerindians Visit....* devised and performed by performance artists Coco Fusco and Guillermo Gómez-Peña. Despite their efforts to create a piece of overt performance, Fusco and Gómez-Peña's performances were read by some viewers/audience members as literal displays of human specimens. As Fusco later noted, "we did not anticipate that we...could be believable" (1995: 134).

6. Marjorie Becker, in her historical study of the state of Michoacán after the Mexican revolution, stresses the mythology that was created through the use of official revolutionary iconography, literature, and art, observing that "in all contexts official representations of peasantry and state [prevailed]" (Becker 1995:xi).

7. Three early accounts include the following references: "after the Mayan culture, the one which reached a high degree of development and which should be

considered in a prominent place is the Tarasca" (Saldívar and Osorio Bolio 1934:156); "during the time of discovery and conquest of the New World, one of the tribes of *indias* semi-civilized was that of the TARASCANS" (León 1934:149). Basauri described Lake Pátzcuaro as the "cradle of one of the most interesting civilizations of America" (1990 [1940]:487).

8. Of course, whiteness is not a unitary category; however, in postrevolutionary Mexico whiteness was formulated as an aspirational goal.

9. As already noted, in the postrevolutionary era, the Lake Pátzcuaro region was afforded particular distinction through associations with Lázaro Cárdenas, governor of Michoacán and president of the Republic.

10. As noted in Chapter 7, a photo by Frederick Starr, published in *Mexican Folkways*, depicted fishermen inside a hut on Janitzio with their fishing nets (1928:5).

11. Another significant alteration between the two editions occurs in the section entitled "Tapatío Traditions" (155) [tapatío refers to the city of Guadalajara]. In the 2001 edition, alongside a caption which simply states "stirring music," the accompanying photo shows two P'urhépecha musicians from Jarácuaro, namely Felix Francisco and his son, Juan, both playing violin, wearing the costume for *The Old Men* (although only the two musicians are visible). In the 2006 edition this photo was dropped and replaced by one depicting a man and boy playing twelve-string guitar and double bass, wearing "cowboy" rather than the usual charro hats used for mariachi, and everyday shirts, with the caption "Mariachi music."

12. In *La Danza de los Sembradores* (*the Dance of the Sowers*) López and his sons presented a scenario of men sowing and ploughing (as undertaken on the fertile soils of Jarácuaro) and women carrying food to the workers. The men were costumed in the traje de manta (as used for the *The Old Men*) while the women wore their everyday clothes. An image of this dance, depicting Pedro López holding a hoe in a Jarácuaro field, with hills and open sky in the background, was used as the cover for a cassette recording by López's ensemble, which included the music for the dance of the sowers: *Danza de los Sembradores* (1989). Produced by the recording company Discos Alegría as part of their series entitled "Folklore Mexicano," the visual imagery on the cover generated associations between folklore, nature, and a preindustrial rural idyll, specifically linked to contemporary life in Lake Pátzcuaro.

13. As noted, the front cover of the printed program for *Hamarándecua* (1930) depicts three women, heads covered with blue rebozos, holding fish. See Erica Segre (2005) for a discussion of the hermeneutics of the veil in Mexican black-and-white photography, with references to the interplay of presence and absence and the tradition of religious Christian painting.

14. These corporeal positions form a stark contrast with the upright and defiant depiction of revolutionary women, with bullet belt slung across the body.

15. Discussing the dance production *La Malinche*, by José Limón (Mexican American choreographer and dancer), Carol Maturo notes that the character of "El Indio wears simple white cotton pleated shirt and wrapped pants worn by landless peasants who fought in the Revolution. In the political mythology of Mexico in 1920s and 1930s, the peon revolutionaries became cultural heroes, their simple clothing adorning Mexico's murals, and thus gaining worldwide exposure" (2008:71–71).

16. For photos, artworks, and descriptions of the costume see González 1928b:34–35, Campos 1928:31, and Bartolo Juárez 1937b.

17. See *Masks: the other face of Mexico* by Victor Moya Rubiok (1978) for an examination of the Mexican context.

18. "Mexico is the land of superimposed pasts. Mexico City was built on the ruins of Tenochtitlán, the Aztec city that was built in the likeness of Tula, the Toltec city that was built in the likeness of Teotihuacán, the first great city on the American continent. Every Mexican bears within him [sic] this continuity

which goes back two thousand years. It doesn't matter that this presence is almost always unconscious and assumes the naïve forms of legend and even superstition. It is not something known, but something lived" (Paz 1985:362–3).

19. Included in this edition is a photo of a devil mask from Pátzcuaro, depicted as a grotesque face with horns, fangs, and fur for a moustache (Toor 1929:134). As with other signifying elements, one mask is interpreted in juxtaposition with others, forming a network of oppositions and correspondences, such that one mask "supposes other real or potential masks by its side" (Lévi-Strauss 1982: 67,144). Thus the Old Man mask of Pátzcuaro presented the image of a real, archetypal human, in juxtaposition with *El Diablo* (the Devil).

20. In the last two decades, two distinct uses of masks have arisen in highly visible and political contexts: the ski mask for the neo-Zapatistas (EZLN), and the mask of a *luchador* (wrestler), worn by the populist, antigovernment hero "Superbarrio" in Mexico City. In assessing the signification of the mask-wearing function, Mexican scholar Claudio Lomnitz notes in his writings on Mexican nationalism that the mask enables "a more abstract identification of a movement with 'the people,' and as such its demands can be put forward in a clearer way to the public.... The use of masks is a Brechtian sort of strategy, effacing the individual and stressing the social persona by relying on images derived from the mass media" (Lomnitz 2001:158–59). The potency of the mask lies in the ubiquity of the image and the presentation of the individual as the messenger of the masses. Parallels may be drawn with the Old Man masks, in as much as their iconic usage encompasses and signifies a mass of people ("indigenous people"), however, while the neo-Zapatistas and Superbarrio are working for political change, the Old Men dancers tend to be performing within the established boundaries of national politics and the tourist industry.

21. In Mendoza's work on the performance of folkloric music and dance in defining and redefining of ethnic and racial distinctions and identities in the Andes, she has shown that different forms of *zapateo* are used as markers of ethnic orientation. In the Cusco region of the Andes a hard, fast, and marked zapateo, with short and quick hopping steps, a hunched-over posture and stooping low to the ground is associated with indigenous, whereas minimized zapateo, an upright posture and slower, sometimes swaying movements are associated with mestizo (1998:178).

22. "There was another dance of old men, which they danced hunched over, with masks of old men, which is more than a little funny and amusing and makes one laugh because of its manner" (Durán 1990:463).

23. Although this is a study of public interpretations of *The Old Men*, of course the dancers and musicians themselves have their own ways of interpreting the dance they perform. Of particular interest is the lack of meanings that many musicians and dancers from Jarácuaro read in the dance. As far as many are concerned, they are enacting a dance that requires no explanation, preferring to revel in the sheer physicality of the movments.

24. Such pairings therefore include direct-indirect, strong-light, and sudden-sustained, which relate directly to the effort category of Laban Movement Analysis.

Chapter 12

1. Research by Patricia Albers and William James concerning photographic representation of ethnicity in postcards in the southwestern United States, particularly relating to American Indians, demonstrated that tourism influences the way in which host groups are represented and that with the growth of tourism, the images changed to satisfy the desires of a wider range of visitors,

displaying "idyllic, exotic scenes apparently designed to meet the expectations of mostly White American tourists" (Nash 1996:71).

2. Ever since the initial focus on the island of Janitzio in the early postrevolutionary period the sheer physical features of the little island have formed an essential component. With its distinctive conical form in profile and its circular form in aerial view, Janitzio has proven to be a useful icon. In 1926, renowned U.S. art photographer Edward Weston captured images of the island that have been displayed in art exhibitions worldwide (Arts Council Collection 1999). In addition to overtly nationalistic and touristic uses, numerous companies engage the image for marketing and publicity; for example, the bottled water company *La Salud* (Health) depicts the profile of Janitzio on their labels with obvious connotations of naturalness and purity.

3. See also Hellier-Tinoco 2010c.

4. Given the economic and business-model references of the photograph, it is a weighty and paradoxical fact that the chairman and CEO of TelCel, Carlos Slim Helú, was identified as the wealthiest person in the world, as of April 2010.

5. My thanks for details in this section to various members of the Mexican and Michoacán Tourist Boards, including: Alejandra Perezmejia, Adjunct Director of Media and Contracts, Regional Office for Europe (PROMOTUR); Julie Ruffini (PROMOTUR); Ivonne Bustani Moukarzel, Vice-director of General Promotional Operations (PROMOTUR), and Alejandra Flores, Office of Press and Publicity of the Secretary of Tourism, Michoacán.

6. I give grateful thanks to Bruce Herman for his insightful information. Herman noted that "I sold that photo to the Mexican tourism board years ago; they have violated the contract in so many ways I don't even pay attention any more.... People appearing in postcards rarely even see the cards let alone get paid; guys like me shoot tons of pics and hope to sell a few. Sometimes it's years between shooting the pic and getting some money out of it. I tend to pay the subjects something right there when I shoot if I have something I think is good and will sell.... The photo business in Latin countries is like the wild West: people stealing images right and left and not much you can do about it. All the laws in Mexico are designed to help the big guys" (personal communication). In addition to the European use, the photograph was published in the Spanish-language Mexican tourist magazine *Michoacán: Cómo y Dónde* (Michoacán: How and Where) (2000).

7. An eagle with a snake in its beak sits on a cactus on an island in the middle of a lake. This image forms the center of the Mexican national flag. Another overt connection to Aztec general knowledge was generated through the phrase "plunge visitors into the heart of this celebration" linking with plunging a knife into the chest of a sacrificee to cut out the heart in Aztec ritual (an oft-reproduced yet mis-represented notion).

8. Pertinently, Roland Barthes, in his writing on photography, made specific associations with photographic images and death, observing that "however 'lifelike' we strive to make it (and this frenzy to be lifelike can only be our mythic denial of an apprehension of death), Photography is a kind of primitive theater, a kind of Tableau Vivant, a figuration of the motionless and made-up face beneath which we see the dead" (1984:32).

9. In three other examples, Rubén M. Campos described rural songs and dances as the "soul of the people" in his Eulogy of Song and Dance at the *Fiesta of Song and Dance* in the P'urhépecha highland town of Paracho in 1924 (Campos 1928:98); in the printed program for *Hamarándecua* in 1930, P'urhépecha fiestas, music and dance were characterized as the "soul of the people"; and in relation to *Noche Mexicana* and the *Exhibition of Popular Arts* in Mexico City in 1921, "a leading commentator...announced that the 'soul of the Republic, dispersed and almost forgotten by our foreign-oriented intellectuals,' had been rediscovered and made palpable by the Noche Mexicana and the Exhibition of Popular Arts" (López 2006:25).

Chapter 13

1. Rowe and Schelling observed that "the way in which cultural actions come to be called folklore needs to be understood as a historical process, involving changes in the practice both of its producers and of those who seek to interpret and control it" (1991:4).

2. Jaime Garduño Argueta discusses the commercialization of cultural patrimony as undertaken by INAH, using the term DisneyINAHlandia (2000).

3. Engaging with the concept of a pluricultural nation, a recent rerelease of a recording of P'urhépecha music explicitly addressed this issue, even as it was aimed at a global and international marketplace with English-only liner notes. Originally released in 1966, having been recorded from the 1940s onward by Henrietta Yurchenco, the rerelease in 2003 was part of the series entitled *The Real Mexico in Music and Song*, with the accompanying sleeve information that "with this type of cultural activity the aim is for Mexicans to be aware of their origin, and also to give value to the different cultures and the 57 languages that are spoken in this great country that is Mexico" (2003). In the twenty-first century, music from the P'urhépecha region is promoted as part of the "real Mexico," authenticating it (and notionally setting up an oppositional binary with an *unreal Mexico*) while also presenting such music as the cultural heritage and patrimony of all Mexicans. Simultaneously, the concept of diversity, difference, and plurality of indigenous peoples, here differentiated through language, is also part of the construct. However, despite the configuration of valorization and pluralism, the production process did not encompass activities of P'urhépecha involvement or decision-making.

4. In a 1996 special issue of *National Geographic* magazine, entitled "Emerging Mexico," a double-page color photo depicted *Night of the Dead* on Janitzio, with the figure of a single elderly woman - her rebozo framing her face and her body curved by the side of a grave-forming the center photo. The caption read "Candles light the way for spirits returning home to Michoacán's island of Janitzio on El Día de los Muertos, the Day of the Dead. Every November 2 Mexicans keep vigil in cemeteries, greeting the souls of loved ones with prayers, flowers, and their favorite foods. Says island resident Teresa Talavera: 'Bad things can happen if we ignore the dead'" (Parfit and Harvey 1996:22–3).

5. It is worth reiterating that a similar essentialist concept of indigenous music has been perpetuated, with references to an "indigenous aesthetic" (Hellmer 1990: 64) and an "indigenous musical concept" (Sánchez 1990: 93, see also Sánchez n.d.).

6. For the process of creating the Deer Dance of the Yaqui culture to be compatible with the Mexican national image of the Yaquis see Spicer 1965:135 (see f.n. 7:24 above).

7. Chamorro noted that in the 1980s, cassettes had an enormous impact particularly due to the availability of cassette players (62). Two radio stations were of great significance: XEZM de Zamora, and XEPUR La Voz de los Purépechas (the Voice of the P'urhépechas), broadcast from Cherán, under the auspices of INI.

8. The issue of making an audio recording in order to claim ownership/authorship is also pertinent. Interestingly, Alonso Bolaños recounts an episode concerning Henrietta Yurchenco in the P'urhépecha region in the 1960s. According to Alonso Bolaños, Yurchenco noted that in 1966 she knew members of the family of Nicolás Juárez, and they complained to her that on many occasions she had recorded other musicians, but that the pieces were composed by Nicolás many years earlier and had been "'stolen'" (2008:121).

9. In general economic terms the significance of the tourist industry is considerable, having generated a large proportion of foreign earnings for the country, particularly in the post-1940 era (Saragoza 2001:91). According to the World Trade Organization statistics, "in 1990, Mexico hosted 16.7 million international visitors, ranked eighth in the world for tourist arrivals, and earned

US$5,467 million. By 1999, Mexico ranked seventh among all nations with its 20.2 million tourists, and benefited from earnings of US$7.9 billion" (Pi-Sunyer et al. 2001:128). See Kemper 1979 for a discussion of tourism in the Pátzcuaro region.

10. MacCannell's model of attraction for the tourist as "an element of desire to become identified with the paradoxical combination of remoteness, inaccessibility, mysteriousness, and fame of the site" (2001:383) is highly pertinent and applicable to *Night of the Dead* on Janitzio.

11. In Mexico City, the Gabriel family from Urandén has sustained themselves economically as mariachi musicians, although in recent years this has become more difficult with an increase in the number of mariachi ensembles and the duplication of hire-locations other than Plaza Garibaldi. Although the family does perform *The Old Men* in Mexico City, for economic reasons they can only undertake this on weekdays when a contract does not present a conflict with a mariachi contract. Payment for a performance of *The Old Men* and P'urhépecha music is generally less than they can earn for a mariachi performance. Making choices on financial grounds therefore becomes important (31–37 🔊).

12. García Canclini transcribes the words of a mask-maker from the lakeside village of Tócuaro, who recounted a conversation with dancers of the *Old Men* from Jarácuaro: " 'I sell masks to those from Jarácuaro who perform the Dance of the Old Men, and after a couple of months they come here again: we want six more masks. But, what did you do with the others? 'They [visitors] bought everything from us, including the pants'. They have more contact that I do, because they go to the restaurants, the big hotels, the important cities to dance and they sell them there' " (1985:21).

13. As I noted previously, photographer Bruce Herman, whose photograph of the Old Man dancer was used by the Mexican Tourist Board for the European billboard poster campaign, stated that his photo was utilized many times beyond the fair use of the contractual agreement.

14. As a final note I again raise questions regarding my complicity as a scholar in propagating essentialist notions of folkloric and folk in relation to the *Dance of the Old Men* and Mexico, specifically concerning two aspects arising in the final stages of book production: the cover image and the Library of Congress classification. Firstly, the image on the cover of this book is a photograph of José Evaristo Gabriel and members of his family—Jesús, José Refugio, and Luis Alberto—as they posed on the roof of their home in Mexico City in 2010. I took this photo with their full consent and paid them for their work. Yet by displaying this image on the book cover I am using the *Dance of the Old Men* to sell a product, and am circulating associations between this stereotypical form and notions of Mexico. Secondly, the Library of Congress classification for this book includes the terms "folk music, Mexican" and "folk dancing, Mexican," thereby encompassing the very core of my discussion that threads through the book. My concerns therefore remain: in global flows, how complicit am I in disseminating and perpetuating notions of Mexico as folkloric?

References

Adams, Charles R. 1976. "Melodic Contour Typology." *Ethnomusicology* 20(2): 179–213.

Adés, Dawn and Alison McClean. 2009. *Revolution on Paper: Mexican Prints 1910–1920.* London: The British Museum Press.

Aguirre Beltrán, Gonzalo. 1970. "The Integration of the Negro into the National Society of Mexico." In *Race and Class in Latin America*, edited by Magnus Mörner, 11–27. New York: Columbia University Press.

Alonso Bolaños, Marina. 2004. "Mexico's Indigenous Universe." In *Music in Latin America and the Caribbean: An Encyclopedic History, Volume 1, Performing Beliefs: Indigenous Peoples of South America, Central America and Mexico,* edited by Malena Kuss, 231–45. Austin: University of Texas Press.

———. 2008. *La "invención" de la música indígena de México: antropología e historia de las políticas culturales del siglo XX.* Buenos Aires: Editorial Sb.

Alter, Stewart. 1994. *The Truth Well Told: McCann-Erickson and the Pioneering of Global Advertising.* New York: McCann-Erickson Worldwide Publishers.

American Automobile Association Travel Guide to Mexico. 1990. Heathrow, Fla.: AAA.

Anderson, Benedict. 1983. *Imagined Communities: Reflections on the Origin and Spread of Nationalism.* London: Verso.

Anderson, Charles. 1970. "The Concepts of Race and Class and the Explanation of Latin American Politics." In *Race and Class in Latin America,* edited by Magnus Mörner, 231–55. New York: Columbia University Press.

Arriaga, Antonio. 1947. "La cultura de los Tarascos del Lago de Pátzcuaro." *Universidad Michoacana* 25/26: 37–42.

Arts Council Collection. 1999. *Edward Weston—Catalogue.* London: Hayward Gallery Publishing.

Audiffred, Miryam. 2000. "La revolución, clave para la danza mexicana." *La Journada online* www.jornada.unam.mx, 30 December 2000.

Austerlitz, Paul. 1997. *Merengue: Dominican Music and Dominican Identity.* Philadelphia: Temple University Press.

Averill, Gage. 1989. "Haitian Dance Bands, 1915–1970: Class, Race, and Authenticity." *Latin American Music Review* 10(2): 204–35.

———. 1991. Notes to *Rara in Haiti, Gaga in the Dominican Republic.* Washington, D.C.: Folkways/Smithsonian (SF 40402).

————. 1994. "'Se Kreyól Nou Ye'/'We're Creole': Musical Discourse on Haitian Identities." In *Music and Black Ethnicity: the Caribbean and South America*, edited by Gerard H. Béhague, 157–85. New Brunswick, N.J.: Transaction Publishers.

Ballesteros Coca, Hector. 1958. *Estudio monográfico de la comunidad de Yunuén*. Pátzcuaro, Michoacán: Centro Regional de Educación Fundamental para la América Latina (CREFAL).

Banks, Marcus. 1996. *Ethnicity: Anthropological Constructions*. London: Routledge.

Barlow, Robert. 1948. "Pastorela de Viejitos. Para solemnizar el nacimiento de nuestro Señor Jesucristo [para Morelia 1848]." *Tlalocan* 2(4): 321–67.

Barre, Marie-Chantal. 1983. *Ideologías indigenistas y movimientos indios*. Distrito Federal, México: Siglo Veintiuno.

Barrero Próspero, Alfredo, and Armando Grandos Hurtado. 1991. *Mandani Arhini P'urhepecha Ujtsïkuecha—Breve antología de la música P'urhépecha*. Morelia, Michoacán: Universidad Michoacana de San Nicolás de Hidalgo.

Barth, Frederick. 1969. *Ethnic Groups and Boundaries: The Social Organization of Cultural Difference*. London: George Allen and Unwin.

Barthes, Roland. 1984. *Camera Lucida*. Translated by Richard Howard. London: Harper Collins.

Bartolo Juárez, Enrique. 1994. *Pirekuas, sones y abajeños de Jarácuaro*. Pátzcuaro y Distrito Federal, México: Dirección General de Culturas Populares de CONACULTA, Proyectos de Apoyo as las Comunidades y Municipios (PACMYC).

Bartolo Júarez, Nicolás. 1937a. *Canciones isleñas del Lago Pátzcuaro*. Jarácuaro, Michoacán: Archivo Regional. Departamento Autónomo Prensa y Publicidad.

————. 1937b. *Sones isleños del Lago Pátzcuaro*. Jarácuaro, Michoacán: Archivo Regional Departamento Autónomo Prensa y Publicidad.

Bartolomé, Miguel Alberto. 1994. "La represión de la pluralidad y los derechos indígenas en Oaxaca." In *Derechos indígenas en la actualidad*, 73–99. Distrito Federal, México: UNAM Instituto de Investigaciones Jurídicas.

Bartra, Roger. 1989. "Culture and Political Power in Mexico." *Latin American Perspectives* 16(2): 61–69.

————. 1999. *La sangre y la tinta. Ensayos sobre la condición postmexicana*. Distrito Federal, México: Océano.

Barz, Gregory, and Timothy J. Cooley, eds. 2008. *Shadows in the Field: New Perspectives for Fieldwork in Ethnomusicology*. New York and Oxford: Oxford University Press.

Basauri, Carlos. 1990 [1940]. *La población indígena de México*. Distrito Federal, México: Secretaría de Educación Pública.

Basave Benítez, A. F. 1992. *México mestizo: análisis del nacionalismo mexicano en torno a la mestizofilia de Andrés Molino Enriquez*. Distrito Federal, México: Fondo de Cultura Económica.

Beals, Ralph. 1946. *Cherán: A Sierra Tarascan Village*. Institute of Social Anthropology, Publication No. 2. Washington, D.C.: Smithsonian Institution.

Beals, Ralph, and Daniel F. Rubín de La Borbolla. 1940. "The Tarascan Project. A Cooperative Enterprise of the National Polytechnic Institute, Mexican Bureau of Indian Affairs, and the University of California." *American Anthropologist* 42: 708–12.

Becker, Marjorie. 1995. *Setting the Virgin on Fire: Lázaro Cárdenas, Michoacán Campesinos, and the Redemption of the Mexican Revolution*. Berkeley: University of California Press.

Beezley, William. 2008. *Mexican National Identity: Memory, Innuendo, and Popular Culture*. Tucson: University of Arizona Press.

Beezley, William, Cheryl English Martin, and William E. French, eds. 1994. *Rituals of Rule, Rituals of Resistance: Public Celebrations and Popular Culture in Mexico.* Wilmington, Del.: SR Books.

Béhague, Gerard. 1973. "Latin American Folk Music." In *Folk and Traditional Music of the Western Continents*, edited by B. Nettl, 179–206. Upper Saddle River, N.J.: Prentice Hall.

Bell, Elizabeth. 2008. *Theories of Performance.* Thousand Oaks, Calif. and London: Sage Publications.

Best Maugard, Adolfo. 1929. "Las Máscaras—Masks." *Mexican Folkways* 5(1): 122–6.

Bigas Torres, Sylvia. 1990. *La narrativa indigenista mexicana del siglo xx.* Guadalajara, Jalisco: Editorial Universidad de Guadalajara.

Blaustein, Richard. 1993. "Rethinking Folk Revivalism: Grass-roots Preservationism and Folk Romanticism." In *Transforming Tradition: Folk Music Revivals Examined*, edited by N. Rosenberg, 258–74. Urbana: University of Illinois Press.

Boggs, Ralph S. 1938. "Appraisal of 'El folklore y la música mexicana.'" *Handbook of Latin American Studies* 3: 175–180.

———. 1939. "Folklore." *Handbook of Latin American Studies* 4: 159–69.

Bonfil Batalla, Guillermo. 1970. "Del indigenismo de la revolución a la antropología crítica." In *De eso que llaman antropología mexicana*, edited by A. Warman, 39–65. Distrito Federal, México: Editorial Nuestro Tiempo.

Booth, George C. 1941. *Mexico's School-made Society.* Stanford, Calif.: Stanford University Press.

Bourdieu, Pierre. 1984. *A Social Critique of the Judgement of Taste.* Cambridge, Mass.: Harvard University Press.

Boyer Múgica, Margarita. 1997. *Francisco J. Múgica: breve ensayo biográfico.* Morelia, Michoacán: Instituto Michoacano de Cultura y H. Ayuntamiento de Tingüindín.

Brading, David 1985. *The Origins of Mexican Nationalism.* Cambridge: Centre of Latin American Studies.

———. 1988. "Manuel Gamio and Official *Indigenismo* in Mexico." *Bulletin of Latin American Research* 7(6): 75–9.

———. 1992. "El patriotismo liberal y la reforma mexicana." In *El nacionalismo en México*, edited by C. Noriega Elío, 179–204. Zamora, Michoacán: El Colegio de Michoacán.

———. 2001. *Mexican Phoenix: Our Lady of Guadalupe: Image and Tradition Across Five Centuries.* Cambridge: Cambridge University Press.

Brandes, Stanley. 1979. "Dance as Metaphor: A Case from Tzintzuntzan, Mexico." *Journal of Latin American Lore* 5(1): 25–43.

———. 1988. *Power and Persuasion. Fiestas and Social Control in Rural Mexico.* Philadelphia: University of Pennsylvania Press.

———. 2006. *Skulls for the Living, Bread for the Dead. The Day of the Dead in Mexico and Beyond.* Hoboken, N.J.: Wiley-Blackwell.

Brass, Paul R. 1991. *Ethnicity and Nationalism: Theory and Comparison.* New Delhi: Sage.

Bravo Ramírez, Francisco J. 1975. *Michuacan: Ensayo económico, político y social.* Distrito Federal, México: Editorial Porrúa S.A.

Brenner, Anita. 1932. *Your Mexican Holiday: A Modern Guide.* New York and London: Putnam.

Brewster, Keith. 2005. "Patriotic Pastimes: The Role of Sport in Post-Revolutionary Mexico." *International Journal of the History of Sport* 22(2): 139–57.

Brody Esser, Janet. 1984. *Máscaras ceremoniales de los Tarascos de la sierra de Michoacán.* Distrito Federal, México: Instituto Nacional Indigenista, Series de Artes y Tradiciones Populares.

Bruno Ruiz, Luis (no date, c.1956). *Breve historia de la danza en México.* Distrito Federal, México: Editorial Porrúa.

Buckland, Theresa Jill. 2001. "Dance, Authenticity and Cultural Memory: The Politics of Embodiment." *Yearbook for Traditional Music* 33: 1–16.

Bugarini, Jesús. 1985. *Zacán: renacimiento de una tradición.* Morelia, Michoacán: Instituto Michoacnao de Cultura, Gobierno del Estado de Michoacán.

Bullé Goyri, Alejandro Ortiz. 2003. "El teatro indigenista de los años veinte: ¿Orígenes del teatro popular mexicano actual?" *Latin American Theater Review* 37(1): 75–93.

Butler, Judith. 1990. *Gender Trouble: Feminism and the Subversion of Identity.* New York and London: Routledge.

———. 1993. *Bodies That Matter: On the Discursive Limits of "Sex."* New York and London: Routledge.

Campbell, Patrick. 1996. *Analysing Performance.* Manchester, U.K.: Manchester University Press.

Campos, Rubén M. 1928. *El folklore y la música mexicana: investigación acerca de la cultura musical en México (1525–1925).* Distrito Federal, México: Secretaría de Educación Pública.

———. 1930. *El folklore musical de las ciudades: investigación acerca de la música mexicana para bailar y cantar.* Distrito Federal, México: Secretaría de Educación Pública.

———. 1932. "Las danzas mexicanas." *Nuestro México, Our Mexico.* 6: 25–9 & 74–75.

———. 1939. "La música popular mexicana de hoy." *Vigesimoséptimo Congreso Internacional de Amercianistas. Actas de la Primera Sesión,* 441–54. Distrito Federal, México: Instituto Nacional de Antropología e Historia, Secretaría de Educación Pública.

Cárdenas Solórzano, Cuauhtémoc. 1985. "Presentación." In *Zacán: renacimiento de una tradición,* edited by Jesús Bugarini, 1–2. Morelia, Michoacán: Instituto Michoacano de Cultura.

———. 1986. "Presentación." In *Michoacán: indumentaría tradicional, el traje regional. Patrimonio de los pueblos,* edited by O. Vázquez, n.p. Morelia, Michoacán: Casa de las Artesanías, Gobierno de Michoacán.

Carrasco, Pedro. 1952. *Tarascan Folk Religion: An Analysis of Economic, Social & Religious Interactions.* Mid-American Institute, publication 17, New Orleans: University of Tulane.

———. 1976. *El catolicismo popular de los Tarascos.* Distrito Federal, México: Secretaría de Educación Pública, Colección SEP-SETENTAS, no. 298.

———. 1986. *La sociedad indígena en el centro y occidente de México.* Zamora, Michoacán: El Colegio de Michoacán.

Carriaga, Daniel. 1969. "Ballet Folklorico de Mexico: Controlled Creativity, Styled Authenticity." *Los Angeles Times,* 1 February.

Carvalho-Neto, Paulo de. 1965. *Concepto de folklore.* Distrito. Federal, México: Editorial Pormaca.

Caso, Alfonso. 1929. "El uso de las máscaras entre los antiguos Mexicanos: The Use of Masks Among the Ancient Mexicans." *Mexican Folkways* 5(1): 111–13.

———. 1942. "La protección de las arts populares." *América Indígena* 2(3): 25–29.

Castañeda, Daniel. 1941. "La música y la revolución mexicana." *Boletín Latino Americano de Música.* Instituto Interamericano de Musicología 5(5): 437–48.

Castañeda, Quetzil. 2001. "The Aura of Ruins." In *Fragments of a Golden Age: The Politics of Culture in Mexico Since 1940,* edited by Gilbert Joseph, Anne Rubenstein, and Eric Zolov, 452–467. Durham, N.C. and London: Duke University Press.

Castelo-Branco, Salwa El-Shawan, and Jorge Freitas Branco, eds. 2003. *Vozes de Povo: A Folclorização em Portugal.* Oeiras, Portugal: Celta Editora.

Castro Agúndez, Jesús. 1958. *Monografía y música de danzas y bailes regionales presentados en las jornadas nacionales deportivas y culturales llevadas a cabo en los años de 1953 a 1958.* Distrito Federal, México: Secretaría de Educación Pública, Dirección General de Internados de Enseñanza Primaria y Escuelas Asistenciales.

Chamorro, J. Arturo. 1981. "Fuentes de la investigación etnomusicológica en Michoacán." In *La Cultura Purhé,* edited by Francisco Mirando, 98–115. Zamora, Michoacán: El Colegio de Michoacán.

———. 1983a. *Abajeños y sones de la fiesta purépecha,* (notes with recording). Distrito Federal, México: INAH.

———. 1983b. *Sabiduría popular.* Zamora, Michoacán: El Colegio de Michoacán.

———. 1992a. "El triunfo de Leco: ideología popular, competencia musical e identidad p'urhépecha." In *Estudios Michoacanos IV,* edited by Sergio Zendejas Romero, 259–78. Zamora, Michoacán: El Colegio de Michoacán.

———. 1992b. *Universos de la música Purhépecha.* Zamora, Michoacán: Centro de Estudios de las Tradiciones, El Colegio de Michoacán.

———. 1994. *Sones de la guerra: rivalidad y emoción en la práctica de la música P'urhépecha.* Zamora, Michoacán: El Colegio de Michoacán.

Chapman, M., E. Tonkin, and M. McDonald, eds. 1989. *History and Ethnicity.* London: Routledge.

Charlot, Jean. 1925. "Esthetics of Indian Dances." *Mexican Folkways* 1(2): 4–8.

———. 1963. *The Mexican Mural Renaissance, 1920–1925.* New Haven, Conn.: Yale University Press.

Chorba, Carrie. 2007. *Mexico, From Mestizo to Multicultural: National Identity and Recent Representations of the Conquest.* Nashville, Tenn.: Vanderbilt University Press.

Cincuenta años de danza. 1984. Distrito Federal, México: Palacio de Bellas Artes, Instituto Nacional de Bellas Artes.

Clifford, James, and George Marcus, eds. 1986. *Writing Culture: The Poetics and Politics of Ethnography.* Berkeley: University of California Press.

Coffey, Mary Katherine. 2002. "Muralism and the People: Culture, Popular Citizenship, and Government in Post-Revolutionary Mexico." *The Communication Review* 5 (1): 7–38.

Cohen, Anthony. 2000. "Introduction: Discriminating Relations: Identity, Boundary and Authenticity." In *Signifying Identities: Anthropological Perspectives on Boundaries and Contested Values,* edited by A. Cohen, 1–13. London and New York: Routledge.

Cohen, Erik. 1988. "Authenticity and Commoditization in Tourism." *Annals of Tourism Research* 15(3): 371–86.

Conquergood, Lorne Dwight. 1995. "Of Caravans and Carnivals: Performance Studies in Motion." *The Drama Review* 39(4): 137–41.

———. 2002. "Performance Studies: Interventions and Radical Research." *TDR: The Drama Review* 46(2): 145–56.

Cooley, Timothy. 2005. *Making Music in the Polish Tatras: Tourists, Ethnographers, and Mountain Musicians.* Bloomington: Indiana University Press.

Cortés, Eladio, ed. 1993. *Dictionary of Mexican Writers.* Santa Barbara, Calif.: Greenwood Press.

Cortés Zavala, Maria Teresa. 1995. *Lázaro cárdenas y su proyecto cultural en Michoacán. 1930–1950*. Morelia, Michoacán: la Universidad Michoacana de San Nicolás de Hidalgo.

Covarrubias, Luis. n.d. (c.1979). *Mexican Native Dances: Regional Dances of Mexico/Danzas regionales de México*. Distrito Federal, México: Editorial México, Fischgrund.

Covarrubias, Miguel. 1929. "Notas sobre máscaras mexicanas—Notes on Mexican Masks." *Mexican Folkways* 5(1): 114–17.

Covarrubias, Miguel, and Vincente T. Mendoza. 1955. "La danza en México." *Artes de México*.

———. 1967. "La danza en México." *Artes de México*.

Cowan, Jane. 1990. *Dance and the Body Politic in Northern Greece*. Princeton, N.J.: Princeton University Press.

Crick, Malcolm. 1989. "Representations of International Tourism in the Social Sciences: Sun, Sex, Sights, Savings and Servility." *Annual Review of Anthropology* 18: 307–44.

"Curriculum Guide for Educators." 2009. Instituto Mazatlán Bellas Artes de Sacramento (Ballet Folklorico IMBA) California, United States of America.

Dacosta Holton, Kimberly. 2005. *Performing Folklore: ranchos folclóricos from Libson to Newark*. Bloomington: Indiana University Press.

Daniel, Yvonne Payne. 1991. "Changing Values in Cuban Rumba: A Lower Class Black Dance Appropriated by the Cuban Revolution." *Dance Research Journal* 23(2): 1–10.

———. 1995. *Rumba: Dance and Social Change in Contemporary Cuba*. Bloomington: Indiana University Press.

———. 1996. "Tourism dance Performances: Authenticity and Creativity." *Annals of Tourism Research* 23(4): 780–97.

Davis, Diane. 2007. "The Modern City." Lecture: Celebrating the City—Mexico City Through History and Culture. The British Academy, 30 October 2007.

Davis, Martha Ellen. 1994. "Music and Black Ethnicity in the Dominican Republic." In *Music and Black Ethnicity: the Caribbean and South America*, edited by Gerard H. Béhague, 119–55. New Brunswick, N.J.: Transaction Publishers.

Dawson, Alexander S. 1998. "From Models for the Nation to Model Citizens: *Indigenismo* and the 'Revindication' of the Mexican Indian, 1920–40." *Journal of Latin American Studies* 30: 279–308.

———. 2004. *Indian and Nation in Revolutionary Mexico*. Tucson: University of Arizona Press.

de la Peña, Guillermo. 2005. "Social and Cultural Policies Toward Indigenous Peoples: Perspectives from Latin America." *Annual Review of Anthropology* 34: 717–39.

———. 2006. "A New Mexican Nationalism? Indigenous Rights, Constitutional Reform and the Conflicting Meaning of Multiculturalism." *Nations and Nationalism* 12(2): 279–302.

de la Peña, Guillermo, T. Linkck, J. Espín, and J. Tapia. 1987. "Algunos temas y problemas en la antropología social del area P'urhépecha." In *Antropología social de la región P'urhépecha*, edited by G. de la Peña, 31–65. Zamora, Michoacán: El Colegio de Michoacán.

de la Torre Otero, Maria Luisa. 1933. *El folklore en México: El arte popular y el folkore aplicados a la educación*. Publisher unknown.

Delpar, Helen. 1992. *The Enormous Vogue of Things Mexican: Cultural Relations between the United States and Mexico*. Tuscaloosa, Ala.: University of Alabama Press.

del Val, José. 1995. "México, indigenismo e identidad." In *Tradición e identidad en la cultura mexicana*, edited by Agustín Jacinto Zavala and Álvaro Ochoa Serrano, 47–53. Zamora, Michoacán: El Colegio de Michoacán y CONACYT.

Derrida, Jacques. 1990. *Du droit à la philosophie*. Paris: Galilée.

————. 1998. *Of Grammatology*. Baltimore, Maryl. The Johns Hopkins University Press.

————. 2001. *Writing and Difference*. London and New York: Routledge.

Desmond, Jane C. 1993/4 and 1997a. "Embodying Difference: Issues in Dance and Cultural Studies." *Cultural Critique* 26: 33–63: and in *Meaning in Motion: New Cultural Studies of Dance*, edited by J. Desmond, 29–53. Durham, N.C.: Duke University Press.

————. 1997b. "Introduction." In *Meaning in Motion: New Cultural Studies of Dance*, edited by J. Desmond, 1–28. Durham, N.C.: Duke University Press.

————. 1999. *Staging Tourism: Bodies on Display from Waikiki to Sea World*. Chicago and London: University of Chicago Press.

Dickens, Guillermina. 1954. *Dances of Mexico*. London: Max Parrish, Royal Academy of Dancing and the Ling Physical Education Academy.

Dimas, Néstor. 1995. *Temas y textos del canto purépecha*. Zamora, Michoacán: El Colegio de Michoacán y El Instituto Michoacano de Cultura.

Dinerman, Ina R. 1974. *Los tarascos; campesinos y artesanos de Michoacán*. Distrito Federal, México: Secretaría de Educación Pública.

Domínguez, Francisco. 1925. *Sones, canciones y corridos michoacanos* (3 volumes). Distrito Federal, México: Secretaría de Educación Pública.

————. 1930a. "Canacuas, danza antigua de guaris." *Mexican Folkways* 6(3): 110–16.

————. 1930b. "La música de las canacuas." *Mexican Folkways* 6(3): 123–27.

————. 1937. "Música yaqui." *Mexican Folkways* 13(1): 32.

————. 1941. *El álbum musical de Michoacán*. Distrito Federal, México: Secretaría de Educación Pública.

Domínguez, Francisco and Carlos González. 1930. *Hamarándecua – costumbres*. Distrito Federal, México: Departamento del Distrito Federal, Dirección General de Acción Educativa.

Dorson, Richard M. 1950. "Folklore and Fakelore." *American Mercury* 70 (1950): 335–48.

———— 1976. *Folklore and Fakelore: Essays toward a Discipline of Folk Studies*. Cambridge, Mass.: Harvard University Press.

Duany, Jorge. 1994. "Ethnicity, Identity, and Music: An Anthropological Analysis of Dominican Merengue." In *Music and Black Ethnicity: the Caribbean and South America*, edited by G. Béhague, 65–90. Miami, Fla.: University of Miami.

Durán, Fray Diego. 1990. *Historia de las indias de Nueva España e islas de la tierra firme*. Distrito Federal, México: Banco Santander. (Francisco González Varela - transcripción) and (1984) México: Editorial Porrúa, S.A. (Angel Ma. Garibay K).

"Educational Work of the National League of Peasants." 1928. *Mexican Folkways* 4(1): 69–70. Author unknown.

Eggener, Keith. 2000. "Contrasting Images of Identity in the Post-War Mexican Architecture of Luis Barragán and Juan O'Gorman." *Journal of Latin American Cultural Studies* 9(1): 27–45.

Entman, Robert M. 1993. "Framing: Toward Clarification of a Fractured Paradigm." *Journal of Communication* 43(4): 51–58.

Erdman, J. L. 1996. "Dance Discourses: Rethinking the History of 'Oriental dance.'" In *Moving Bodies: Rewriting Dance*, edited by G. Morris, 288–305. London: Routledge.

Feld, Steven. 1988. "Aesthetics as Iconicity of Style, or 'Lift-Up-Over-Sounding': Getting into the Kaluli Groove." *Yearbook of Traditional Music* 20: 74–113.

Fish, Stanley. 1980. *Is There a Text in this Class? The Authority of Interpretive Communities*. Cambridge, Mass.: Harvard University Press.

Florescano, Enrique. 1993. "La creación del Museo Nacional de Antropología y sus fines científicos, educativos y políticos." In *El patrimonio cultural de México*, edited by Enrique

Florescano, 145–64. Distrito Federal, México: Consejo Nacional para la Cultura y Las Artes, Fondo de Cultura Económica.

———. 1994. *Memory, Myth, and Time in Mexico: From the Aztecs to Independence*. Austin: University of Texas Press.

———. 1999. *Memoria Indígena*. Distrito Federal, México: Taurus.

———. 2001a. *Etnia, estado y nación. Ensayo sobre las identidades colectivas en México*. Distrito Federal, México: Taurus.

———. 2001b. *Memoria mexicana*. Distrito Federal, México: Taurus.

Fogelquist, Mark Stephen. 1975. "Rhythm and Form in the Contemporary Son Jalisciense." University of California: Master of Arts Dissertation.

Foster, George M. 1948. *Empire's Children: The People of Tzintzuntzan*. Washington, D.C.: Smithsonian Institution, Institute of Social Anthropology.

———. 1967. *Tzintzuntzan: Mexican Peasants in a Changing World*. Boston: Little Brown and Co.

Foster, Susan Leigh. 1995. "Choreographing History." In *Choreographing History*, edited by S. Foster, 1–21. Bloomington: Indiana University Press.

Foucault, Michel. 1982. "The Subject and Power." In *Michel Foucault: Beyond Structuralism and Hermeneutics*, edited by H. L. Dreyfus and P. Rabinow, 208–26. Chicago: The Harvester Press.

Fox, Richard G. 1990. "Introduction." In *Nationalist Ideologies and the Production of National Cultures*, edited by R. Fox, 1–14. Washington, D.C.: American Anthropological Association, Monograph No. 2.

Friedlander, Judith. 1975. *Being Indian in Hueyapan: A Study of Forced Identity in Contemporary Mexico*. New York: St. Martin's Press.

Frola, Francisco. 1942. "La danza en México." *América: Revista de la Asociación de Escritores y Artistas Americanos* 13 (2/3): 67–69.

Fusco, Coco. 1995. *English Is Broken Here*. New York: The New Press.

Gamboa, Fernando, Luis Felipe Obregón, and Santiago Aria Navarro (n.d.) "*Los viejitos: danza del estado de Michoacán. Cucuchucho de Lago de Pátzcuaro.*" Distrito Federal, México: Secretaría de Educación Pública, Dirección General de Asuntos Indígenas.

Gamio, Manuel. 1924. "Posibilidades del arte indígena en México." *Boletín de la Unión Panamericana*. Washington, D.C.

———. 1925. "El aspecto utilitario del folclore. The Utilitarian Aspect of Folklore." *Mexican Folkways* 1(1): 7–9.

———. 1960 [1916]. *Forjando Patria*. Distrito Federal, México: Porrúa.

García Canclini, Néstor. 1985. *Notas sobre las máscaras, danzas y fiestas de Michoacán*. Morelia, Michoacán: Comite Editorial de Gobierno de Michoacán.

———. 1993. *Transforming Modernity: Popular Culture in Mexico [Las Culturas populares en el capitalismo]*. Austin: University of Texas Press.

———. 1995. *Hybrid Cultures: Strategies for Entering and Leaving Modernity [Culturas Híbridas]*. Minneapolis, Minn.: University of Minneapolis Press.

———. 1996. "Modernity after Postmodernity." In *Beyond the Fantastic: Contemporary Art Criticism from Latin America*, edited by Gerardo Mosquera, 20–52. Cambridge, Mass.: MIT Press.

———. 2008. "Policies for Cultural Creativity" *Power of Culture*. http://www.powerof-culture.nl/uk/archive/commentary/canclini.html.

García Contreras, Manuel, coordinador general. 1986. *Católogo de danzas y fiestas de Michoacán*. Morelia, Michoacán : Comité Editorial del Gobierno de Michoacán.

García Mora, Carlos. 1997. "Étnias y lenguas en Charapan: consideraciones Purepechistas. In *Lengua y etnohistoria P'urépecha: Homenaje á Benedict Warren*, edited by C. Paredes Martínez, 40–63. Morelia, Michoacán: La Universidad Michoacana de San Nicolás de Hidalgo.

Garduño Argueta, Jaime. 2000. "Disneylandia." *La Jornada*, 15 March 2000.

Garland, Peter. 1991. *In Search of Silvestre Revueltas: Essays 1978–1990*. Santa Fe, N. Mex.: Soundings Press.

Garza, José. 2000. "La memoria indígena continúa inquebrantable y reproduce tradiciones y costumbres: Florescano." *La Jornada*, 10 February 2000.

Geertz, Clifford. 1988. *Works and Lives. The Anthropologist as Author*. Stanford, Calif.: Stanford University Press.

Gellner, Ernest. 1964. *Thought and Change*. London: Weidenfeld and Nicholson.

———. 1983. *Nations and Nationalism*. Oxford: Basil Blackwell.

Giddens, Anthony. 1990. *The Consequences of Modernity*. Cambridge: Cambridge University Press.

Gitlin, Todd. 1980. *The Whole World Is Watching: Mass Media in the Making and Unmaking of the New Left*. Berkeley, Calif., Los Angeles, Calif., & London: University of California Press.

Gledhill, John. 1993. "Michoacán is Different?: Neoliberalism, Neocardenismo and the Hegemonic Process." In *Mexico: Dilemmas of Transition*, edited by Neil Harvey, 91–117. London and New York: The Institute of Latin American Studies and British Academic Press.

Goertzen, Chris. 1997. *Fiddling for Norway: Revival and Identity*. Chicago and London: University of Chicago Press.

Goffman, Irving. 1974. *Frame Analysis: An Essay on the Organization of Experience*. New York: Harper & Row.

Gómez Bravo, Lucas, Ireneo Rojas Hernández, and Felipe Chávez Cervantes. 1987. *Pirekuecha*. Morelia, Michoacán: La Universidad Michoacana de San Nicolás de Hidalgo.

Gómez-Peña, Guillermo. 2004. " 'Culturas-in-Extremis' Performing Against the Cultural Backdrop of the Mainstream Bizarre." In *The Performance Studies Reader*, edited by Henry Bial, 345–56. London and New York: Routledge.

González, Carlos. 1925. "La ceremonía de la ofrenda a los difuntos en el cementerio de la isla de Janitzio, la noche del primer al segundo de noviembre." *Ethnos* 3a. época, 11–16.

———. 1928a. "The Cemetery at Night" and "El Cementerio de Noche" [photos] *Mexican Folkways* 4(1): 66–67.

———. 1928b. "The Dance of the Moors—*La Danza de los Moros*." *Mexican Folkways* 4(1): 31–36.

González, Luis. 1981. *Los días del presidente Cárdenas. Historia de la revolución mexicana. Período 1934–40*. Distrito Federal, México: El Colegio de México.

González Navarro, Moisés. 1970. "*Mestizaje* in Mexico during the National Period." In *Race and Class in Latin America*, edited by Magnus Mörner, 145–69. New York: Columbia University Press.

Gostkowski, Gustave. 1900. *Au Mexique: Études, notes et renseignements utiles au capitalistes, à l'immigrant, et au touriste*. Paris: Maurice de Brunoff.

Grau, Andrée. 1998. *Dance*. London and New York: Dorling Kindersley.

Greenwood, Davydd. 1977. "Culture by the Pound: An Anthropological Perspective on Tourism as Cultural Commoditization." In *Hosts and Guests: The Anthropology of Tourism*, edited by Valene Smith, 37–52. Philadelphia: University of Pennsylvania Press.

Gutiérrez, Natividad. 1999. *Nationalist Myths and Ethnic Identities: Indigenous Intellectuals and the Mexican State.* Lincoln, Neb. and London: University of Nebraska Press.

Guzmán Gomez, Alba. 1991. *Voces indígenas: educación bilingüe bicultural en México.* Distrito Federal, México: Dirección General de Publicaciones del Consejo Nacional para la Cultura y las Artes, Instituto Nacional Indigenista.

Guzmán A., José Napoleón. 1985. *Francisco J. Mújica. Semblanza de un revolucionario Michoacano.* Morelia, Michoacán: Gobierno del Estado de Michoacán-Departamento de Investigaciones Históricas de la Universidad Michoacana de San Nicolás de Hidalgo.

Hagedorn, Katherine J. 2001. *Divine Utterances: The Performance of Afro-Cuban Santería.* Washington, D.C.: Smithsonian Institution Press.

"Hanover 2000: de pinxi, the Belgian specialist in interactive experiences, has created the two key attractions of the Mexican Pavilion." Press Release, de pinxi. Brussels, 5 June 2000.

Harker, David. 1985. *Fakesong: The Manufacture of British 'Folksong' 1700 to the Present Day.* Milton Keynes: Open University Press.

Harris, Max. 2000. *Aztecs, Moors and Christians.* Austin: University of Texas Press.

Hayes, Joy Elizabeth. 2006. "National Imaginings on the Air: Radio in Mexico, 1920–1950." In *The Eagle and the Virgin: Nation and Cultural Revolution in Mexico, 1920–1940,* edited by Mary Kay Vaughan and Stephen Lewis, 243–58. Durham, N.C. and London: Duke University Press.

Hellier, Ruth. 1999a. "La Corona: símbolo de un 'cargo,' cerveza y flores. La tradición en La Pacanda." *Piel de Tierra* 3: 7–8.

———. 1999b. "Los Sombrereros de Jarácuaro." *Úkata, revista del arte popular michoacano* 3(23): 5–6.

———. 2001a. "Removing the Mask: La Danza de los Viejitos in Post-Revolution Mexico, 1920–1940." Unpublished Doctoral Thesis: University of Central England.

———. 2001b. "Viva el mariachi: migration and musicians in Michoacán, Mexico." *Latin American Music Seminar.* University of London. Institute of Latin American Studies.

Hellier-Tinoco, Ruth. 2003a "Experiencing People: Relationships, Responsibility and Reciprocity." *British Journal of Ethnomusicology* 12(1): 19–34.

———. 2003b. "Review Essay: Special Feature: New Books and Compact Discs in Mexican Music." *British Journal of Ethnomusicology* 12(2): 107–15.

———. 2004. "Power Needs Names: Hegemony, Folklorisation and the *Viejitos* Dance of Michoacán, Mexico." In *Music, Power and Politics,* edited by Annie J. Randall, 47–64. London and New York: Routledge.

———. 2005. "Becoming-in-the-World-with-Others: Inter-Act Theatre Workshop." *Research in Drama Education: Special Edition on Ethics* 10(2): 159–73.

———. 2006. Review of *¡Llegaron Los Camperos!—Concert Favorites of Nati Cano's Mariachi Los Camperos* and *Aztec Dances—Xavier Quijas Yxayotl.* In *World of Music* 48(1): 159–61.

———. 2009a. "Dead Bodies/Live Bodies: Myths, Memory and Resurrection in Contemporary Mexican Performance." In *Performance, Embodiment and Cultural Memory,* edited by Colin Counsell and Roberta Mock, 114–39. Newcastle: Cambridge Scholars Publishing.

———. 2009b. "Mexico, But Not Mariachi." *Classroom Music,* Rhinegold Publishing. London. Autumn Term 2, 2009/10.

———. 2010a. Book Review of *Sounds of the Modern Nation: Music, Culture, and Ideas in Post-Revolutionary Mexico* by Alejandro L. Madrid. In *Ethnomusicology* 54 (1): 141–46.

———. 2010b. "Corpo/Reality, Living-Dead, and Voyeurs: Night of the Dead on the island of Janitzio, Mexico." *Performance Research* (*Memento Mori*) 15 (1): 23–31.

————. 2010c. "Saludos de México (el auténtico)!: postales, anuncios espectaculares, turismo y cuerpos actuantes." *Fractal* 47: 79–98.

————. (forthcoming) *Performing Memories, Myths, and Histories: Contemporary Theatre and Performance in Mexico*. Bristol and Portland: Intellect Books.

Hellmer, José Raul. 1963. *La Música tradicional en Michoacán*: Vol. III. Folklore Mexicano. Recordings by José Raul Hellmer 1953–63. Revised and rereleased by CENIDIM. Notes with cassette. Distrito Federal, México: CENIDIM.

————. 1990. "La música mexicana indígena hoy" and "La música mestiza." *Heterofonía*. 2–3(21): 62–67. [original published in English 1960].

Henson, James. 1999. "The Color of Money: Race, Ideology and Foreign Enterprise in Postrevolutionary Mexico." *Sincronía* (web journal of University of Guadalajara) Summer/Verano 1999.

Hernández C., Maria Magdalena, and Alma Ruth Rojas A. 1982. *Jarácuaro*. Morelia, Michoacán: Consejo Nacional para la Cultura y las Artes, Culturas Populares.

Hernández Rincón, Federico, and Hiram Dordelly. 1986. *Sones para violín: material didáctico para la enseñanza de la primera a la cuarta posiciones*. Distrito Federal, México: INBA and CENIDIM.

Hershfield, Joanne. 2006. "Screening the Nation." In *The Eagle and the Virgin: Nation and Cultural Revolution in Mexico, 1920–1940*, edited by Mary Kay Vaughan and Stephen Lewis, 259–78. Durham, N.C. and London: Duke University Press.

Herz, May. *Day of the Dead. El Día de Muertos. How We Celebrate It Today, History and Origins*. www.inside-mexico.com/featuredead. Accessed 20 April 2010.

Hobsbawm, Eric. 1990. *Nations and Nationalism since 1780: Programme, Myth, Reality*. Cambridge and New York: Cambridge University Press.

Hobsbawm, Eric, and Terence O. Ranger, eds. 1983. *The Invention of Tradition*. Cambridge: Cambridge University Press.

Hutchinson, Syndey. 2009. "Introduction." *Journal of American Folklore* 122(486): 378–90.

Hyde, Alan. 1997. *Bodies of Law*. Princeton, N.J.: Princeton University Press.

Ibargüengoitia, Jorge. 1998. *Instrucciones para vivir en México*. Distrito Federal, México: Joaquín Mortíz.

Ibarra, Jr., Alfredo. 1952. "Los viejitos." *Orientación musical: revista mensual de cultura artística* 10: 122–123.

Israde, Yanireth. 2000. "El folklore mexicano, de luto por Amalia Hernández." *La Jornada*, 5 November 2000.

Jabbour, Alan. 1993. "Foreword." In *Transforming Tradition: Folk Music Revivals Examined*, edited by N. Rosenberg, xi –xiii. Urbana and Chicago: University of Illinois Press.

Jacinto Zavala, Agustín. 1988. *Mitología y modernización*. Zamora, Michoacán: El Colegio de Michoacán.

————. 1996. "Tarecuato: Tradición oral versus modernización." In *Estudios Michoacanos VI*, edited by Augstín Jacinto Zavala, 88–110. Zamora, Michoacán: El Colegio de Michoacán.

Jacinto Zavala, Agustín, and Álvaro Ochoa Serrano, co-ords. 1995. *Tradición e identidad en la cultura mexicana*. Zamora, Michoacán: El Colegio de Michoacán y CONACYT.

Jauss, Hans Robert. 1982. *Toward an Aesthetic of Reception*. Translated by Timothy Bahti. Minneapolis: University of Minnesota Press.

Johnston, Edith. 1935. *Regional Dances of Mexico*. Dallas, Tex.: Banks Upshaw and Company.

Joseph, Gilbert, and Timothy J. Henderson, eds. 2002. *The Mexico Reader*. Durham, N.C. and London: Duke University Press.

Joseph, Gilbert, and Daniel Nugent. 1994. *Everyday Forms of State Formation: Revolution and the Negotiation of Rule in Modern Mexico*. Durham, N.C.: Duke University Press.

Joseph, Gilbert, Anne Rubenstein, and Eric Zolov. 2001. *Fragments of a Golden Age: The Politics of Culture in Mexico Since 1940*. Durham, N.C. and London: Duke University Press.

Kaeppler, Adrienne L. 1977. "Polynesian Dance as 'Airport Art.'" In *Asian and Pacific Dance: Selected Papers from the CORD Conference and SEM Conference*, 1974 CORD Annual 8: 74–84. New York: Committee for Research on Dance.

Kamenetsky, Christa. 1972. "Folklore as Political Tool in Nazi Germany." *Journal of American Folklore* 85(337): 221–236.

Keen, Benjamin. 1996. *A History of Latin America*. Boston: Houghton Mifflin Company.

Kemper, Robert V. 1979. "Tourism in Taos and Pátzcuaro: A Comparison of two Approaches to Regional Development." *Annals of Tourism Research* 6(1): 91–110.

———. 2001. "Tourism in MesoAmerica." In *The Oxford Encyclopedia of Mesoamerican Cultures*, edited by David Carrasco, volume 3: 250–2. New York: Oxford University Press.

Kirshenblatt-Gimblett, Barbara. 1998. *Destination Culture: Tourism, Museums, and Heritage*. Berkeley and Los Angeles: University of California Press.

Kirshenblatt-Gimblett, Barbara and Edward M. Bruner. 1992. "Tourism." In *Folklore, Cultural Performances, and Popular Entertainments*, edited by Richard Bauman, 300–307. New York and Oxford: Oxford University Press.

Knight, Alan. 1990. "Racism, Revolution and Indigenismo." In *The Idea of Race in Latin America*, edited by R. Graham, 71–113. Austin: University of Texas Press.

———. 1994a. "Peasants into Patriots: Thoughts on the Making of the Mexican Nation." *Mexican Studies/Estudios Mexicanos* 10(1): 135–61.

———. 1994b. "Popular Culture and the Revolutionary State in Mexico, 1910–1940." *Hispanic American Historical Review* 74(3): 393–444.

Krauze, Enrique. 1997. *Mexico: Biography of Power, A History of Modern México, 1810–1996*. Trans. Hank Heifetz. New York: HarperPerennial.

Kuri-Aldana, Mario. 1975. *Danzas de la region lacustre del estado de Michoacán* Vol. 1. Collección: Música de las danzas y bailes populares de México. Distrito Federal, México: FONADAN, SEP. 8 pp. booklet.

Kuss, Malena, ed. 2004. *Music in Latin America and the Caribbean: An Encyclopedic History, Volume 1, Performing Beliefs: Indigenous Peoples of South America, Central America and Mexico*. Austin: University of Texas Press.

"La cacería del pato en el lago de Pátzcuaro." 1925. *Ethnos* 3a Epoca, 1 (5): 126–128.

Lau, Frederick. 1996. "Forever Red: The Invention of Solo *Dizi* Music in Post-1949 China." *British Journal of Ethnomusicology* 5: 113–131.

Lavalle Josefina. 1988. *El Jarabe…el jarabe ranchero o jarabe de Jalisco*. Distrito Federal, México: INBA and Centro Nacional de Investigación, Documentación e Información de la Danza "José Limón."

Lehmann, Hans-Thies. 2006. *Postdramatic Theatre*. Trans. Karen Jürs-Munby. London: Routledge.

León M., F. Adrian, and Hilario Contreras. 1944. "Pastorela de viejos (Para el año de 1912)." *Tlalocan* 1(3): 169–93.

León, Nicolás. 1890. "Anomalías y mutilaciones étnicas del sistema dentario entre los Tarascos pre-colombinos." *Anales del Museo Michoacano* 3: 168–73.

———. 1904. *Los Tarascos: Notas históricas étnicas y antropológicas*. Distrito Federal, México: Museo Nacional de México.

———— 1934. "Los indios Tarascos del Lago de Pátzcuaro." *Anales del Museo Nacional*, 5a. Epoca. 1–1. México: Museo Nacional de Arqueología, Historia y Etnografía, 149–68.

Lévi-Strauss, Claude. 1982. *The Way of the Masks*. Seattle: University of Washington Press.

Lewis, Stephen E. 2006. "The Nation, Education, and the 'Indian Problem' in Mexico, 1920–1940." In *The Eagle and the Virgin: Nation and Cultural Revolution in Mexico, 1920–1940*, edited by Mary Kay Vaughan and Stephen Lewis, 176–95. Durham, N.C. and London: Duke University Press.

Llano, Enrique and Marcel de Clerck. 1939. *Danses indiennes du Mexique*. Bruxelles: Marcel Hayez.

Lomnitz, Claudio. 2001. *Deep Mexico, Silent Mexico: An Anthropology of Nationalism*. Minneapolis, M.N.: University of Minnesota Press.

————. 2005. *Death and the Idea of Mexico*. Brooklyn, N.Y.: Zone Books.

Londré, Felicia Hardison, and Daniel J Watermeier. 2000. *The History of North American Theater: The United States, Canada, and Mexico: from Pre-Columbian Times to the Present*. New York: Continuum.

López, Rick. 2006. "The Noche Mexicana and the Exhibition of Popular Arts: Two Ways of Exalting Indianness." In *The Eagle and the Virgin: Nation and Cultural Revolution in Mexico, 1920–1940*, edited by Mary Kay Vaughan and Stephen Lewis, 23–42. Durham, N.C. and London: Duke University Press.

López Castro, Gustavo. ed. 1988. *Migración en el occidente de México*. Zamora, Michoacán: El Colegio de Michoacán.

Los viejitos: danza del estado (n.d.) Morelia, Michoacán: Secretaría de Educación Pública: Dirección de Asuntos Indígenas.

Los viejitos: danza regional del estado de Michoacán. (n.d.) Morelia, Michoacán: Escuela Secundaria Técnica No. 16, Morelia.

Loza, Steven. 2006. "Challenges to the Euroamericentric Ethnomusicological Canon: Alternative Tools for Graduate Readings, Theory and Method." *Ethnomusicology* 50(2): 360–371.

Lumholtz, Carl. 1904. *Unknown Mexico*. New York: Charles Scribner's Sons.

————. 1945. *El México desconocido. Cinco años de exploración entre las tribus de la Sierra Madre Occidental, en la Tierra Caliente de Tepic y Jalisco, y entre los tarascos de Michoacán*. México: Ediciones Culturales de Publicaciones Herreras/Editoral Nacional, Tomo II.

MacAloon, John. 1995. "Interval Training." In *Choreographing History*, edited by S. Foster, 32–53. Bloomington: Indiana University Press.

MacCannell, Dean. 1973. "Staged Authenticity: Arrangements of Social Space in Tourist Settings." *American Journal of Sociology* 79(3): 589–603.

————. 1984. "Reconstructed ethnicity, tourism, and cultural identity in third world communities." *Annals of Tourism Research* 11(3): 375–391.

————. 1992. *Empty Meeting Grounds. The Tourist Papers*. London and New York: Routledge.

————. 1999. *The Tourist: A New Theory of the Leisure Class*. Berkeley: University of California Press.

————. 2001. "Remarks on the Commodification of Cultures." In *Hosts and Guests Revisited: Tourism Issues of the 21st Century*, edited by V. Smith and M. Brent, 380–90. New York: Cognizant Communication Corporation.

Madrid, Alejandro, L. 2009. *Sounds of the Modern Nation: Music, Culture, and Ideas in Post-Revolutionary Mexico*. Philadelphia: Temple University Press.

Manuel, Peter. 1989. "Andalusian, Gypsy and Class Identity in the Contemporary Flamenco Complex." *Ethnomusicology* 33(1): 47–65.

Marinetti, Filippo Tommaso, Emilio Settimelli, and Bruno Corra, 1995 [1915]. "The Futurist Synthetic Theatre." In *Twentieth Century Theatre: A Sourcebook*, edited by Richard Drain, 19–22. London and New York: Routledge.

Márquez Joaquín, Pedro. 1997. "Problemas de traducción en textos del siglo XVI." In *Lengua y etnohistoria P'urépecha: Homenaje á Benedict Warren*. Carlos Paredes Martínez, coord, 218–30. Morelia, México: La Universidad Michoacana de San Nicolás de Hidalgo.

Martínez, Rubén. 2001. "Corazón del Rocanrol." In *Fragments of a Golden Age: The Politics of Culture in Mexico Since 1940*, edited by Gilbert Joseph, Anne Rubenstein, and Eric Zolov, 373–414. Durham, N.C. and London: Duke University Press.

Maturo, Carol. 2008. "Visual Communication: Props and Costume." In *José Limón and La Malinche: The Dancer and the Dance*, edited by Patricia Seed, 55–78. Austin: University of Texas Press.

Mayer-Serra, Otto. 1941a. *Panorama de la música mexicana desde la Independencia hasta la actualidad*. Distrito Federal, México: El Colegio de México.

———. 1941b. "Silvestre Revueltas and Musical Nationalism in Mexico". *The Musical Quarterly* 27: 123–45.

———. 1941c. "Silvestre Revueltas y el nacionalismo musical en México." *Boletín Latino Americano de Música* V/V.: 543–46.

———. 1960. *The Present State of Music in Mexico, El estado presente de la musica en México*. Washington, D.C.: Pan-American Union, [Spanish and English].

Medina, Guillermo A. 1986. *CREFAL: presencia y acción en américa latina y el caribe*. Pátzcuaro, Michoacán: CREFAL.

Memoria de Gestión. http://www.sep.gob.mx/wb2/sep/sep_4409_antecedentes (accessed April 2008).

Mendieta y Núñez, Lucio. 1940. *Los Tarascos: monografía, história, etnográfica y económica*. Distrito Federal, México: Instituto de Investigaciones Sociales, UNAM.

Mendoza, Moisés. 1937. "Las danzas populares de México." *El Nacional*, 1 October.

———. 1939. "Danzantes indígenas en el palacio de bellas artes." *El Nacional*, 28 July.

Mendoza, Vicente T. 1956. *Panorama de la música tradicional en México*. Distrito Federal, México: Instituto de Investigaciones Estéticas, UNAM.

Mendoza, Zoila. S. 1998. "Defining Folklore: Mestizo and Indigenous Identities on the Move." *Bulletin of Latin American Research* 17(2): 165–83.

———. 2000. *Shaping Society Through Dance: Mestizo Ritual Performance in the Peruvian Andes*. Chicago and London: University of Chicago Press.

———. 2008. *Creating our Own: Folklore, Performance, and Identity in Cuzco, Peru*. Durham, N.C.: Duke University Press.

Mendoza-Walker, Zoila. 1994. "Contesting Identities Through Dance: Mestizo Performance in the Southern Andes of Peru." *Repercussions: Critical Alternative Viewpoints Music Scholarship* 3(2): 50–80.

Mexican Life: Mexico's Monthly Review. 1943. Vol. 19.

Meyer, M. 1995. "Dance and the Politics of Orality: A Study of the Irish *Scoil Rince*." *Dance Research Journal* 27(1): 25–39.

Meyer, Michael C., William L. Sherman, and Susan M. Deeds. 1999. *The Course of Mexican History*. New York: Oxford University Press.

Michel, Concha. 1932. "Pastorela o coloquio." *Mexican Folkways* 7(1): 5–30.

———. 1951. *Cantos indígenas de México*. Distrito Federal, México: Instituto nacional indgenista.

Michoacán: cómo y dónde. 2000. México: Guía México Desconocido.

Michoacán: lagos azules y fuertes montañas. 1992. México: Secretaría de Educación Pública.

Miller, Marilyn. 2004. *Rise and Fall of the Cosmic Race: The Cult of Mestizaje in Latin America.* Austin, Texas: University of Texas Press.

Modotti, Tina. 1928. "Bread of the Dead." *Mexican Folkways* 4(1): 64.

———. 1929. "Sobre fotografía." *Mexican Folkways* 5(4): 196–98.

Monsiváis, Carlos. 1987. "Muerte y resurrección del nacionalism mexicano." *Nexos* 109: 13–22.

———. 1995. *Los rituales del caos.* Distrito Federal, México: Ediciones ERA.

Mörner, Magnus. 1970. "Historical Research on Race Relations in Latin America during the National Period." In *Race and Class in Latin America*, edited by Magnus Mörner, 199–230. New York and London: Columbia University Press.

Morris, Stephen D. 1999. "Reforming the Nation: Mexican Nationalism in Context." *Journal of Latin American Studies* 31: 363–97.

Moser, Hans. 1962. "Vom Folklorismus in unserer Zeit." In *Zeitschrift für Volkskunde 58.* S. 177–209.

———. 1964. "Der Folklorismus als Forschungsproblem der Volkskunde." In *Hessische Blätter für Volkskunde 55.* S. 9–57.

Mosk, Sanford A. 1950. *Industrial Revolution in Mexico.* Berkeley, Calif.: University of California.

Moya Rubiok, Victor José. 1978. *Máscara: la otra cara de México.* Distrito Federal, México: UNAM.

Mulvey, Laura. 1975. "Visual Pleasure and Narrative Cinema." *Screen* 16(3): 6–18.

Nagel, Joane. 1994. "Constructing Ethnicity: Creating and Recreating Ethnic Identity and Culture." *Social Problems* 41(1): 152–76.

Nash, Dennison. 1996. *Anthropology of Tourism.* New York: Pergamon.

Nash, June C. 1997. "When Isms become Wasms." *Critique of Anthropology* 17(1): 11–32.

———. 2001. *Mayan Visions: The Quest for Autonomy in an Age of Globalization.* New York and London: Routledge.

Nava López, E. Fernando. 1991. "La clasificación de un campo semántico de creación humana: la música." *Anales de Antropología* 28: 409–36.

———. 1993. "Expresiones P'urhépechas del canto." *Anales de Antropología* 30: 409–32.

———. 1998. "Musical traditions of the P'urhépecha (Tarascos) of Michoacán, Mexico." Unpublished manuscript.

———. 1999. *El campo semántico del sonido musical P'urhépecha.* Distrito Federal, México: Instituto Nacional de Antropología e Historia.

———. 2004. "Musical Traditions of the P'urhépecha (Tarascos) of Michoacán." In *Music in Latin America and the Caribbean: An Encyclopedic History, Volume 1, Performing Beliefs: Indigenous Peoples of South America, Central America and Mexico*, edited by Malena Kuss, 247–60. Austin: University of Texas Press.

Ness, Sally Ann. 1992. *Body, Movement and Culture: Kinesthetic and Visual Symbolism in a Philippine Community.* Philadelphia: University of Pennsylvania Press.

Nettl, Bruno. 1978. "Persian Classical Music in Tehran: The Processes of Change." In *Eight Urban Musical Cultures*, edited by B. Nettl, 146–85. Urbana: University of Illinois Press.

———. 1985. *The Western Impact on World Music: Change, Adaptation and Survival.* New York: Schirmer Books.

Noble, John. 1995. *Mexico (A Travel Survival Kit).* Victoria, Australia: Lonely Planet Publications.

———. 2006. *Mexico (Country Guide).* Victoria, Australia: Lonely Planet Publications.

Nolasco Armas, Margarita. 1970. "La antropología aplicada en México y su destino final: el indigenismo." In *De eso que llaman antropología mexicana*, edited by Arturo Warman, 66–93. Distrito Federal, México: Editorial Nuestro Tiempo.

Novack Cynthia J. 1995. "The Body's Endeavors as Cultural Practices." In *Choreographing History*, edited by S. Foster, 177–84. Bloomington: Indiana University Press.

Núñez y Domínguez, José de J. 1927. "El 'Corpus' en mi tierra." *Mexican Folkways* 3(4): 191–202.

Nuñez, Theron. 1963. "Tourism, Tradition, and Acculturation: Weekendismo in a Mexican Village." *Ethnology* 2: 347–52.

Ochoa, Álvaro, and Herón Pérez. 2001. *Cancionero michoacano 1830–1940. Canciones, cantos, coplas y corridos*. Zamora, Michoacán: El Colegio de Michoacán.

Ogazon, Estela. 1981. *Máscaras mexicanas*. Distrito Federal, México: Museo Universitario de Ciencias y Arte, UNAM.

Olsen, Patrice Elizabeth. 1997. "Issues of National Identity: Obregón, Calles and Nationalist Architecture, 1920–1930." *Sincronía* An E-Journal of Culture Studies from the University of Guadalajara. Spring/Primavera 1997.

O'Malley, Ilene. 1993. *The Myth of the Revolution: Hero Cults and the Institutionalisation of the Mexican State, 1920–1940*. New York: Greenwood Press.

Onstott, Jane. 2001. *National Geographic Traveler: Mexico*. Washington, D.C.: National Geographic Society.

———. 2006. *National Geographic Traveler: Mexico*. Second Edition. Washington, D.C.: National Geographic Society.

Ortiz Monasterio, Leonor. 1985. "Prólogo." In *Zacán: renacimiento de una tradición*, edited by Jesús Bugarini, 5–12. Morelia, Michoacán: Instituto Michoacano de Cultura, Gobierno del Estado de Michoacán.

Paredes, Américo. 2001 [1982]. "Folklore, *Lo mexicano*, and the Proverb." In *The Chicano Studies Reader: An Anthology of Aztlán, 1970–2000*, edited by Chon Noriega, Karen Mary Davalos, Chela Sandoval, Rafael Pérez-Torres, and Eric R. Ávila, 271–280. Los Angeles, Calif.: UCLA Chicano Studies Research Center Publications.

Parfit, Michael (text) and David Alan Harvey (photographs). 1996. "Emerging Mexico: Bright with Promise, Tangled in the Past." *National Geographic: Special Issue: Emerging Mexico* 190(2): 7–23.

Paz, Octavio. 1972 [1950]. *El laberinto de la soledad*. New York: Grove Press.

———. 1985. *The Labyrinth of Solitude, The Other Mexico, and Other Essays*. New York: Grove Press.

Pegg, Carol. 1995. "Ritual, Religion and Magic in West Mongolian (Oirad) Heroic Epic Performance." *British Journal of Ethnomusicology* 4: 77–99.

Pérez-González, Benjamin. 1997. "El proyecto tarasco. Antecedentes y trascendencia." In *Lengua y etnohistoria P'urépecha: Homenaje á Benjamin Warren*, Carlos Paredes Martínez, coord. 264–272. Morelia, Michoacán: La Universidad Michoacana de San Nicolás de Hidalgo.

Phelan, Peggy. 1993. *Unmarked: The Politics of Performance*. London: Routledge.

———. 1995. "Thirteen Ways of Looking at Choreographing Writing." In *Choreographing History*, edited by S. Foster, 200–210. Bloomington: Indiana University Press.

Pietri, Anne-Lise, and René Pietri, 1976. *Empleo y migración en la región de Pátzcuaro*. Distrito Federal, México: Instituto Nacional Indigenista.

Pilcher, Jeffery M. 1998. *¡Que vivan los tamales! Food and the Making of Mexican Identity*. Albuquerque: University of New Mexico Press.

————. 2001. "Mexico's Pepsi Challenge: Traditional Cooking, Mass Consumption, and National Identity." In *Fragments of a Golden Age: The Politics of Culture in Mexico Since 1940*, edited by Gilbert Joseph, Anne Rubenstein, and Eric Zolov, 71–90. Durham, N.C. and London: Duke University Press.

Pi-Sunyer, Oriol, R. Brooke Thomas, and Magalí Daltabuit. 2001. "Tourism on the Maya Periphery." In *Hosts and Guests Revisited: Tourism Issues of the 21st Century*, edited by V. Smith and M. Brent, 122–40 New York: Cognizant Communication Corporation.

Poniatowska, Elena. 2001. "Foreword." In *Fragments of a Golden Age: The Politics of Culture in Mexico Since 1940*, edited by Gilbert Joseph, Anne Rubenstein, and Eric Zolov, i–vx. Durham, N.C. and London: Duke University Press.

————. 2007. *La noche de Tlatelolco: testimonios de historia oral*. Distrito Federal, México: Ediciones Era.

Pool, Stafford. 1995. *Our Lady of Guadalupe. The Origins and Sources of a Mexican National Symbol 1531–1797*. Tuscon and London: The University of Arizona Press.

Poole, D. A. 1990. "Accommodation and Resistance in Andean Ritual Dance." *Drama Review* 34(2): 98–126.

"Presentación." 1990. Foreword to *La población indígena de México*, by Carlos Basauri, 9–10. Distrito Federal, México: Secretaría de Educación Pública [no author stated].

Programa nacional de desarrollo de los pueblos indígenas, 1991–1994. 1990. Distrito Federal, México: Instituto Nacional Indigenista.

Próspero Román, Salvador. 1987a. *La música p'urhépecha de michoacán (La orquesta de quinceo: juan crisóstomo valdés y francisco salmerón equihua)*. Morelia, Michoacán: Universidad Michoacana de San Nicolás de Hidalgo.

————. 1987b. *La música y sus manifestaciones en la cultura P'urhépecha*. Morelia, Michoacán: Universidad Michoacana de San Nicolás de Hidalgo.

Pruneda, Alfonso. 1951. "Preliminar." In *Cantos indígenas de México*, by Concha Michel, 7–8. Distrito Federal, México: Instituto Nacional Indgenista.

Puig Casauranc, J.M. 1928. "Notas." In *El folklore y la música mexicana: investigación acerca de la cultura musical en México (1525–1925)*, Ruben M. Campos, no page. Distrito Federal, México: Secretaría de Educación Pública.

Rabkin, George. 1985. " 'Is There a Text on This Stage?' Theatre/Authorship/Interpretation." *Performing Arts Journal* 26(7): 142–59.

Ramírez Gil, Felipe. 1989. "El contorno melódico como elemento esencial de análisis: su aplicación en la Pirekua." *Relaciones: Estudios de Historia y Sociedad* 38: 77–88.

Ramos, Samuel. 1998 [1934]. *El perfil del hombre y la cultura en México*. Distrito Federal, México: Colección Austral.

Ramsey, Kate. 1997. "Vodou, Nationalism, and Performance: The Staging of Folklore in Mid-Twentieth-Century Haiti." In *Meaning in Motion: New Cultural Studies of Dance*, edited by Jane C. Desmond, 345–78. Durham, N.C.: Duke University Press.

Redfield, Robert. 1942. "La sociedad folk." *Revista Mexicana de Sociología* 4(4): 13–41.

————. 1947. "The Folk Society." *The American Journal of Sociology* 52(4): 293–308.

Reed, Susan A. 1998. "The Politics and Poetics of Dance." *Annual Review of Anthropology* 27: 503–32.

Reily, Suzel Ana. 1994. "Macunaíma's Music: National Identity and Ethnomusicological Research in Brazil." In *Ethnicity, Identity and Music. The Musical Construction of Place*, edited by M. Stokes, 71–96. Oxford/Providence, R.I.: Berg.

Reyes Rocha, José, María Luisa Miaja Isaac, and Abelardo Torres Cortés. 1991. *La educación indígena en Michoacán*. Morelia, Michoacán: Gobierno del Estado, Instituto Michoacano de Cultura.

Rhodes, Robin. 1999. "The Mexican Indigenous Rights Movement: The Life and Rights of the Nahua of the Puebla Sierra." *Sincronía*. Otoño/Fall 1999.

Riveroll, Robert. 1947. *Mexican Dances*. Distrito Federal, México: Riveroll's Art Gallery.

Rodríguez, Olavo Alán. 1994. "The Afro-French Settlement and the Legacy of Its Music to the Cuban People." In *Music and Black Ethnicity: the Caribbean and South America*, edited by G. Béhague, 109–17. Miami: University of Miami.

Rodríguez, S. 1996. *The Matachines Dance: Ritual Symbolism and Interethnic Relations in the Upper Rio Grande Valley*. Albuquerque: University of New Mexico Press.

Rodríguez, Victoria Eli. 1994. "Cuban Music and Ethnicity: Historical Considerations." In *Music and Black Ethnicity: the Caribbean and South America*, edited by G. Béhague, 91–108. Miami: University of Miami.

Rodríguez Peña, Hilda. 1988. "La danza popular." In *La antropología en México. Panorama histórico*, edited by C. García Mora, Vol. 4, 336. Distrito Federal, México: Instituto Nacional de Antropología e Historia.

Romero Flores, Jesús. 1936a. *Costumbres típicas de Michoacán*. Distrito Federal, México: Departamento de las Bellas Artes, Sección de Música.

———. 1936b. *Michoacán histórico y legendario*. Distrito Federal, México: Talleres Gráficos del Museo Nacional de Arqueología, Historia y Etnografía.

———. 1938. *Leyendas y cuentos Michoacanos*. Distrito Federal, México: Ediciones Botas.

Roque, Ignacio. 2007. "Pátzcuaro y Janitzio reviven su tradicional 'Noche de Muertos.'" *La Crónica de Hoy*, 3 November 2007.

Roseberry, William. 1994. "Hegemony and the Language of Contention." In *Everyday Forms of State Formation: Revolution and the Negotiation of Rule in Modern Mexico*, edited by Gilbert Joseph and Daniel Nugent, 355–66. Durham, N.C.: Duke University Press.

Rosenberg, Neil V. ed. 1993. *Transforming Tradition: Folk Music Revivals Examined*. Urbana: University of Illinois Press.

Rowe, William, and Vivienne Schelling. 1991. *Memory and Modernity: Popular Culture in Latin America*. New York: Verso.

Royce, Anya Peterson. 1977. *The Anthropology of Dance*. Bloomington: Indiana University Press.

Saavedra, Rafael M. 1972. "Los viejitos." *El Sol de México*, 8 September 1972.

Sáenz, Moisés. 1928. "Las Escuelas Rurales y el progreso del indio. Rural Schools and the Progress of the *Indio*." *Mexican Folkways* 4(1): 73–5.

———. 1936. *Carapan: bosquejo de una experiencia*. Lima: Imprenta Gil.

Said, Edward. 2002. *Power, Politics, and Culture*. New York: Vintage Books.

Saldívar, Gabriel. 1937. *El Jarabe, baile popular mexicano*. Distrito Federal, México: Talleres Gráficos de la Nación.

Saldívar, Gabriel, and Elisa Osorio Bolio. 1934. *História de la música en México*. Distrito Federal, México: Secretaría de Educación Pública.

Sánchez, George. J. 1993. *Becoming Mexican American*. New York and Oxford: Oxford University Press.

Sánchez, Rosa Virginia. 1990. "Música impresa: *Sones para violin*." *Heterofonía* 102–103 (21): 92–3.

———. n.d. *Folklore Mexicano vol III* Cassette notes: 3. INI.

Sandburg, Carl. 1927. *The American Songbag*. New York: Harcourt, Brace and Company.

Sandoval Pérez, Margarito. 1998. *Arte y folklore en Mexican Folkways*. Distrito Federal, México: UNAM.

Saragoza, Alex. 2001. "The Selling of Mexico: Tourism and the State, 1929–1952." In *Fragments of a Golden Age: The Politics of Culture in Mexico Since 1940*, edited by Gilbert Joseph,

Anne Rubenstein, and Eric Zolov, 91–115. Durham, N.C. and London: Duke University Press.

Savigliano, Marta. 1995. *Tango and the Political Economy of Passion*. Boulder, Col.: Westview.

Sayer, Derek. 1994. "Everyday Forms of State Formation: Some Dissident Remarks on 'Hegemony.'" In *Everyday Forms of State Formation: Revolution and the Negotiation of Rule in Modern Mexico*, edited by Gilbert Joseph and Daniel Nugent, 367–77. Durham, N.C.: Duke University Press.

Scharrer Tomm, Beatriz. 1995. "Prólogo." *En el México indio*. Frederick Starr [1908] 9–25. Distrito Federal, México: CNCA, Dirección General de Publicaciones.

Schechner, Richard. 1988. *Performance Theory*. New York and London: Routledge.

——— 2002. *Performance Studies: An Introduction*. New York and London: Routledge.

Schmidt, Arthur. 2001. "Making It Real Compared To What? Reconceptualizing Mexican History Since 1940." In *Fragments of a Golden Age: The Politics of Culture in Mexico Since 1940*, edited by Gilbert Joseph, Anne Rubenstein, and Eric Zolov, 23–68. Durham, N.C.: Duke University Press.

Scott, James C. 1994. "Foreword." In *Everyday Forms of State Formation: Revolution and the Negotiation of Rule in Modern Mexico*, edited by Gilbert Joseph and Daniel Nugent, vii–xii. Durham, N.C.: Duke University Press.

Scruggs, T.M. 1999. "'Let's Enjoy as Nicaraguans': The Use of Music in the Construction of a Nicaraguan National Consciousness." *Ethnomusicology* 43(2): 297–321.

Scully, Michael and Virginia. 1933. *Motorists' Guide to Mexico*. Dallas, Tex.: Southwest Press.

Seeger, Anthony. 1994. "Whoever We Are Today, We Can Sing You a Song about It." In *Music and Black Ethnicity: the Caribbean and South America*, edited by G. Béhague, 1–15. Miami, Fla.: University of Miami.

Segre, Erica. 2005. "The Hermeneutics of the Veil in Mexican Photography: of *rebozos, sábanas, huipiles* and *lienzos de Verónica.*" *Hispanic Research Journal* 6(1): 39–65.

Sepúlveda, Maria Teresa. 1974. *Los cargos políticos y religiosos en la región del Lago de Pátzcuaro*. Distrito Federal, México: INAH.

Shay, Anthony. 2002. *Choreographic Politics*. Middletown, Conn.: Wesleyan University Press.

Slonimsky, Nicolas. 1946. *The Music of Latin America*. London: George Harrap and Co.

Sol, Máximo. 1938a. "El folklore en la literatura Mexicana." *Heraldo Michoacano*, 19 September 1938.

Solórzano, Armando and Raul G. Guerrero. 1941. "Ensayo para un estudio sobre la 'Danza de los Concheros de la Gran Tenochtitlán.'" *Boletín Latino Americano de Música. Instituto Interamericano de Musicología* 5(5): 449–76.

Spicer, Edward. 1965. "La danza yaqui del venado en la cultura mexicana." *América Indígena* 25(1): 117–39.

Standish, Peter, and Steven Bell. 2004. *Customs and Culture of Mexico*. Santa Barbara, Calif.: Greenwood Press.

Stanford, Thomas. 1972. "The Mexican Son." *Yearbook of the International Folk Music Council* 4: 66–85.

Starr, Frederick. 1908. *In Indian Mexico: A Narrative of Travel and Labor*. Chicago: Ferbes and Company.

——— . 1928. "Fishermen Malsing Nets. Island of Janitchio, Mich" [photo]. *Mexican Folkways* 4(1): 5.

——— . 1995. *En el México indio*. Distrito Federal, México: Consejo Nacional para la Cultura y la Artes/ Dirección General de Publicaciones.

Stavenhagen, Rodolfo. 1979. *Problemas étnicos y campesinos*. Distrito Federal, México: Consejo Nacional para la Cultura y la Artes/Instituto Nacional Indigenista.

Stern, Steve. 1995. *The Secret History of Gender: Women, Men, and Power in Late Colonial Mexico*. Chapel Hill: University of North Carolina Press.

Stevenson, Robert. 1999. "Music." In *Handbook of Latin American Studies* 56: 679–712.

Stokes, Martin. 1994. "Introduction: Ethnicity, Identity and Music." In *Ethnicity, Identity and Music: The Musical Construction of Place*, edited by Martin Stokes, 1–27. Oxford: Berg.

Taylor, Diana. 2003. *The Archive and the Repertoire: Performing Cultural Memory in the Americas*. Durham, N.C. and London: Duke University Press.

Taylor, Jane. 1987. "Tango." *Cultural Anthropology* 2(4): 481–93.

Tenorio-Trillo, Mauricio. 1996. *Mexico at the World's Fairs: Crafting a Modern Nation*. Berkeley and Los Angeles: University of California Press.

Terry, T. Philip. 1935. *Terry's Guide to Mexico*. Boston: Houghton Mifflin.

Toor, Frances. 1925. "The Festival of the Dead." *Mexican Folkways* 1(2): 17–22.

———. 1928. "Noticias de los pueblos." *Mexican Folkways* 4(1): 65–70.

———. 1929. "El uso actual de las máscaras—The present day use of masks." *Mexican Folkways* 5(1): 127–31.

———. 1930. "Notas sobre las Canacuas." *Mexican Folkways* 6(3): 108.

———. 1931. *El cancionero Mexicano*. Publisher unknown.

———. 1938. *Frances Toor's Motorist Guide to Mexico*. Mexico City: Frances Toor Studios.

———. c 1944. *New Guide to Mexico*. New York: R.M. McBride and Company.

———. 1947. *A Treasury of Mexican Folkways*. Mexico City: Mexico Press.

Torreblanca, Marcelo. 1980. "*Danza de los viejitos: Estado de Michoacán*. Curso de Verano. Recopilación de datos históricos por el Prof. Marcelo Torreblanca E." Unpublished.

Tortajada Quiroz, Margarita. 1995. *Danza y poder*. Distrito Federal, México: INBA/Cenidi Danza.

———. 2000. *La danza escénica de la Revolución mexicana, nacionalista y vigorosa*. Distrito Federal, México: el Instituto Nacional de Estudios Históricos de la Revolución Mexicana.

Turino, Thomas. 1984. "The Urban-Mestizo Charango Tradition in Southern Peru: A Statement of Shifting Identity." *Ethnomusicology* 28(2): 252–70.

———. 1990. "Structure, Context and Strategy in Musical Ethnography." *Ethnomusicology* 34(3): 339–412.

———. 1993. *Moving Away from Silence: Music of the Peruvian Altiplano and the Experience of Urban Migration*. Chicago: University of Chicago Press.

Turner, Victor. 1982. *From Ritual to Theater*. New York: PAJ Publications.

Urry, John. 2002. *The Tourist Gaze: Leisure and Travel in Contemporary Societies*. London: Sage Publications.

Vargas Tentori, Alfredo. 1952. Thesis for UNAM-CREFAL. Pátzcuaro, Michoacán: CREFAL and Mision Cultural lacustre Num. 1 de la Secretaría de Educación Pública del Gobierno de México, con centro de operaciones en Janitzio.

Vasconcelos, José. 1926. "The Latin-American Basis of Mexican Civilization." In *Aspects of Mexican Civilization: Lectures of the Harris Foundation*, edited by J. Vasconcelos and Manuel Gamio, 3–102. Chicago: University of Chicago Press.

———. 1948 [1925]. *La raza cósmica: misión de la raza iberoamericana*. Paris: Agencia Mundial de Librería and Mexico, DF: Colección Austral, Espasa-Calpe Mexicana.

———. 1963. *José Vasconcelos, A Mexican Ulysses, An Autobiography*, trans. W. Rex Crawford. Bloomington: Indiana University Press.

Vaughan, Mary Kay. 1982. *The State, Education and Social Class in Mexico, 1880–1928*. DeKalb, Ill.: University of Northern Illinois Press.

―――. 1997. *Cultural Politics in Revolution: Teachers, Peasants, and Schools in Mexico, 1930–40*. Tucson: University of Arizona Press.

―――. 2001. "Transnational Processes and the Rise and Fall of the Mexican Cultural State: Notes from the Past." In *Fragments of a Golden Age: The Politics of Culture in Mexico Since 1940*, edited by Gilbert Joseph, Anne Rubenstein, and Eric Zolov, 471–487. Durham, N.C. and London: Duke University Press.

Vaughan, Mary Kay, and Stephen Lewis, eds. 2006. *The Eagle and the Virgin: Nation and Cultural Revolution in Mexico, 1920–1940*. Durham, N.C. and London: Duke University Press.

―――. 2006. "Introduction." In *The Eagle and the Virgin: Nation and Cultural Revolution in Mexico, 1920–1940*, edited by Mary Kay Vaughan and Stephen Lewis, 1–20. Durham, N.C. and London: Duke University Press.

Vázquez, Octavio, co-ord. 1986. *Michoacán: indumentaría tradicional, el traje regional. Patrimonio de los pueblos*. Morelia, Michoacán: Casa de las Artesanias.

Vázquez León, Luis. 1992. *Ser indio otra vez: La purepechización de los tarascos serranos*. Distrito Federal, México: Consejo Nacional para la Cultura y Las Arts.

Vázquez Valle, Irene. 1976. *El son del sur de Jalisco*. Guadalajara: Gobierno del Estado de Jalisco.

Vertí, Sebastián. 1991. *Tradiciones mexicanas*. Distrito Federal, México: Editorial Diana.

Wade, Peter. 2000. *Music, Race, and Nation. Música Tropical in Colombia*. Chicago and London: The University of Chicago Press.

Wagley, Charles. 1950. "Review of *Empire's Children: The People of Tzintzuntzan* by George M. Foster." *The Hispanic American Historical Review* 30(2): 218–20.

Warman, Arturo. 1970. "Todos santos y todos difuntos." In *De eso que llaman antropología mexicana*, edited by Arturo Warman, 9–38. Distrito Federal, México: Editorial Nuestro Tiempo.

―――. 1972. *La danza de Moros y Cristianos*. Distrito Federal, México: Colección SEP.-SETENTAS. Núm. 46.

Warren, Benedict. 1963. *Vasco de Quiroga and His Pueblo-Hospitals of Santa Fe*. Washington, D.C.: Academy of American Franciscan History.

―――. 1997. "Los estudios de la lengua de Michoacán. Cuestiones para investigación." In *Lengua y etnohistoria P'urépecha: Homenaje á Benedict Warren*, edited by C. Paredes Martínez, 27–39. Morelia, Michoacán: La Universidad Michoacana de San Nicolás de Hidalgo.

Waters, Wendy. 2006. "Remapping Identities: Road Construction and Nation Building in Postrevolutionary Mexico." In *The Eagle and the Virgin: Nation and Cultural Revolution in Mexico, 1920–1940*, edited by Mary Kay Vaughan and Stephen Lewis, 221–42. Durham, N.C. and London: Duke University Press.

West, Robert C. 1948. *The Cultural Geography of the Modern Tarascan Area*. Washington, D. C.: Smithsonian Institution, Institute of Social Anthropology.

Wood, Robert E. 1997. "Tourism and the State: Ethnic Options and the Construction of Otherness." In *Tourism, Ethnicity, and the State in Asian and Pacific Societies*, edited by Michael Picard and Robert E. Wood, 1–34. Hawaii: University of Hawaii Press.

Zantwijk, Rudolf Alexander van. 1974. *Los servidores de los santos. La identidad social y cultural de una comunidad tarasca en México*. Distrito Federal, México: SEP – INI.

Zárate Hernández, José Eduardo. 1993. "Procesos políticos en la cuenca lacustre de Pátzcuaro." In *Estudios Michoacanos IV*, edited by Sergio Zendejas Romero, 205–32. Zamora, Michoacán: El Colegio de Michoacán.

Zizumbo Villareal, Lilia. 1986. "Pátzcuaro: El turismo en Janitzio." In *Estudios Michoacanos I*, edited by Carlos Herrejón Peredo, 151–69. Zamora, Michoacán: El Colegio de Michoacán.

Zolov, Eric. 1999. *Refried Elvis: The Rise of the Mexican Counterculture*. Berkeley and Los Angeles: University of California Press.

———. 2001. "Discovering a Land 'Mysterious and Obvious': The Renarrativizing of Postrevolutionary Mexico." In *Fragments of a Golden Age: The Politics of Culture in Mexico Since 1940*, edited by Gilbert Joseph, Anne Rubenstein, and Eric Zolov, 234–72. Durham, N.C. and London: Duke University Press.

Theater and Event Programs

Danzas Auténticas Mexicanas: Programa. 1937. México: Departamento Autónomo de Prensa y Publicidad. 18–25 September 1937.

Danzas Auténticas Mexicanas: Programa. 1939. México: Departamento Autónomo de Prensa y Publicidad.

Hamarándecua—Costumbres. 1930. México: Departamento del Distrito Federal, Dirección General de Acción Educativa (authors: Francisco Domínguez and Carlos González).

Noche de Muertos. 2000. Pamphlet (Folleto). Michoacán: Secretaría de Turísmo.

Noche de Muertos. 2007. Pamphlet (Folleto). Michoacán: Secretaría de Turísmo.

The Ballet Folklorico of Mexico – Amalia Hernandez. The University Musical Society of The University of Michigan, Concert Program, February 26, 1969.

The EXPO-Guide. 2000. Germany: EXPO 2000 (World's Fair) Hannover Gmbh.

Newspaper and Magazine Articles

Danzantes indígenas en el Palacio de Bellas Artes. *El Nacional*, 28 July 1939. Moisés Mendoza.

Disneylandia. *La Jornada*, 15 March 2000. Jaime Garduño Argueta.

El folklore mexicano, de luto por Amalia Hernández. *La Jornada*, 5 November 2000. Yanireth Israde.

En pro del turismo en lugares indígenas. *Heraldo Michoacano*, 15 October. 1938.

En torno de la educación indígena. *Heraldo Michoacano*, 12 October 1938.

Festival artistico de la raza Purhépecha: Martha Sahagún y Lázaro Cárdenas, Invitados especiales. *Xiranhua* (Periodismo Indígena P'urhépecha de México), 11 October 2005.

Festival cultural. *Heraldo Michoacano*, 20 October 1938.

Festival de canto y danza [advert]. *Heraldo Michoacano*, 7 May 1954.

Front page photo. *Heraldo Michoacano*, 29 October 1938.

Homenaje al creador de la Danza de los Viejitos en festival P'urépecha. *La Jornada*, 10 October 2000.

La conmemoración del Día de la Raza. *Heraldo Michoacano*, 13 September 1938.

La memoria indígena continúa inquebrantable y reproduce tradiciones y costumbres: Florescano. *La Jornada*, 10 February 2000. José Garza.

Las 'Canacuas'—El arte coreográfico tarasco simbolizado. *Heraldo Michoacano*, 28 September 1938.

Las danzas populares de méxico. *El Nacional*, 1 October 1937. Moisés Mendoza.

Magno festival en el CREFAL. Actos de gran significación. Celebración del III aniversario del centro piloto. *Heraldo Michoacano*, 9 May 1954. E. Avilés y Avilés.

Murió Tata Gervasio, creador de la tradicional danza de 'Los Viejitos.' *La Voz de Michoacán*, 25 November 1999.

Pátzcuaro y Janitzio reviven su tradicional 'Noche de Muertos.' *La Crónica de Hoy*, 3 November 2007. Ignacio Roque.

Será ejecutada la Danza de 'Los Viejitos' en S. Antonio, Texas, en la Fiesta de la Raza. *Heraldo Michoacano*, 12 October 1938.

Un recorrido inolvidable: Maravilló Janitzio a los periodistas. *La Voz de Michoacán*, 6 November 1968. Alejandro César Herrera.

Web Site Report

"Listo, Festival de la Raza P'urhépecha de Zacán" www.cbtelevision.com.mx/cultura/listo-festival-de-la-raza-purhpecha-de-zacan/ accessed 15.10.2008.

Press Releases

"Hanover 2000: de pinxi, the Belgian specialist in interactive experiences, has created the two key attractions of the Mexican Pavilion." Press Release, 5 June 2000. de pinxi, Brussels.

"Los Viejitos." 1974. Boletín de Prensa (Press Release), 3 September 1974, FONADAN, Mexico.

Web Sites

http://en.wikipedia.org/wiki/Day_of_the_Dead accessed 2.2.2010.
www.alegria.org/modules/eguide/event.php?eid=119 accessed 5.11.2008.
www.bestday.com/Morelia_Michoacan/Attractions accesssed 12.07.2008.
www.inside-mexico.com/featuredead accessed 4.20.2010.
www.lonelyplanet.com/worldguide/mexico accessed 5.21.2005.
www.mexico21.org.mx accessed 8.21.2000.
www.visitmexico.com accessed 5.7.2006.
www.yr.com accessed 9.22.2006.

Government Papers

Correspondence: 28 November 1939. Lázaro Cárdenas and Nicolás Bartolo Juárez. Archivo General de la Nación.

Informe 15.9.1921. Informe rendido por el C. General Francisco J. Múgica, Gobernador Constitucional acerca del estado de la Administración Pública, durante el periodo corrido del 22 de Septiembre de 1920 al 15 de Septiembre de 1921, y contestación del C. Presidente del Congreso. XXXVLL Congreso Constitucional del Estado de Michoacán de Ocampo.

Informe 16.9.1929. Informe de Gobierno de 1928–1929 que rinde el General de División Don Lázaro Cárdenas de Rio XLII Legisladora 16 Sep. 1928–16 Sep. 1929. XLII Congreso Constitucional del Estado de Michoacán de Ocampo.

Informe 16.9.1931. Informe de Gobierno de 1930 a 1931 que rinde el Lic. Gabino Vázquez, 16 de Sep. 1930–15 Sep. 1931, XLIII Congreso Constitucional del Estado de Michoacán de Ocampo. Sección de Archivo y Biblioteca.

Informe 1.9.1936. Informe rendido el 1er. de septiembre de 1936 por el c. Presidente de la República General Lázaro Cárdenas, al H. Congreso de la Unión. Mexico: Secretaria de Hacienda y Crédito Público, 1936.

La Educación Pública en México. Desde el 1er. de diciembre de 1934 hasta el 30 de noviembre de 1940. Mexico: Poder Ejecutivo Federal, 1941, T. I.

Radio Educación (Archived Programs) (www.radioeducacion.edu.mx)

FONADAN Fondo Nacional para el Desarrollo de la Danza Popular Mexicana. Departamento de Etnomusicología. Series: Música de las danzas y bailes tradicionales de México. Marcelo Torreblanca, Mario Kuri-Aldana, Felipe Ramírez Gil.

A 354. 1974. Los Viejitos (C451/2, C837. 1985). Conjunto Atardecer, Los Viejitos (Gervasio López, Felix Francisco, Pedro López, Dimas Esteban). Los Viejitos de Jarácuaro (Gervasio López, Felix Francisco, Pedro López, Atilano López, Dimas Esteban).

A 535. 1976 (C665 and C792.1983.) Los Viejitos de Jarácuaro (Benedicto Santiago, Nicolás Constantino, Salvador Santiago).

C 752: Los Hermanos Cortés.

Discography

Avelinita. Orquesta de Cuerdas Mirando el Lago. P'uréri ukata.

Dalia Tsïtsïki: Pirekuas y abajeños de los purépecha. Corason. COCD119. 1994.

Danza de los Sembradores. JLD-80. 1989.

Danzas de la Region Lacustre del Estado de Michoacán Vol. 1 Collección *Música de las Danzas y Bailes Populares de México.* FONADAN, SEP. 1975.

Folklore Purepecha in *Music of Mexico: Michoacán* (Banda Melchor Ocampo) Vols. 1 & 2. Alborada Records KGM-012 and KGM-095. 1992 & 1994.

Homenaje a Grandes Compositores de la Meseta Purhépecha de Michoacán, con los Nietos del Lago de la Isla de Urandén, Municipio de Pátzcuaro. Alborada Records. 2003.

Juchari Kuinchekuecha (Nuestras Fiestas) el Grupo Purépecha de Charapan. 2001.

La Música Tradicional en Michoacán Vol. III. 1990. Folklore Mexicano, recordings by J. R. Hellmer 1953–1963. Revised and rereleased by CENIDIM. 1990.

Los Grandes Compositores de la Isla de Jarácuaro, Michoacán, Vol. 1. Gilberto Cázares Ponce. Tía Nina, La voz del Alma Purépecha. 2007.

Los Nietos del Lago y Grupo los Gallitos: La Danza de los Viejitos de Urandén. Fono-México TAR-676.

Los P'urépechas de Jarácuaro: Michoacán y sus Danzas P'urépechas. Alborada Records KGM 211. 1999.

Los Viejitos de Jarácuaro. Danza Tradicional de Michoacán. Con el conjunto de cuerdas Los Purépechas de Jarácuaro. Alborada Records CDIM 2070. 2000.

Los Viejos Alegres. Con la orquesta de cuerdas Flor de Dalia. Self produced: Procopio Cázares Patricio. Jarácuaro. No date.

Música de Ichupio, Michoacán, México. Orquesta de Cuerdas Mirando el Lago. Pedro Dimas and Paul Anastasio. SwingCatEnterprises. 2002.

Música Indígena P'urhépecha, Vol I 1973, Series *Maestros del Folklore Michoacano.* Arturo Macías. Discos Peerless No. 1663.

Música y Canciones Purhépecha. Los Nietos del Lago de la Isla de Urandén, Michoacán. Alborada Records. 2004.

The Real Mexico in Music and Song. Nonesuch Records 7559–79724–2. Warner Music Group Company. [Originally released in 1966 (H-72009)]. 2003.

Filmography

Inauguración del CREFAL, 9 May 1951.Video. CREFAL. Pátzcuaro, Mexico.
Janitzio. 1935. Director: Carlos Navarro.
Maclovia. 1948. Director: Emilo Fernández.
Qué lindo es Michoacán. 1943. Director: Ismael Rodríguez.
Rituales Tarascos. 1961. Noticiario Mexicano and CREFAL. Pátzcuaro, Mexico.
The Three Caballeros. 2008, [1944]. Director: Norman Ferguson. Walt Disney.

Theater Performances

Aztec. 1991. Maurice Gilmour and the Leicestershire T.I.E. Company (Simon Cuckson, Ruth Hellier, Jane Perkins, Paul Waring), UK.

Index

abajeño, 84, 188, 266, 286n.3
academic disciplines, in postrevolutionary
      period, 26–7, 59–63
  See also archeology; ethnography;
      ethnomusicologists; folklore
academic journals, 27, 30. See also Ethnos
academics and intellectuals. See individuals
Academy of Mexican Dance, 122, 282n.7
Acapulco, 19, 126, 127, 129, 132, 151, 229, 257
actors, and embodied actions, 39, 73, 77,
      80, 81, 101, 128, 210, 234, 262, 281n.11
advertising, 8, 125, 219–20, 224
  of Danzas Auténticas Mexicanas, 109
  for the European tourist campaign with
      the Dance of the Old Men, 15–17, 16,
      33, 152, 226–30, 246, 277n.23
  of McCann-Erickson, and Young and
      Rubicam, 229–30
  Night of the Dead in Lake Pátzcuaro, 21
  and Lake Pátzcuaro, 24, 33, 225
  for tourism, using the Ballet Folklórico
      de México, 126, 141
AeroMéxico, 247
aesthetics, designations and
      classifications, 66
  of dance and music, 64–5, 88, 140–2,
      281n.5
  of Danzas auténticas mexicanas and
      Hamarándecua, 100–10

affirmation, through cultural display, 46, 158
agency, 189–90, 206, 243, 248, 256,
Aire Libre, Teatro al (Open-Air Theater).
      See theater
Alejo Reynoso, family (Pacanda), 159–60,
      179, 255, 285n.19
Alborada Records, 15, 177, 192
All Saint's Day and All Soul's Day. See Night
      of the Dead
American Songbag (Sandburg), 63
appropriation, of music, dance, and
      ritual, 269, 6883 (see also performism)
archeology, 282n.13
  as indigenista vision, 59–60, 275
  in the Lake Pátzcuaro region, 9, 68–9
architecture, in postrevolutionary
      period, 64
  and the Palace of Fine Arts, 108
archives: film, newspaper, scholarly,
      sound, 15, 30, 105
art and artist, designation of, 78, 83, 108,
      116, 132, 140–2, 281n.5
  and European influence, 32, 56, 64,
      281n.5
  and the Zacán Artistic Festival. See
      Festival Artístico de la Raza
      P'urhépecha
artifact, P'urhépecha people as. See
      objectification; objects

CPSIA information can be obtained
at www.ICGtesting.com
Printed in the USA
BVOW01s0021091116
467291BV00002B/65/P